The Balanced Plate

The Essential Elements
of Whole Foods
and Good Health

The Balanced Plate

More Than 150 Flavorful Recipes
That Nourish Body, Mind, and Soul

Renée Loux

Foreword by Dean Ornish, MD

RODALE

Rodale books may be purchased for business or promotional use or for special sales. For information, please write to: Special Markets Department, Rodale Inc., 733 Third Avenue, New York, NY 10017

Printed in the United States of America
Rodale Inc. makes every effort to use acid-free ⊗, recycled paper ♺.

Interior design by Patricia Field
Cover design by Carol Angstadt

Library of Congress Cataloging-in-Publication Data

Loux, Renée.
    The balanced plate : the essential elements of whole foods and good health / Renée Loux; foreword by Dean Ornish, MD.
        p. cm.
    Includes bibliographical references and index.
    ISBN-13 978–1–59486–471–1 paperback
    ISBN-10 1–59486–471–3 paperback
    1. Cookery (Natural foods)   I. Title.
TX74167   2006
641.5'63—dc22   2006011776

Distributed to the trade by Holtzbrinck Publishers

2   4   6   8   10   9   7   5   3   1   paperback

We inspire and enable people to improve their lives and the world around them
For more of our products visit **rodalestore.com** or call 800-848-4735

Contents

Acknowledgments

Above all and beyond the beyond, to my beloved husband, Shep, for whom even the most loving, joyful, eloquent, poetically strung words are but a faint reflection of my heart and soul… I love you more than anything, ever.

For my Mama and Daddio, within the great gift of life, you have shown me the kind of love and support that I wish all daughters could know . . . even when I left a full scholarship at a university to move to Hawaii and open a raw food restaurant, which was a little ahead of the curve. Brava! Courage, hard work, and a lot of luck make dreams come true.

To my lamb-brother Lyle; his beautiful wife, Erika; and baby Ella-phant (whom I am certifiably obsessed with!).

To Dean Ornish, whose extraordinary work and noble dedication continue to have revolutionary benefits for the hearts (physically and endearingly) of so many. Above all, you are truly a wonderful, intelligent, compassionate being. In kindred parallel with my dear Shep, we are both grateful to see another couple so deeply in love and breaking the mold. Cheers, to many, many more.

To HH the Dalai Lama, who embodies happiness and compassion with such strength and sweetness and who holds so much with such a light heart and a contagious giggle, even in the face of great challenge. May the world catch the wave.

To Margaret Hecht, whose soul I have fallen in love with for lifetimes before and to come.

To Lavina Currier, whom I adore to no end, my heart runs deep with gratitude for all you have opened in my life.

To my love-muffin Alicia Silverstone, because everything falls away when we are together.

To Bob Thurman, for the wisdom of humor and a truly brilliant mind that I hope is contagious.

To Marty Kreigel, who can comprehensively answer my every question in any field with an uncanny depth of knowledge, compassion, and genuine heart.

To Eddie and Nicki, for sharing deep roots of wisdom and wings of freedom.

To Liz Penta, my dearest friend and genuine superwoman, for whom I wish the world. You walk in this world with such rare integrity and mindfulness. We need to clone you.

To John Medeski, who truly soaks up the marrow of life and has schooled me on many of the finer things.

To Michele Nischan, a pioneer and gifted chef with incredible vision and follow-through. You inspire me with great hope.

To Joy Peirson and Bart Potenza, who are the light at the Candle in New York and in the lives of all who know them. Shine on!

To Dominique Pandolfi, for sincere beauty, true grace, and a deep pulse of friendship through many incarnations, and for fabulous photos.

To Helen Hunt, who is thoroughly a beautiful woman, mother, and being. And Matthew and Makena, who tickle me to have a family of my own. Yes!

To Mark Tarbell, one of the best chefs and nicest people on the planet. Your kindness and talent are effervescent.

To Steve Murphy, the main man, for catching the vision and impeccable style.

To Margot Schupf, for the cool brilliance of taking this project under her wing with poise and finesse, thank you!

To Jen DeFilippi, for compassionate composure, wisdom, and guidance, and more than any author would dare to dream for in a collaborative editing dance.

To Joel Gotler, my superagent extraordinaire, who walks in many worlds with dexterity and consideration.

Lastly, to the gifted chefs who have tantalized my palate and inspired greatness—Daniel Bouloud, Anton Mossiman, Charlie Trotter, Roxanne Klein, Dan Barber, Rose Gray, and Ruth Rogers, and perhaps most of all Mr. Roger Verge, whose light has spilled profoundly into my life.

Lokha Samasta Sukhino Bavantu—May all beings everywhere be happy and free.

Approach love and cooking
with reckless abandon.

—HH THE DALAI LAMA

Foreword

Renée Loux has written an exquisite book. She gives us recipes for sumptuous dishes made from a balance of wholesome ingredients. But she also gives us something even more valuable and enduring: a new way of thinking about food and how it impacts our lives. Does it taste good or is it good for me? Well, both. Renée describes for us how delicious food can be healthy food—healthy for our bodies, healthy for the environment, and healthy for our children. These are foods that taste good and make you feel good and look good. Renée brings to the table the unbounded joy of someone in love with life and good health. She recognizes that delicious food is a major part of living a balanced life. As she describes it, this book is the product of her life-long love affair with food.

Awareness—in this case, of our food and how it is prepared—is the first step in healing. When we become more aware, more mindful of how the choices we make each day affect us—for better and worse—and how quickly we can experience these changes, then we have the freedom to make different choices and pave a new road.

Part of the value of scientific research is to help raise our awareness of how diet and lifestyle directly affect our health. For almost 30 years, I have directed a series of scientific studies proving how powerful changes in diet and lifestyle can be. These studies used the latest in high-tech, state-of-the-art measures to prove the power of simple, low-cost, and low-tech lifestyle changes. We were able to show that even severe heart disease often can be reversed when people make bigger changes in diet and lifestyle than had been previously recommended. If you can reverse heart disease, you can usually prevent it. We focused on heart disease since it's the leading killer of men and women in the United States, but the benefits of changing diet and lifestyle go far beyond that. In our more recent studies, we showed in a randomized controlled trial that similar changes in diet and lifestyle may slow, stop, or even reverse the progression of prostate cancer. What is true of prostate cancer is likely to be for breast cancer as well.

Not everyone needs to make sweeping changes in diet and lifestyle to effect change. If you're at high risk or are trying to reverse heart disease or prevent the recurrence of cancer, then you probably need to make bigger changes in diet and lifestyle than someone who just wants to lose a few pounds and is otherwise healthy (and needs only the proverbial "ounce of prevention"). If you just want to lower your cholesterol or blood pressure, you can begin by making moderate changes in diet and lifestyle. If that's enough to achieve your goals, great; if not, then consider making bigger changes.

You have a wide spectrum of dietary choices; it's not all or nothing. If you go on a diet and feel constrained, you are more likely to drop it. But if you see your food choices each day as part of a spectrum, then you are more likely to feel free and empowered. An optimal diet for most people is low in refined carbohydrates (sugar, white flour, alcohol) and high in complex carbohydrates (fruits, vegetables, whole grains, legumes, soy products); low in fat, especially saturated and trans fats, and high in omega-3 fatty acids; low in animal protein and high in plant-based proteins. To the degree you move in a healthful direction on this spectrum, you're likely to feel better, look better, lose weight, and gain health.

If you indulge yourself one day, you can eat more healthfully the next. If you're a couch potato one day, exercise a little more the next. Then you're less likely to feel restricted. Studies have shown that those who eat the healthiest diets are the ones who allow themselves some indulgences. Also important to maintaining health is moderate exercise. Choose a way of exercising that you enjoy. The more you exercise, the more fit you become, but even a little goes a long way. Just walking 20 to 30 minutes a day—and not even all that fast—may reduce premature death by 50 percent or more.

Perhaps most important, hundreds of scientific studies have documented the powerful effects of love and intimacy in our lives.

People who feel lonely and depressed are many times more likely to get sick and die prematurely than those who have a strong connection to another, caring relationships, and community support.

Emotional stress plays an important role in just about all illnesses, both directly and indirectly. For example, emotional stress makes arteries constrict and blood clot faster, which, in turn, may cause a heart attack. Also, people are more likely to smoke, overeat, drink too much, work too hard, and so on when they are feeling stressed. Thus, stress management is an important part of what I recommend when it comes to balance and prevention. These techniques include, among others:

- Yoga-based stretching
- Breathing techniques
- Meditation and imagery
- Support groups
- Quitting smoking
- Personal, positive affirmations

Even a few minutes a day of yoga and meditation can make a big difference—the consistency is more important than the duration. In most forms of meditation, you repeat a sound, a phrase, or a verse from a prayer over and over and over again. You can focus on a sacred object such as rosary beads or a picture or icon. It can be a favorite prayer. It can be secular. It can be anything. Or you can simply observe your breathing: in and out, over and over.

When you focus your mind, a number of good things begin to happen. First, you get better at concentrating, so whatever you do, you do better. Second, when you pay attention to something, you enjoy it more fully. Food, sex, music, art, massage, anything sensual becomes more pleasurable when you pay attention to it. Also, your mind begins to quiet down and you can begin to experience more of an inner sense of peace and joy and well-being. And you realize that this mindfulness is our natural state until we disturb it, so it's very empowering. When we feel stressed, we can, for example, stop blaming others and instead focus on what we can do about that stress. One of the things we can do is to bring mindfulness into all aspects of our daily lives.

Meditation is the practice of paying attention. Renée encourages us to do just that with our food—to be mindful in its selection, in its preparation, in its eating. In *The Balanced Plate*, she shows us how to select the cleanest ingredients, how to prepare them most wholesomely and deliciously, and how to thoroughly celebrate eating. One of the gifts of this book is the knowledge that the selection, preparation, and eating of food can become joyful meditations in their own right.

In that context, how you eat is as important as what you eat. When you pay attention to your food, eating becomes a form of meditation. You enjoy the food more fully, so you can eat fewer calories with greater pleasure. And you begin to notice how the food affects you. When you eat a meal high in sugar, salt, and fat, you feel tired and sluggish an hour or two later. When you eat from a balanced plate, you feel light, clear, and energized afterward. Try it and see.

Close your eyes when you put a bite of food in your mouth; savor the texture, the flavor, the temperature. Involve as many of your senses as you can. Experiment with a ripe piece of fruit or a small piece of high-quality chocolate. Notice how the flavors change and linger as the food goes down your throat. I love chocolate, so I try to find the richest, darkest chocolate. I stop what I'm doing, look at the chocolate, smell it, savor it, and let it melt in my mouth. Notice how the flavors change as it melts and goes down your throat. You can take several minutes with a single piece of chocolate, and it can be exquisitely satisfying.

In this book, Renée brings just such an extraordinarily satisfying approach to food and to life. Her passionate and balanced approach is at once sensually gratifying and thoroughly wholesome.

And, oh yes, don't miss the chocolate mousse.

Dean Ornish, MD
Founder and President,
Preventive Medicine Research Institute
Clinical Professor of Medicine,
University of California, San Francisco
Author, Dr. Dean Ornish's Program
for Reversing Heart Disease; Eat More,
Weigh Less; *and* Love & Survival

PART ONE

Introduction to the Balanced Plate

Food is our common ground, a universal experience.

—JAMES BEARD

Food is a celebration and a true common denominator. Today, we see food as a necessity, sometimes as an indulgence, and certainly as a commodity, but we seem to have lost the awareness that food interconnects us all as humans and links us to the elements of the earth and the rhythm of the seasons. Most of us have forgotten that food is a fundamental part of who we are, what we are, and where we are going.

It is no secret that we are literally made of what we eat, drink, and breathe. It is also no secret that heart disease kills more Americans than all other causes of death combined, that one in two men and one in three women will be diagnosed with cancer, and that uncontaminated groundwater is becoming scarce.[1,2] Is there a connection? The connection is clear as a looking glass.

There are countless factors that influence health—directly and tangentially—in our complex, changing world. The root of health is sustained and nourished by good food, pure water, and clean air. Whether we realize it or not, every day we are exposed to an unseen bevy of hazards in the food we eat, the water we drink, and the air we breathe. It is no mystery why so many are sick, stressed out, and overweight. Never before has there been so much within the reach of so many, and yet the simple task of feeding ourselves poses such problems. We have lost our connection to the power of food, the design of the elements, and the intelligence of the earth. We have lost our sense of balance . . . but we can return to it, and with pleasure.

Restoring balance and good health is an elementary exercise in getting back to the basics and enjoying the ride. Reconnecting to our relationship with food is the first step in cultivating lifelong happiness and health. Through culture, tradition, and history, food is one of the few choices each of us can make with such profound personal and collective effects. This book is written with all of my heart, passion, and hope to live fully, without compromise, and soak up the marrow of life in the best of health.

Covering the natural elements of health, harmony, and beyond, I have outlined what you can do for your body, mind, and spirit, and for the planet to reclaim balance. In the chapters that follow, I will show you how to identify environmental hazards and how to avoid them, or counter that which is unavoidable by:

- Determining the true cost of food, finding out where it really comes from, and choosing the safest, most nutritious options
- Choosing balanced whole foods over processed, denatured foods for optimal health and satisfaction
- Learning about the principles, elements, and approaches of different whole food diets to help you identify the nature of food and what works for you
- Setting the stage for holistic well-being by identifying health hazards in the kitchen and elsewhere at home, and then reconnecting with natural elements to foster a nourishing environment
- Fueling your beautiful body with pure, sumptuous, fabulous food that you can share with the ones you love

With effervescence, I invite you to return to the balanced plate again and again for a long life of good fortune, cheer, and happy endings. *Me ke aloha.*

CHAPTER I

The True Cost of Food

A significant part of the pleasure of eating is in one's accurate
consciousness of the lives and the world from which the food comes.

—WENDELL BERRY

Food is arguably our most valuable human resource. The simple act of eating has profound consequences for our bodies and the world. For millennia, food has been grown in rational proportions, with care for symbiotic regional ecosystems, healthy soil, and water management, and with crops rotated seasonally and designed to survive the changing elements. In the last 50 years, however, the food industry has radically changed. This change not only pervades the growing of food but also the processing, distribution, politics, and consumption of food. Farm productivity has increased more than 80 percent since 1960, but the population living and working on farms has dropped from 40 percent to 2 percent.[3,4] Family-run farms are on the verge of extinction, and in today's global economy, the dependence on seasonal, regional food no longer exists. Moreover, modern farming has truncated tried-and-true systems with a chemical revolution. We are growing more

Definition of "Organic"

As defined by the National Organic Standards Board (NOSB):

"Organic agriculture is an ecological production management system that promotes and enhances biodiversity, biological cycles, and soil biological activity. It is based on minimal use of off-farm inputs and on management practices that restore, maintain, and enhance ecological harmony. . . .

"'Organic' is a labeling term that denotes products produced under the authority of the Organic Foods Production Act. The principal guidelines for organic production are to use materials and practices that enhance the ecological balance of natural systems and that integrate the parts of the farming system into an ecological whole. . . .

"Organic agriculture practices cannot ensure that products are completely free of residues; however, methods are used to minimize pollution from air, soil, and water. . . .

"Organic food handlers, processors, and retailers adhere to standards that maintain the integrity of organic agricultural products. The primary goal of organic agriculture is to optimize the health and productivity of interdependent communities of soil life, plants, animals, and people."[5]

food on less land with higher profit margins, lower prices, and the loss of a majority of the once-prolific varieties of any given food for two, three, or maybe four standard varieties, which dominate the market without contest.

Like it or not, we find ourselves in the midst of a battle for the future of food every time we go to the market. Every dollar we spend on food has ecological and social impact. In one corner, cheap, industrialized, chemical-laden, standardized varieties of food rise to epic proportion. In the other corner grow the safe, strong, responsible roots of sustainable, organic foods. It is a

neck-and-neck fight. Cost and convenience versus quality and diversity. A hard-won match.

Growing food with sustainable methods ensures safe, nutritious food and a future for our children's children. Waving away the option of safe, sustainable food for cheap, industrial agriculture sets into motion a series of repercussions that may never be recovered from or reversed. There is an old proverb that reads, "We are only as rich as our soil and as wealthy as our water." If that is indeed the case, we are living on borrowed principle, which is a high risk in any managed portfolio.

The gravity of the situation is a little hard

to feel, especially because the attractive, abundant displays of produce in the supermarket look harmless, healthy, and so inviting. For consumers rummaging through these bins, it is hard to believe that the malady of industrial agriculture could be capable of undermining our collective future, especially when the apple looks so shiny, red, and uniform.

Most of us don't think of apples as big business, but industrial agriculture is hugely profitable. The food industry in America generates $1 trillion annually, occupying 13 percent of our GNP (gross national product) and employing 13 percent of our labor force.[6] That is *big* business by any standard.

Fortunately, industrial agriculture is not the only contender in the democracy of business. We are putting our money where our mouths are, literally. Today, organically grown food is one of the fastest-growing sectors of the food industry.[7] More people who are faced with the question of the true cost of food find that the answer is to make the powerful choice of safe, sustainable, organically grown food.

Top 10 Reasons to Go Organic

Regardless of diet, organics are a smart priority. Opting for organics is an effectual choice for personal and planetary health. Buying organically grown food—free of harmful chemicals, bursting with more nutrition, taste, and sustainable sustenance—is a direct vote for immediate health and the hopeful future of generations to come.

1. Avoid Chemicals

Eating organically grown food is the only way to avoid the cocktail of chemical poisons present in commercially grown food. More than 600 active chemicals are registered for agricultural use in America,[9] to the tune of billions of pounds annually.[10] The average application equates to about 16 pounds of chemical pesticides per person every year. Many of these chemicals were approved by the Environmental Protection Agency (EPA) before extensive testing. The National Academy of Sciences reports that 90 percent of the chemicals applied to food have not been tested for long-term health effects before being deemed "safe." Further, the FDA tests only 1 percent of food for pesticide residue.[11] The most dangerous and toxic pesticides require special testing methods, which are rarely if ever employed by the FDA.

> The average conventional apple has 20 to 30 poisons on its skin even after washing.[8]

2. Benefit from More Nutrients

Organically grown foods have more nutrients—vitamins, minerals, enzymes, and micronutrients—than commercially grown foods because the soil is managed and nourished with sustainable practices by responsible standards. The *Journal of Alternative and Complementary Medicine* conducted a review of 41 published studies comparing the nutritional value of organically grown and conventionally grown fruits, vegetables, and grains and concluded that there are significantly more of several nutrients in organic crops.[12] Further, the study verifies that five servings of organically grown vegetables (such as lettuce, spinach, carrots, potatoes, and cabbage) provide an adequate allowance of vitamin C, whereas the same number of servings of conventionally grown vegetables do not. On average, organically grown foods provide:

- 21.1 percent more iron (than their conventional counterparts)
- 27 percent more vitamin C
- 29.3 percent more magnesium
- 13.6 percent more phosphorus

3. Enjoy Better Taste

Try it! Organically grown food generally tastes better because nourished, well-balanced soil produces healthy, strong plants. This is especially true with heirloom varieties, which are cultivated for taste over appearance.

4. Avoid GMO

Genetically engineered (GE) food and genetically modified organisms (GMO) are contaminating our food supply at an alarming rate, with repercussions beyond understanding (see "GMO: Untested, Unlabeled, and We Are Eating Them" on page 15). GMO foods do not have to be labeled in America. Because organically grown food cannot be genetically modified in any way, choosing organic is the only way to avoid foods that have been genetically engineered.

5. Avoid Hormones, Antibiotics, and Drugs in Animal Products

Conventional meat and dairy are the highest-risk foods for contamination by harmful substances. More than 90 percent of the pesticides Americans consume are found in the fat and tissue of meat and dairy products.[13] The EPA reports that a majority of pesticide intake comes from meat, poultry, fish, eggs, and dairy products because these foods are all high on the food chain. For instance, a large fish that eats a smaller fish that eats even smaller fish accumulates all of the toxins of the chain, especially in fatty tissue. Cows, chickens, and pigs are fed animal parts, by-products, fish meal, and grains that are heavily and collectively laden with toxins and chemicals. Lower-fat animal products are less dangerous, as toxins and chemicals are accumulated and concentrated in fatty tissue.

Antibiotics, drugs, and growth hormones are also directly passed into meat and dairy products. Tens of millions of pounds of antibiotics are used in animal feed every year.[14] The union of concerned scientists estimates that roughly 70 percent of antibiotics produced in the United States are fed to animals for nontherapeutic purposes.[15] US farmers have been giving sex hormones and growth hormones to cattle to artificially increase the amount of meat and milk the cattle produce without requiring extra feed. The hormones fed to cows cannot be broken down, even at high temperatures. Therefore they remain in complete form and pass directly into the consumer when meat is eaten. Hormone supplementation is the biggest concern with beef, dairy products, and farmed fish. In the United States, the jury is still out. However, Europe's

Debunking Organic Myths

MYTH: Organic food costs more money.

REALITY: The common opinion that organic food is more expensive is curtailed by the complicated reality that lies just beneath the price tag. Buying organic food in bulk, at farmer's markets, and in season keep the cost within the reach of most people.

MYTH: Conventional farming is more productive than organic farming.

REALITY: Organic methods are as efficient, economical, and financially competitive as conventional methods. According to a report that documents 15 years of research by Rodale Institute's long-term Farming Systems Trial, organic farming is economically sound, ergonomic, and better for the soil and the environment. The experiment compared highly productive, intensive corn and soybean crops using both conventional and organic management. The study proved that after a transitional period of about 4 years, crops grown using organic methods yielded as well as, and often better than, those grown conventionally.[16]

scientific community agrees that there is no acceptably safe level for daily intake of any of the hormones currently used in the United States and has subsequently banned all growth hormones.[17, 18] The major concerns for US consumers include the early onset of puberty, growth of tumors, heightened cancer risks, and genetic problems.[19, 20] Growth hormones in milk (rBGH or rBST) are genetically modified and have been directly linked to cancer, especially in women.[21]

Many scientists and experts warn that rampant use of antibiotics in animal feed, like penicillin and tetracycline, will breed an epidemic that medicine has no defense against.[22] Karim Ahmed, PhD, a senior scientist at the Natural Resources Defense Council (NRDC) states that it "is perhaps one of the most serious public health problems the country faces. We're talking about rendering many of the most important antibiotics ineffective."

Choosing organic animal products is unyieldingly important, especially for children, pregnant women, and nursing mothers.

6. Preserve Our Ecosystems

Organic farming supports eco-sustenance, or farming in harmony with nature. Preservation of soil and crop rotation keep farmland healthy, and chemical abstinence preserves the ecosystem. Wildlife, insects, frogs, birds, and soil organisms are able to play their roles in

The use of pesticides has doubled every 10 years since 1945.[23] Crop loss has doubled.[24]

the tapestry of ecology, and we are able to play ours, without interference or compromise.

7. Reduce Pollution and Protect Our Water and Soil

Agricultural chemicals, pesticides, and fertilizers are contaminating our environment, poisoning our precious water supplies, and destroying the value of fertile farmland. Certified organic standards do not permit the use of toxic chemicals in farming and require responsible management of healthy soil and biodiversity.

According to Cornell entomologist David Pimentel, it is estimated that only 0.1 percent of applied pesticides reach the target pests. The bulk of pesticides (99.9 percent) is left to impact the environment.[25]

8. Preserve Agricultural Diversity

The rampant loss of species occurring today is a major environmental concern. It is estimated that 75 percent of the genetic diversity of agricultural crops has been lost in the last century.[26] Leaning heavily on one or two varieties of a given food is a formula for devastation. For instance, consider that only a handful of varieties of potatoes dominate the current

> Respect all food, and avoid its waste...because
> it is life itself.
>
> —THOMAS KILLER

marketplace, whereas thousands of varieties were once available.[27] Now, dig back to recent history's potato famine in Ireland, where a blight knocked out the whole crop, which consisted of just a few varieties, and millions of people died of starvation. Today, most industrial farms also grow just one crop rather than an array of crops on one piece of land. Ignorance is bliss? Or amnesia is disastrous?

Crop rotation is a simple and effective technique used in organic agriculture to reduce the need for pesticides and improve soil fertility.

Most conventional food is also extremely hybridized to produce large, attractive specimens, rather than a variety of indigenous strains that are tolerant to regional conditions such as droughts and pests. Many organic farms grow an assorted range of food, taking natural elements and time-tested tradition into account. Diversity is critical to survival.

9. Support Farming Directly

Buying organic food is an investment in a cost-effective future.

Commercial and conventional farming is heavily subsidized with tax dollars in America. A study at Cornell University determined the cost of a head of commercial iceberg lettuce, typically purchased at 49 cents a head, to be more than $3.00 a head when hidden costs were revealed. The study factored in the hidden costs of federal subsidies, pesticide regulation and testing, and hazardous waste and cleanup. Every year, American tax dollars subsidize billions of dollars for a farm bill that heavily favors commercial agribusiness.

Peeling back another layer of the modern farming onion reveals a price tag that cannot be accurately measured but certainly includes other detrimental associated costs such as health problems, environmental damage, and the loss and extinction of wildlife and ecology.

10. Keep Our Children and Future Safe

Putting our money where our mouths are is a powerful position to take in the $1 trillion food industry market in America. Spending dollars in the organic sector is a direct vote for a sustainable future for the many generations to come.

The Dirty Dozen

Eating organically grown food is a clear, intelligent, delicious choice. Finding and affording only organic food is sometimes tough. We do the best we can. Certain foods are worth the extra effort, or worth simply avoiding when organic is not available. The "dirty dozen" are the foods most commonly and highly contaminated with pesticides and chemicals, even after washing and peeling. The research used to compile this list is from extensive independent tests run by the FDA and the USDA from more than 100,000 samples of food. The chemical pesticides detected in these studies are known to cause cancer, birth defects, nervous system and brain damage, and developmental problems in children.[28–31] In other words, panic if it ain't organic.

1. Meat: Beef, Pork, and Poultry

The EPA reports that meat is contaminated with higher levels of pesticides than any plant food. Many chemical pesticides are fat-soluble and accumulate in the fatty tissue of animals. Animal feed that contains animal products compounds the accumulation, which is directly passed to the human consumer. Antibiotics, drugs, and hormones are a standard in animal husbandry, all of which accumulate and are passed on to consumers as well. Ocean fish carry a higher risk for heavy metals than pesticides, though many freshwater fish are exposed to high levels of pesticides from contaminated water.

2. Dairy: Milk, Cheese, and Butter

For reasons similar to those for meat, the fat in dairy products poses a high risk for contamination by pesticides. Animals concentrate pesticides and chemicals in their milk and meat. Growth hormones and antibiotics are also serious concerns and are invariably found in commercial milk, cheese, and butter.

3. Strawberries, Raspberries, and Cherries

Strawberries are the crop that is most heavily dosed with pesticides in America. On average, 300 pounds of pesticides are applied to

Because we do not think about future generations, they will never forget us.

—HENRIK TIKKANEN

The Most Common and Dangerous Chemical Pesticides in the United States

Chlorinated Hydrocarbons

Chlorinated hydrocarbons include DDT (which is now banned, though still present in our soil) and dieldrin (which is legal and considered to be five times as toxic as DDT).[32] These chemicals are fat-soluble and accumulate in the fatty tissue of the body.[33, 34] Cancer, nerve damage, and death are among the most serious effects of exposure.[35, 36]

Organophosphates

The most common group of compounds used as pesticides (including about half of the insecticides used in the United States)[37] are organophosphates. These are the same chemicals used as nerve agents in World War II.[38] These pesticides are highly toxic and proven carcinogenic compounds.[39] Direct brain damage and nerve damage are associated with exposure.[40] Organophosphates are especially harmful to developing nervous systems in infants and children.[41]

every acre of strawberries (compared to an average of 25 pounds per acre for other foods). Thirty-six different pesticides are commonly used on strawberries, and 90 percent of strawberries tested register pesticide contamination above safe levels. Raspberries trump strawberries with the application of 39 chemicals: 58 percent of the raspberries tested registered positive for contamination. Cherries are almost as dodgy with 25 pesticides and 91 percent contamination.

4. Apples and Pears

With 36 different chemicals detected in FDA testing, half of which are neurotoxins (meaning they cause brain damage), apples are almost as contaminated as strawberries. Ninety-one percent of apples tested positive for pesticide residue. Peeling nonorganic apples reduces but does not eliminate the danger of ingesting these chemicals. Pears rank hazardously near apples with 35 pesticides and 94 percent contamination.

5. Tomatoes

It's standard practice for more than 30 pesticides to be sprayed on conventionally grown tomatoes. The thin skin does not stop chemicals from infiltrating the whole tomato, so peeling won't help you here.

Clean Cotton-Pickin' Choice

Cotton is one of the most universally comfy, breathable, and soft fibers of any natural or man-made fabric. Pure cotton is a luxurious textile for clothing, sheets, towels, table linens, and even underwear and socks. But conventional cotton is one of the biggest agricultural bullies and most environmentally destructive constituents of all time. The simple act of growing just a pound of cotton for a T-shirt takes an enormous toll on the environment and significantly affects the health of folks living in cotton-growing areas.

The True Cost of Cotton[42, 43]

- 25 percent of all pesticides and insecticides used globally are on cotton—though cotton occupies only 3 percent of farmland.
- 600,000 tons of pesticides are used on cotton crops in America alone—that's 300 pounds per acre, or $\frac{1}{3}$ of a pound of pesticides for every pound of cotton!
- An average cotton crop is sprayed 30 to 40 times per growing season.
- Five of the top nine pesticides used on cotton in the United States are known to cause cancer—all nine are classified by the EPA as "Category I and II," which are the most dangerous of all chemicals.
- The most acutely toxic pesticide registered by the EPA, aldicarb, is standard for cotton crops. The number of states where aldicarb is detected in groundwater? Sixteen.
- In California, it is illegal to feed cotton leaves, stems, and short fibers to livestock because of the concentrated pesticide residues. Instead, the short fibers are used to make mattresses, pillows, tampons, swabs, and cotton balls. How many tampons does the average woman use in a lifetime? A lot.

Organics to the Rescue!

Fortunately, there are positive alternatives to conventional cotton. Organically grown cotton is the way to go. Organic cotton farming employs fields where pesticide use has been discontinued for at least 3 years to rebuild soil fertility and safety. No synthetic fertilizers or pesticides are used to grow organic cotton. Choose organic cotton to rest assured and for a clean tomorrow.

See the Resource Guide on page 378 for organic cotton companies.

6. Potatoes

Potatoes are one of the most popular vegetables, but they also rank among the most contaminated with pesticides and fungicides. Twenty-nine pesticides are commonly used, and 79 percent of potatoes tested exceed safe levels of multiple pesticides.

7. Spinach (and Other Greens, Including Lettuce)

The FDA found spinach to be the vegetable most frequently contaminated with the most potent pesticides used on food. Eighty-three percent of the conventionally grown spinach tested was found to be contaminated with dangerous levels of at least some of the 36 chemical pesticides commonly used to grow it.

8. Coffee

Most coffee is grown in countries where there are little to no standards regulating the use of chemicals and pesticides on food. The United States produces and exports millions of tons of pesticides, some of which are so dangerous that they are illegal to use on American farmland. Foreign countries import these chemicals to cultivate food, which is sold back to the United States. Coffee is an unfortunate culprit in this vicious cycle of malevolent agriculture. Purchasing "Fair Trade" coffee provides insurance that the premium price paid for this treasured

What about Kids?

There are "critical periods" in human development when exposure to a toxin can permanently alter the way an individual's biological system operates. For that reason, the EPA raises well-founded concerns about children being at higher risk for exposure to pesticides. Consider that:

- A child's internal organs are still developing, and immature enzymatic, metabolic, and immune systems may provide less natural protection.[44]
- In relation to their body weight, infants and children eat and drink more than adults, possibly increasing their exposure to pesticides in food and water.[45]
- Pesticides may harm a developing child by blocking the absorption of important food nutrients necessary for normal healthy growth.[46]
- If a child's excretory system is not fully developed, the body may not fully remove pesticides.[47]

beverage supports farms and workers with more equanimity and reward.

9. Peaches and Nectarines

Forty-five different pesticides are regularly applied to succulent, delicious peaches and nectarines in conventional orchards. The thin skin does not protect the fruit from the dangers of these poisons. Ninety-seven percent of nectarines and 95 percent of peaches tested for pesticide residue show contamination from multiple chemicals.

10. Grapes (Especially Imported Grapes)

Because grapes are a delicate fruit, they are sprayed multiple times during different stages of growth. The thin skin does not offer much protection from the 35 different pesticides used as a standard in conventional vineyards. Imported grapes are even more heavily treated than grapes grown in the United States. Several of the most poisonous pesticides banned in the United States are still used on grapes grown abroad. Eighty-six percent of grapes test positive for pesticide contamination; samples from Chile showed the highest concentration of the most poisonous chemicals.

11. Celery

Conventionally grown celery is subjected to at least 29 different chemicals, which cannot be washed off because, of course, celery does not have any protective skin. Ninety-four percent of celery tested was found to have pesticide residues in violation of safe levels.

12. Bell Peppers (Red and Green)

Bell peppers are one of the most heavily sprayed foods, with standard use of 39 pesticides. Sixty-eight percent of bell peppers tested had high levels of chemical pesticide residues. The thin skin of peppers does not offer much protection from spraying and is often waxed with harmful substances.

It's bizarre that the produce manager is more important to my children's health than the pediatrician.

—MERYL STREEP

GMO: Untested, Unlabeled, and We Are Eating Them

Genetically engineered food is a massive unchecked science experiment growing at alarming speed. The science of modifying genes is still so new that its side effects and long-term repercussions are absolutely unknown.

All living organisms have a genetic code, which is in part responsible for the expression and characteristics of the life form. For instance, you are made up of your parents' genes, which are made up of their parents' genes, and so forth. These genes determine the color of your eyes and skin, the shape of your earlobes, and the many functions and expressions of the trillions of cells in your body. This architecture is a fundamental part of how life, including plants, has evolved over billions of years. The science behind GMO involves invasively splicing genes together to create new ones that have never existed anywhere in nature.

The benevolent purpose of genetic engineering is an attempt to improve food, such as increasing the yield and resistance to pests by inoculating a plant with the beneficial traits of another organism. Crossing the pollen of different tomatoes to grow juicier, sweet fruit offers delicious results, and it's a natural practice that has been used by farmers in the field for a very long time. In a natural context, this is a noble profession, but unfortunately, this is not how the story of genetic engineering is playing out, nor where it ends. Crossing tomato plants with fish genes so the tomatoes will be resistant to cold weather is a new chapter with an uncertain ending.[48] And splicing carcinogenic pesticides to grow in every cell of the plant is an antagonistic part of the story told only behind closed doors and deliberately omitted from the labels of food in America. Genetically engineered food is an issue every person should be seriously concerned about.

To begin with, genetically engineered food requires very volatile science to override billions of years of genetic safeguards in order to successfully splice genes together. This process is done in a lab with a "gene gun." Genes are forced into the structure of the host much the way bacteria or tumors invade cells and tissue. Antibiotic "markers" are attached to the genes to ensure the new genes have successfully occupied the host. Let it be known that all GMO food contains antibiotics.[49]

One of the most pervasive concerns about GMO food is that there is no way to contain it.[50] A genetically engineered plant will produce pollen with these modified traits, which cannot be contained because pollen is airborne on the wind and carried by insects. Once GMO are unleashed, there is absolutely no recall. Natural species cannot coexist with GMO. It is definitive that the genetically engineered species will take over. The clock is ticking.

Principal GMO Health Concerns

1. Pesticides

The most common engineering of GMO involves splicing chemical pesticides into food crops.[51] Although it would seem that the purpose of growing a plant that contains these toxic chemicals in every cell would be to reduce the application of pesticides in the field, it is quite the opposite. Plants engineered with pesticides are simply able to tolerate larger doses of chemicals without dying. This raises more than one problem:

- Food from plants that have pesticides genetically spliced into them is saturated with contamination of chemicals far exceeding "safe" levels. The pesticides cannot be washed off or reduced by peeling away the skin.[52]
- These crops are additionally dosed with a heavy application of pesticides, compounding the dangers of these chemicals.[53]
- Studies show that an increased use of pesticides is not decreasing crop loss. Initially, pesticides kill insects and pests, but regular and excessive use of pesticides is breeding super-insects and weeds that are resistant to the chemical pesticides, and more crops than ever are lost.[54]

2. Resistance to Antibiotics

Antibiotic genes are used as "markers" to identify which host cells have accepted inserted foreign genes.[55] The antibiotics remain in the plant tissue and can be passed to humans and animals when eaten. The main concern is that a constant low dose of antibiotics in food will make antibiotics medically less effective, especially against newly emerging strains of *E. coli* and *Salmonella*.[56]

GMO and Food Labels

Genetically engineered food does not have to be labeled in America.[57] Roughly 75 percent of US processed foods—boxed cereals, other grain products, breads, chips, cookies, candy, frozen dinners, cooking oils, and more—contain some genetically modified ingredients.[58] Nearly every (nonorganic) product containing corn, soy, or canola or cottonseed oil, and a growing amount of wheat and rice, is contaminated with genetically modified organisms.

The Endangered Species List

Organic Papayas in Hawaii

In 1998, the University of Hawaii engineered papaya seeds to be resistant to a "black-ring" virus that was plaguing the fruit with unsightly black spots. At first, it was a grand success. Then it became clear that the engineered papayas were becoming susceptible to a host of other problems as a result of the engineering. The fields of nearby organic papaya farms soon became contaminated with the GMO papayas, as the genetically modified pollen travels when the trees flower in open air. This posed a crippling problem to the organic farming industry because more than half of the papaya crop is exported to Japan, where GMO food is banned.[59] Further, crops began to fail as the GMO papayas fell vulnerable to many other problems. Extensive testing soon revealed that the natural papaya species were being invaded by the GMO papaya. Just 6 years later, conservative estimates found that at least 50 percent of the non-intended papaya crops (wild papayas and organic papayas) were contaminated with GMO.[60] It is just a matter of time before natural, wild, and organic papayas are extinct in Hawaii.

3. Allergies and Toxic Effects of Gene Insertion

The crossing of one plant's genes with another is one thing, but the thought of splicing fish genes in a tomato is disconcerting to many. Ethics aside, new proteins are created from inserting genes from animals and non-food organisms like bacteria into plants.[61] These new proteins may have toxic or allergy-causing effects, especially in allergy-prone children. Further, as these genetically modified organisms roam freely through open pollen, it is absolutely unknown how they will mutate and interface with each other and other plants.

4. Pharm-Crops: Exposure to Drugs and Industrial Chemicals

The newest and most alarming developments with genetically engineered food are pharm-crops, pharmaceutical drugs and vaccines grown on food.[62] Very little information is available to the public sector, but permits have been issued to grow birth control, AIDS vaccines, herpes simplex vaccines, and animal-disease vaccines on food in open fields.[63] Corn is one of the most common host plants, and this is a fundamental reason to eat only organically grown corn (it must be free from GMO to be labeled "Certified Organic"), because cross-pollination from crops with drug-inserted genes cannot be contained.

The Fateful Five of Genetic Engineering

"The Fateful Five" are the dominant hosts of GMO. Unless otherwise specified, put your money on the fact that these foods are genetically modified. Certified organic food is considered safe from GMO contamination, and labels that read "GMO-free" are generally trustworthy.

1. Corn and Corn Products. Nonorganic corn syrup, fructose, high fructose corn syrup, glucose syrup, baking powder, corn oil, corn flour, cornmeal, cornstarch, soda, candy, candy bars, cookies, corn chips, and tortillas

2. Soy and Soy Products. Nonorganic soy sauce, tofu, soy protein isolates, soymilk, soy oil, soy cheese, lecithin, and soy lecithin fillers in meat products and vegetarian meat products

3. Rice

4. Wheat

5. Canola Oil (and Cottonseed Oil). I hope no one is eating cottonseed oil, because it is not regulated at all by the FDA.

Local versus Global

What is the true cost of food? It's far more than the price sticker or the supermarket circular reads. In addition to the billions of dollars spent annually on pesticides and GMO efforts, the price tag of our food more often than not includes shipping and handling from foreign ports.

A vast amount of the food we eat is grown far from the table at home. Wholesale market studies conclude that the average piece of food travels about 1,550 to 2,485 miles from farm to table.[64] This is 25 percent farther in the United States and 50 percent farther in the United Kingdom than just 20 years ago.[65] For consumers, the global market of food offers unparalleled choices for any kind of food, any time of year. This luxury is not without cost, however, consuming and exhausting staggering amounts of fuel and generating alarming amounts of pollution at the expense of culture, variety, and the stability of microeconomy.

"Transcontinental Lettuce"

In *Homegrown,* Brian Halwell reports that "the transcontinental head of lettuce, grown in Salinas Valley of California and shipped 5,000 kilometers to Washington, DC, requires about 36 times as much fossil fuel energy in transport as it provides in food energy when it arrives. By the time this lettuce gets to the United Kingdom, the ratio of fuel energy consumed jumps to 127."

The short-term benefits of food grown far from home pose long-term problems by eroding the stability of a diversified economy and agriculture. Subsidies, cheap oil, demographics, and innovation in food processing and storage have radically altered the economic balance of agriculture. Some economists argue that long-distance and imported food trade is better, cheaper, and more efficient because it enables the consumer (whether an individual, store, or country) to buy food at the lowest cost. The unseen cost of this marginalized perspective is much more complicated and without a doubt compromises social, ecological, and economic diversity.

Why Are We So Dependent on Food Grown Far Away?

Demographics

As urban and suburban areas sprawl, farmland is squeezed farther away from the centers of population.

Land Cost and Real Estate

Spiking real estate values crush the economic viability of small farms, especially in populated regions.

Big Business in Agriculture

The food industry in America is a $1 trillion industry with an unlimited market. Heavy transportation subsidies, including cheap fuel, obscure the crippling cost of shipping food to solely benefit Big Business in agriculture. Big Business is consuming independent companies and smaller, family-run farms to dominate the supply-demand market of the food industry. Retailers, even in the natural-organic food sector, are heavily influenced by the supply of what is cheap and consistent. Independent farms cannot compete with the power of consolidation. A tragic, common example can be seen in large retail stores that deal with consolidated suppliers over local farmers, and their shelves are stocked with produce from

The Power of Buying Locally Grown Food

- Buying locally grown food reestablishes agricultural diversity such as heirloom strains and varieties that are acclimated to region and geography. Growing and eating a wider variety of food benefits everyone in the food chain and reestablishes local ecology.

- Spending money on locally grown food stabilizes the regional economy and keeps money in the local economy longer. Dollars spent locally cycle through the microeconomy to create jobs, raise the standard of living, and boost the economy. Localized economies are less vulnerable than the fluctuating international market, especially when it comes to the food industry.

- Local food costs less and creates less waste.

anywhere in the country or world, regardless of local supply.

Advanced Technology in Storage and Transport

Advancements in refrigeration and storage methods, including natural and chemical preservatives, additives, and advanced techniques to control the stability of fresh produce (such as gassing fruits), make long-distance shipping and extended shelf life of produce possible.

Convenience: "Global Vending Machine"

The luxury of having any food, anytime, in any season tempts us to override the consideration of long-term sustainability. Getting mangoes to New York requires thousands of miles of transport. I know, I know, they are so divinely good, which is part of the problem.

Calendar of Produce

Seasonally available fresh produce is part of the foundation of a balanced plate. Following the rhythm of the growing seasons is a natural way to get a good variety of foods and, therefore, balance. Of course, it is possible to purchase imported items year-round, but seasonal produce has by far the best flavor because it is fresher and therefore has more nutrition. A local farmer's market is the finest place in town for direct access to seasonal goodies. Each month of the year offers a cornucopia of produce for a balanced plate.

JANUARY	FEBRUARY	MARCH	APRIL
VEGETABLES	**VEGETABLES**	**VEGETABLES**	**VEGETABLES**
CELERY	ARTICHOKE^	ARTICHOKE*	ARTICHOKE*
FENNEL^	ASPARAGUS^	ASPARAGUS	ASPARAGUS*
WINTER SQUASH	CELERY	CELERY	BEANS, FRESH FAVA^
GREENS:	FENNEL	FENNEL*	CELERY
BOK CHOY+	**GREENS:**	MOREL MUSHROOMS^	FENNEL
CHICORY	CHARD	PEAS—EDIBLE POD^	MOREL MUSHROOMS*
COLLARD GREENS^	CHICORY	**GREENS:**	PEAS—EDIBLE POD*,
KALE	COLLARDS	CHARD	ENGLISH/SHELLING^
SPINACH	KALE	COLLARD*	**GREENS:**
BRASSICA:	SPINACH	FRISÉE^	CHARD+
BROCCOLI	WATERCRESS	KALE	COLLARDS
BRUSSELS SPROUTS	**BRASSICA:**	MESCLUN^	DANDELION
CABBAGES—GREEN,	BROCCOLI*	NETTLES	KALE+
RED, NAPA, SAVOY	BRUSSELS SPROUTS+	SPINACH	LETTUCES
CAULIFLOWER	CABBAGES	TATSOI	NETTLES
ROOTS:	CAULIFLOWER	**BRASSICA:**	SPINACH
CARROT	**ROOTS:**	BROCCOLI	SPRING SALAD MIX*
CELERY ROOT/CELERIAC	CARROT	CABBAGES*	**BRASSICA:**
DAIKON+	CELERY ROOT/CELERIAC	CAULIFLOWER*	BROCCOLI
JERUSALEM ARTICHOKE	JERUSALEM ARTICHOKE	**ROOTS:**	CABBAGES
POTATO—WHITE+	POTATOES—RED AND	CARROT*	**ROOTS:**
RUTABAGA+	RUSSET	CELERY ROOT/CELERIAC	BEET^
TURNIP+	RADISH	JERUSALEM ARTICHOKE	CELERY ROOT/CELERIAC
ALLIUM:	TURNIP	RADISH	**ALLIUM:**
GREEN ONION ^		**ALLIUM:**	GREEN GARLIC+
LEEK		GREEN GARLIC*	LEEK
		LEEK	SWEET ONIONS—TEXAS^
		SPRING ONION	
FRUITS	**FRUITS**	**FRUITS**	**FRUITS**
AVOCADO—FUERTE+,	AVOCADO—HAAS	AVOCADO—HAAS	AVOCADO—HAAS
HAAS^	CHERIMOYA	CHERIMOYA	RHUBARB—FIELD*
KIWIFRUIT	RHUBARB	KIWIFRUIT	**CITRUS:**
RHUBARB—HOTHOUSE^	WATER CHESTNUT*	RHUBARB	GRAPEFRUIT
CITRUS:	**BERRIES:**	**BERRIES:**	ORANGE—NAVEL+
LEMON*	RASPBERRIES^	STRAWBERRIES	
ORANGE—NAVEL^,	STRAWBERRIES^	**CITRUS:**	
BLOOD^	**CITRUS:**	LEMON—MEYER	
TANGERINE/MANDARIN	GRAPEFRUIT*	LIME—KEY	
ORANGE*	ORANGES—NAVEL^,	ORANGE—NAVEL	
PEAR:	BLOOD+	TANGERINE/MANDARIN	
ANJOU	TANGERINE/MANDARIN	ORANGE	
BOSC+	ORANGE		

SYMBOL KEY: ^ = *COMING INTO SEASON*   * = *AT ITS PEAK*   + = *WINDING DOWN*

MAY	JUNE	JULY	AUGUST
VEGETABLES	**VEGETABLES**	**VEGETABLES**	**VEGETABLES**
ARTICHOKE+ ASPARAGUS+ BEANS— FAVA* CELERY+ CHIVES CORN^ GREEN BEANS^ FENNEL+ MOREL MUSH- ROOMS+ PEAS—EDIBLE POD*, ENGLISH/ SHELLING SUMMER SQUASH^ GREENS: ARUGULA CHARD+ DANDELION FIDDLEHEAD FERN KALE LETTUCE MIZUNA SALAD MIX+ SORREL* SPINACH+ BRASSICA: BROCCOLI+ CABBAGES+ CAULIFLOWER ROOTS: BEET CARROT NEW POTATOES^ RADISH+ ALLIUM: GREEN GARLIC+ RAMPS* SWEET ONION, VIDALIA*	CORN^ CUCUMBER^ EGGPLANT^ PEAS—ENGLISH/ SHELLING+ SUMMER SQUASH^ TOMATOES^ GREENS: KALE LETTUCES ROOTS: CARROT+ BEET+ POTATOES ALLIUM: GARLIC^ RED ONION SWEET ONION— VIDALIA*, WALLA WALLA+	BASIL^ CORN* CUCUMBER^ EGGPLANT^ GREEN BEANS OKRA^ PEPPER, BELL^ POTATOES SUMMER SQUASH* TOMATO^ ALLIUM: GARLIC RED ONION* SWEET ONION— VIDALIA, WALLA WALLA+	BASIL BEANS—SHELLING, CRANBERRY^ BLACK-EYED PEAS^ CORN* CUCUMBER* EGGPLANT GREEN BEANS* OKRA* PEPPER, BELL SUMMER SQUASH* TOMATO*
FRUITS	**FRUITS**	**FRUITS**	**FRUITS**
AVOCADO MANGO^ PEACH^ RHUBARB— FIELD+ BERRIES: BLACKBERRIES^ CHERRIES^ RASPBERRIES^ STRAWBERRIES MELONS: CANTALOUPE^ HONEYDEW^ WATERMELON^	APRICOT* FIGS—BLACK MISSION^ GRAPE^ MANGO NECTARINE^ PEACH^ PINEAPPLE BERRIES: BLACKBERRIES* BLUEBERRIES^ BOYSENBERRIES* RASPBERRIES* STRAWBERRIES CITRUS: LIME* MELONS: CANTALOUPE^ HONEYDEW^ WATERMELON^	CURRANTS^ FIGS—BLACK MISSION, CALIMYRNA GRAPES^ MANGO NECTARINE* PEACH* PINEAPPLE PLUM^ BERRIES: BLUEBERRIES* CHERRIES+ CITRUS: LIME ORANGE, VALENCIA^ PEARS: ASIAN^ BARTLETT^	MANGO* NECTARINE+ PEACH* PLUM* BERRIES: BLACKBERRIES+ BLUEBERRIES+ RASPBERRIES* FIGS: ADRIATIC BLACK MISSION BROWN TURKEY CALIMYRNA GRAPES: RED FLAME* THOMPSON SEEDLESS CITRUS: LIME+ ORANGE—VALENCIA* PEARS: ASIAN^ BARTLETT*

*SYMBOL KEY: ^ = COMING INTO SEASON   * = AT ITS PEAK   + = WINDING DOWN*

SEPTEMBER	OCTOBER	NOVEMBER	DECEMBER
VEGETABLES	**VEGETABLES**	**VEGETABLES**	**VEGETABLES**

ARTICHOKE^
BASIL*
BEANS—
  SHELLING*
CELERY^
CUCUMBER*
EGGPLANT*
KOHLRABI^
OKRA*
PEPPER—BELL,
  HOT
TOMATO
 	
GREENS:
KALE^
LETTUCES
 	
ROOTS:
CELERY ROOT/
  CELERIAC
 	
ALLIUM:
GARLIC*
ONION
SUMMER
  SQUASH+
WINTER
  SQUASH^
	ARTICHOKE*
	BASIL+
	BEANS—
	  SHELLING+
	CARDOON*
	CELERY
	EGGPLANT+
	GREEN BEANS
	KOHLRABI
	PEPPER—
	  BELL+, HOT+
	PUMPKIN
	TOMATO+
	WILD
	  MUSHROOMS*
	WINTER
	  SQUASH^
	
	GREENS:
	ARUGULA
	CHARD^
	KALE
	LETTUCES
	PARSLEY
	SPINACH^
	TURNIP
	
	BRASSICA:
	BROCCOLI^
	BRUSSELS
	  SPROUTS^
	CABBAGES^
	
	ROOTS:
	BEET^
	CELERY ROOT/
	  CELERIAC
	DAIKON^
	PARSNIP
	POTATOES
	RADISH
	RUTABAGA
	SWEET POTATO
	TURNIP^
	YAM^
		ARTICHOKE+
		CELERY^
		DILL*
		GREEN BEANS+
		KOHLRABI+
		PEPPER—
		  BELL+, HOT+
		WINTER
		  SQUASH*
		
		GREENS:
		BOK CHOY
		CHARD^
		ENDIVE
		KALE
		SALAD MIX
		
		BRASSICA:
		BROCCOLI
		BRUSSELS
		  SPROUTS
		CABBAGE^
		
		ROOTS:
		BEET
		CARROT^
		CELERY ROOT/
		  CELERIAC
		DAIKON*
		JERUSALEM
		  ARTICHOKE^
		PARSNIP
		POTATOES
		RADISH
		RUTABAGA
		SWEET
		  POTATO*
		TURNIP^
		YAM*
		
		ALLIUM:
		GARLIC
		LEEK
			CELERY
			PARSLEY
			WILD MUSH-
			  ROOMS*
			WINTER SQUASH
			
			GREENS:
			BOK CHOY
			SALAD MIX
			SPINACH
			
			BRASSICA:
			BROCCOLI
			BRUSSELS
			  SPROUTS*
			CABBAGE
			CAULIFLOWER
			
			ROOTS:
			CARROT
			CELERY ROOT/
			  CELERIAC
			DAIKON+
			JERUSALEM
			  ARTICHOKE
			PARSNIP+
			POTATOES
			SWEET POTATO*
			TURNIP*
			YAM*

FRUITS	**FRUITS**	**FRUITS**	**FRUITS**

APPLE*
FIGS+
GRAPE*
MANGO+
MELONS+
PERSIMMON—
  FUYU (FIRM)^
  HACHIYA (SOFT)^
PLUM+
POMEGRANATE^
 	
CITRUS:
ORANGE—
  VALENCIA*
 	
PEARS:
ASIAN*
BARTLETT+
QUINCE^
	AVOCADO—
	  HAAS+,
	  FUERTE^
	PERSIMMON—
	  FUYU (FIRM)*
	  HACHYA
	  (SOFT)*
	POMEGRANATE*
	PRICKLY
	  PEAR^
	
	BERRIES:
	CRANBERRY^
	RASPBERRIES+
	
	CITRUS:
	LEMON^
	KUMQUAT^
	ORANGE—
	  VALENCIA+
	
	NUTS:
	ALMOND*
	CHESTNUT*
	PISTACHIO*
	WALNUT*
	
	PEARS:
	BOSC^
	COMICE^
	QUINCE*
		APPLE+
		AVOCADO^
		CRANBERRY*
		GUAVA*
		PERSIMMON*
		POMEGRAN-
		  ATE+
		PRICKLY PEAR*
		STARFRUIT*
		
		CITRUS:
		LEMON^
		ORANGE—
		  NAVEL^
		TANGERINE/
		  MANDARIN
		  ORANGE
		
		PEARS:
		ANJOU^
		BOSC*
		COMICE*
		QUINCE+
			AVOCADO—HAAS,
			  FUERTE
			CHERIMOYA^
			CRANBERRY+
			CURRANT
			DATES
			KIWIFRUIT
			LATE POMEGRAN-
			  ATE+
			
			CITRUS:
			GRAPEFRUIT^
			LEMON
			ORANGE—
			  NAVEL^
			TANGERINE/
			  MANDARIN
			  ORANGE*

SYMBOL KEY: ^ = COMING INTO SEASON   * = AT ITS PEAK   + = WINDING DOWN

CHAPTER 2

Nutritional Cross-Training: Many Roads, One Table

The purpose of the art of cooking is to manage a part of the environment—minerals, water, biological life, atmosphere, pressure, and time—to become the simplest dishes in the most practically and delicately condensed form suitable for the smoothest transformation into a healthy, happy, free man.

—MICHIO KUSHI

There are many roads leading to the table. It seems food ranks up there with religion and politics in terms of heated debates and staunch positions. Low carb or low fat? Whole grains or high protein? Steamed, grilled, or just plain raw? Peeling back the practice and expressions of these positions often reveals more similarities than differences. Food seems very much like religion in that we are all talking about the same things, calling them different names, and practicing different approaches to the same table—that is, healthy food that tastes great.

Macrobiotics, raw foods, and Ayurveda are all individually developed and insightful systems. All have been around for a very long time, each with several incarnations of practice. Though the extreme practice of any one leaves little room for another, the fundamental principles of these systems are in agreement: eating the freshest seasonal, regional, naturally grown whole foods, at the peak of nutrition, prepared in a way that suits the body best for balance, harmony, energy, and health.

The goal of cross-training is to get the body into epic, versatile shape. In terms of physical training, it draws from many different types of exercise to condition the body for peak performance across the board. For nutrition and the culinary arts, I use the term in a similar fashion, to create a balanced plate that draws from several dietary systems and traditions for a more versatile approach to optimal health and fantastic flavor.

This is not a quick-fix diet book, and these systems are not presented as strict dietary programs. Step-by-step programs are usually a temporary solution and tend to fade as all fads do. *The Balanced Plate* is a lifestyle primer based on a whole foods philosophy that is fit for a lifetime. Rather than offering a program full of absolutes, which I believe is neither accurate nor appropriate for everyone, I hope that you will use the following overview of systems to tailor a whole foods cross-training plan that appeals to you and can evolve with the seasons and the cycles of your life. As all things change, a more deeply developed relationship with food will help steady the course and balance the plate of life.

Whole Foods:
The Complete Package for a Balanced Plate

The study of nutritional science is pretty complex and easily misconstrued. Understanding the needs of the body gets very complicated very quickly. Certain nutrients require cofactors to be utilized; some minerals need to be in a certain ratio with others in order to be absorbed properly; particular vitamins act as coenzymes to make others work. It's more than enough to make the average home cook throw in her apron and order take-out. So how can you be sure you're getting all the nutrients your body needs? Easy. By eating a diet rich in whole foods—the foundation of a balanced plate.

Whole foods are a complete package, consumed as close to their natural state as possible. Fresh vegetables, fruits, whole grains and beans, nuts and seeds, seaweed, herbs and spices, high-quality oils, and natural seasonings—ideally grown naturally and organically—are all part of the balanced plate of whole foods. These foods have had little to no processing and retain most, if not all, of their original nutritive value and fiber.

Unprocessed whole foods are not denatured by high-tech refinery or adulterated by artificial ingredients, additives, colorings, or preservatives; therefore they are fertile with naturally occurring nutrients and prosperous with the subtle complexity of genuine, full flavor.

The Intelligence of Whole Foods

The real intelligence of whole foods is the natural intelligence of plants. Using energy from sunlight, plants transform inorganic nutrients from the soil into organic bioavailable nutrients fit for humans to feast and thrive on. The complex spectrum of macronutrients—protein, fat, and carbohydrates—and micronutrients—vitamins, minerals, and phytonutrients—is soundly represented in the cornucopia of whole foods.

Just as the intelligence of our bodies requires cooperation (a few trillion cells strong!), the matrix of a plant's nutrition also requires cooperation. Nutrients are designed to function in a sophisticated, synergistic relationship with one another. All of the essential nutrients we need to live depend on a balanced ratio and the cooperation of others for maximum utilization. Some vitamins and minerals act as vital cofactors to make others available. For example, adequate amounts of vitamin D are necessary for calcium to be absorbed and employed. Potassium works to decrease the loss of calcium in the body and must be in a balanced ratio with sodium to support the pump that feeds and flushes cells. Vitamin C enhances iron uptake and works to regenerate vitamin E for optimal antioxidant action.

The study of this complex puzzle gets tricky quickly, but choosing whole foods simplifies the equation. The intelligence of naturally occurring nutrients from whole foods is that all of the necessary elements and catalysts are consistently present. Our bodies immediately recognize the nutritive value of whole foods and know how to process them effectively. On the other hand, processed, isolated, and denatured foodstuffs are like an alphabet missing the vowels: difficult to translate into anything intelligible. Our bodies are so good to us, putting up with so many constant demands and complicated functions. The least we can do is regularly treat ourselves to fine, clean fuel and chew well with gratitude.

Choosing Whole Foods

It seems so many of us want to enjoy the most of what is available with the least stress and sacrifice. Eating whole foods is simply that.

There are more obvious whole foods choices, such as favoring fresh tomatoes over ketchup (though in many school lunch programs, ketchup is considered a vegetable) or fresh summer corn over the corn syrup in

Enriched Foods

"Enriched" food products are really a misnomer. Foods that have been artificially fortified with vitamins and nutrients are not the same as foods with naturally occurring vitamins and nutrients. Many nutritionists will agree that our bodies cannot do much with nutrients like these—our bodies simply cannot absorb much of them at all because they are just pieces of the puzzle and do not include the complex of cofactors that enable them to be utilized. The best source of all vitamins, minerals, and nutrients is whole food.

soda pop or chips, but there is a spectrum in between where smart choices can make enjoying favorite foods a more nourishing experience.

Vegetables and fruits are best fresh, in season, and organically grown. Organic frozen produce is fine from time to time, when seasonal delicacies like berries and sweet peas are not fresh from the farm, but cans of veggies and fruit probably have more to offer as a weight to set a vegetable terrine (page 320) than as staples in the pantry. I think a more lenient exception can be made for organic canned beans; though they are not as full of nutrients or as tender as sprouted and blanched or freshly cooked beans, they are certainly handy for tossing together a Three Bean Salad (page 221) in a pinch or whipping up hummus in a jiffy.

In the bean corner, soy products come in just about every shape and medium, most of which are really processed. Products like tofu and soymilk definitely have protein and

nutrients, but they're a far cry from the simple greatness of edamame (the whole soybean in or out of its shell). The closer it is to its whole, natural state, generally the better it is for you.

Choosing the fortified nutrition of whole grains like quinoa and brown rice over the stripped character of white rice, pasta, and bread is a classic whole foods move. This isn't to say pasta and bread are verboten, just choose wisely. Hearty multigrain bread, for instance, is a more wholesome and smarter choice than, say, artificially enriched white bread. There are also some great organic pasta products made from whole wheat and quinoa, though to be quite honest, some of them are pretty horrible, too. I am not trying to make pasta the enemy—a little fresh pasta with Quick Rustic Tomato Sauce (page 336), a heap of veggies, and salad can be oh-so-good. It is all about balance. It's not about prying things you love from your kitchen, but adding more of the things you do love to the table. A more joyful objective is to make the best choices whenever possible and try to balance out due indulgences.

On the sweet side, unrefined sweeteners like maple syrup, agave, and honey tantalize the sweetest tooth and still contain a good amount of minerals without jacking blood-sugar levels around nearly as much as the leeching rush of refined sugar. Kudos to that! Less-refined sugar, like organic evaporated cane juice, Sucanat, or organic sugar, is the better choice when granulated sugar is called for, and it's free from the chemicals used to grow and process conventional white sugar.

As for oils, unrefined and unfiltered is generally the way to go. So many of the precious compounds, like chlorophyll, riboflavin, and antioxidants, are intact in unrefined oil, whereas the good stuff in commercially produced oils is commonly bleached and filtered out because it shortens shelf life. Naturally refined oils, like grapeseed oil and some sesame oils, do have a place with certain techniques because they can stand higher heat without breaking down to smoke. Therefore, the process of refining is important and varies from company to company; natural refining is gentle and does not use chemicals or harsh solvents. As far as filtered oil goes, unfiltered is generally best. A good extra-virgin olive oil should be slightly cloudy with good stuff and have sediment on the bottom. The one exception is flax oil, which is more stable when it is filtered because the particulate matter that makes it through pressing tends to speed up its breakdown. Otherwise and overall, less is more—less processing, mo' bettah. See "Oils" on page 96 for a full spread of guiding info.

With so many of the savvy ingredients that bump recipes up to the stratosphere of phenomenal flavor, like soy sauce, wasabi, vanilla extract, and so forth, choose pure products without artificial colors, flavorings, or preservatives. Most of the high-quality products are made traditionally, in pre–chemical revolution fashion, and naturally embody a whole foods philosophy.

The philosophy of whole foods is a solid foundation to cover the essential bases of sound nutrition with any given culinary approach. Taking the guesswork out of getting the full allowance of essential nutrition by choosing complete, whole foods for a balanced plate leaves more room to romp, ramble, and play with passion and possibility.

In art and dream, may you proceed with abandon. In life, may you proceed with balance and stealth.

—PATTI SMITH

Macrobiotics:
Balanced Basics for All Seasons

Macrobiotics takes a big, long view of life. The word is derived from Greek—"macro" meaning "big, large, long" and "bio" meaning "life"—and macrobiotics is as old as the hills. The term *macrobiotic* has been used all over the world throughout history by philosophers and physicians to signify living in health and harmony with nature and one's surroundings; eating a simple, balanced diet; and enjoying a long life. I don't know about you, but I want to sign right up for that!

The macrobiotic system is rooted in balance. The long and short of it is that balance in all things is the key to health and happiness. The roots of this system are found in ancient cultures, the teachings of Buddhism, the Old and New Testaments, and Taoism. The branches of macrobiotic principles reflect its core roots of balance, reaching through the micro- and macrospectra of human health, emotions, philosophy, spirituality, planetary history, and evolution.

One of the driving principles of macrobiotics considers that food and food quality affect our lives deeply. The concept that food is the fundamental, primary medicine to bring balance to the body is surprisingly as revolutionary today as it was 5,000 years ago, even with the current tremendous advances in science and modern medicine.

A Brief History of Macrobiotics

The concept of macrobiotics has been around in perpetuity. In its current manifestation as a methodized system, the practical principles of macrobiotics originated in the late 19th century by a physician named Sagen Ishisuka. Dr. Ishisuka extensively studied both Western and Eastern medicine and established a theory of nutrition and medicine based on applying the Western medical sciences of medicine, biology, chemistry, biochemistry, and physiology to traditional Oriental medicine. Using an elementary practice to recover from severe kidney and skin disease, he went on to successfully treat innumerable patients, for the most part simply by having them return to natural, balanced foods. His theory was based on a few basic principles:

- Food is the basis of health, happiness, and a long life.
- The best food is natural, whole, and unrefined.
- The best food is locally grown and eaten in season.
- Sodium and potassium in food are the most important antagonistic and complementary elements for the harmony of yin and yang in the body.

Though his prescription mirrored the simple

Japanese diet of traditional food, it was radically against the grain of the European dairy, meat, and refined foods diet that was sweeping Japan by popular storm. He acquired an extensive following and a highly respected posse of associates who were known as the Soku-Yo-Kail. One of Dr. Ishisuka's prodigies, Nishibata Nanabu, treated a patient, a young man named Joichi Sakurazawa who suffered from a serious illness, using Dr. Ishisuka's treatment of eating natural, balanced food. Joichi Sakurazawa became a student of these principles and went on to study at Columbia University and sit with the great minds of the time, including Albert Einstein and Albert Schweitzer, and become a contemporary founder of the methodology of the macrobiotic system using the pen name George Oshawa. Oshawa is widely regarded as the "father of macrobiotics" and was hugely responsible for systematizing this well-respected philosophy and approach to health and healing. He introduced macrobiotics to Europe and his students—namely Michio and Aveline Kushi—subsequently to North America in the late 1960s. Go, team.

The Balance of Yin and Yang

With an emphasis on locally grown, natural whole foods, eating macrobiotically is in accord with the principle balance of yin and yang properties. Using food as a fundamental tool, the deeper expression of macrobiotics extends into the whole of a lifestyle, observing and balancing yin and yang in the nature of all things. George Oshawa, one of the main macrobiotic cats of all time, said, "Food is the key to health, and health is the key to peace." Deep.

The concept of yin and yang describes two primal opposing yet complementary forces that govern all life and can be found in all things in the universe. Yin and yang are an ancient dichotomy and reflect a sensible relationship to food. To this end, food is considered in terms of yin and yang according to taste, properties, and effects on the body. Yin foods have a cold, damp, expansive, sweet nature. Yang foods have a hot, dry, contractive, salty nature. Macrobiotic principles attempt to achieve harmony by keeping the natural forces of yin and yang in food in balance, thereby allowing the person to enjoy good health and a long life. The ideal diet is based on foods with a natural balance of yin and yang, such as vegetables and grains. Of course, none of us can eat like the Buddha at all times. Therefore, when eating foods that are extreme in nature, such as chocolate, which is extremely delicious, it is important to eat other foods to balance the scales, like at some point eating a big bowl of steamed broccoli. The idea is to cultivate a dependable balance, and in my opinion not to get crazy about it, but to have the tools to

> Let food be thy medicine,
> and medicine be thy food.
>
> —HIPPOCRATES

correct imbalances and enjoy indulgences without all of the baggage.

The Guiding Principles of Macrobiotics

The interpretation of the macrobiotic system varies depending on the practitioner or teacher. The basic principles are permeated by a good dose of common sense. The core values are not radical and can be embraced with any system of health and good food.

Seasonal, Regional, Organic Food

Food that is fresh in season, grown locally and organically, is a smart base for everyone. As the seasons change, so do our bodies. The cornucopia that emerges and subsides with the seasons is a brilliant way to get a good variety of foods to please the palate and nourish the body. Food grown close to home is fresher and better. Way to go!

Food grown locally, or in the home region, makes good sense, not only for freshness, but to support the local economy and to curb the expense and resources required to ship, store, and broker food from far away. Buying food in a farmer's market is one of the simplest and

most profound acts one can make personally and globally for a sustainable future. Economic studies show that money spent in a local community will stay in the community longer. That makes good homegrown sense.

Fresh, Whole Food

Traditional macrobiotics advises eating food in its highest life force. While the jury is still out on the interpretation of what "life force" is, the energy of a growing plant is irrefutable.

Fresh food is at the peak of nutrition. Whole food is a complete package. Fresh, whole food is in a league of optimal nourishment and nutrition. Canned, frozen, processed, and preserved food is in an eroded state of compromise. Note to self: Evaluate the difference between fresh snap peas from the farm stand in the zenith of summer and the soggy misfortune of canned peas from the school cafeteria.

With less time from the farm to the plate, more nutrients are available for our bodies and more flavors and textures are present to indulge the senses.

Balanced Variety of Food

A good array of food is ideal to meet the complex needs of the body. Traditional

A Note about Indulgence

In my days of very pious eating, a well-known friend who indulged in a life of debauchery would lecture to me, "Too much of anything is still too much, including moderation, Renée. Live a little!" I would rebut to his portly frame, "Your arteries are likely plastered with enough cholesterol to kill an elephant, and I will laugh longer because I will last longer," at which he would heartily laugh. He has since trimmed down and tuned up after heart trouble and a brush with diabetes, and I have mellowed my militant health agenda. We still taunt and tease one another shamelessly.

I eat well almost all of the time and keep trim and fit so I can indulge without guilt just some of the time. I figure a bit of naughtiness flanked by plenty of good habits keeps me resilient and free from being a complete social derelict. I do, after all, have a penchant for fine wine and chocolate. And I do profess that pleasure is an inherent part of health.

macrobiotic principles are anchored by the concept of yin and yang. The concept of yin-yang is as old as the hills and recognized in most health and scientific systems. Yin-yang, positive-negative, hot-cold, acid-alkaline, damp-dry, male-female. Name it, and call it what you will. Philosophically, one can consider the polarity of all things, from balance to extremes, which manifests through food. The macrobiotic system is designed to cultivate a steady balance in the body by choosing a broad range of plant-based foods that balance, match, and complement each other. An ideal portfolio of food will represent species from all stages of biological development. This includes ancient foods such as seaweed and unhybridized wild and heirloom vegetables, root vegetables, leafy green vegetables, nuts and seeds, cultivated grains and beans, and seasonal fruits. The concept that we are a product of everything that has come before us may be nourished and balanced.

Apropos, changing up favorite foods and rotating the approach to preparing food will keep everything fresh. As in physical training, it is important to vary the exercise of a good, core program to garner the utmost benefits.

Moderation of Extreme Foods and Flavors

Less is more. Moderate use of oil, salt, seasoning, and heat cultivates buoyant health and an easy balance for the body. Foods that are extremely sour, salty, sweet, spicy, or bitter are harsh and overstimulating to the body.

Given that balance is the ideal natural state of being, foods with extreme flavors are an imposition that stresses the body in its effort to maintain a healthy equilibrium. Analogously, extreme heat and cold are rough on food and destructive to the precious good stuff. High-temperature cooking and freezing do not get the thumbs-up.

Extreme foods enable the cycle of craving, a symptom of imbalance. For instance, too many sweets cause plenty of problems on their own and often feed a craving for salty, oily foods, which cycles back to a hankering for more sweet stuff and so forth.

Traditional macrobiotics has a well-earned reputation for being bland. To the unaccustomed palate, "moderately seasoned" can be confused with "no taste at all," and lessening stimulating tastes can be insipid. But when we begin to relax and simplify flavors, our taste buds grow more appreciative of and sensitive to subtle flavors.

Natural Seasonings

Natural seasonings complement and bring out the gorgeous natural flavors of food. Natural seasonings are not highly refined or plagued with additives, preservatives, or artificial flavoring. Highly refined foods strip the body of precious nutrients, and artificial additives and preservatives are damaging and toxic to our precious insides. No good.

Macrobiotic Principles of the Universe

As Interpreted by George Oshawa

Macrobiotics has a deep reach, through the tangible, to the philosophical and existential realms of life. Simple and sensible. I like that.

The seven universal principles of the infinite universe are:

1. Everything is a differentiation of one Infinity.
2. Everything changes.
3. All antagonisms are complementary.
4. There is nothing identical.
5. What has a front has a back.
6. The bigger the front, the bigger the back.
7. What has a beginning has an end.

The idea is to show up and get out of the way of good-quality, fresh produce and well-prepared foods to let the flavors naturally bloom. There are many choice condiments, such as shoyu (soy sauce), tamari, vinegar, sweeteners, and salt, that are unrefined and free of additives and preservatives.

Macrobiotics includes a bevy of ingredients unknown to many a Western palate. Discover the flavors of the umeboshi plum and vinegar (dynamic salty, sour, sweet pickled plum and brine), mirin (sweet rice wine), shiso leaf (the herb that makes pickled ginger pink!), ponzu (a sour, salty, sweet condiment), yuzu (a Japanese citron), and gomasio (a staple seasoning made from roasted and ground sesame and salt). Oh my! Check in with Chapter 3, Kitchen Elements, to inspire an ancient and new world of flavor.

A Clean and Peaceful Atmosphere of Cooking and Eating

Mindful preparation of food and thorough enjoyment of eating are precious parts of the cycle. I regularly stamp my feet with happiness, giddily wave my hands, and make joyful little noises when I eat. I am in unabashed wonder at the deep crimson of the beet, the mandala of the cross section of a head of purple cabbage, the complex aroma that fills the kitchen from a rich vegetable broth. Fortunately, most of my dear friends are equally enthusiastic. Recognize that the sunrise and the rainfall grow plants and make possible our very human senses of taste and smell and tactile delight in eating. Okay, I admit, I can be caught eating over the sink while running out the door, though a peaceful pocket of mindful dining feels as deeply nourishing as the food itself. A leisurely, loving meal is one of the finest indulgences I can conjure, especially when I don't have to do the dishes.

Here and Now

The macrobiotic system emerged long before the chemical revolution and the belief in "plastics for a better tomorrow" that reigned as truth. Understanding food to be one of the most fundamental elements to cultivate balance not only in our bodies, but also with our environment, may be more profoundly true now than at the turn of the last century. Today, there are a growing number of elements in our food and environment that are competing to disrupt the balance in our bodies and with our environment. Now more than ever, food is a profoundly important medicine and prime factor in maintaining health. The spirit of this book genuinely reflects macrobiotic principles, with a focus on food for a balanced plate and a deeper expression extending into the whole of a lifestyle—cultivating and balancing yin and yang in the nature of all things. For as Dr. Seuss said, "Remember that life's a great balancing act."

Five Tastes of Macrobiotics

There are five major tastes that show up on the radar of our tongues, which make up the harmony of flavor we experience: sour, salty, sweet, spicy (also called pungent), and bitter. Historically, it was believed that different flavors are sensed by different parts of the tongue. For example, sweet flavors were supposedly registered by the tip of the tongue, salty and sour on the sides, and bitter in the back. The popularized taste map, which still shows up in anatomy books, may be more fiction than science. In fact, all tastes are elicited from all regions of the tongue, though some areas may be more sensitive to certain flavors.

The relationship of the five tastes maps the blueprint of the character of food. Macrobiotics chooses simple, natural seasonings to represent the five tastes for a gentle balance of flavor. There are a few additional tastes recognized by other systems. "Astringent" is a sixth taste distinguished by Ayurveda, and "umami" has recently emerged as an altogether new flavor comprised of the savory flavor found in protein-rich foods, some vegetables, soy sauce, miso, seaweed, and mushrooms.

Our sense of smell is estimated to be 10,000 times more sensitive than our sense of taste. The aroma of food more accurately describes the depth and complexity we associate with flavor, because the actual dynamics of taste are very basic.

Five Tastes of Macrobiotics

The concept of the five tastes is part of the core of a balanced plate. Balancing flavor is true culinary cross-training and pervasive in all culinary contexts and traditions. The simple balance of these tastes educes an ample expression of the character of flavor. In the spirit of Goldilocks, not too much, not too little, just right.

SOUR	SALTY	SWEET	PUNGENT/ SPICY	BITTER
BROWN RICE VINEGAR LEMON APPLE CIDER VINEGAR UMEBOSHI PLUM, PASTE, AND VINEGAR PICKLES SAUERKRAUT SHISO LEAVES	SEA SALT MISO SHOYU (SOY SAUCE) TAMARI UMEBOSHI PLUM, PASTE, AND VINEGAR SHISO LEAVES SEAWEED GOMASIO (GROUND ROASTED SESAME AND SALT)	BROWN RICE SYRUP AMASAKE BARLEY MALT SYRUP APPLES, APPLE JUICE, AND APPLESAUCE CARROTS PARSLEY LIGHT MISO	GINGER GREEN ONIONS/ SCALLIONS ONIONS DAIKON AND RADISHES WATERCRESS ARUGULA	DANDELION GREEN NORI WAKAME GOMASIO (GROUND ROASTED SESAME AND SALT)

Raw and Living Foods: Vibrant Balance

Eating raw food is one of the oldest and newest approaches to eating for life. Today's raw foodies are flying the coop from the pigeonholed concept of carrot sticks and hunks of raw cauliflower. Over the last decade, fabulous talent and technology have brought raw foods into the spotlight of respected culinary regard. Preparing raw food is an innovative approach to the culinary arts, and the proven health benefits of a raw foods diet are phenomenal. Many say raw food provides pure, clean energy, grows age-defying skin, keeps our bodies trim and fit, and all our organs happy and young. In short, raw and living foods are part of an intelligent prescription for a balanced plate.

The premise of raw and living food nutrition is based on sensible science and experience. The quantum of the universe, including your magnificent body, is made of only two things: matter and energy. Organic raw and living foods are the finest matter available, alive with the energy of nutrients and enzymes, made deliciously bioavailable with ease, vibrancy, and sustainability.

Raw and living foods typify the apex of whole foods nutrition and the quintessence of energy and vitality. Regardless of just how much raw food any of us eat, it is an undeniable truth that fresh, organic, living food does the body good.

What Are Raw and Living Foods?

Raw and living foods are whole and unprocessed, fresh and unrefined—in the strict definition, they are not heated above 112°F. Raw foods contain the complete spectrum of their naturally occurring vitamins, minerals, and nutrients, complete with the enzymes needed to turn the food into pure, clean energy the body can use. We are not talking about just carrot and celery sticks, or even simply fruit, vegetables, nuts, and seeds. There is a blossoming trend in culinary art ingenuity, restaurants, products, and recipes that reveals some really fantastic foods that have been created with these ideals in mind. Fresh juices, nut milks, shakes, smoothies, soups (chilled and warmed), wraps and rolls with dipping sauces, spreads, pâté, sushi, delectably layered dishes, desserts, and even chocolate are delicious examples of the abundant repertoire of raw and living foods. Preparing raw and living foods for a multitude of flavors and textures requires a different approach to the culinary arts, but one with seemingly limitless possibilities. The cornucopia of irresistible recipes and options for both the novice and the well-seasoned chef makes integrating raw and living elements into any type of diet both easy and enjoyable.

A Good Place to Start

Everybody eats some raw foods, even if it is a slice of tomato on a sandwich. Foods like guacamole and salsa are raw by nature and welcomed to the table of most. Smoothies are a quick, convenient way to start the day, and some are so delicious that they seem indulgent. Including salad is a complementary pleasure to any lunch or dinner. Choosing high-quality ingredients like extra-virgin olive oil, good sea salt, and a bevy of fresh herbs and spices not only seasons food with delicious appeal but also nourishes and balances the body. Many people find eating raw food to be contagious, especially after getting a taste of how good they feel and the clean-burning energy these foods provide. Including raw and living foods in your diet opens up the spectrum of food choices with new flavors, textures, and ingredients, for abundant returns. The more, the merrier.

Principal Benefits of Raw and Living Foods

Complete Package

As you know by now, food in its whole state is a complete package. Raw food is the ultimate whole food because it is consumed in the state provided by nature. Now, I am going to make a preemptive statement about "cooking" food: I don't believe that fire belongs on the sidelines in the kitchen. Of course, I see

that certain foods are clearly more nutritious raw, and this has been my main orientation for more than a decade. But I also see that certain foods need to be broken down—especially the tough cellulose of some vegetables, grains, and beans—so our bodies can thoroughly absorb their nutrients. This can be done by marinating with lemon and salt, fermenting, culturing, or by sensitive and mindful cooking.

Peak of Nutrition

Fresh, organic raw and living food is at the peak of nutrition, and it's a source of pure energy full of life force. The life force of living foods can be called the *electrical energy* that activates the *chemical energy* in our bodies, enabling *mechanical energy* to use that fine matter at its highest potential in every action in our cells, tissue, bones, and blood.

Some nutrients are partially destroyed and others completely destroyed by heat, light, air, and water. In fact, studies suggest that 40 to 60 percent of protein is destroyed by cooking. Half the goods for twice the work? Not a good deal. Hence, a fundamental principle of eating raw food is choosing food at the height of nutrition to fuel the body with pure energy.

Enzymes and Easy Digestion

Enzymes are the sparks of life. They make things happen. They are tiny specialized proteins that catalyze essential activity in the body. From blinking an eye to secreting saliva, from repairing tissue and beating the heart, to the essential process of digestion, every metabolic action in the body requires enzymes. These actions include the multitude of chemical reactions in the body required to sustain life, including and especially the big job of digestion.

Enzymes are very delicate molecules and highly sensitive to heat. It is widely accepted that enzymes are destroyed by temperatures in excess of 110° to 112°F. Cooked, processed, refined, or pasteurized foods are, therefore, devoid of these precious team players. So what happens when naturally occurring enzymes in food are knocked off? The body has to manufacture them, which requires a lot of energy. Enzymes are naturally secreted in saliva and by the stomach, intestines, and pancreas. But food that is completely devoid of enzymes demands these glands and organs to work overtime to provide enough of the right enzymes to master the task of digestion. Our bodies are occupied with maintenance and repair without the burden of expending undue energy just to be fed. Digestion requires a bounteous amount of energy as it is, which is why your mother forbade swimming immediately after lunch. The same lunch made from fresh, raw food will not require the standard copious amounts of energy to digest, which leaves much more time to play and energy to replenish, repair, and maintain tissues, blood, and organs. A far better deal and much more fun.

Juicy with Organic Water

Fresh, organic fruits and vegetables are full of organic water, which keeps the body juicy and well hydrated. Water is one of the most important elements for our bodies and the first to hitchhike out of food when it is heated. The valuable organic water in fresh fruits and vegetables is the kind our bodies can truly drink into their cells. Further, the organic water is the medium in fresh foods where valuable nutrients reside, like precious water-soluble vitamins. They just can't survive a broken home (even with therapy).

How Much Raw Food Is Enough?

Other than death and taxes, there are no absolutes. What works for me may not be quite right for you. And what works today may not apply a year from now. I truly believe in and respect the individual needs of every body.

I am all for what feels good. For years I thrived on an exclusive diet of raw food. Now I eat primarily raw foods and dabble in other culinary delights with fresh, organic standards. I find my body and choices shift with the seasons, climate, social situation, demand of schedule, and emotional terrain.

A minimum of 50 percent raw food is ideal for a lot of people. Many strike a healthful

The Family of Enzymes

AMYLASE breaks down carbohydrates—both starch and sugar—which are the primary fuel for the body and brain. Found in fresh fruits, vegetables, and honey.

PROTEASE breaks down protein. The word *protease* sounds kind of sexy, and it is. Breaking down protein to be available for use by the body builds a beautiful body, lean muscles, and happy organs. Found in all green vegetables and especially abundant in pineapple and papaya.

LIPASE breaks down fats and oils. Healthy fats and oils grow supple skin and luminous hair, and they're responsible for the health and happiness of every single cell in our bodies and brains. Found in unrefined oils, avocados, olives, and raw seeds and nuts.

balance by eating 80 percent raw food. Eating 100 percent raw food requires responsibility and time-intensive dedication. For some (myself included), it can be great for periods of time, especially in the zenith of summer, or for cleansing and detoxifying. It can be helpful to remember that our primary habits make up the foundation of our health, and a little recreation is good.

As there are certain foods that are more imperative to eat only when they are organically grown (see "The Dirty Dozen" on page 10), certain foods are much more nutritious and fortifying in a natural, raw state. Oil leads that list. Fresh, cold-pressed, unrefined oils nourish every cell in the body and offer a delicious, clean-burning fuel. Certain oils can tolerate higher temperatures without being destroyed, which is important with any kind of cooking. See "Oils" on page 96 for a comprehensive chart.

The Culinary Art of Raw and Living Foods

Raw and living foods have gained in popularity and respect both for their nutritional validity and as rising stars in the culinary arts. Preparing raw and living food requires an innovative approach to the world of food. Techniques and talent that cultivate texture, match and develop flavor, and turn on the natural intelligence of fine raw food are being integrated into the kitchens of the world's most respected chefs.

Many of the great techniques for preparing raw food are fairly time intensive, such as sprouting, fermenting, and dehydrating. Then again, other preparations are lickety-split-quick, such as making blended soups, smoothies, salads, and dressings. Then there are a number of approaches with a midgrade time demand. The recipe section in this book is seasoned with some of each, as well as with a broad range of cooked-food recipes with a sliding scale of intensity. It is about finding balance and figuring out what works best for you.

I really do believe that enjoying food is part of sound nutrition. For me, making food and cooking are part of the enjoyment. I feel nourished when I feed others. There are some days I have the leisurely pleasure of being in the kitchen for hours, but most days, time is of the essence. Those are the moments when I am grateful to just steam some broccoli rather than marinate it for 2 days to make it palatable, for I am one of many who do not care for raw broccoli. With this, I believe in the intelligence of a hybrid approach. For instance, I would rather lightly steam the broccoli just until it is bright green and drizzle it with some excellent extra-virgin olive oil and fine sea salt rather than sauté it in oil. The steamed broccoli seems much more alive to me than when it is sautéed, and the benefits of the olive oil are so much greater when it is not heated. When it comes to preparing raw foods for the balanced plate, just remember that you want to maximize nutritional value with the least amount of effort. I strongly believe that raw food provides a pillar for health and optimal nutrition. It may just be the fountain of youth.

Ayurveda:
Ancient Balance of the Elements

Ayurveda is a deep and complex system with roots in ancient India. Translated from Sanskrit, *Ayurveda* literally means "knowledge of life." It is thought to be the oldest healing system still in practice. The purpose of Ayurveda is to heal and maintain the quality and longevity of life. A core principle of Ayurveda recognizes that nature heals disease, meaning that your body heals itself. We simply aid and assist nature's process with food, medicine, activity, and lifestyle. Food stands as the principal medicine of Ayurveda, but the depth and breadth of this holistic system takes into account physical, metaphysical, emotional, spiritual, and philosophical aspects of life for sound nutrition. The Ayurvedic system has bewildering multiplicity. What follows is a very general overview of a brilliant complex system.

When diet is wrong, medicine is of no use.
When diet is correct, medicine is of no need.

—ANCIENT AYURVEDIC PROVERB

Basic Ayurvedic Principles

There are several components of the formula of health in the Ayurvedic system.

- Balance of the five elements in the body
- Equilibrium of the three *doshas*, called the *tridosha* (vata, pitta, and kapha), and proper expression of their attributes, which manage the various tissues, structures, and functions of the body
- The vitality and balance of digestive fire and the biological fire of metabolism, called *agni*
- Balance, production, and elimination of the three waste products, called *malas* (urine, feces, and sweat)
- Normal function of the five senses
- Harmonious function of the body, mind, and consciousness

The Five Elements

Ayurveda identifies five elements that embody all matter. The entire cosmos is a relationship and balance of these five elements. Apropos, human beings, as a microcosmos of the universe, are made up of and embody the five elements as well.

ETHER: SPACE. In the human body: spaces and cavities of the body—mouth, gastrointestinal (GI) tract, respiratory tract, abdomen, thorax, capillaries

AIR/MOTION: In the human body: pulse of heart, contraction of lungs, nervous system, nerve and sensory impulse and response

FIRE/LIGHT AND HEAT: In the human body: metabolism, digestion, intelligence and thinking, vision (sight)

WATER/FLUID: In the human body: secretion, digestive juices, mucous membranes, blood

EARTH/MATTER: In the human body: All structures of the body

The Tridosha System

The tridosha is an organizational system that recognizes three physical constitutions, or doshas: *vata, pitta,* and *kapha*. Each dosha is compromised of all five elements (ether, air, fire, water, earth); however, two elements predominate in each. Every dosha has specific attributes that are expressed by physical, mental, and emotional complexions.

Each one of us exhibits aspects of all three doshas, though most people favor one dominant dosha. It is said that the predisposition of a person's dosha is determined by genetics, diet, lifestyle, environment, and the constitutions and emotions of his or her parents at the time of conception. It is useful to take into consideration that a person's dosha is not carved into stone, but that the attributes of a body may be changed in spite of dominant tendencies. Food is the principal tool to influence and balance the body.

The word *dosha* is a bit confusing because it literally translates to mean "fault" or "impurity." The connotation is that the extreme expression of one dosha in the body signifies an imbalanced system. The ideal of health is a balance of all doshas and all elements in the body, as different systems, actions, and tissues in the body are governed by different doshas.

VATA

ELEMENT: Air and Ether

DERIVATIVE: of Sanskrit verb "vah," meaning "to move," "to carry," "vehicle." "That which moves" is called "vata."

GOVERNS: activity and movement in body

SEAT: lungs, throat, esophagus, nasal cavity, thorax

RESPONSIBILITIES: expansion and contraction

FRAME: tends toward extremes, very tall or very short; thin bone structure and slight build

SKIN: dark or pale complexion; dry, rough, cold; sometimes cold hands and feet; fewer moles that tend to be dark in color

EYES: usually dark; sometimes small or sunken

HAIR: darker; dry; sometimes curly

NAILS: dry, brittle

APPETITE AND DIGESTION: variable appetite, usually not strong

TENDENCY TO CRAVE: sweet, sour, and salty foods; often hot drinks

ELIMINATION: tends toward constipation

NATURE/EMOTIONS: enthusiastic, excitable, often creative and dramatic

ENERGY: usually very active, alert, restless, talks and walks quickly, sometimes fatigues easily

MENTAL: quick learning and understanding, often short memory; less willpower; sometimes lacks confidence

SLEEP: sleeps less than other constitutions; often disturbed or restless

SYMPTOMS WHEN OUT OF BALANCE: challenged by dryness and constipation; flighty, moody, ungrounded, anxious, scattered, forgetful, stressed out

NURTURED BY: grounding food; regular schedules; calming activity

PITTA

ELEMENT: Fire and Water

DERIVATIVE: of Sanskrit verb "tap," meaning "to heat," "to be austere"

GOVERNS: metabolism, digestion, thinking

SEAT: Stomach and small intestines

RESPONSIBILITIES: regulate body heat; metabolism, appetite, and digestion; learning, thinking, and understanding

FRAME: medium height and build; not overly thin or overweight

SKIN: Coppery, yellowish, or red complexion; often fair; more freckles than other constitutions

EYES: green, gray, copper brown; bright, sharp eyes

HAIR: fine, silky; lighter brown, blond, red

NAILS: softer

APPETITE AND DIGESTION: good, strong; strong metabolism

TENDENCY TO CRAVE: sweet, bitter, astringent; often cold drinks

ELIMINATION: soft, plentiful, liquid; tends toward excessive perspiration and frequent urination

NATURE/EMOTIONS: passionate, strong emotions, fiery

ENERGY: ambitious, focused, passionate

MENTAL: good power of comprehension, quick learner, sharp, intelligent, natural leader, strong opinions

SLEEP: medium duration, good sleep

SYMPTOMS WHEN OUT OF BALANCE: angry, jealous, resentful, tunnel-visioned, hyperactive, competitive, rashes, diarrhea, heartburn

NURTURED BY: cooling, fresh food; letting go of control; keeping cool—does not tolerate extreme heat and light well

KAPHA

ELEMENT: Earth and Water

DERIVATIVE: of two Sanskrit words, "ka," meaning "water," and "pha," meaning flourish. "That which is flourished by water" is kapha.

GOVERNS: cells, tissues, organs

SEAT: large intestine

RESPONSIBILITIES: lubricate joints and organs; build and maintain strong muscles and bones; cellular secretion; memory retention

FRAME: solid; medium; stocky; well-developed muscles; tendency to carry extra weight

SKIN: bright complexion; thick, soft, oily, lustrous skin

EYES: dark or blue

HAIR: thick, dark, soft, sometimes wavy

NAILS: strong

APPETITE AND DIGESTION: regular appetite; slow digestion

TENDENCY TO CRAVE: pungent, bitter, astringent foods

ELIMINATION: soft, slow, heavy, moderate

NATURE/EMOTIONS: tolerant, calm, forgiving; sometimes greedy and possessive

ENERGY: good stamina; slow and steady, calm

MENTAL: slower learner, but with definite and long retention of knowledge

SLEEP: sound, prolonged

SYMPTOMS WHEN OUT OF BALANCE: sad, melancholy, retention of weight; resistant to change, apathy, lethargy

NURTURED BY: spicy, warm foods; activities to keep moving

Agni: The Fire Within

Agni is the biological fire of metabolism, including digestion. It is considered to be the key to health and disease.

Agni is similar to the function and an integral part of the fiery nature of pitta in the body, which governs digestion and metabolism. The subtle difference is that pitta is the container of this energy and agni is the content. Agni is also related to vata, with a shared nature of movement. An imbalance of any dosha can impair agni with deleterious effects on the metabolism.

Eating with the Seasons

From an Ayurvedic perspective, balance naturally changes with the seasons. Each season mirrors one or more elements and various attributes of the tridosha. For instance, in the heat of the summer (which reflects the fire of pitta), cool, fresh foods, which naturally calm and balance the nature of pitta, are more desirable. In the dry, cold season of winter (which reflects the cool, dry *vata* nature), warming spices and earthy, substantial foods soothe the soul. Choosing seasonally available foods to nourish and balance the body is a healthy choice and one that serves up good common sense.

A clear example of agni is its manifestation as gastric fire. The enzyme system is dependent on agni, which functions as a catalytic agent. It is the action of agni that stimulates digestion and breaks down food to be absorbed and assimilated by the body.

Agni is also responsible for maintaining the nutrition of the body's tissues and is therefore present in every tissue and cell of the body. As a steward of the autoimmune system, agni destroys unhealthy microorganisms, bacteria, and toxins in the stomach, small intestine, colon, and blood, which is essential to maintain a healthy intestinal ecology. The action of circulation and the healthy maintenance of skin color are also a function of agni, so kindle your agni for a lovely complexion.

Improper Function of Agni

When agni is weakened because of an imbalance in the tridosha, the metabolism can be severely affected and the immune system drastically compromised. If agni is not functioning well, food is not digested and cannot be absorbed. Subsequently, undigested food accumulates in the colon, putrefying into a fetid material called *ama.* Processed food, poor food combining, and overeating all snuff out agni and cause ama to accumulate in the large intestine. Modern-day agriculture and industry also produce toxic ama in the form of chemicals, pesticides, and other agricultural and environmental poisons that were not around in the days of the ancient rishi. Ama is considered to be the root of all disease, clogging the channels of the body such as the intestines, arteries, capillaries, and blood vessels. This rank substance can be reabsorbed into the blood and accumulates to cause stagnation, weaken organs, and impair the immune response of the body. Eating equable food from a balanced plate keeps ama from collecting and agni kindled for full-fledged health and harmony.

Six Tastes of Ayurveda

Ayurveda recognizes six tastes of food: sour, salty, sweet, pungent (spicy), bitter, and astringent. Each taste has its own qualities, or *guanas,* which in turn act on the body and affect balance. Many foods have more than one taste and are meant to work in combination. There are three aspects of taste:

- The immediate experience of taste and how it affects the body is called *rasa.* This includes the emotional impact and association of taste, especially sweet.
- The effect taste has on digestion is called *virya.* For instance, a hot, spicy virya enhances digestion; a cool virya slows digestion.
- The subtle, long-term effect of taste on the body and metabolism is called *vipak*—for instance, whether a food promotes a lightness in the body or causes weight gain.

SOUR

ELEMENTS: Earth and Fire

SUM EFFECT OF SOUR TASTE: moderately moist; mildly heavy

RASA (IMMEDIATE EFFECT): warming, stimulating

VIRYA (EFFECT ON DIGESTION): warming, heating, stimulating; promotes digestion

VIPAK (LONG-TERM EFFECT): warming body over time

EFFECT ON VATA TYPES (AIR AND ETHER): balancing

EFFECT ON PITTA TYPES (FIRE AND WATER): aggravating

EFFECT ON KAPHA TYPES (WATER AND EARTH): aggravating, by causing retention of water

SOUR TASTE IN FOOD: lemon, vinegar, pickles

SALTY

ELEMENTS: Fire and Water

SUM EFFECT OF SALTY TASTE: stimulating; warming; mildly moist and heavy (less than sweet, more than sour); small amount good for digestion; too much causes water retention (more than sour), irritation, damage to the heart, promotes weight gain (though less than sweet)

RASA (IMMEDIATE EFFECT): heating, warming

VIRYA (EFFECT ON DIGESTION): heating, stimulating

VIPAK (LONG-TERM EFFECT): warming; moist; grounding

EFFECT ON VATA TYPES (AIR AND ETHER): good because it holds moisture; vata tends to be dry

EFFECT ON PITTA TYPES (FIRE AND WATER): aggravating because it is heating

EFFECT ON KAPHA TYPES (WATER AND EARTH): not great; though it stimulates digestion, it causes water retention and weight gain

SALTY TASTE IN FOOD: seaweed, shoyu (soy sauce)

Definition of Metabolism

In *Ayurveda: The Science of Self-Healing,* Dr. Vasant Lad defines metabolism as "the sum of all the biophysical and chemical processes through which living organisms function and maintain life. Also the transformation of substances (such as ingested food) by which energy is made available for the use of the organism."

SWEET

ELEMENTS: Earth and Water

SUM EFFECT OF SWEET TASTE: satisfying; calming, not stimulating; short-term feels good, long-term causes inertia and weight gain

RASA (IMMEDIATE EFFECT): cooling; slowness; calm; satiation; gratification

VIRYA (EFFECT ON DIGESTION): inhibits digestion

VIPAK (LONG-TERM EFFECT): heavy, moist; causes weight gain

EFFECT ON VATA TYPES (AIR AND ETHER): good and grounding

EFFECT ON PITTA TYPES (FIRE AND WATER): soothing and balancing

EFFECT ON KAPHA TYPES (WATER AND EARTH): unbalancing; cool, moist, earthy, and watery qualities lead to inertia and weight gain

SWEET TASTE IN FOOD: sugar, fruit, honey, maple syrup

PUNGENT (SPICY)

ELEMENTS: Air and Fire

SUM EFFECT OF PUNGENT TASTE: hottest of all tastes; light, dry, clearing from beginning to end; stimulates digestion

RASA (IMMEDIATE EFFECT): hot, stimulating, drying, light

VIRYA (EFFECT ON DIGESTION): very stimulating

VIPAK (LONG-TERM EFFECT): heating, stimulating, drying, lightness

EFFECT ON VATA TYPES (AIR AND ETHER): small amounts okay to help stimulate digestion; too much is aggravating because heat and dryness cause too much movement and dehydration, which is not good for vata

EFFECT ON PITTA TYPES (FIRE AND WATER): very unbalancing

EFFECT ON KAPHA TYPES (WATER AND EARTH): excellent; drying and warming, which is what kapha needs

PUNGENT TASTE IN FOOD: chili peppers, garlic, onion, hot spices

BITTER

ELEMENTS: Air and Ether

SUM EFFECT OF BITTER TASTE: coldest and lightest of all tastes; fairly dry; excellent balance for salty, sour, and sweet taste (which are moist and heavy)

RASA (IMMEDIATE EFFECT): cooling

VIRYA (EFFECT ON DIGESTION): cool, light, and dry, but stimulating; good

VIPAK (LONG-TERM EFFECT): warming, light, and drying effect over time; coolness moderated by warming effect

EFFECT ON VATA TYPES (AIR AND ETHER): not good, too drying and light

EFFECT ON PITTA TYPES (FIRE AND WATER): helpful; cold, light, and dry, good for digestion

EFFECT ON KAPHA TYPES (WATER AND EARTH): balancing; light and dryness good for kapha and digestion

BITTER TASTE IN FOOD: dark leafy greens (kale, collard greens, chard, broccoli rabe, escarole, endive, chicory)

ASTRINGENT

ELEMENTS: Air and Earth

SUM EFFECT OF ASTRINGENT TASTE: drying and slightly light; contracting effect on digestion; constricts blood vessels flowing to digestive tract

RASA (IMMEDIATE EFFECT): cool, dry

VIRYA (EFFECT ON DIGESTION): mildly inhibits digestion; cool (cooler than sweet, not as cold as bitter)

VIPAK (LONG-TERM EFFECT): mildly light and dry, becomes less so and more pungent over time

EFFECT ON VATA TYPES (AIR AND ETHER): not good, too dry and cool

EFFECT ON PITTA TYPES (FIRE AND WATER): cool; good for pitta

EFFECT ON KAPHA TYPES (WATER AND EARTH): dryness good for kapha

ASTRINGENT TASTE IN FOOD: Very few foods are predominantly astringent. Pomegranates, cranberries, teas, red wine, and some unripe fruits are examples of more astringent foods. Many foods have an astringent secondary flavor. Most beans and grains are primarily sweet with a secondary taste of astringency.

Health and Disease

It is said that "health is order; disease is disorder." Maintaining health is a continuous relationship between order and disorder and greatly depends on managing the internal environment of the body as it constantly reacts to the external environment of the world we live in.

Yoga: Cross-Training for the Body, Mind, and Spirit

The roots of yoga branch through an extensive family tree that delineates many schools of thought, practice, and medicine. The exact origins are unknown, but yoga is believed to be the oldest physical discipline in existence. The first detailed description of the principles and goals of yoga are recorded in the *Upanishads,* written between the 5th and 8th centuries BC. Amazing that material written 10,000 years ago is still a current affair.

There are many definitions of the word *yoga,* all of which allude to the intelligence and complexity of a vast system with many interpretations, including a close relationship with Ayurveda. The core definition of yoga is generally translated as "union," "merger," or "integration." The union of yoga infers a merger of body, mind, and spirit, harmony with one's environment, and joining the individual self with the ultimate cosmos. In essence, it is a system to understand our essential nature as humans. It is a path to cultivate harmony inside, outside, and with the world at large. Deep, but practical.

In the West, yoga is known mostly as a physical practice. The kind of yoga taught in classes, gyms, and studios is part of the *hatha* yoga system, also called *hatha vidya.* The word *hatha* represents opposing energies: positive-negative, sun-moon, male-female, hot-cold. It is similar but not exactly analogous to the concept of yin-yang of other Eastern philosophies. The main aim of yoga is to bring balance to these opposing energies and use the best of both of them. Yoga endeavors to balance, calm, and restore the body, mind, and spirit through physical exercise, controlled breathing, relaxation, and meditation.

Yoga is commonly thought of simply as a string of postures, called *asanas,* that make up a physical workout to tone and beautify the body. While it does make the body beautiful, hatha yoga embraces a much broader holistic system that envelops ethical precepts, moral observances, dietary prescriptions, control of breath, and meditation, as well as its popular physical practice to remove blockages and disease from the body and restore balance and harmony to the physical, mental, and energetic bodies. A regular yoga practice brings balance and beauty to the body and beyond.

Yoga is a pillar of my health and well-being; it is my home base. I've practiced it almost every day for about 12 years, and I find that it appeases my mind, pacifies my soul, and tones my body to be long and strong. Organizing my body with conscious breathing spills over into the more mundane parts of my life, and I dig deep to call on it when I am stuck in traffic, waiting on line, or dealing with an automated

> I was first initiated into Yoga by my parents...
> in the daily ritual of taking food. In this
> context, *Yoga* means *to join*. Something outside
> joins in me, whether it is mother's milk or the
> food we take.
>
> —KRISHNAMACHARYA

phone system. I go to classes from time to time, only with teachers I know and trust (thank you, Eddie and Nicki), but practice on my own mostly, always allowing for at least 15 minutes of breathing first thing in the morning (no matter what!) and 10 minutes of calm, easy stretching before bed so I sleep like a baby. Namaste.

The Science of Yoga

What the ancient lineage of yoga has recognized for thousands of years has sparked the interest of science in the last half-century or so. Science has observed the ability of some advanced practitioners of yoga to control mental and physical responses of the body that are normally considered beyond control.

Thousands of empirical research studies by health professionals in India and the West have been conducted to examine the therapeutic potential of yoga. The results show that the physical practice of yoga, meditation, and breathing certainly influence, regulate, and control the physiological restrictions of the body such as blood pressure; heart rate; metabolic rate; respiratory, nervous system, and immune function; brain waves; and body temperature. A little stretching and breathing go a long way!

The Yoga of Food

Given the meaning of yoga as joining, merging, and integration, eating is yogic, too. We literally become the food we eat, and the food we eat becomes us, hence a daily part of a yoga practice. There is magic in mindfulness. That mindfulness may be a constant, unseen opportunity to awaken more, soak up more, live more, love more.

Many systems recognize the concept of life force. Some call it *chi, qui, mana,* or *prana,* though all may agree it can be found in food, in air, and in the clarity of focus. The mindful focus on the miracle of food may certainly be spiritual nutrition to feed the soul.

Food Guidelines for Balancing
Basic Constitution with Ayurveda

The following chart outlines foods you should favor or avoid to balance each of the doshas. These guidelines are only a general design. Remember that most of us embody more than one dosha. In terms of identifying foods to avoid, it is less about abstinence and more about knowing when you need to favor other foods to help maintain balance. As you become familiar with this guide, the sense of which foods fit you will become clear and your internal barometer should take over.

	VATA		PITTA		KAPHA	
	FAVOR	**AVOID**	**FAVOR**	**AVOID**	**FAVOR**	**AVOID**
FRUITS	APPLES, SWEET* APPLES (COOKED) APPLESAUCE APRICOTS AVOCADOS BANANAS BLUEBERRIES CHERRIES COCONUT FIGS (FRESH) GRAPEFRUIT GRAPES KIWI LEMONS LIMES MANGOES MELONS ORANGES PAPAYAS PEACHES PINEAPPLES PLUMS PRUNES (SOAKED OR COOKED) RAISINS (SOAKED OR COOKED) RASPBERRIES RHUBARB STRAWBERRIES TAMARIND WATERMELON	APPLES, SWEET* APPLES, TART CRANBERRIES FIGS (DRY) PEARS PERSIMMONS POMEGRAN-ATES PRUNES (DRY) RAISINS (DRY)	APPLES, SWEET APPLES (COOKED) APPLESAUCE APRICOTS AVOCADOS BLUEBERRIES CHERRIES* COCONUT DATES FIGS (DRY) FIGS (FRESH) GRAPES* KIWI* LIMES* MANGOES MELONS ORANGES PAPAYAS* PEARS PINEAPPLES PLUMS POMEGRAN-ATES PRUNES (DRY) PRUNES (SOAKED OR COOKED) RAISINS (DRY) RASPBERRIES* STRAWBER-RIES* WATERMELON	APPLES, TART BANANAS GRAPEFRUIT KIWI* LEMONS PEACHES PERSIMMONS RASPBERRIES* STRAWBER-RIES* RHUBARB TAMARIND	APPLES, SWEET APPLES, TART* APPLES (COOKED) APPLESAUCE APRICOTS BLUEBERRIES CHERRIES CRANBERRIES GRAPES KIWI LEMONS* LIMES PEACHES PEARS PERSIMMONS POMEGRAN-ATES PRUNES (DRY) PRUNES (SOAKED OR COOKED) RAISINS (DRY) RASPBERRIES* STRAWBER-RIES*	APPLES, TART* AVOCADOS BANANAS COCONUT DATES FIGS (FRESH) GRAPEFRUIT MELONS* ORANGES PAPAYAS PLUMS RHUBARB TAMARIND WATERMELON

*SYMBOL KEY: * OKAY IN MODERATION*

	VATA		PITTA		KAPHA	
	FAVOR	**AVOID**	**FAVOR**	**AVOID**	**FAVOR**	**AVOID**

VEGETABLES	ASPARAGUS
	BEETS
	  (COOKED)
	BEETS (RAW)
	CABBAGE
	  (COOKED)
	CARROTS
	CILANTRO
	CORN*
	CUCUMBERS
	DAIKON
	FENNEL
	GARLIC
	GREEN BEANS
	JERUSALEM
	  ARTICHOKES
	LEAFY GREENS
	LEEKS
	  (COOKED)
	LETTUCE
	ONIONS
	  (COOKED)
	PARSLEY
	PARSNIPS
	PEAS (COOKED)
	POTATOES,
	  SWEET
	PUMPKIN
	RADISHES
	  (COOKED)
	RUTABAGAS
	SPINACH
	  (COOKED)
	SPINACH (RAW)
	SPROUTS
	SQUASH,
	  SUMMER
	SQUASH,
	  WINTER
	TOMATOES
	  (COOKED)
		ARTICHOKES
		BROCCOLI
		BRUSSELS
		  SPROUTS
		BURDOCK
		CABBAGE
		  (RAW)
		CAULIFLOWER
		CELERY
		DANDELION
		EGGPLANT
		HORSERADISH
		KALE
		LEEKS (RAW)
		MUSHROOMS
		OLIVES, GREEN
		PEAS (RAW)
		PEPPERS,
		  SWEET
		PEPPERS, HOT
		POTATOES,
		  WHITE
		RADISHES
		  (RAW)
		TOMATOES
		  (RAW)*
		WHEATGRASS
			ARTICHOKES
			ASPARAGUS
			BEETS
			  (COOKED)
			BROCCOLI
			BRUSSELS
			  SPROUTS
			CABBAGE
			  (COOKED AND
			  RAW)
			CARROTS*
			CAULIFLOWER
			CELERY
			CILANTRO
			CUCUMBERS
			DAIKON
			EGGPLANT
			FENNEL
			GREEN BEANS
			JERUSALEM
			  ARTICHOKES
			KALE
			LEAFY GREENS
			LEEKS
			  (COOKED)
			LETTUCE
			MUSHROOMS
			OLIVES, BLACK
			ONIONS
			  (COOKED)
			PARSLEY
			PARSNIPS
			PEAS (COOKED
			  AND RAW)
			PEPPERS,
			  SWEET
			POTATOES,
			  SWEET AND
			  WHITE
			PUMPKIN
			RADISHES
			  (COOKED)
			RUTABAGA
			SQUASH,
			  WINTER AND
			  SUMMER
			TOMATOES
			  (COOKED)
			WATERCRESS*
			WHEATGRASS
			ZUCCHINI
				BEETS (RAW)
				BURDOCK
				DAIKON
				DANDELION*
				EGGPLANT*
				GARLIC
				HORSERADISH
				LEEKS (RAW)
				OLIVES, GREEN
				ONIONS (RAW)
				PEPPERS, HOT
				RADISHES
				  (RAW)
				SPINACH
				  (COOKED AND
				  RAW)
				TOMATOES
				  (RAW)
					ARTICHOKES
					ASPARAGUS
					BEETS
					  (COOKED AND
					  RAW)
					BROCCOLI
					BRUSSELS
					  SPROUTS
					BURDOCK
					CABBAGE
					  (COOKED AND
					  RAW)
					CARROTS
					CAULIFLOWER
					CELERY
					CILANTRO
					DAIKON
					DANDELION
					EGGPLANT
					FENNEL
					GARLIC
					GREEN BEANS
					HORSERADISH
					JERUSALEM
					  ARTICHOKES
					KALE
					LEAFY GREENS
					LEEKS
					  (COOKED AND
					  RAW)
					LETTUCE
					MUSHROOMS
					ONIONS
					  (COOKED AND
					  RAW)
					PARSLEY
					PEAS (COOKED
					  AND RAW)
					PEPPERS,
					  SWEET AND
					  HOT
					POTATOES,
					  WHITE
					RADISHES
					  (COOKED AND
					  RAW)
					RUTABAGA
					SPINACH
					SPROUTS
					SQUASH,
					  WINTER
					TOMATOES
					  (COOKED)
					WATERCRESS
					WHEATGRASS
						CUCUMBERS
						OLIVES, BLACK
						PARSNIPS
						POTATOES,
						  SWEET
						PUMPKIN
						SQUASH,
						  SUMMER
						TOMATOES
						  (RAW)
						ZUCCHINI

	VATA		PITTA		KAPHA	
	FAVOR	**AVOID**	**FAVOR**	**AVOID**	**FAVOR**	**AVOID**

GRAINS	AMARANTH
	OATS (COOKED)
	PASTA*
	POLENTA*
	QUINOA
	RICE, BASMATI,
	  BROWN,
	  JASMINE
	SEITAN
	SPROUTED
	  BREAD
	WHEAT
	WILD RICE
		BARLEY
		BREAD (WITH
		  YEAST)
		BUCKWHEAT
		CORN
		COUSCOUS
		MILLET
		OATS (DRY)
		RYE
		SPELT
		TAPIOCA
			AMARANTH
			BARLEY
			COUSCOUS
			OATS (COOKED)
			PASTA
			POLENTA*
			QUINOA
			RICE, BASMATI,
			  BROWN*,
			  JASMINE
			SEITAN
			WILD RICE
				BREAD (WITH
				  YEAST)
				BUCKWHEAT
				CORN
				MILLET
				MUESLI*
				OATS (DRY)
				POLENTA*
				RICE, BROWN*
				RYE
					AMARANTH
					BARLEY
					BUCKWHEAT
					CORN
					COUSCOUS
					MILLET
					OATS (DRY)
					PASTA
					POLENTA
					QUINOA
					RICE, BASMATI,
					  JASMINE
					RYE
					SEITAN
					SPELT
					SPROUTED
					  BREAD
					TAPIOCA
					WILD RICE
						BREAD (WITH
						  YEAST)
						OATS (COOKED)
						PASTA*
						RICE, BROWN
						SEITAN
						WHEAT

	VATA		PITTA		KAPHA	
	FAVOR	**AVOID**	**FAVOR**	**AVOID**	**FAVOR**	**AVOID**

SWEETENERS	BARLEY MALT
	FRUIT JUICE
	FRUIT
	  CONCEN-
	  TRATES
	HONEY
	MAPLE SYRUP*
	MOLASSES
	RICE SYRUP
	SUGAR CANE
	  JUICE (DRIED,
	  UNBLEACHED)
		MAPLE SYRUP*
		WHITE SUGAR
			BARLEY MALT
			FRUIT JUICE
			FRUIT
			  CONCEN-
			  TRATES
			MAPLE SYRUP
			RICE SYRUP
			SUGAR CANE
			  JUICE (DRIED,
			  UNBLEACHED)
				HONEY*
				MOLASSES
				WHITE SUGAR
					FRUIT JUICE
					FRUIT
					  CONCEN-
					  TRATES
					HONEY
						BARLEY MALT
						MAPLE SYRUP
						MOLASSES
						RICE SYRUP
						SUGAR CANE
						  JUICE (DRIED,
						  UNBLEACHED)
						WHITE SUGAR

*SYMBOL KEY: * = OKAY IN MODERATION*

	VATA		PITTA		KAPHA	
	FAVOR	**AVOID**	**FAVOR**	**AVOID**	**FAVOR**	**AVOID**
CONDIMENTS	BLACK PEPPER* CHILI PEPPERS* GOMASIO MUSTARD PICKLES SALT SCALLIONS SOY SAUCE SPROUTS* TAMARI VINEGAR	CHOCOLATE HORSERADISH	BLACK PEPPER* SALT TAMARI	CHILI PEPPERS CHOCOLATE GOMASIO HORSERADISH MUSTARD PICKLES SALT SCALLIONS SOY SAUCE VINEGAR	BLACK PEPPER CHILI PEPPERS HORSERADISH MUSTARD SCALLIONS	CHOCOLATE GOMASIO PICKLES SALT SOY SAUCE VINEGAR

	VATA		PITTA		KAPHA	
	FAVOR	**AVOID**	**FAVOR**	**AVOID**	**FAVOR**	**AVOID**
SEAWEED	ARAME DULSE HIJIKI KELP KOMBU	NONE, ALL ARE OKAY IN MODERATION	ARAME* DULSE* HIJIKI* KOMBU*	KELP	ARAME* DULSE* HIJIKI* KOMBU*	KELP

*SYMBOL KEY: * = OKAY IN MODERATION*

	VATA		PITTA		KAPHA	
	FAVOR	**AVOID**	**FAVOR**	**AVOID**	**FAVOR**	**AVOID**

SPICES	ALLSPICE
	BLACK PEPPER
	CARAWAY
	CARDAMOM
	CAYENNE
	CINNAMON
	CLOVES
	CORIANDER
	CUMIN
	FENNEL SEED
	FENUGREEK
	GINGER (DRY
	  AND FRESH)
	MACE
	MUSTARD
	NUTMEG
	PAPRIKA
	POPPY SEEDS
	SALT
	STAR ANISE
	TURMERIC
	VANILLA
		NONE, ALL
		ARE OKAY IN
		MODERATION
			BLACK PEPPER
			CARAWAY
			CARDAMOM
			CINNAMON
			CORIANDER
			CUMIN
			FENNEL SEED
			GINGER
			  (FRESH)
			ORANGE PEEL
			SALT
			TURMERIC
			VANILLA
				ALLSPICE
				CAYENNE
				CLOVES
				FENUGREEK
				GINGER (DRY)
				MACE
				MUSTARD
				NUTMEG
				PAPRIKA
				POPPY SEEDS
				STAR ANISE
					ALLSPICE
					BLACK PEPPER
					CARAWAY
					CARDAMOM
					CAYENNE
					CINNAMON
					CLOVES
					CORIANDER
					CUMIN
					FENNEL SEED
					FENUGREEK
					GINGER (DRY
					  AND FRESH)
					MACE
					MUSTARD
					NUTMEG
					PAPRIKA
					POPPY SEEDS
					SALT
					STAR ANISE
					TURMERIC
					VANILLA
						NONE, ALL
						ARE OKAY IN
						MODERATION

	VATA		PITTA		KAPHA	
	FAVOR	**AVOID**	**FAVOR**	**AVOID**	**FAVOR**	**AVOID**

HERBS	BASIL (DRY
	  AND FRESH)
	BAY LEAF
	CILANTRO
	DILL
	FENNEL
	MARJORAM
	MINT
	OREGANO
	PARSLEY
	ROSEMARY
	SAFFRON
	SAGE
	SAVORY
	TARRAGON
	THYME
		NONE, ALL
		ARE OKAY IN
		MODERATION
			BASIL (FRESH)
			CILANTRO
			DILL
			FENNEL
			MINT
			PARSLEY
			SAFFRON
			TARRAGON
				BASIL (DRY)
				BAY LEAF
				MARJORAM
				OREGANO
				ROSEMARY
				SAGE
				SAVORY
				THYME
					BASIL (DRY
					  AND FRESH)
					BAY LEAF
					CILANTRO
					DILL
					FENNEL
					MARJORAM
					MINT
					OREGANO
					PARSLEY
					ROSEMARY
					SAFFRON
					SAGE
					SAVORY
					TARRAGON
					THYME
						NONE, ALL
						ARE OKAY IN
						MODERATION

SYMBOL KEY: * = OKAY IN MODERATION

	VATA		PITTA		KAPHA	
	FAVOR	**AVOID**	**FAVOR**	**AVOID**	**FAVOR**	**AVOID**
LEGUMES	ADZUKI BLACK BLACK-EYED PEAS CANNELLINI GARBANZO KIDNEY LENTILS, BROWN, GREEN AND YELLOW LIMA BEANS MISO NAVY BEANS PEAS (DRIED) PINTO SOYBEANS SPLIT PEAS TEMPEH TOFU*	LENTILS, RED* MUNG BEANS MUNG DAL TOFU*	ADZUKI BLACK BLACK-EYED PEAS CANNELLINI GARBANZO KIDNEY LENTILS, BROWN AND RED LIMA BEANS MUNG BEANS MUNG DAL NAVY PEAS (DRIED) PINTO SOYBEANS SPLIT PEAS TEMPEH	LENTILS, GREEN AND YELLOW MISO	BLACK BEANS GARBANZO LENTILS (ALL) MUNG BEANS* NAVY PEAS (DRIED) PINTO SOY MILK TEMPEH TOFU (HOT)*	KIDNEY MISO SOYBEANS TOFU (COLD)

	VATA		PITTA		KAPHA	
	FAVOR	**AVOID**	**FAVOR**	**AVOID**	**FAVOR**	**AVOID**
NUTS	ALMONDS, DRY, SOAKED BRAZIL NUTS CASHEWS COCONUT HAZELNUTS MACADAMIA PEANUTS PECANS PISTACHIOS WALNUTS	NONE, ALL ARE OKAY IN MODERATION	ALMONDS, SOAKED COCONUT	ALMONDS, DRY BRAZIL NUTS CASHEWS HAZELNUTS MACADAMIA PEANUTS PECANS PISTACHIOS WALNUTS	AVOID NUTS IN GENERAL	AVOID NUTS IN GENERAL

	VATA		PITTA		KAPHA	
	FAVOR	**AVOID**	**FAVOR**	**AVOID**	**FAVOR**	**AVOID**
SEEDS	CHIA FLAX PSYLLIUM* PUMPKIN SESAME AND TAHINI SUNFLOWER	POPCORN PSYLLIUM*	FLAX POPCORN PSYLLIUM PUMPKIN SUNFLOWER	CHIA SESAME AND TAHINI	CHIA FLAX* POPCORN PSYLLIUM* PUMPKIN* SUNFLOWER*	PSYLLIUM* SESAME AND TAHINI

SYMBOL KEY: * = OKAY IN MODERATION

	VATA		PITTA		KAPHA	
	FAVOR	**AVOID**	**FAVOR**	**AVOID**	**FAVOR**	**AVOID**
OILS	COCONUT GRAPESEED OLIVE OIL SAFFLOWER SESAME SOY SUNFLOWER	CORN OIL FLAX SEED	COCONUT FLAX SEED GRAPESEED OLIVE OIL SOY SUNFLOWER WALNUT	ALMOND APRICOT CORN SAFFLOWER SESAME	ALMOND CORN FLAX SEED* SESAME SUNFLOWER	APRICOT COCONUT FLAX SEED* GRAPESEED OLIVE OIL SAFFLOWER WALNUT

	VATA		PITTA		KAPHA	
	FAVOR	**AVOID**	**FAVOR**	**AVOID**	**FAVOR**	**AVOID**
BEVERAGES	ALMOND MILK ALOE VERA APPLE CIDER APRICOT JUICE BEER* BERRY JUICE BLACK TEA* CAROB CARROT JUICE CHAI GRAIN COFFEE GRAPE JUICE GRAPEFRUIT JUICE GREEN VEGGIE JUICE LEMONADE MANGO JUICE MISO BROTH ORANGE JUICE PAPAYA JUICE PRUNE JUICE* TOMATO JUICE* WINE, DRY WHITE* WINE, SWEET*	APPLE JUICE BLACK TEA* CARBONATED DRINKS CHOCOLATE COFFEE COLD DRINKS CRANBERRY JUICE HARD ALCOHOL ICED TEA PEAR JUICE PINEAPPLE JUICE POMEGRANATE JUICE PRUNE JUICE* SOYMILK (COLD, HOT) TOMATO JUICE* WINE, DRY RED	ALMOND MILK ALOE VERA APRICOT JUICE BEER* BERRY JUICE BLACK TEA CAROB* CHAI GRAIN COFFEE GRAPE JUICE GREEN VEGGIE JUICE MANGO JUICE MISO BROTH* ORANGE JUICE* PEACH JUICE PEAR JUICE POMEGRANATE JUICE PRUNE JUICE RICE MILK SOYMILK (HOT) WINE, DRY WHITE*	APPLE CIDER CARBONATED DRINKS CARROT JUICE CHOCOLATE COFFEE COLD DRINKS CRANBERRY JUICE GRAPEFRUIT JUICE HARD ALCOHOL ICED TEA LEMONADE PAPAYA JUICE PINEAPPLE JUICE SOYMILK (COLD) TOMATO JUICE WINE, DRY RED WINE, SWEET	ALOE VERA APPLE CIDER APPLE JUICE APRICOT JUICE BERRY JUICE BLACK TEA CAROB CARROT JUICE CHAI COFFEE* CRANBERRY JUICE GRAIN COFFEE GRAPE JUICE GREEN VEGGIE JUICE MANGO JUICE PEACH JUICE PEAR JUICE PINEAPPLE JUICE* POMEGRANATE JUICE PRUNE JUICE SOYMILK (HOT) WINE, DRY WHITE* WINE, DRY RED*	ALMOND MILK BEER CARBONATED DRINKS CHOCOLATE COFFEE* COLD DRINKS GRAPEFRUIT JUICE HARD ALCOHOL ICED TEA LEMONADE MISO BROTH ORANGE JUICE PAPAYA JUICE RICE MILK SOYMILK (COLD) TOMATO JUICE WINE, SWEET

*SYMBOL KEY: * = OKAY IN MODERATION*

CHAPTER 3

Kitchen Elements

In nature there is fundamental unity running through
all the diversity we see about us.

—GANDHI

Earth, water, air, and fire embody the attributes of all earthly delights. These elements are the fiber of sustenance and the foundation of a balanced plate. They are also the tools for creating balance and cultivating a nourished environment at home. Good stuff.

The quality of the elements you introduce into your kitchen—and, therefore, into your body—reflects the contingent quality of life and fundamentally influences just how magnificently the scene plays out. The cleanest ingredients and products are key to realizing wholeness, balance, and good health. Natural seasonings, pure water, clean air, and intelligent cooking methods are the foundation of wellness. As I've mentioned before, our bodies are formed by the food we eat, the water we drink, and the air we breathe, so eat, drink, breathe, and be merry—but do it well and with consideration for the elements in your kitchen. From harmony grow happiness, freedom, and good health.

Earth: Stocking the Whole Foods Pantry

Earth elements are the building blocks of creation in the kitchen. Natural seasonings like herbs, spices, salts, and some of the other dynamic ingredients that will be discussed in this section are all fruits of the earth, and they bring fortified nutrition and outrageous flavor to the table. Some of what follows may be new and some fondly familiar. All of these earthly delights are worth getting to know as parts of a balanced whole foods diet and for use in sculpting epicurean masterpieces at the drop of a hat.

Earth elements profile all carnal flavors—salty, sour, sweet, spicy, bitter, and astringent—and their characteristic attributes and their subtleties—warming, cooling, moist, dry, sharp, and soft. Using these natural condiments to balance, complement, and draw out the flavors of food is like striking a harmonious chord with many octaves.

Natural seasonings are an essential choice for good health and great food. Seasoning food with natural, unrefined ingredients enhances the organic flavor of food and the rapport of a dish and is a nourishing complement, not an imposition. Artificial flavors, preservatives, and chemical additives are an imposition that should be avoided at all costs. With so many remarkable natural elements, anything is possible. The only thing worth missing with artificial ingredients is the toll they take on our health.

I invite you to explore and play with any of these goodies that may be new to your palate and plate. I encourage you to stock the shelves of your pantry, spice rack, and fridge with the noble tools of fine flavor and unusual ingredients. Any little thing not found in a store will surely be in the surf of the Internet. Let your senses guide you, and watch the magic unfurl.

Herbs and Spices

Herbs and spices have been used medicinally for ages and are still valued for their properties to promote health, aid digestion, and calm, stimulate, and balance the body. Suffice it to say that a well-appointed spice rack is key to adorning, balancing, and complementing the flavors of almost any dish in a pinch.

Generally speaking, herbs grow in the temperate zones of the world and have green leaves, which are superior when used fresh. Spices are generally the product of tropical plants, including roots, bark, seeds, buds, and fruit; they are typically dried and used whole or ground.

Herbs and spices are used to stimulate all of the senses, through aroma, texture, and visual appeal, not just taste. The flavors of herbs and spices are more accurately derived from their aromas. The transformative aroma rides on the delicate essential oils of the plant's leaves, seeds, stem, or bark. These precious essential oils are best captured and naturally preserved by deliberate drying and storage.

Some dried herbs and spices are reputed as drab and dull, but certain types stand up stronger and longer than others. Shelf life is always a factor, and some dried herbs and spices will stay fresh and pungent for extended periods when stored well. As a rule, dried herbs and spices should be used or discarded within 6 months. Whole spices, such as peppercorns, cinnamon sticks, or cumin seeds will keep fresh for a year. Heat, light, and oxygen are destructive culprits to the delicate and complex aromatic and flavorful esteem of quality herbs and spices. Though it seems handy to let them perch in open view right next to the stove, stashing them in an airtight jar or double-bagged in a cool, dark cabinet or drawer is the best bet. Most dried herbs and spices are packaged in small, airtight jars for good reason—they hold a quantity that can be used in a reasonable amount of time and kept perky and fresh. Empty small jam or mustard jars are snazzy and perfect to recycle for storing herbs and spices purchased loose in the bulk section.

Please note: The following guide includes only part of the spectrum of the world-winds of spices and herbs. I have chosen to cover those you will find later in the recipe section. The nature of these precious culinary gifts may offer insight for matching and substitution. Go with your creativity and intuition to take a magic carpet ride where the seven seas meet and the four winds blow.

Herbs: The Spirit of Balanced Flavor

Herbs constitute a broad range of plants that are used to enhance the flavor and aroma of food. The word *herb* is derived from the Latin term *herba,* meaning "grass," connoting a "green crop."

Herbs have grown wild and been cultivated for millennia for use as food and medicine. Not only do herbs offer appetizing aroma and dynamic flavor, but they are often laden with health-promoting properties to stimulate and aid digestion. Good stuff!

Many cultures and systems recognize the importance of balance in foods. Ayurvedic principles fundamentally use herbs and spices to balance the physical body and well-being. In other Asian systems, nutrition and medicine have long been integrated, which intelligently relies on food, herbs, and spices to balance the flavor, texture, and color of food for optimal balance.

In the culinary world, certain herbs are essential in classic cuisines. As a chef, I am anything but classically trained. I have found such fun, freedom, and ingenuity in approaching food with passion and a sense of adventure. With a deep sense of gratitude for the many pioneers who have come before us (including the seafaring champions who braved the spice routes, and the genius forged by chefs like Roger Verge, Anton Mossiman, Daniel Bouloud, Charlie Trotter, Michele Nischan, and many more), I encourage home cooks to shed their inhibitions and experiment with the aromas and flavors of the herbal world.

BASIL

NATURE: Sweet-pungent-spicy.

BOTANY: *Ocimum* species; the many varieties of basil are annuals, all belonging to the mint family.

ETHNIC ORIGIN AND HISTORY: Native to tropical Asia, where it has been cultivated for more than 3,000 years. The Greeks called it the royal herb. Now grown throughout the temperate world.

VARIETIES:

■ Sweet basil *(O. basilicum):* Common, broad-leafed basil, bright green, smooth leaves, white flowers.

■ Opal basil *(O. b. purpurascens):* Also called purple basil, dark purple leaves, pink flowers. Very aromatic with clear mint and clove character.

■ Bush basil *(O. b. minimum):* Also called dwarf basil, very similar to sweet basil in aroma and flavor, compact bush with small leaves, white flowers, and a peppery aroma. Easy to grow in a pot.

■ Cinnamon basil *(O. b. cinnamon):* Native to Mexico, smaller, smooth leaves, darker green with a flush of pink. Sweet aroma with a clear note of cinnamon and undertone of camphor or eucalyptus.

■ Holy basil *(O. canctum):* Also known as *bai gaprow.* Very aromatic. Notes of mint and camphor and a musky undertone. Bitter raw. Gaining notoriety as a powerful antioxidant and health aid.

■ Lemon basil and lime basil *(O. b. citriodorum, americanum):* Smaller leaves, compact bush, white flowers. Distinct lemon flavor and lime flavor, respectively.

■ Thai basil *(O. b. horapa):* Also known as *bai horapa.* Smaller, dark green leaves, purple stem and flowers. Sweet, peppery aroma, clear notes of licorice and anise in flavor.

PART USED: Leaves and flowers.

AROMA: Complex, sweet, spicy, licorice overtones, clove undertones. Many variations.

FLAVOR: Warm, slightly peppery, a touch pungent, clove and mint undertones. Many variations.

COMPLEMENTARY SPICES: Black pepper, chives, cilantro, garlic, marjoram, mint, oregano, parsley, rosemary, savory, thyme.

- Basil is generally sold in bunches, and sometimes loose.
- Basil leaves are delicate and bruise easily, so avoid bunches with broken and blackened leaves and stems.
- Wrap in a slightly damp paper towel or thin dishtowel in a plastic bag in the fridge. Keeps for 3 to 5 days. Remove any bruised leaves as needed during storage and use.
- My mom tears or chops basil leaves, places them in ice cube trays, and fills the trays with filtered water to freeze in the height of summer when basil is at its best and her herb box is overflowing. Will keep frozen for 3 months or so.

GROW YOUR OWN!: Basil is easy to grow once it is going. Buying "starts" is a great jump start, as seeds take a while to germinate. Most basil is fairly tender and prefers shelter, full sun, and rich, well-drained soil. Pinch off budding flowers to prolong the growth and encourage a healthy bush. Colder latitudes will benefit from growing on a windowsill or in a greenhouse (even in summer). Harvest all summer until the first frost.

NUTRITION AND TRADITION:

- Key in Mediterranean cooking, especially Italian cuisine (think pesto).
- A natural companion for tomatoes—in salad, soup, and sauces.
- I have an affinity for mint with basil.
- Brilliant with raspberries (and mint).
- A little bit is surprisingly choice with chocolate. Try with the Chocolate of the Gods Mousse with Raspberries and Mint on page 354.

BAY LEAF

NATURE: Sweet-astringent-cooling.

BOTANY: *Laurus nobilis;* also called laurel leaf, or bay laurel. The broad leaf of an evergreen tree.

ETHNIC ORIGIN AND HISTORY: Native to eastern Mediterranean regions, but long cultivated in Europe and America. Greeks and Romans hailed bay leaf as a symbol of wisdom, honor, celebration, and triumph, and classically crowned kings, artists, and Olympic athletes with wreaths of the glossy, strong leaves.

VARIETIES: Many varieties, only two used commonly.

- Turkish: 1- to 2-inch, oval leaves. More subtle.
- Californian: 2- to 3-inch, narrower leaves. Stronger.

PART USED: Fresh and dried leaves.

AROMA: Sweet, balsamic, overtones of nutmeg, undertones of camphor and eucalyptus.

FLAVOR: Cool, astringent, slightly sweet; fresh bay is slightly bitter.

COMPLEMENTARY SPICES: Allspice, black pepper, garlic, marjoram, oregano, parsley, sage, savory, thyme.

BUYING AND STORING:

- Fresh bay leaf is infinitely superior to dried bay leaf. Fresh bay has a touch of bitterness, which will fade after storing in the fridge for a day or two.
- Fresh bay leaf may be dried until brittle by laying it out in a dark, ventilated place.
- Dried bay leaf will retain its aroma and flavor for up to a year when stored in an airtight container. Stale bay leaf has no flavor or aroma.

GROW YOUR OWN!: Bay does well grown in a pot. Bay trees do well in warm regions, though they may be moved indoors in the winter in temperate climes (hence it's great that they grow well in a pot!). Leaves may be picked all year. Produces small yellow flowers in the spring (in warm regions), followed by inedible purple berries.

NUTRITION AND TRADITION:

- Used to flavor stock, soups, sauces, stews, marinades, and pickles.
- Bay leaf yields flavor slowly, and flavor blossoms during slow, long cooking. Classic and essential to bouquet garni, used to flavor slow-cooked dishes.
- Always remove before serving. Too much will make a dish bitter.

CHIVES

NATURE: Pungent-spicy-warming.

BOTANY: *Allium schoenoprasum*; chives are the smallest and most delicate members of the onion family (*Allium* species). Hollow, grasslike stems and edible lavender-colored flowers.

ETHNIC ORIGIN AND HISTORY: Chives and wild onions are indigenous to temperate Europe and North America.

VARIETIES: One common variety available for cooking, but infinite wild varieties grow all over Europe and North America.

PART USED: Stems and flowers.

AROMA: Light, onion aroma.

FLAVOR: Mildly spicy, onion flavor.

COMPLEMENTARY SPICES: Basil, cilantro, fennel, paprika, parsley, tarragon.

BUYING AND STORING:

- Look for fresh, perky bunches.
- Chives may be cut and placed in ice cube trays with water to freeze for a few months.
- Dried chives are pretty, but do not have much flavor or aroma.

GROW YOUR OWN!:

- Easy to grow in pots or in the ground.
- Perennials will grow in just about any soil, but require plenty of regular water,

as the small bulbs and roots do not grow deeply.

- Propagate by dividing clumps of bulbs and planting.
- Plants die off in the winter and come back in early spring.
- Cut chives, rather than pulling them up, to keep the clumps well established and strong. Always leave some greens on the plant to keep the bulb roots strong.

NUTRITION AND TRADITION:

- Chives should be added at the end of a dish and not cooked, as they lose their flavor and aroma.
- Essential to the French blend of *fines herbes*.

CILANTRO

NATURE: Sweet-pungent-spicy.

BOTANY: *Coriandrum sativum*; called coriander in some cultures and Chinese parsley in others; a bright green-leafed herb also prized for its seed, called coriander seed.

ETHNIC ORIGIN AND HISTORY: Native to Mediterranean regions and western Asia.

VARIETIES: One common variety.

PART USED: Leaves, sprigs, roots, seeds.

AROMA: Refreshing, sweet, lemon overtones.

FLAVOR: Delicate, complex, sweet, hint of lemon, pepper, and mint.

COMPLEMENTARY SPICES: Basil, chili, chives, garlic, ginger, lemongrass, mint, parsley.

BUYING AND STORING:

- Fresh leaves are very delicate. Remove any parts that are not perky. Wrap in a paper towel or a thin dishtowel in a plastic bag in the fridge for about 4 days.
- Bunches may also be kept in a glass of water in the fridge, covered with a plastic bag, changing the water every 2 to 3 days to last even a few extra days.
- May be chopped and frozen with water in ice cube trays for a few months.
- Dried cilantro is not worth mentioning, nor worth buying.

GROW YOUR OWN!:

- Although cilantro has delicate leaves, it is an easy annual to grow, even from seed.
- Loves a warm, sunny spot and plenty of water.

NUTRITION AND TRADITION:

- Cilantro is an herb that some people are wild for and others despise, with claims that it tastes soapy (I personally am an ardent fan!).
- Cilantro is known to draw heavy metals out of the body, especially mercury.
- The delicate, complex flavor and aroma cannot withstand heat, so add after cooking.
- Key in Vietnamese and Southeast Asian dishes.

NATURE: Sweet-cooling.

BOTANY: *Anethum graveolens*; an annual plant grown for its feathery leaves, also called dill weed, which resemble fennel leaves, and also for its seeds.

ETHNIC ORIGIN AND HISTORY: Native to southern Russia, western Asia, and eastern Mediterranean regions. Dill has been cultivated and grown wild for thousands of years and hailed as a symbol of good luck by 1st-century Romans.

VARIETIES:

- European dill: also called dill weed, preferred for its leaves, rather than its more pungent seeds.
- Indian dill: grown primarily for seed, which is lighter, longer, and narrower; used in curries.

PART USED: Fresh and dried leaves; seeds.

AROMA:

- Leaves: clean, sweet, fragrant aroma, with hints of lemon and anise.
- Seeds: somewhat like caraway, as both contain *carvone* in their essential oils.

FLAVOR:

- Leaves: somewhere between parsley and anise.
- Seeds: similar to anise and fennel, warm with a sharp note, clean aftertaste.

COMPLEMENTARY SPICES: Coriander, cumin, garlic, ginger, mustard, tarragon, turmeric.

BUYING AND STORING:

- Fresh dill is delicate and does not last long (2 to 3 days in a plastic bag in the fridge before it droops).
- Look for bunches that are crisp and fresh, not wilting.
- Dried dill does not translate the distinctive flavor of fresh, but will keep for up to a year in an airtight container in a cool, dry place.
- Dill seed, stored similarly, will keep for up to 2 years. Ground dill seed does not retain flavor or aroma.

GROW YOUR OWN!:

- Dill is easy to grow from seed and prefers shelter, full sun, plenty of water, and well-drained soil. Happy in pots or in the ground, though the taproot is easily damaged and does not like to be transplanted.
- Successive planting will supply plants throughout the growing season.
- Dill will come to flower, then seed, and will self-seed if left alone.
- Avoid planting dill and fennel near each other, as they will cross-pollinate and create hybrids (which actually could be interesting, but the seeds will be sterile).

NUTRITION AND TRADITION:

- When using dried dill weed, do so in the later stages of cooking as the flavor and fragrance diminish quickly.

- The flavor of dill seed, which is stronger and more pungent than the leaves, is actually enhanced by cooking.
- The leaves and seeds are used in crunchy dill pickles, made famous in New York delis.
- Quintessential in classic potato salad.

MINT

NATURE: Cooling-warming-drying.

BOTANY: *Mentha* species; broadly divided into two groups: spearmint and peppermint.

ETHNIC ORIGIN AND HISTORY: Native to southern Europe and Mediterranean regions. One of the most popular and pervasive flavors in the world. Excellent in both sweet and savory foods.

VARIETIES: More than 30 varieties, of which only a few are commonly used and available.

- Common peppermint (*M. piperita*): tall stems, small, darker-green leaves, quintessential peppermint flavor.
- Chocolate mint (*M. piperita citrata*): in the peppermint category, dark green to purple leaves, purple stem, scent of after-dinner chocolate mints. Fantastic for desserts.
- Common spearmint (*M. spicata*): most widely grown, quintessential appearance of mint, sweet and cooling, clean aftertaste.
- Apple mint (*M. suaveolens*): a type of spearmint with downy, larger leaves and an apple-mint aroma. Excellent with fresh apple. Leaves are better chopped as they are not as attractive as other mints.
- Pineapple mint (*M. suaveolens variegata*): a type of spearmint, smaller than apple mint, with light green leaves trimmed in cream. Young leaves have a distinct tropical fruit aroma; more mature leaves are mintier.

PART USED: Fresh and dried leaves.

AROMA:

- Spearmints: mellow, refreshing.
- Peppermints: stronger, with menthol overtones.

The earth does not belong to man; man belongs to the earth. This we know. Whatever befalls the earth befalls the sons of the earth. Man did not weave the web of life; he is merely a strand in it. Whatever he does to the web, he does to himself.

—CHIEF SEATTLE, 19TH-CENTURY NATIVE AMERICAN

FLAVOR:

- Spearmints: sweet, a sharp, pleasant pungency with lemon notes.
- Peppermints: slightly sweet with a fiery bite, tangy with a touch of spice, cool, clean aftertaste.

COMPLEMENTARY SPICES: Basil (mint and basil are divine companions), black pepper, cardamom, chili pepper, cumin, dill, ginger, marjoram, oregano, paprika, parsley, thyme, chocolate!

BUYING AND STORING:

- Bunches of fresh mint will last longest (just a few days) in a glass of water in the fridge.
- My mom chops the leaves and puts them in ice cube trays with water to freeze for a few months when the mint is abundant. Works well.
- Dried mint maintains its pungency and has concentrated flavor, but lacks the sweetness of fresh leaves.

GROW YOUR OWN!:

- Mint grows like a weed and will take over a garden if it is not separated. Unless you have the space, it is probably better to grow it in a pot.
- Seeds for varieties easily available on the Internet.
- Mint is a perennial plant that prefers partial shade to full sun and plenty of water.

NUTRITION AND TRADITION:

- Mint has both a cooling and warming nature. It has a drying effect, which makes it a helpful digestive aid.
- The aroma of mint is from the menthol contained in the plant, which has cooling, slightly numbing effects.
- Balances heating spices, especially chili peppers and curries.
- Excellent with chocolate and raspberries.
- Fabulous in a tall, cold glass of water with lemon and cucumber in the dog days of summer.

OREGANO AND MARJORAM

NATURE: Spicy-bitter-sweet.

BOTANY: *Origanum* species; oregano (*O. vulgare*) and marjoram (*O. majorana*) are different herbs from the same species, both closely related to thyme. Low, bushy perennial of the mint family.

ETHNIC ORIGIN AND HISTORY: Mediterranean regions. "Oregano" is Greek for "joy of the mountain."

VARIETIES: Many varieties of oregano, of which only one (common, *O. vulgare*) is readily available. One common variety of marjoram (*O. majorana*).

PART USED: Leaves.

AROMA:

- Oregano: spicier, slightly sharp and sweet, peppery, camphor undertone.
- Marjoram: sweeter, subtly spicy.

FLAVOR:

- Oregano: warm, peppery, slightly sharp and spicy with a touch of bitter and a note of lemon.
- Marjoram: similar, but sweeter.

COMPLEMENTARY SPICES: Basil, black pepper, chili, cumin, garlic, paprika, parsley, rosemary, sage, thyme.

BUYING AND STORING:

- Look for strong leaves in fresh oregano. Marjoram is a little more tender.
- Dried oregano and marjoram have more intense flavors but lack the subtle sweetness. Both will keep for a year, stored in an airtight container in a cool, dry place.

GROW YOUR OWN!:

- Oregano and marjoram plants may be purchased at most nurseries, though they can be grown from seed.
- Propagate by dividing the roots and planting.
- They need plenty of sun and well-drained soil to thrive.
- Prune back plants in the late fall to keep the plants bushy and prevent them from growing straggly.
- Leaves may be picked throughout the growing cycle. Harvest for drying just after the flower buds form.
- Marjoram is a perennial, but it can be grown as an annual in warmer climates.

NUTRITION AND TRADITION:

- Marjoram is more delicate than oregano and does not lend itself to long cooking.
- The essential oil of oregano is a great natural antifungal and antibacterial.

PARSLEY

NATURE: Sweet-balancing.

BOTANY: *Petroselinum crispum*; biennial plant, cultivated throughout the temperate world.

ETHNIC ORIGIN AND HISTORY: Native to eastern Mediterranean regions. Grown in Germany in the 1500s and valued for its roots rather than leaves. Parsley leaves were used to ward off drunkenness in ancient times (not so effectively, it seems!).

VARIETIES: There are more than 30 varieties, though only 2 are commonly available.

- Curly parsley: most popular, with decorative curly leaves.
- Flat parsley/Italian parsley: flat leaf, stronger flavor.
- Parsley root: a lovely root, like a small parsnip or turnip (depending on variety), with a subtle nutty flavor marrying parsley and celery.

PART USED: Leaves most commonly used; stems for juices and stocks; root is used as a vegetable, like parsnips.

AROMA: Clean, lemon overtones with a touch of spice.

FLAVOR: Herbaceous, clean, and slightly tangy with a soft note of mild pepper.

COMPLEMENTARY SPICES: Practically everything.

BUYING AND STORING:

- Fresh parsley is sold in bunches, which should be bright green with no signs of wilting or yellowing.
- To store, shake off excess moisture and wrap in a paper towel or a very thin dishtowel in a plastic bag in the fridge. Will keep for 3 to 5 days.
- Dried parsley is not much worth mentioning (i.e.: do not buy, period).
- My mom chops parsley up and puts it in ice cube trays filled with water to freeze when her herb box is overflowing. A pretty good runner-up to fresh.

GROW YOUR OWN!: Parsley may be germinated, by soaking in warm water overnight, and sowed in the ground or an herb box. They take a few weeks to germinate and grow. Thin seedlings to give them room to grow. The plant will grow back 2 years in a row before needing to be planted again. It is good to sow seeds every year so there is no lapse when one batch runs to seed in its second year.

- Harvest starting in late spring.
- P.S. My mom, who lives in New Paltz, New York (near Woodstock, where it gets cold!), has had parsley plants live through the winter in mild years, allowing her to harvest herbs all year round. She has a great green thumb.

NUTRITION AND TRADITION:

- Rich in vitamins A, C, and K (which strengthens collagen to aid blood clotting).
- Parsley is known to cleanse the urinary tract. Very tonifying for the bladder and kidneys.
- Traditionally used to treat jaundice.

ROSEMARY

NATURE: Spicy-bitter-astringent-warming.

BOTANY: *Rosmarinus officinalis*; rosemary is the silver-green needles, like pine, of a dense, woody evergreen perennial, which is a member of the mint family.

ETHNIC ORIGIN AND HISTORY: Native to Mediterranean regions, where it still grows wild. Recorded in use since 500 BC and grown in England since Roman times. Long cultivated in temperate climes throughout Europe and America.

VARIETIES: One common variety.

PART USED: Needlelike leaves, sprigs, stems, flowers.

AROMA: Strongly aromatic, warm, peppery, pine and camphor undertones.

FLAVOR: Warm and peppery, slightly bitter, nutmeg and camphor notes, balsamic, astringent aftertaste. Flavor fades after leaves are cut. Flowers are milder tasting.

COMPLEMENTARY SPICES: Basil, bay leaf, chives, garlic, lavender, mint, oregano, parsley, sage, savory, thyme.

BUYING AND STORING:

- Fresh rosemary is readily available and keeps fresh for several days in a plastic bag in the fridge or in a glass of water or vase, in or out of the fridge.
- Dried rosemary retains much of its flavor, and the leaves are easy to crumble, though fresh rosemary is available year-round.

GROW YOUR OWN!:

- Rosemary is difficult to grow from seed but easy to propagate by cutting.
- Leaves and sprigs may be cut any time of year, and pruning plants well in the spring will keep them bushy.
- Rosemary bushes love full sun and well-drained soil.

NUTRITION AND TRADITION:

- Use rosemary wisely as the flavor is strong and is not diminished by long cooking.
- Essential element to the French spice blend *herbs de Provence,* which also includes thyme, marjoram, savory, bay leaves, and sometimes lavender and fennel seed.

SAGE

NATURE: Spicy-astringent-warming.

BOTANY: *Salvia* species; sage is a perennial shrub, with narrow, oval, gray-green velvety leaves, that thrives in warm, dry soils.

ETHNIC ORIGIN AND HISTORY: Native to northern Mediterranean regions.

VARIETIES: Many varieties. Common sage (*S. officinalis*) is most easily available and has broad- and narrow-leafed varieties. Young leaves are green and less pungent than gray, older leaves.

PART USED: Fresh and dried leaves; flowers.

AROMA: Mild to strong, warm, astringent, slightly spicy.

FLAVOR: Spicy notes and astringent overtones, with balsamic, mint, and camphor notes, may be musky or sweet.

COMPLEMENTARY SPICES: Bay leaf, caraway, ginger, marjoram, parsley, savory, thyme.

BUYING AND STORING:

- Sometimes easier to grow than to buy. Fresh leaves will keep for several days when wrapped in a paper towel in a plastic bag in the fridge.
- Dried sage, which is more potent but can be musty and acrid in flavor, will keep for up to 6 months when stored in an airtight container in a cool, dry place.

GROW YOUR OWN!:

- Sage loves warm, dry soil. It does not like freezing temperatures.
- Easier to grow from starts than from seed, and happy in a pot.
- Leaves may be harvested from spring to autumn. Cut back plants after flowering to keep them bushy.

NUTRITION AND TRADITION:

- Sage is helpful in digesting fatty and oily foods and was traditionally coupled with them.
- Use sparingly as it has a strong flavor that does not diminish much with heat.

TARRAGON

NATURE: Sweet-balancing.

BOTANY: *Artemisia dracunculus;* perennial, aromatic herb, with narrow, pointed leaves.

ETHNIC ORIGIN AND HISTORY: Native to Siberia and western Asia. The Arabs introduced it to Europe in the 16th century when they ruled Spain, and the French appropriated its culinary finesse.

VARIETIES: Several varieties, the best and most common of which is French tarragon (*A. d. sativa*).

PART USED: Fresh leaves and sprigs.

AROMA: Sweet, pine and licorice notes.

FLAVOR: Subtle yet strong, spicy anise undertones, basil overtones, and a sweet finish. Cooking diminishes the aroma but the flavor stays.

COMPLEMENTARY SPICES: Basil, bay leaves, chives, dill, fennel, parsley.

BUYING AND STORING:

- Some markets sell tarragon, usually in small, plastic clamshell packages, but it is easy to grow your own.
- Fresh sprigs will keep for about 5 days in a plastic bag in the fridge.
- Dried tarragon is a faint image of the aroma and flavor of fresh sprigs.

GROW YOUR OWN!:

- Tarragon loves full sun and rich, dry soil.
- Until plants are well established, they need to be brought inside in cold months.
- The white roots of the plants should be divided in the spring to propagate. Do this every 3 years to preserve the flavor of the plant, even if you do not intend to plant more.

NUTRITION AND TRADITION:

- Classic in bouquet garni, for slow-cooked dishes, soups, and stews.
- Excellent in vinaigrettes and marinades.
- Lovely sprinkled in a salad.

NATURE: Spicy-pungent-warming-drying.

BOTANY: *Thymus* species; a hardy, small evergreen shrub with tiny aromatic leaves that is a perennial member of the mint family. Varieties grown in hot regions are much stronger in flavor than those grown in cool places.

ETHNIC ORIGIN AND HISTORY: Native to the Mediterranean basin.

VARIETIES: There are hundreds of varieties of thyme, both wild and cultivated, each with a slightly different aroma.

- Common thyme *(T. vulgaris):* most popular thyme; a sturdy, upright shrub with gray-green leaves. Broad and narrow-leafed varieties.
- Lemon thyme *(T. citriodorus):* a compact, upright shrub with a fresh, lemon note, and the second most popular thyme.
- Creeping thyme *(T. serphyllum):* mild with very, very small leaves.
- Conehead thyme *(T. capitatus):* also called Persian thyme, the most popular in the Middle East.

PART USED: Leaves and sprigs.

AROMA: Warm, earthy, and peppery.

FLAVOR: Spicy like oregano, citrus notes, overtones of mint, undertones of camphor, clean aftertaste.

COMPLEMENTARY SPICES: Basil, bay leaves, chili, clove, garlic, lavender, marjoram, nutmeg, oregano, paprika, parsley, rosemary, savory.

BUYING AND STORING:

- Look for perky stems with good green color. Avoid browning leaves.
- Fresh leaves will keep in a plastic bag in the fridge for up to a week.
- Many nurseries and garden stores will have a good variety to grow. Make sure it has a good aroma when brushed with your hand.
- Dried thyme retains flavor decently and will keep for 4 to 6 months in an airtight container in a cool, dry place.

GROW YOUR OWN!:

- Thyme loves full sun, heat, and well-drained soil.
- Propagate by dividing the roots and planting.
- Pick leaves whenever needed, the more the better, or the plant will become straggly.
- Harvest for drying just before it flowers.

NUTRITION AND TRADITION: An essential component of the French herb blend for slow cooking, bouquet garni.

Spices: Seasonings of the Trade Winds

The word *spice* is derived from the Latin word *species,* meaning "specific kind," and later it was used in reference to "goods" or "merchandise," which spices were highly regarded as. Traded for millennia, spices have inspired great adventures and journeys to faraway lands, founded fortunes and empires, jeopardized political treaties, and induced great scandal and intrigue.

Spices season food with the trade winds of flavor and bring an essence that none other can provide. Their properties are complex, unique, and tantalizing. May they find their way to the spirit and soul of your food and body.

SAVORY SPICES

CARAWAY

NATURE: Bitter-sweet-pungent-spicy.

BOTANY: *Carum carvi;* fruits (seeds) of an herbaceous, biennial shrub in the parsley family.

ETHNIC ORIGIN: Western Asia, northern and central Europe.

PART USED: Dried seeds (fruits).

AROMA: Pungent, nutty, delicate hint of anise and slight undertone of dried orange peel.

FLAVOR: Bittersweet, sharp, spicy, nutty.

CLASSIC CULINARY USE FOR FOOD:

- Great with mild vegetables like cabbage, cauliflower, potatoes, and beans.
- Common in central and eastern European food, especially in Jewish cuisine and German and Austrian fare.
- Classic in pumpernickel and rye breads, cabbage, and sauerkraut.
- Found in Hungarian goulash.
- Also in North Africa's Tunisian *tabil* (caraway, coriander, garlic, and chili) and spicy *harissa* (chili, garlic, cumin, coriander, caraway, and olive oil) and Moroccan cuisine (like the traditional caraway soup).

COMPLEMENTARY SPICES: Coriander, garlic, parsley, thyme.

BUYING AND STORING: Store in an airtight container in a cool, dry place for 4 to 6 months. Often used whole or slightly crushed, so best purchased as such. Ground caraway loses its aroma and fortitude quickly.

NOTES:

- Popular in medieval fare in rustic breads, beans, soups, and cabbage.
- The Romans favored it for vegetables.
- The essential oils of caraway are used to flavor spirits such as aquavit and Kümmel.

CHILI PEPPERS

NATURE: Spicy-pungent-heating.

BOTANY: *Capsicum* species; fruit of a sub-tropical and tropical plant. *Capsaicin* in the seeds, white fleshy parts, and skin is responsible for the peppery pungent bite. The content of capsaicin depends on the variety of the chili and the degree of ripeness.

ETHNIC ORIGIN: Central and South America.

PART USED: Fresh and dried fruits.

AROMA: Mildly nose-prickling spicy, sweet.

FLAVOR: Mild to explosively hot (generally, the smaller in size, the hotter the heat; the larger, the milder), pungent, some overtones of sweet.

CLASSIC CULINARY USE FOR FOOD:

- Used throughout Asia, Africa, and the Americas. India is the largest producer and consumer.
- Mexican cuisine uses fresh and dried chili as a staple seasoning.
- Korean kimchee is rarely shy with hot chili pepper.

COMPLEMENTARY SPICES: Most spices including bay leaves, coriander, garlic, ginger, lemon, lemongrass, lime.

BUYING AND STORING:

- Fresh chili peppers should be firm, shiny, and perky with smooth skin.
- Keep for a week or so wrapped in a

Hot, Hot, Hot

There are as many varieties of chili peppers as colors in the rainbow. Below I have included varieties found in the recipes in this book. Try different sizes, heats, and flavors to match your dish. Remember, start with a little bit. You can always add more. Once a dish is overspiced, it is hard to recover other flavors.

CAYENNE PEPPER (DRIED AND GROUND): Most common ground chili. Very hot to extremely hot, depending on variety. Pungent, tart, some slightly smoky.

CHIPOTLE PEPPER (DRIED, WHOLE, OR GROUND): A smoke-dried jalapeño pepper. Tan to coffee colored. Smoky sweet, chocolaty smell and flavor. My favorite!

JALAPEÑO PEPPER: Bright green, some with darker patches. Medium size. Mild to medium-hot. Red and fully ripe are sweeter and less hot.

CHILI POWDER (DRIED, GROUND BLEND): Chili powder is a blend of chili pepper and other spices. A fantastic seasoning for the right dishes.

paper towel in a plastic bag in the fridge.

- Dried chili pepper varies as per the country of origin, type, and characteristic flavors. Dried chili will keep almost indefinitely in an airtight container in a cool, dry place.

NOTES:

- Removing the seeds and veins significantly reduces the heat.
- Capsaicin stimulates digestive juices and increases circulation, which induces sweating and actually cools the body. Hence, the popularity of hot and spicy food in traditionally subtropical and tropical climes.
- Chili oil is a great seasoning that may be made at home! Fill a jar one-third full with dried chili peppers and the rest with vegetable oil (like olive oil or grapeseed oil). Close tightly and let stand for up to 1 month for increasing heat.

CORIANDER

NATURE: Warm-earthy-bitter.

BOTANY: *Coriandrum sativum;* seeds of cilantro plant.

ETHNIC ORIGIN: Western Asia, Mediterranean.

PART USED: Mature, dried seeds (fruits).

AROMA: Sweet, woody, peppery undertones, floral overtones.

FLAVOR: Bitter-sweet, earthy-warm, freshly ground has a hint of orange zest.

CLASSIC CULINARY USE FOR FOOD: North Africa: *harissa* and *tabil;* Cyprus: with crushed green olives; Middle East: stews and vegetable dishes; Europe and the United States: pickling spice; West India: masalas; Mexico: paired with cumin; England: cakes and cookies; pairs well with autumn fruits like apples, pears, and squashes.

COMPLEMENTARY SPICES: Chili pepper, cilantro, cinnamon, cumin, fennel, garlic, ginger, nutmeg.

BUYING AND STORING:

- Whole coriander seeds are widely available and significantly more aromatic when crushed than the preground powder. The aroma dissipates quickly after grinding, so grind in small batches.
- Whole seeds keep fresh for 4 to 6 months in a sealed glass jar stored in a cool, dry place.

NOTES:

- The bitterness mellows when dry-roasted in a skillet before crushing.
- Round, Moroccan coriander is much more common and more bitter than the sweeter, oval Indian variety.

NATURE: Bitter-spicy-sweet-warm.

BOTANY: *Cuminum cyminum;* fruit (seed) of a small, herbaceous plant, which is a member of the parsley family. Similar appearance to caraway. Two varieties: common, amber or brown cumin is lighter in color and plumper in shape; and black cumin (rarer and highly prized), which is darker, leaner, sweeter, and more complex in flavor.

ETHNIC ORIGIN: Common cumin is from the Nile Valley of Egypt; true black cumin is from Kashmir and northern Pakistan.

PART USED: Dried seeds (fruits).

AROMA: Strong, acrid yet warm, spicy, sweet, deep.

FLAVOR: Sharp, slightly bitter, pungent, warm.

CLASSIC CULINARY USE FOR FOOD:
- In all cuisines that favor spicy food, cumin is used in breads, chutneys, relishes, spice mixtures, and stews and with vegetables.
- Great with cabbage, onions, potatoes, lentils, rice, and squash.
- Early Spanish tradition complemented cumin, saffron, anise, and cinnamon.
- Moroccan grain dishes like couscous.
- Sparingly in Mexican cuisine.
- Ground coriander and cumin are a classic Indian coupling.

COMPLEMENTARY SPICES: Bay leaf, black pepper, caraway, coriander, curry leaf, fennel seed, garlic, ginger, mustard, oregano, paprika, thyme, turmeric.

BUYING AND STORING:
- Common cumin is widely available.
- Black cumin is available in Asian and specialty markets.
- Whole seeds are best. Ground cumin has a very short shelf life.
- Store in an airtight container in a cool, dry place for several months.

NOTES: The aroma of cumin is enhanced when dry-roasted before being ground.

FENNEL SEED AND POLLEN

NATURE: Sweet-drying.

BOTANY: *Foeniculum vulgare;* fennel is a bulbous aboveground perennial vegetable, with pale green celerylike stems. Common fennel is the variety from which the elongated, oval, greenish-brown seeds are harvested. Fennel pollen is just that—the pollen from flowering fennel—and is a dusty golden-green with a strong, distinctive taste.

ETHNIC ORIGIN: Mediterranean.

PART USED: Young leaves, flowers, pollen, stems, and seeds.

AROMA: Warm, anise and licorice, camphor and eucalyptus overtones.

FLAVOR: Slightly sweet, anise-licorice, camphor and eucalyptus notes; seeds are also slightly astringent with a bittersweet aftertaste; pollen is very strong (use sparingly), somewhere between anise and fennel with bittersweet overtones.

CLASSIC CULINARY USE FOR FOOD:

- Fennel as a vegetable is excellent in salads, slaws, and sauces.
- Sicilians use it in pasta.
- Pollen is intoxicatingly heady for grilled vegetables.
- Fennel seed is a great pickling spice and is used in Germany to flavor sauerkraut.
- The seed is used in breads in Iraq and is an essential element to Chinese five-spice blend.
- In India, the seed is used with vegetables, beans and lentils, garam masala, and spiced gravies.

COMPLEMENTARY SPICES: Black pepper, cinnamon, cumin, ginger, mint, parsley, thyme.

BUYING AND STORING:

- Fennel as a vegetable should be stored in a plastic bag in the fridge and will keep fresh for 2 to 4 days.
- Seeds will keep fresh for more than a year when stored in an airtight container in a cool, dry place.
- Wild fennel pollen is an intensely flavored golden-green dust and is found only in very special markets and more easily over the Internet.

NOTES:

- Fennel seed makes a great breath freshener and digestive aid when chewed after a meal, as is done in India.
- Fennel, akin to anise and licorice, is prized as a blood-sugar balancing food. The Greeks called it *marathon,* meaning "to grow thin," for its slimming and balancing properties.

GINGER

NATURE: Warming-spicy-sweet.

BOTANY: *Zingiber officinale;* ginger is an underground stem, called a rhizome, that grows lush leaves and flowers (which are inedible) in subtropical and tropical regions.

ETHNIC ORIGIN: Asia, and Southeast Asia.

PART USED: Fresh rhizomes.

AROMA: Warm, refreshing, woody undertones, sweet citrus overtones.

FLAVOR: Hot, tangy, biting.

CLASSIC CULINARY USE FOR FOOD:

- Pervasive in many Asian cuisines, including Japanese, Chinese, Korean, Southeast Asian, Vietnamese, and Indian fare.
- Dried ginger is used in Middle Eastern and European dishes (as back in the day,

it was dried on the boats en route to these locales).

COMPLEMENTARY SPICES: Basil, black pepper, chili, cilantro, garlic, lemongrass, lime, mint, scallions, tamarind, turmeric.

BUYING AND STORING:

- Jamaican and Hawaiian ginger are prized as the most choice.
- There are two types of fresh gingerroot: Young ginger has a thin, pale skin, with tender, more mild and less fibrous flesh; mature ginger has a tougher skin that generally requires peeling. Look for smooth skin and a fresh, spicy fragrance. If the ginger is wrinkled, the root is past its prime and the flesh will be fibrous and dry.
- Fresh ginger can be wrapped in plastic and stored for up to 3 weeks and frozen for up to 6 months. To use frozen ginger, slice off a piece of the unthawed root and return the rest to the freezer.
- Dried ginger is a powder with characteristics very different from that of fresh ginger. Dried ginger generally cannot replace fresh ginger, but is delicious in gingerbread, gingersnaps, and spiced sweets.

NOTES:

- Ginger was recorded as a staple in the diet of Confucius, the renowned Chinese philosopher.
- Pickled ginger is a refreshing and decorative condiment, called *garni*, made with rice vinegar and sugar, popular with Japanese food.

LEMONGRASS

NATURE: Sour-spicy.

BOTANY: *Cymbopogon citrates;* an ornate, tropical grass. Now cultivated on almost every continent, including Asia, Australia, west Africa, Mexico, Brazil, and in California and Florida.

ETHNIC ORIGIN: Southeast Asia, Indonesia, Thailand, Vietnam, and Malay Islands.

PART USED: Slightly bulbous, pale green lower part of the stalk.

AROMA: Mild, spicy citrus.

FLAVOR: Clean, tart, unique citrus, peppery overtones.

CLASSIC CULINARY USE FOR FOOD:

- In Southeast Asian soups, salads, stir-fries, stews, and curries. Especially good with coconut.
- For broth, stew, or curry: Remove the outer two layers and bruise the stalk, cook with dish, and remove before serving.
- When intended to be used in a soup or salad: Remove the outer layers and slice very finely from the bottom. Stop when the stalk becomes too tough to easily cut thinly, as the fiber is tough and unpleasant to chew.

- May also be pounded for stir-fried dishes, curries, and vegetable dishes.

COMPLEMENTARY SPICES: Basil, chili, cilantro, cinnamon, garlic, ginger, turmeric.

BUYING AND STORING:

- Fresh stalks are available in Asian and specialty markets. The stalks should be firm and not wrinkled. Wrapped in plastic, fresh stalks will keep for 2 to 3 weeks in the fridge. Wrapped well, they may be frozen for up to 6 months.
- Freeze-dried lemongrass retains respectable flavor, but air-dried lemongrass loses its aromatic, volatile essential oils.

NOTES: Grated lemon rind may be used as a substitute for fresh lemongrass when needed.

MUSTARD

NATURE: Pungent-spicy-bitter.

BOTANY: *Brassica* species; the acrid seeds of several species of plants, belonging to the same family as broccoli, Brussels sprouts, cauliflower, collards, kale, and kohlrabi.

ETHNIC ORIGIN: Southern Europe and western Asia.

PART USED: Dried seeds.

AROMA: Whole mustard seeds have almost no aroma. When ground, mustard is pungent. Cooking releases its acrid, earthy aroma.

FLAVOR: Spicy, bitter, sweet.

CLASSIC CULINARY USE FOR FOOD:

- Pickling and preserving spice.
- Prepared mustard as a condiment. The seeds are soaked in water to activate the enzyme *myrosinase,* which gives it the spicy kick. Then to halt the enzyme, an acidic liquid such as vinegar (tangy), wine (more spicy), or beer (some real heat!) is used.

COMPLEMENTARY SPICES: Bay leaf, black pepper, chili, coriander, cumin, dill, fennel, garlic, honey, parsley, tarragon, turmeric.

BUYING AND STORING:

- Mustard seeds may be stored for up to a year in a cool, dry place.
- Powdered mustard should be used or discarded within 4 to 6 months.
- Prepared mustards will keep for several months even after being opened, though they will dry out and slowly lose their flavor.

NOTES:

- Add powdered mustard in the later stages of cooking as the flavor diminishes.
- Mustard greens are also excellent and have a kick. Young mizuna is delicious in a green salad or finely chopped over tomatoes.

NATURE: Sweet-spicy-bitter-drying.

BOTANY: *Capsicum annuum* species; paprika is made from dried, ground red peppers (longer and thinner than traditional red bell peppers). There is not a single "paprika" pepper, rather it's made from a number of red capsicums. Some varieties are spicier and some milder; all are subtly sweet.

ETHNIC ORIGIN: Central and South America, though planted throughout the Ottoman Empire in Turkey and Hungary as early as 1604, where it has found a home in traditional cuisines.

PART USED: Dried fruits, ground into a powder.

AROMA: Delicate, slightly sweet, and slightly spicy. Some varieties have caramel notes, some are a bit smoky, and others are more fruity.

FLAVOR: Varies. Slightly sweet, a touch of spice and smoke, gently pungent, a hint of bitterness.

CLASSIC CULINARY USE FOR FOOD: Used to color and flavor vegetables, especially potatoes, rice, beans, noodles, and soups.

- Hungary and Serbia: Principal spice and coloring in traditional cuisine.
- Balkan countries and Turkey: A common table condiment along with chili flakes, rather than black pepper.
- Morocco: Commonly found in spice blends and marinades.
- India: A staple to add a red color to dishes.
- Spain: Married with olive oil and onions, called *sofrito*, and used in many slow-cooked dishes. Also, essential to *romesco* sauce, a classic sauce from Catalonia, Spain, made from ground tomatoes, red bell peppers, onion, garlic, almonds, and olive oil.

COMPLEMENTARY SPICES: Caraway, cardamom, garlic, ginger, oregano, parsley, pepper, rosemary, saffron, thyme, turmeric.

BUYING AND STORING:

- Paprika is a powdered spice that varies in color and grade of grind, from very fine to coarse. All varieties should be stored in an airtight container and kept out of the light.
- Hungarian and Balkan paprikas are generally spicier varieties.
- Spanish, Moroccan, and Portuguese varieties are milder.

NOTES: Paprika should not be overcooked as it will become bitter.

PEPPER AND PEPPERCORNS

NATURE: Spicy-warm-pungent.

BOTANY: *Piper nigrum;* peppercorns are a berry that grows on a climbing vine in grapelike clusters. The essential oil content is responsible for its flavor, and the amount of the alkaloid *peperine* accounts for its bite.

There are many varieties of peppercorn: black, white, pink, and red. All are from the same plant; each is picked at different stages of maturity, cured, and dried differently. White peppercorns are pungent, but less aromatic and spicy, because the hull is removed, where much of the essential oils reside.

Pepper was the original quest of the historical spice trade and alternative routes to the Far East. At one time in Rome, pepper was traded, ounce for ounce, with gold.

ETHNIC ORIGIN: India's Malabar Coast and Indonesia.

PART USED: Immature and ripe fruits (berries).

AROMA: Pungent, warm, woody undertones, slightly fruity and lemon overtones.

FLAVOR: Spicy, biting, hint of sweet, clean aftertaste.

CLASSIC CULINARY USE FOR FOOD: Everything.

COMPLEMENTARY SPICES: Everything.

BUYING AND STORING:

- Sun-dried peppercorns are superior to those subjected to artificial heat drying, where some of the precious volatile oils are lost.
- Large, uniform peppercorns command the highest price. Tellicherry and Lampong are the best varieties.
- Whole peppercorns will keep for about a year in an airtight container. Ground pepper loses its flavor in 3 to 4 months.

NOTES:

- Stimulates gastric juices and is a digestive aid as such.
- Black peppercorns are harvested when the fruit is young and still green, then dried, whence it becomes wrinkled and dark in color.
- White peppercorns are picked when the berries are a ripening yellowish-red. They are then soaked to remove the skin and sun dried.

SAFFRON

NATURE: Pungent-bitter-warming.

BOTANY: *Crocus sativus;* saffron is the dried stigmas of the violet-colored saffron crocus, which flowers in the autumn. Each flower contains three stigmas, which must be picked at dawn. Deep to brilliant red and orange-red.

ETHNIC ORIGIN: Mediterranean and western

Asia. Today, Spain is the main producer.

PART USED: Stigmas, known as threads or filaments.

AROMA: Distinctive, rich, warm, pungent, musky undertone, floral-honey overtones.

FLAVOR: Delicate yet penetrating and lingering, warm, earthy, and slightly bitter and musky.

CLASSIC CULINARY USE FOR FOOD:

- Used to flavor and color food, especially grains and wine.
- Saffron is usually infused into the liquid of a dish. Threads may also be ground up and mixed into dishes.
- When added earlier in cooking, it will lend more color. When added in the later stages of cooking, saffron will impart more aromatic flavor.
- Classic in Provençal bouillabaisse and risotto alla Milanese.
- Good with grains, asparagus, carrots, leeks, mushrooms, spinach, and winter squashes.
- I use it in Moroccan Saffron Quinoa Tabbouleh (page 300).

COMPLEMENTARY SPICES: Cinnamon, fennel, ginger, nutmeg, paprika, pepper.

BUYING AND STORING:

- Purchase saffron from a reliable source. Because it is easily adulterated, tourist markets around the world pass off marigolds, safflower, and turmeric as saffron. Saffron has a very distinctive, penetrating aroma that gives away the real deal.
- Threads will keep their flavor and aroma for 2 to 3 years, stored in an airtight container away from light and heat.

NOTES:

- A little bit goes a long way. Overspicing with saffron will bring bitterness.
- It takes about 80,000 flowers to yield just 5 pounds of stigmas, which produce only 1 pound of dried saffron. Hence, no mystery why it is the most expensive spice in the world.
- Saffron was also used as a dye in ancient civilizations, such as for the robes of Buddhist monks.

Cooking should be a carefully balanced reflection of all the good things of the earth.

—JEAN AND PIERRE TROISGROS

TAMARIND PASTE

You'll often find that a recipe calls for a quantity of tamarind paste, so here are some easy instructions for working with what you find at the market.

Making Paste from Fresh Tamarind

Break open the pods and peel away all of the papery skin. Remove the flesh from the strings that hold it in place and remove the seeds. Add barely enough warm water to cover the flesh and soak for 15 to 20 minutes to soften. Use clean fingers to work it into a paste. If there are any remaining tough pieces of pulp left when all of the soft parts have dissolved, pull them out, squeeze dry, and discard. The paste should be the consistency of fruit concentrate.

Making Paste from Tamarind Blocks

Break off a chunk of the block about the size of an egg. Break into a few pieces and remove seeds if there are any. Add barely enough warm water to cover the flesh and soak for 15 to 20 minutes to soften. Use clean fingers to work it into a paste. When all of the soft parts have dissolved, pull out any remaining tough pieces of pulp, squeeze dry, and discard. The paste should be the consistency of fruit concentrate.

TAMARIND

NATURE: Sour-sweet-astringent.

BOTANY: *Tamarindus indica;* long, beanlike pods from tall, evergreen shade tree. Tamarind trees will bear fruit for up to 200 years. Tartaric acid is responsible for the tart taste, which varies in intensity depending on the type of tree and region.

ETHNIC ORIGIN: Northeast Africa (likely Madagascar).

PART USED: Sour-sweet pulp of ripe pods.

AROMA: Mild.

FLAVOR: Sour, sweet, tart, fruity.

CLASSIC CULINARY USE FOR FOOD:

- Choice for sweet and sour dishes.
- Used in India and southeast Asia as an acidic element, the way Western cuisine uses lemon and vinegar.
- Used in the Middle East, South and Central America, and the West Indies for drinks.
- Excellent for taming and balancing the fiery effect of spicy chili peppers and hot spices.
- Dusted with sugar or candied as a sweet.

- Essential to Worcestershire sauce.

COMPLEMENTARY SPICES: Black pepper, chili, cilantro, cumin, garlic, ginger, mustard, turmeric.

BUYING AND STORING:

- Tamarind is available in East Indian and Asian markets as whole pods (beans); as a dried block, with or without seeds; as a paste; and in a thick liquid concentrate or syrup, which resembles a tart molasses.
- The skin of whole pods is brittle and a gray- to caramel-brown. The pulp is dark brown, sticky, and quite fibrous with veins. The longer fresh tamarind sits around, the more the pulp will pull away from the skin, which will crack and crumble.
- All processed tamarind will keep almost indefinitely.

NOTES:

- Tamarind offers an incredible sour, sweet, tart portfolio of flavors.
- To use a tamarind block, soak a small piece (1 tablespoon) in warm or hot water for 10 to 20 minutes to soften. Mash to loosen the pulp and remove any veins or seeds. Tamarind concentrate can be used like a freshly made paste. Though convenient to use, it tends to be much darker.

TURMERIC

NATURE: Bitter-spicy-pungent-warming-drying.

BOTANY: *Curcuma longa;* turmeric is a perennial rhizome (stemming root), closely related to ginger, with bright orange-yellow flesh. *Curcumin* is the compound responsible for the bright color.

ETHNIC ORIGIN: Southern Asia.

PART USED: Fresh and dried root.

AROMA: Gingery, spicy, warm, citrus overtones, musky undertones; dried turmeric has deeper, woody undertones.

FLAVOR: Fresh turmeric is agreeably earthy, bitter, spicy, gingery, and pungent, with floral and citrus overtones; dried turmeric powder is similar, with earthy, wood undertones.

CLASSIC CULINARY USE FOR FOOD:

- Used sparingly as it easily overpowers other spices.
- Used for its bright orange-yellow color, for many regional vegetable, bean, lentil, and grain dishes.
- In Indian and the West Indies' curry and masala spice blends.
- Found in Southeast Asian pastes with lemongrass, ginger, garlic, shallots, tamarind, and chili.
- Especially good with coconut milk, ginger, scallions, and cilantro.

- In North African *tagines* and stews as well as Moroccan spice blends.
- In the West, turmeric is used to color cheese, margarine, and mustard, and widely used in pickles and relishes.

COMPLEMENTARY SPICES: Black pepper, chili, cilantro, clove, coriander, cumin, curry leaf, fennel, garlic, ginger, lemongrass, mustard, paprika.

BUYING AND STORING:

- Fresh turmeric should be firm with smooth skin. It can be found in Asian markets and may be stored for up to 2 weeks when wrapped in a paper towel in a plastic bag in the fridge. Freezes well for up to 6 months. To use, cut off an unthawed piece of the desired size and return the rest to the freezer.
- Dried turmeric will keep for at least a year in an airtight container.

NOTES: Turmeric will stain just about any-thing (and is used as a dye), so be mindful when using it.

WASABI

NATURE: Spicy-pungent-cleansing.

BOTANY: *Eutrema wasabi;* a gnarled, knobby root, also called Japanese horseradish, that grows in cold, pure running water.

ETHNIC ORIGIN: Mountainous regions of Japan.

PART USED: Roots, commonly ground and dried into powder.

AROMA: Fierce, penetrating, nose-prickling spicy.

FLAVOR: Sharp, clean, eye-watering hot kick and bite, fresh, clean aftertaste.

CLASSIC CULINARY USE FOR FOOD:

- Classic accompaniment to sushi, served as a paste, which is mixed with soy sauce for dipping.
- Mixed with soy sauce and dashi (soup stock) to make wasabi-joyu, a popular sauce and marinade.
- Great as a piquant kick to vinaigrette and creamy dressings.
- Epic with avocado.
- Wasabi does not retain its flavor when cooked, so it must be added to cold foods.

COMPLEMENTARY SPICES: Ginger, mustard, scallion, soy sauce.

BUYING AND STORING:

- Fresh wasabi root, which looks like horseradish, is difficult to find, but abso-lutely incredible.
- Look for pure wasabi powder. Some wasabi powders are mixed with horse-radish and mustard, which is okay, though they carry a harsher flavor. Avoid wasabi adulterated with artificial green coloring and additives.
- Powdered wasabi, usually sold in a can,

will keep fresh for a few months in an airtight container, though it eventually loses its potency and develops a stale aftertaste.

- Wasabi is also sold as a paste, often in a tube, which must be refrigerated. Wasabi paste loses its flavor much more quickly than the powder and is often artificially dyed.

NOTES: Dried wasabi powder will develop its penetrating aroma and flavorful kick only when mixed with water and left to steep for 5 to 10 minutes.

SWEET SPICES

CARDAMOM

NATURE: Pungent-bittersweet.

BOTANY: *Elettaria cardamomum;* pale green, tough-skinned fruits (pods and seeds) of a large perennial bush in tropical regions. Member of the ginger family. Each pod contains about 6 to 12 seeds. Stickiness between the seeds is a sign of superior freshness.

ETHNIC ORIGIN: Rain forests of the Western Ghats in southern India; a close variety is also native to Sri Lanka. Now grown in Tasmania, Vietnam, Papua New Guinea, and Guatemala (the world's largest exporter).

PART USED: Dried seeds.

AROMA: Penetrating, fruity, camphor and eucalyptus overtones (from *cineole* in the essential oils), smoky undertones.

FLAVOR: Warm, pungent, bittersweet, lemony, eucalyptus-camphor tones, clean aftertaste.

CLASSIC CULINARY USE FOR FOOD:

- Good for both savory and sweet dishes.
- Used to flavor rice and slow-braised dishes.
- Great with autumn and winter fruits, like apples, pears, oranges, and winter squashes, as well as sweet potatoes and other root vegetables.
- Brewed with coffee in Arab countries (yum!).
- Classic in Indian spice mixtures, such as masalas, as well as Lebanese, Syrian, and Ethiopian foods.
- Popular in Scandinavian cuisine since the times Vikings traveled the trade routes from Constantinople. Found in German and Russian spiced cakes, pastries, and breads.

COMPLEMENTARY SPICES: Black pepper, caraway, cinnamon, cloves, coffee, coriander, cumin, ginger, nutmeg, paprika, saffron.

BUYING AND STORING:

- Cardamom seeds are best purchased in their whole pods (small), which should be plump and green. The best quality is green-amber in color. Also available as a whole seed outside the pod; it is small, round, and dark in color, though the volatile oils diminish when exposed to air. Ground cardamom is usually of inferior quality, easily adulterated, and usually ground with the pods.
- Pods will keep up to 1 year, stored in an airtight container in a cool, dark place, though the color and aroma will fade slowly.

NOTES:

- Use sparingly as it is very strong and becomes bitter.
- Cardamom is a great digestive aid and breath-freshener.
- Indian pilafs are seasoned with whole spices, added to the rice before cooking, such as cardamom, cinnamon sticks, cloves, cumin seeds, and black peppercorn.

CINNAMON

NATURE: Warm-sweet-drying.

BOTANY: *Cinnamomum zelanicum;* from the bark of an evergreen tree of the laurel family grown in the subtropics and tropics.

ETHNIC ORIGIN: Sri Lanka.

PART USED: Dried bark, rolled into quills, commonly known as cinnamon sticks; or ground into a fine powder.

AROMA: Very agreeable, warm yet intense, sweet and delicately spicy, woody.

FLAVOR: Warm, sweet, undertone of clove, overtone of orange-citrus.

CLASSIC CULINARY USE FOR FOOD: All manners of sweets and desserts; well placed in savory foods like rice and mulled wine.

COMPLEMENTARY SPICES: Other warm-sweet spices, cardamom, chocolate, cloves, ginger, nutmeg, vanilla.

BUYING AND STORING:

- Whole cinnamon sticks are superior to ground cinnamon. The essential oils, specifically the eugenol in the oils, are delicate and are preserved much better as a whole stick.
- Cinnamon sticks will keep their aroma and flavor for up to 2 years stored in an airtight container in a cool, dry place.
- The paler the cinnamon, the finer the grade.
- Ground cinnamon loses its flavor quickly (1 to 2 months), so purchase in small amounts.

Cinnamon Sticks

There are many grades of cinnamon sticks, classified by the thickness of the quill. Thin quills have the finest flavor and are the highest grade. Small inner pieces of bark, called feathers and chips, are the lowest grade. Feathers and chips are generally used to produce ground cinnamon.

CLOVE

NATURE: Spicy-bittersweet-warming.

BOTANY: *Syzyium aromaticum;* cloves are the unopened flower buds of a small, tropical evergreen tree. As in cinnamon, *eugenol* in the essential oil gives the distinctive taste.

ETHNIC ORIGIN: Molucca Islands in Indonesia.

PART USED: Dried flower buds.

AROMA: Warm, assertive, undertones of pepper, overtones of camphor and eucalyptus.

FLAVOR: Sharp, fruity, bitter, leaves a numbing sensation in the mouth.

CLASSIC CULINARY USE FOR FOOD: Used in both sweet and savory foods. Used sparingly since the strong flavor overpowers other spices.

- Classic in baked goods, pumpkin pie, sweets, and preserves.
- Europe: used as a pickling spice and sparingly in stews.
- India: essential in garam masala.
- China: essential in five-spice powder (with star anise, cassia, fennel seed, and sichuan pepper).
- France: essential in *quatre épices* (with black pepper, nutmeg, and dried ginger).

COMPLEMENTARY SPICES: Allspice, bay leaves, cardamom, chili, cinnamon, coriander, curry leaf, fennel, ginger, nutmeg.

BUYING AND STORING:

- Whole cloves are much more potent than ground powder. Whole cloves are very tough and must be ground in an electric mill or grinder.
- Good cloves will release a bit of oil when pressed with a fingernail.

NOTES: As a kid, I used to make holiday ornaments by sticking a whole orange with the stems of cloves until it was covered completely. Mmmm . . . the aroma lingers with my nostalgic memories.

NATURE: Bittersweet-warm.

BOTANY: *Myristica fragrans;* fruit of tropical evergreen tree. The kernel of the oval fruit is smooth and gray-brown, housed in a hard shell, which is wrapped in a webbed, bright red, lacy aril, or membrane. The membrane is actually another prized spice called mace, with a bittersweet flavor and aromatic, floral aroma with hints of clove and pepper.

ETHNIC ORIGIN: Banda Islands of Indonesia, once called the Spice Islands.

PART USED: Kernel of the seed (fruit).

AROMA: Warm, sweet, rich, camphor and eucalyptus overtones, spicy undertones.

FLAVOR: Sweet with deep, bittersweet undertones, aromatic, perfumed overtones, hint of clove and wood.

CLASSIC CULINARY USE FOR FOOD:
- Used in both savory and sweet foods, though more commonly favored for sweet desserts like spiced cakes, honey cakes, and rich fruitcakes.
- Italians add it to vegetable dishes and beans. (I use it in my Insider Italian Lentils, page 310.)
- The French include it with pepper and cloves in slow-cooked stews and ragouts.
- The Dutch add lavish amounts to cauliflower and cabbage.
- Excellent in spiced teas like chai.

COMPLEMENTARY SPICES: Black pepper, cardamom, cinnamon, cloves, coriander, cumin, ginger, thyme, vanilla.

BUYING AND STORING:
- Best purchased whole. Nutmeg is easy to grate on a nutmeg grater or any fine metal grater.
- Keeps fresh almost indefinitely when stored in an airtight container. Ground nutmeg loses its aroma and flavor quickly. Banda Penang nutmeg is prized as the best and is superior to West Indian nutmeg.

STAR ANISE

NATURE: Bittersweet-pungent (licorice-anise).

BOTANY: *Illicim verum;* the tough, brown, irregular, eight-pointed star pod and seed of an evergreen shrub of the magnolia family. It bears fruit after 6 years and will continue to bear for a century. Contains the essential oil *anethol,* also found in anise seed.

ETHNIC ORIGIN: Southern China, Vietnam.

PART USED: Whole star anise, seed, and pod.

AROMA: Fennel, licorice, anise, sweet, warm, pungent.

FLAVOR: Sweet, assertive, pungent, a touch of

bitterness, licorice overtones, mildly numbing undertones like clove, clean aftertaste.

CLASSIC CULINARY USE FOR FOOD: A principal cornerstone of classic Chinese five-spice. Good with root vegetables and fruits like figs and tropical fruits.

- China: as a marinade for steamed dishes and braised with soy sauce.
- Vietnam: simmered dishes and stocks.
- I use it as a spice for brewing Molokai Chai (page 168).

COMPLEMENTARY SPICES: Chili, cinnamon, coriander, fennel seed, garlic, ginger, lemongrass.

BUYING AND STORING:

- Best purchased whole, as ground spice loses flavor quickly.
- Store in an airtight container away from light. Whole star anise will keep for up to a year when stored properly.

VANILLA

NATURE: Sweet.

BOTANY: *Vanilla planifolia;* the word *vanilla* is a diminutive of the Spanish word *vaina,* meaning "pod." Vanilla beans are the stamen (fruit) of a perennial, climbing orchid. Subtropical and tropical. Vanillin crystals, called *givre,* are where the aroma and flavor reside among the thousands of tiny black seeds inside the long, thin pod.

There are several varieties of vanilla, each with unique, subtle identities:

- Bourbon vanilla from Madagascar and Réunion (Africa)—rich, sweet, very creamy flavor.
- Indonesian vanilla—slightly smoky, strong flavor.
- Mexican vanilla—considered one of the most complex and delicate varieties.
- Tahitian vanilla—very floral and fruity.

ETHNIC ORIGIN: Central America, originally sophisticatedly cultivated and cured by the Aztecs.

PART USED: Cured pods (beans), macerated and extracted into alcohol or vegetable glycerin.

AROMA: Rich, perfumed, sweet, some varieties with hints of licorice and tobacco.

FLAVOR: Sweet and creamy flavor, some varieties slightly smoky and spicy.

CLASSIC CULINARY USE FOR FOOD: Classically used in sweets, especially chocolate. Surprisingly delicious in savory dishes, such as chowders and with root vegetables such as turnips and potatoes.

COMPLEMENTARY SPICES: Chili, chocolate, cinnamon, cloves, saffron.

BUYING AND STORING:

- Good vanilla beans are deep brown to black and wrinkly, moist, and supple with an immediate aroma. The best

The True Cost of Vanilla

Vanilla must be pollinated by hand (part of why it is the world's second-most expensive herb, after saffron) because there is only one type of bee that pollinates the vanilla orchid, and that bee is now extinct.

vanilla beans have a light white frosting of vanillin crystals. The best varieties are found in specialty markets and online.

- Store vanilla beans in a sealed jar in a cool, dark, dry place. Can keep fresh for more than a year.
- Vanilla extract is preserved in alcohol or in vegetable glycerin. Look for "pure vanilla extract" to avoid colorings and synthetic ingredients. Alcohol is a great natural preservative and is best used in baking, where the bitterness of the alcohol dissipates from the heat. Nonalcohol vanilla extract is in vegetable glycerin, which is quite sweet on its own; this extract is best for raw recipes and recipes that do not involve heat.

NOTES:

- Fresh vanilla beans have no aroma or taste. Both of these seductive senses develop only after careful fermentation.
- Vanilla pods are harvested by hand when they begin to turn yellow on the flower. They are plunged into boiling water to prevent them from maturing further. Then they are dried in the sun by day and wrapped in blankets to sweat at night. The pods shrivel and darken. Enzymes in the fruit catalyze a chemical change that bears aromatic compounds, specifically vanillin.
- Eleven pounds (5 kilograms) of fresh vanilla beans yield about 2¼ pounds (1 kilogram) of cured vanilla beans.

All of us have in our veins the exact same percentage of salt in our blood, sweat, and tears that exists in the ocean . . . we are tied to the ocean . . . and when we go back to the sea . . . we are returning from whence we came. . . .

—JOHN F. KENNEDY

Salt: Mineral Balance from the Sea

As humans, we have an intimate relationship with salt. Not only does salt taste good, it sustains life. Salt water has a mineral profile similar to our blood, sweat, and tears. The ocean of electrolyte salts in our bodies is what harnesses the electrical current in our bodies. It is an element we literally cannot live without.

As the impetus for pioneering trade routes across incalculable oceans and vast deserts, salt has been the cornerstone of political alliances, security for great empires, and provocative cause for revolution. Salt has been valued throughout human history as a way to preserve and season food, as well as for medicinal values, and even as money.

Salt is a stoic element that in essence does not change. It will dissolve into liquid and dry back into crystals again and again without changing its natural form.

All salt comes from the sea. Sea salt is harvested from ocean water and dried. Natural sea salt has about 60 trace minerals, which are essential for the needy nuances of our bodies. Rock salt and salt mines are deposits in the earth left from where ancient seas once were. Salt that is mined from ancient seabeds of the earth usually lacks some of the minerals found naturally in seawater because they are washed away by rainwater over thousands of years. Depending on geography, though, some rock salts may contain other valuable minerals from the earth.

The Balancing Qualities of Salt

Salt has a dual nature. It has attributes that are concurrently stimulating and grounding, cooling and warming, moist and dry, strengthening and softening. Salt is best used in balance, both as a seasoning and for health.

Salt stimulates digestion and healthy secretion of hydrochloric acid in the stomach. Both the Ayurvedic and macrobiotic systems value the active quality of salt not only for strengthening digestion but also for overall energy and endurance.

The moist nature of salt helps regulate warmth and coolness to balance the body. Part of this is due to the tonifying and stimulating actions that salt has on the kidneys to aid and regulate fluid balance in the body. The right amount of salt promotes healthy fluid metabolism, but too much stimulation can stress the kidneys and dehydrate the body. The moist, stimulating qualities of salt are especially good in the dryness of cool and cold seasons.

The influence of salt on fluid balance can help soften tissues, muscles, glands, intestinal blockages, and abdominal hardness. Too much salt, however, can raise pressure in the arteries. Because sodium has an affinity for water, excess quantities can settle in vascular fluids and cause arteries to become too firm and hard.

SEA SALTS

Sea salt is the essence of the sea and includes a valuable portfolio of trace elements and minerals to nourish our bodies and season food. There is a wide range of sea salts from different parts of the world, each with different qualities, texture, color, grain, and subtle collection of flavor.

High-quality sea salts are harvested and dried with integrity to offer the best of their natural attributes. The finest sea salt is dried either by the sun or tended at low temperatures to preserve precious elements, minerals, and delicate flavors. I find matching salt with dishes brings subtle harmony and magic to the balance of flavor.

CELTIC SEA SALT (FRENCH)

Celtic sea salt is a pure, naturally moist, pale gray sea salt. It is hand-harvested from the pristine Atlantic waters off Brittany, France, using the same traditional methods used 2,000 years ago. Dried in the sun to preserve abundant, valuable trace minerals, Celtic sea salt has a mild, pure flavor. It is available in coarse grind, fine grind, and extra-fine grind.

OSHIMA ISLAND SALT (JAPANESE)

This sun-dried sea salt is harvested and crafted on the majestic volcanic island of Oshima off the coast of Japan. It is highly mineralized with an exceptionally pure taste and clean finish.

SMOKED SEA SALTS

Smoked sea salt is naturally smoked over wood fires to infuse a deep smoky aroma and flavor. There are several choice smoked salts on the market. When purchasing, be sure products are natural and not infused with artificial flavor.

■ HALEN MÔN SMOKED SEA SALT (UK): An absolutely divine, pure, organic, Welsh salt from the Atlantic off the island of Anglesey, this salt is smoked over oak wood chips to yield a deep-seated aroma and distinctly smoky-sweet flavor. Fine, delicate flakes, which melt easily to infuse a tantalizing smoky flavor. Perfect

Vanilla Salt Glow Scrub

Salt has beautifying properties to make skin glow. Grains of salt naturally slough off dead skin, allowing supple young skin to emerge. The balance of salt and emollient oil in this recipe makes skin radiant and soft all over.

> **1 cup sea salt**
> **½ cup oil (coconut, almond, apricot, or sesame)**
> **1 tablespoon jojoba oil (optional)**
> **2 teaspoons pure vanilla extract**

Mix the sea salt, oil, jojoba oil (if desired), and vanilla together in a glass jar.
To use, rub over skin in a circular motion and rinse well.
Store sealed and stir before using. Keeps indefinitely.

---

as a graceful seasoning to finish a dish.

- **MAINE SMOKED SEA SALT**: A sea salt from Maine that is cool-smoked over a well-tended fire of hickory and alder wood for a mild, yet distinct flavor and aroma.
- **SALISH SMOKED SALT (PACIFIC NORTHWEST)**: Salish smoked salt is prepared in the traditional methods of the Salish tribe of the Puget Sound region of Washington State. Coarsely ground sea salt is smoked over the fire of red alderwood, indigenous to the Pacific Northwest. Best used in marinades or as a rub as the grains are quite coarse and need a little time to dissolve.

SOUL OF THE SEA (HAWAIIAN)

Soul of the Sea salt is harvested from the pure ocean waters of Molokai, one of the small outer islands of Hawaii, where time stands still. It is solar dried with ancient and modern technology to lock in the naturally occurring trace minerals and elements, electrolytes, and complex flavors.

- **PAPOHAKU WHITE**: Glittering, snow-white crystals with immaculate taste and silky texture.
- **HALEAKALA RED**: Infused with the legendary, medicinal red alaa clay of Hawaii. Burnt crimson color and a slightly nutty flavor.
- **KILAUEA BLACK**: Glistening crystals like black pearls. Complex, clean flavor.

FLAKE SALTS AND FINISHING SALTS

Fine salts with exquisite texture and unique character are well worth considering as finishing salt. They are premium quality and best used in the last stages of seasoning, to finish a dish.

FLEUR DE SEL (FRENCH)

Fleur de Sel, or flower of salt, is an artisan sea salt of delicate crystals, which naturally form just on the surface of ponds where sea salt evaporates. Its name comes from the distinct smell of violets that develops as the salt dries. True *Fleur de Sel* is from the Guérande region in France. Like fine wine regions, different areas within Guérande produce salts with their own characteristics. Naturally moist, *Fleur de Sel* has a fine, clean flavor that is exceptional as a finishing salt.

HIMALAYAN CRYSTAL SALT (HIMALAYAS)

Himalayan Crystal Salt is hand-harvested from veins of salt high in the Himalayas. This salt is 250 million years old (yes, really) with a pink glow like rose quartz. Given its age, it is absolutely pristine, with a strong flavor as pure and clean as salt comes. One of the many intriguing things about this salt is how heavy in weight it is. Because it has been under such intense pressure for such a long time, it is extraordinarily dense and therefore powerfully salty. It is believed that the lengthy duress over a quarter billion years has compressed the structure of Himalayan salt into a perfect crystal. A little goes a long way.

- FINE GRIND: Finely ground close to a powder with a pale pink hue, a very potent flavor, and clean finish.
- COARSE GRIND: Rough pieces, similarly with a strong, clean salty flavor and pink hue. Best used in a ceramic mill designed for salt to manage the potency and distribution of salty flavor in a dish (i.e., to avoid small, crunchy rocks in a dish).
- CRYSTAL STONES: Exquisite, dense chunks of salt that look like rough chunks of rose quartz, measuring about an inch or so. To use, they must be dissolved in water to make a brine (salty water), which is great as a liquid salt to season dressings, marinades, sauces, and soups.

Crystal Sole: A Balanced Ocean of Energy

Sole is a tonic made with stones of Himalayan Crystal Salt and pure water, and it may be beneficial for healthfully balancing the body. Drinking sole may help harmonize and balance the acid-alkaline pH of the body and cleanse the intestines. It is also said to normalize blood pressure. Everyone is different, though, so check in with yourself and your physician before deciding what will work for you.

To make sole: Place a number of Himalayan Crystal Salt stones in a jar of pure water overnight (I recommend Fiji water). The amount of stones and water will vary according to the size of the jar. If all of the salt stones dissolve, add more until the water is totally saturated and cannot dissolve any more salt. The water will naturally become completely saturated at 26 percent (26 parts of salt to 100 parts of water), no more no less. This ratio has a magical spell around it, relating to both the saline waters of the ocean and the percentage of salt in our bodily fluids.

The recommended dose of sole is 1 teaspoon daily. It can be taken by mixing it in a glass of water (spring water is recommended) and drinking it on an empty stomach, mixing it into a quart of water to drink throughout the day, or including it with food as a liquid salt for seasoning, marinades, dressing, and soup.

The regularity of taking sole is said to be the key to unlocking its healing benefits.

For more information, check out the book *Water and Salt: The Essence of Life*, by Dr. Barbara Hendel and Peter Ferreira.

MALDON SEA SALT (UK)

Maldon sea salt is a fragile, crumbly, pyramid-shaped crystal of salt. Harvested from the "spring tides" of North Sea waters off the east coast of England, this flake salt contains all of the valuable trace elements of seawater and the complex flavors of delicate sea spray.

MURRAY RIVER SALT (AUSTRALIAN)

Some of the finest salt is ecologically harvested from a salt deposit beneath the Murray River in Australia. These delicate flakes are an unusual burnt-peach color. They melt quickly and evenly into food, with a clean, mild flavor. Perfect for finishing or to serve in a small bowl to show off its pretty color.

Oils: The Courier of Balanced Flavor

Oil is both a courier of fantastic flavor and a staple nutrient we cannot live without. Choosing high-quality oil and treating it with care bring delicious, nutritious returns that every cell in our bodies will celebrate.

- Go organic!
- Use unrefined oil to benefit from its amazing, healthy properties. Refined oils are often treated with chemical solvents to eliminate flavor and color.
- If heating or cooking with oil, use a variety that can tolerate the temperatures.
- Light damages oil. Store oil in green or brown glass, or in metal containers in a cool, dark place to keep it fresh.

COCONUT OIL/COCONUT BUTTER

Coconut butter and coconut oil are interchangeable terms for the oil extracted from coconuts. Misunderstood as an unhealthy oil, cold-pressed, unrefined coconut butter is an excellent oil. Its natural saturation makes coconut butter very heat stable, meaning it can tolerate high temperatures without being destroyed. Though coconut butter has far more saturated fat than unsaturated fat, it is important to understand that not all saturated fat is created equal: The fat in coconut is a medium-chain fatty acid that is directly converted into energy in our bodies and not stored as fat. It is a great source of energy and fuel.

In the kitchen, coconut butter is a great stand-in for butter. It acts just like butter—semisolid at room temperature, solid in the fridge, with an incredibly buttery texture, which works well in both savory and sweet foods. I find it very agreeable, digestible, and absolutely delicious. I choose Omega Nutrition coconut butter most often as it is naturally defragranced and has a clean, clear taste and almost no aroma. I use aromatic coconut oil in suitable dishes, such as Thai recipes or in Coconut Macaroons (page 371), but I find it interferes and overpowers other flavors if the dish is not intended to taste like coconut.

Coconut oil embodies several incredible properties. It is one of the few fats that does not require the liver to emulsify it for digestion and provides clean-burning energy. Coconut oil also contains *lauric acid,* a precious compound also found in mother's milk with incredible antibacterial and antiviral properties.

Coconut Butter Hair Treatment

This easy at-home treatment conditions dry locks and soothes dry scalps beautifully.

Apply up to ¼ cup of coconut oil to the scalp and hair, working it in thoroughly and lovingly. It is wonderful to do this with a friend or lover and massage each other's scalp.

After applying the oil, cover hair with a shower cap or towel, if desired (not your best towel as the oil will stain). Leave on for 20 minutes and up to 2 hours for a deep conditioning treatment. Wash out with a mild shampoo. More than one wash may be required for hair to come completely clean.

Topically, coconut oil is a beautifying emollient. Because of the small molecular structure of coconut oil, it is absorbed easily by the skin. Coconut oil not only softens dry, rough, and wrinkled skin, it protects against damage and aids in skin healing and repair. Its antibacterial properties may be helpful for certain skin conditions, including psoriasis, eczema, and inflammation. I use the fragrant varieties to rub on my body to keep my skin soft and supple. Yum.

COLOR: Very pale yellow to clear, opaque at cool room temperature or in the fridge.

AROMA: Mild to strong floral coconut.

FLAVOR: Buttery, mild to strong quintessential coconut flavor, slightly sweet.

QUALITIES: Warming, moist and lubricating, excellent source of energy.

NOTES:

- Aroma and flavor vary with product.
- I love Omega Nutrition coconut butter, which has little to no aroma and a clean taste that does not compete with other flavors.
- Maximum suitable heat: medium-high heat ≈ up to 425°F (218°C).
- Good for: baking, sautéing (though it may foam a bit).

MAKEUP OF COCONUT OIL

SUPER-UNSATURATED (OMEGA-6): 2 PERCENT
MONOUNSATURATED (OMEGA-9): 5 PERCENT
SATURATED: 93 PERCENT

Flax oil is one of the most nutritious oils. It is rich in omega-3 for beautiful skin and hair, a healthy brain, and happy cells. Flax oil is very delicate and must be refrigerated, with a shelf life of just a few months. It is best for dressings and cold preparation as the precious essential fatty acids cannot survive heat.

COLOR: Pale to deep golden

AROMA: Nutty

FLAVOR: Mildly nutty, earthy

QUALITIES: Fortifying, lubricating, nourishing

NOTES:

- Should be purchased refrigerated and stored in the fridge. Look for bottles with an expiration date.
- Maximum suitable heat: no heat or low heat ≈ up to 120°F (49°C).
- Good for: dressings and sauces.

MAKEUP OF FLAX OIL

SUPER-UNSATURATED (OMEGA-3): 57 PERCENT
POLYUNSATURATED (OMEGA-6): 16 PERCENT
MONOUNSATURATED (OMEGA-9): 18 PERCENT
SATURATED: 9 PERCENT

Beautifying Omega-3

Fatty acids are the main components of all fats. Omega-3 is one of the precious essential fatty acids (EFAs), meaning we must have it to live and can only obtain it from food. Omega-3 is so important because our body uses it to build other fatty acids such as omega-6 and omega-9.

Every cell in our bodies needs EFAs. They make up the membrane of every cell and work to hold oxygen in the membrane, which enables electricity and information to pass in and out of the cell. Thank you, EFAs! Along with making up our protective brain sheaths, EFAs are essential for producing and reproducing healthy cells, and repairing damaged cells. The most obvious and favorable benefit of EFAs is beautiful, supple skin and shiny hair—a great reason to include them every day.

The best sources of omega-3 are flaxseed and its oil, borage seed and its oil, hemp seed and its oil, and cold-water fish and fish oil, but how much is enough? Recommendations for EFA intake vary, but 2 to 3 teaspoons of flax oil or 2 tablespoons of ground flaxseed daily is a good start.

Grapeseed oil is a by-product of winemaking and has been used in Europe for hundreds of years. In the kitchen, it is a neutral diplomat with a mild taste that does not interfere with other flavors, which is especially helpful in baking. Its high smoke point makes it safer to use at high temperatures. On the scales of nutrition, it is rich in vitamins E, C, and beta-carotene and shares many of the healthful properties of other grape products, including red wine. It contains *phytochemicals* that have strong antioxidant properties and *flavonoids,* which act as an internal antiseptic, improve circulation, and strengthen blood vessels.

COLOR: Pale yellow

AROMA: Mild, neutral aroma.

FLAVOR: Mild, neutral taste.

QUALITIES: Warming, clean-burning.

NOTES:

- Good for recipes where oil should not take a flavorful note, especially baking.
- Maximum suitable heat: medium-high heat ≈ up to 425°F (218°C).
- Good for: baking, roasting vegetables.

MAKEUP OF GRAPESEED OIL

SUPER-UNSATURATED (OMEGA-3): 1 PERCENT
POLYUNSATURATED (OMEGA-6): 69–78 PERCENT
MONOUNSATURATED (OMEGA-9): 15–20 PERCENT
SATURATED: 1–6 PERCENT

OLIVE OIL

Olive oil is one of the oldest and most prized oils. There are many varieties of olive oil from different countries with a range of aroma, flavor, and color. Olive oil is graded by degree of acidity. Labels can be misleading. Beware of labels such as "pure olive oil," which are generally low-quality blends. "Extra-virgin" is the best, period, and the only one I use.

COLOR: Good olive oil should range from golden-green to deep-green.

AROMA: Distinct, but varies from mild and fruity to slightly spicy.

FLAVOR: Mild, fruity, buttery, slightly spicy, full-bodied.

QUALITIES: Warm, moist, supple.

NOTES:

- Flavor and aroma vary with different olive oils. Milder olive oils take a backseat, allowing other flavors to bloom, whereas stronger varieties are best to boast their distinctive flavor.
- Maximum suitable heat: medium heat ≈ up to 350°F (177°C).
- Good for: dressings, sauces, sautéing, soups.

- *Extra-Virgin:* Oil from the first pressing of olives with less than 1 percent acidity. Superior flavor. Beautiful clear to cloudy green.
- *Virgin:* Also from the first pressing with more acidity (1 to 3 percent).
- *Olive Oil or Pure Olive Oil:* Blend of refined and virgin oil. Usually 1 percent acidity, but lacks flavor and character.
- *Refined Olive Oil:* Olive oil that has been chemically treated to neutralize flavor.

- *Light Olive Oil:* An American labeling term for olive oil that has been finely filtered, resulting in a very light color, fragrance, and taste.

MAKEUP OF OLIVE OIL

POLYUNSATURATED (OMEGA-6): 8 PERCENT
MONOUNSATURATED (OMEGA-9): 82 PERCENT
SATURATED: 10 PERCENT

SESAME OIL

Sesame oil has a clean, light taste. As prized in the East as olive oil is prized in the West, sesame oil is a delicious, healthful choice to marry with many foods, especially Asian flavors. Unrefined sesame oil is high in antioxidants, including sesamol, which protects the oil from turning rancid easily. Nutritional medicine in ancient and modern India concur that sesame oil is one of the most stable of all oils to store and cook with.

The Damaging Effects of Light on Oil

Light damages oil, even in a sealed container. Prolonged exposure will turn oil rancid. Oil will become rancid far before it can be detected by sight or smell. If it looks or smells rancid, you can bet it has been rancid for too long a time to consider. Keep it in dark glass or completely covered to keep it fresh!

- Without any protection, oil absorbs 82 percent of the light spectrum.
- Clear glass offers less than 10 percent protection.
- Green glass offers 32 percent protection.
- Brown glass offers 48 percent protection.
- Darkness offers 100 percent protection.

Unrefined sesame oil is a versatile oil, favored in the Orient and India for its healthful, balancing, and beautifying properties. It lubricates dryness of the body, inside and out. It has moist, warm qualities, which can relieve constipation and over-dryness. Traditionally, sesame oil is taken to detoxify the body and keep internal and external tissue supple. Topically, sesame oil can be used to soften dry and cracked skin and is traditionally used to treat skin problems, especially fungal diseases.

COLOR: Pale to deep amber.

AROMA: Mild, slightly nutty, touch of sweet.

FLAVOR: Clean, light, very mild nuttiness, like faint sesame seeds.

QUALITIES: Warm, moist, lubricating, detoxifying.

NOTES:

- Toasted sesame oil has a deep amber color and the strong aroma and flavor of sesame. Because it is refined, processed, and cooked, toasted sesame oil can become rancid more quickly than other oils.
- Maximum suitable heat: medium heat (light sautéing) ≈ up to 350°F (177°C).
- Good for: dressings and sauces, light sautéing.

MAKEUP OF SESAME OIL

POLYUNSATURATED (OMEGA-6): 41 PERCENT
MONOUNSATURATED (OMEGA-9): 46 PERCENT
SATURATED: 13 PERCENT

Vinegar: Complementary Balance

As long as there have been undistilled alcoholic beverages, there has been vinegar. Doubtless, the discovery of vinegar was an accidental occurrence, as vinegar is a natural by-product of making alcoholic beverages. Suffice it to say, this alchemical "discovery" was independently made all over the world, using different ingredients with analogous techniques. Findings of ancient Sumerian civilizations reveal the practice of producing vinegar and its use as a condiment and preservative for food, as an antibiotic, and as a detergent for cleaning, just as it is used today.

Any liquid containing less than 18 percent alcohol can be fermented into vinegar. The process that turns alcohol into vinegar comes by way of natural, airborne bacteria, called *Acetobacter aceti,* which convert the sugars in alcohol into *acetic acid,* the constituent that lends vinegar its sour, pungent flavor.

The old-school technique to make vinegar is simply to leave alcohol (wine or beer) open to the air until it turns sour. The

French developed a more sophisticated way to produce vinegar with regular, quality results, called the Orleans Method. The word *vinegar* is derived from the French *vin aigre,* meaning "sour wine." The basic procedure involves putting wine in wooden casks (barrels) to slowly ferment for 2 to 6 months. The vinegar is then filtered into other casks of various woods and sizes to mature for a period of months or years. Red wine is left to mature longer than white wine, and of course, the finer the wine, the more flavorful, complex, and fine the vinegar.

Most commercially produced vinegar follows the research developed by Louis Pasteur in the mid-19th century. This technique involves pouring wine slowly over wood chips, where it trickles through and takes on some of the flavor of the wood. Airborne bacteria (*Acetobacter aceti*), naturally present around the loose wood chips, oxidize the sugars of the alcohol into vinegar. While this is an effective process for en masse production, the subtleties and character of the wine are mostly lost, yielding a flat vinegar, which cannot compete with the complex nuances of vinegar made with traditional techniques and time. The factors that determine the different varieties of vinegar are:

- Type and quality of the ingredients
- How the liquid is fermented
- The vessel used to ferment
- The time allowed for aging and maturation

Please note: I have included notes only on those varieties of vinegar that are found in the recipes in this book. May your sense of adventure only begin here and carry you to palatal pleasure.

APPLE CIDER VINEGAR

MADE FROM: Fermented apple cider.

COLOR: Amber-honey.

AROMA: Delicate apple.

FLAVOR AND ACIDITY: Poignant, fairly pungent and sour, touch of sweet; mild 5 percent acidity.

CHOICE PICK: The best is unpasteurized and unfiltered. Some sold "with the mother," which includes some of the "mother" starter used to catalyze fermentation.

NOTES:

- Apple cider vinegar is a natural tonic to promote healthy digestion and balance the acid-alkaline environment of the stomach and digestive tract.
- Good for pickling and in marinades for substantial salads like potato salad and beet salad.

MADE FROM: Wine of Trebbiano grapes, good wood (used in barrels for storage), and time.

COLOR: Dark, deep chocolate.

AROMA: Smooth, complex, pungent, sweet (the older it is, the more complex the bouquet).

FLAVOR AND ACIDITY: Complex, pungent-sweet acidity varies from stronger, mid-range acidity to low acidity; the older it is, the smoother, sweeter, and more complex.

CHOICE PICK: The best balsamic is aged for months to years, whence the bouquet of mature flavor blossoms. There is some very good balsamic vinegar that is a mere 10 years old. The price goes up with age, and as with many prized wines, the older the better. I have a penchant for old balsamic vinegar, and a treasure trove that ranges from 12-year-old, through 50-, 75-, 100-, and 150-year-old, to (ready?) 350-year-old balsamic vinegar. The flavor is so complex it transcends description. I think I could live on the fumes alone, and use it just a dribble at a time (especially considering the price tag attached to that 2-ounce bottle).

> Vinegar is an economical and naturally chemical-free cleaning agent (I use distilled or apple cider vinegar). It works well on glass and can be mixed with salt and/or baking soda to scrub tiles, toilets, and sinks.

I recommend a good organic balsamic (that will cost $4 to $8 for a nice bottle) and a good mid-grade aged balsamic, 10 to 25 years old (that will run $20 to $40).

NOTES:

- In many recipes that call for aged balsamic, I offer an approximation of regular balsamic vinegar and a touch of maple syrup. Works wonders and seduces the senses with that certain *je ne sais quoi*.

- Balsamic and maple syrup may be simmered and cooked down to reduce to a thicker viscosity for more authentic substitution.

- I got turned on to old balsamic vinegar in a little restaurant on the Italian Riviera where they served it with sweet, fresh, wild strawberries. I almost blew a gasket in surprise of how dynamically complementary the flavors were. It was a taste that fueled my lifelong search for unexpectedly complementary flavors. Flip to page 354 and try the recipe for Chocolate of the Gods Mousse with Raspberries and Mint for your own eye-opening, gustatory adventure. *Infatti squisito!*

RICE VINEGAR AND BROWN RICE VINEGAR

Made from fermented rice or rice wine (sake, which is technically a flat beer, not a wine, as it is made from grain, not grapes), with a mellow, mildly sweet flavor. The color of rice vinegar ranges from almost clear to warm brown depending on the rice and technique. I prefer brown rice vinegar as it is the least refined and has the most subtly complex character.

UMEBOSHI PLUM VINEGAR

Technically not a vinegar because it contains salt, umeboshi plum vinegar is actually the brine from pickling umeboshi plums and prized for its balancing nature. It is one of my most favored condiments, as its dynamic flavor is both salty and sour, with sweet, citrus and cherry tones. The beautiful magenta-pink color comes from the red shiso leaf (or perilla) that the small Japanese plums are pickled with.

WINE VINEGAR (RED AND WHITE)

Red and white wine vinegars are made from wine from red and white grapes, respectively. The quality and flavor of wine vinegar is clearly dependent on the type and quality of wine. The finest are made slowly, in small batches in oak barrels, and aged for several weeks to years. I prefer red wine vinegar over white as it is much more complex, though use it sparingly, since it has quite a sour fortitude.

If more of us valued food and cheer
and song above hoarded gold,
it would be a merrier world.

—J.R.R. TOLKIEN

Macrobiotic and Asian Fusion Ingredients

Traditional Asian condiments are both flavorful and nourishing. Artisanal, organic products are worth seeking out for their deep, well-rounded features with quality that cannot be surpassed.

TAMARI (WHEAT-FREE SOY SAUCE)

INGREDIENTS AND PROCESS: Soybeans, sea salt, water, and koji culture (*Koji mycelium* or *Aspergillus hacho*)

Tamari literally means "liquid pressed from soybeans." It is very similar to shoyu (soy sauce), but made only from soybeans, where shoyu is made with soybeans and wheat. For that reason, it is popular with anyone who is wheat sensitive.

Originally, tamari was a by-product of soybean miso. It was collected as the thick, dark brown liquid that gathered in casks of fermenting miso and, as such, was prized as a rare delicacy because only so much would pool from each batch of miso.

Today, tamari is brewed and fermented much like shoyu, maintaining similar characteristics to the original.

COLOR: Deep brown.

AROMA: Deep, complex.

FLAVOR: Salty, deep, rich.

VARIETIES: One common variety.

NOTES:

- Tamari has a slightly stronger flavor than shoyu. It is good for longer-cooked dishes, like soups and stews.
- Tamari may be used in the same ways as shoyu and is excellent for those who are allergic to wheat.

NUTRITION PORTFOLIO OF TAMARI (FOR 1 TABLESPOON)*

WATER: 66 PERCENT	IRON (FE): 0.43 MG	B_1 (THIAMIN): 0.01 MG
ENERGY: 45 KCAL	MAGNESIUM (MG): 7 MG	B_2 (RIBOFLAVIN): 0.03 MG
PROTEIN: 10.51 PERCENT	MANGANESE (MN): 0.09 MG	B_3 (NIACIN): 0.07 MG
FAT: 0.10 PERCENT	PHOSPHORUS (P): 23 MG	B_5 (PANTOTHENIC ACID): 0.07 MG
CARBOHYDRATE: 5.57 PERCENT	POTASSIUM (K): 38 MG	B_6 (PYRIDOXINE): 0.04 MG
CALCIUM (CA): 4 MG	SODIUM (NA): 1,005 MG	FOLATES (INCLUDING FOLIC ACID): 3 MG
COPPER (CU): 0.024 MG	ZINC (ZN): 0.08 MG	

(* from USDA Nutrient Database for Standard Reference)

INGREDIENTS AND PROCESS: Soybeans, roasted wheat, sea salt, and koji culture (*Aspergillus oryzae*).

Shoyu (traditional soy sauce) is made from a centuries-old method of fermenting soybeans and wheat. The process involves a special "koji" culture (*Koji mycelium* or *Aspergillus oryzae*), which converts the hard-to-digest soy proteins to amino acids, starches to simple sugars, and fats to fatty acids. It matures in wooden casks for several months to several years for the flavor to develop (like good vinegar and wine). The fermentation of shoyu makes these macro-nutrients easy for the body to absorb, and tasty at that.

COLOR: Deep brown.

AROMA: Deep, complex.

FLAVOR: Salty, deep, rich.

VARIETIES:

- Nama shoyu: a live, unpasteurized shoyu; rich, complex aroma; strong, salty flavor. Abundant in healthy microorganisms, such as *Lactobacillus* (because it is unpasteurized), which is helpful for digestion, assimilation, and intestinal balance.

- White shoyu (blond shoyu): White shoyu is a pale yellow soy sauce, available in Japanese markets, with a lovely taste and simple bloom. A bit milder and good for seasoning recipes that are designed to be pale in color. Excellent with a bit of brown rice vinegar on peeled and sliced cucumbers with chives.

NOTES: Look for "shoyu" rather than soy sauce, as shoyu is brewed and cultured with traditional techniques. Look for "organic" or "GMO-free" shoyu, because, sadly, anything containing soy that is not labeled as such is sure to contain ingredients contaminated with genetically modified organisms. Commercial soy sauce is generally produced with chemical extraction and solvents, and often contains preservatives, all of which are best avoided.

NUTRITION PORTFOLIO OF SHOYU (FOR 1 TABLESPOON)*

WATER: 71 PERCENT

ENERGY: 53 KCAL

PROTEIN: 5.2 PERCENT

FAT: 0.08 PERCENT

CARBOHYDRATE: 8.5 PERCENT

CALCIUM (CA): 3 MG

COPPER (CU): 0.02 MG

IRON (FE): 0.31 MG

MAGNESIUM (MG): 7 MG

MANGANESE (MN): 0.07 MG

PHOSPHORUS (P): 20 MG

POTASSIUM (K): 35 MG

SODIUM (NA): 902 MG

ZINC (ZN): 0.08 MG

B_1 (THIAMIN): 0.01 MG

B_2 (RIBOFLAVIN): 0.02 MG

B_3 (NIACIN): 3.35 MG

B_5 (PANTOTHENIC ACID): 0.05 MG

B_6 (PYRIDOXINE): 0.02 MG

FOLATES: 2 MG

(* from USDA Nutrient Database for Standard Reference)

MISO

INGREDIENTS AND PROCESS: Miso is made from beans or grains (most commonly soy, rice, and barley) that are mixed with sea salt and inoculated with koji culture (*Koji mycelium* or *Aspergillus oryzae*). It is aged for several months to several years, during which time the aspergillus oryzae produces abundant amounts of enzymes, which break down the nutrients into simple, absorbable form.

COLOR: Varies with type of miso; creamy white, pale yellow, smooth red, cocoa brown; may be smooth or chunky.

AROMA: Varies with type of miso; rich, complex, sweet, nutty.

FLAVOR: Salty, savory; varies with type of miso; some sweeter, some stronger.

VARIETIES: The ingredients and variations in length of aging produce many varieties of miso. They vary greatly in flavor, texture, color, and aroma. Generally, light-colored sweeter miso is milder and aged for only several months. Darker miso is stronger and aged for 2 or more years.

NOTES: A truly health-giving condiment that embodies the quintessence of Japanese cooking, miso has a full-bodied, complex flavor that complements dishes with a salty flavor. Good for thick sauces and marinades.

NUTRITION PORTFOLIO OF MISO (FOR 1 TABLESPOON)*

WATER: 66 PERCENT	IRON (FE): 0.43 MG	B_1 (THIAMIN): 0.01 MG
ENERGY: 45 KCAL	MAGNESIUM (MG): 7 MG	B_2 (RIBOFLAVIN): 0.03 MG
PROTEIN: 10.51 PERCENT	MANGANESE (MN): 0.09 MG	B_3 (NIACIN): 0.07 MG
FAT: 1 PERCENT	PHOSPHORUS (P): 23 MG	B_5 (PANTOTHENIC ACID): 0.07 MG
CARBOHYDRATE: 5.57 PERCENT	POTASSIUM (K): 38 MG	B_6 (PYRIDOXINE): 0.04 MG
CALCIUM (CA): 4 MG	SODIUM (NA): 1,005 MG	FOLATES (INCLUDING FOLIC ACID): 3 MG
COPPER (CU): 0.024 MG	ZINC (ZN): 0.08 MG	

(* from USDA Nutrient Database for Standard Reference)
*Average mean, as ingredients of different miso vary

Umeboshi plums and plum products are prized for their balancing properties. With a dynamic sour-salty-sweet flavor, umeboshi is a versatile seasoning and helpful digestive aid. I cannot remember life before my discovery of umeboshi, as it is one of my favorite food elements of all time.

INGREDIENTS AND PROCESS: Umeboshi plums are actually apricots grown only in Japan, which are harvested immature and pickled with pure water, sea salt, and red shiso leaf (or perilla), which lends the plums a beautiful deep pink color. Umeboshi plum paste is simply mashed umeboshi plums. Often not as high in quality, plum paste is less expensive but arguably more convenient than whole plums. Also see "Umeboshi Plum Vinegar" on page 104.

COLOR: Soft, deep pink.

AROMA: Tangy, mild.

FLAVOR: Dynamic, sour, salty, sweet.

VARIETIES: There are many varieties of whole umeboshi plums grown and prepared by different families, some larger and more juicy, others smaller and more tart, but there are just a few types of whole plums widely available in the market. See the Natural Import Company in the Resource Guide (page 378) for the best varieties available.

NOTES: An excellent digestive aid, umeboshi stimulates gastric juices and eases the burden of overeating.

Packed with iron, calcium, and phosphorus, umeboshi plums and plum products stimulate gastric juices and ease the burden of overeating. These alkaline minerals also make umeboshi an excellent digestive aid. At the time of publication, the USDA Nutrient Database for Standard Reference did not include a detailed nutrition portfolio of umeboshi.

Chocolate: Food of the Gods

Sensuous and emotive, chocolate has long been considered a food of the gods, with a scandalous history to boot. Few people will disagree that chocolate induces euphoria. Some say chocolate is one of the true aphrodisiacs and a natural antidepressant. Undoubtedly, chocolate has an assortment of sought-after nutrients, minerals, and feel-good compounds.

The History and Botany of Desire

Chocolate comes from the tropical cacao tree called *Theobroma cacao,* which literally translates as "food of the gods." Cacao beans are found nestled in the tender pith of cocoa pods (fruits) that grow directly from the trunk of the tree like exotic, elongated melons. Each fruit contains 20 to 50 purple-brown cacao seeds, which take about 6 months to ripen and must be carefully harvested by hand. Native to Central and South America, cacao is grown everywhere around the equator of the globe, including the Caribbean, Africa, Southeast Asia, the South Pacific, and even Hawaii.

Ancient Mayan and Aztec civilizations were the original stewards of chocolate. Traditionally, chocolate was prepared as a bitter drink, called *xocoatl,* meaning "bitter water," and was believed to bring universal wisdom and knowledge.

Cacao beans and chocolate spread with colonialism. Chocolate was long revered as a sacred treasure in the ancient Americas. Reigning emperor Montezuma was a most famous, passionate devotee, reputed to drink 50 goblets of chocolate elixir every day. When Cortez brought chocolate back to Spain in 1528 from his expeditions in the New World, it was hidden in monasteries for nearly a century and enjoyed only by nobility. Even then, it was slow to catch on until the hot chili pepper of traditionally prepared chocolate was replaced by sugar. This was major. Newly sweetened chocolate percolated in popularity, though it remained a luxurious indulgence for the upper snuff of Europe. It was not until 1657 when the more egalitarian nature of the English made chocolate a rarefied craze for a mass audience in the first chocolate houses in London. Come one, come all!

Divine Process

Like wine grapes and coffee, cacao beans are blended and fermented. The beans are then dried and roasted to specific temperatures to elicit their euphoric aroma and flavor before being cracked open for their nib, or heart. Processing chocolate requires the skillful craft of an artisan. Fine chocolate is slowly roasted to perfection with a low, steady heat. Like fine wine and good coffee, there is a significant difference between the really good stuff and the mediocre rabble.

Properly roasted nibs are finely ground into what is called chocolate liquor (nonalcoholic), a viscous liquid of cocoa butter and cocoa solids. Chocolate in its most familiar form is made by first separating the cocoa butter (oil) from the cocoa solids and then reintroducing them in a process called conching, which makes or breaks the sensuous texture and complex flavor of fine chocolate. Higher-quality chocolate is conched for longer periods of time, then *tempered* (carefully cooled) for a lustrous shine, snap, and smooth texture. Oh, tease me!

Raw Chocolate

"Raw" cacao beans and nibs are now available on the market; they have only been fermented and dried, never roasted. Some say raw cacao is superior in nutrition and purity; however, many connoisseurs believe that the complex flavors and aroma can only be drawn out through careful roasting at precise temperatures. In my experience, raw cacao has its benefits, but it's terribly bitter and dull in taste. Raw cacao has a very damp, moist quality, which can be aggravating to many conditions. Properly roasted cacao has been roasted slowly at low temperatures to preserve precious constituents and allow flavor to bloom.

The scientists who have been increasingly studying chocolate for its beneficial properties have indeed been using roasted chocolate. Their results concur: The bevy of feel-good compounds, antioxidants, and flavonoids has strong staying power through the careful roasting process of cacao beans.

Feel-Good Compounds

With more than 300 naturally occurring compounds in pure chocolate, it is easy to explain the pleasurable effects of this indulgence as well as its claims as a healthful decadence.

ANTIOXIDANTS

The antioxidants present in chocolate are regarded with healthy respect for their ability to keep the body youthful and beautiful as well as build a healthy heart. In plants, antioxidants are designed as protective agents to improve reproductive success; we humans just ride on those coattails. The antioxidants in chocolate join the prized family of compounds found in high levels in green and black tea, coffee, wine, and blueberries.

Though cocoa butter does contain naturally saturated fat, pure chocolate is considered heart-healthy, in moderation. This is because chocolate contains antioxidant compounds called *phenolics,* which protect blood vessels and prevent fatty substances in the bloodstream from oxidizing and clogging arteries. The bitter taste of pure chocolate is in part due to the presence of this fantastic family.

THEOBROMINE AND CAFFEINE

Theobromine is a gentle, long-lasting stimulant celebrated for its mood-improving effects. Caffeine is also present in chocolate, though only in small amounts. One ounce of pure chocolate contains about as much caffeine as 3 ounces of black tea. Though caffeine has its downsides, moderate doses improve circulation and make the brain feel fit as a fiddle.

PHENYLETHAMINE (PEA)

Phenylethamine is a potent stimulant with a natural presence in chocolate. This compound is related to amphetamines and increases neurotransmitters (brain chemicals) that control our ability to think clearly, pay attention, and stay alert. I am tickled to think eating chocolate could make me a little smarter.

ANANDAMIDE (BLISS CHEMICAL)

Anandamide, a chemical produced by our brains (as a neurotransmitter), is also found naturally in pure chocolate. This little chemical sparked a flurry of investigation at Harvard, where researchers decisively agreed that this compound is a significant part of the good feeling chocolate munching provides. Interestingly enough, anandamide, which is typically broken down quickly after it is produced in the brain, might have a longer shelf life in chocolate due to other compounds present in the cacao bean that inhibit its breakdown. Hence, we feel good longer after eating good chocolate.

SEROTONIN AND MAO INHIBITORS

Eating chocolate naturally releases serotonin in the brain, a hormone that induces feelings of pleasure similar to sunlight. MAO inhibitors beneficially block certain enzyme activities to allow serotonin and other good brain juice to circulate longer, as well as naturally diminish a ravenous appetite.

Chocolate Tidbits

- The melting point of chocolate is just below our natural body temperature, which is why it literally "melts in your mouth."
- The world consumption of chocolate tops more than 600,000 *tons* a year! That is some serious indulgence.
- Americans consume almost half of the world's production of chocolate: 3.5 billion pounds a year, which equates to 11 pounds of chocolate per person per year. The British outdo Americans, averaging 16.5 pounds per person per year, only to be surpassed by the Swiss, who consume 22 pounds per person per year!

CHOICE CHOCOLATE

I am a chocolate devotee, seeking and tasting from the near and far reaches of the globe. I won't tease you with stories of smuggled chocolate hand pounded and traditionally roasted by tribal women. These are some of the best and most widely available brands.

COCOA POWDER

Pure cocoa powder is made from cocoa solids that have been hydraulically pressed to remove almost all of the cocoa butter from the whole bean. The cocoa solids are dried in cakes and pulverized into powder.

- GREEN & BLACK'S COCOA POWDER: Organic, fair-trade, roasted carefully at low temperatures. Absolutely choice.
- SCHARFFEN BERGER NATURAL COCOA POWDER: Scharffen Berger really knows chocolate, though sadly it is not organic.
- RAPUNZEL KOKOA COCOA POWDER: Beautifully processed, organic, fair-trade cocoa powder produced in the Swiss town of St. Gallen.

DUTCH PROCESS COCOA

Invented by a Dutch chocolatier, Dutch process cocoa is treated with natural alkali (like sodium or potassium carbonate) to neutralize the harsh acidic compounds found in cacao beans. Dutch process cocoa has a very dark color, sometimes with a reddish cast, and a milder taste. It is prized for baking as it will rise more easily, where other cocoa powder used for baking will require more leavening such as baking soda (sodium bicarbonate), which is also an alkali.

CACAO BEANS AND CACAO NIBS

These are the pure, real deal. Unadulterated, unprocessed, 100 percent chocolate. Cacao beans are generally found in their skins, which are laborious to peel off. Cacao nibs are peeled, slightly crushed, and oh-so-convenient. Cacao beans and cacao nibs are available raw, but my humble mouth agrees, the lightly toasted varieties (such as Scharffen Berger's Cacao Nibs) have much more complex, subtle flavors and are the cat's meow!

- SCHARFFEN BERGER'S CACAO NIBS: Be careful, these are addictive. The chocolate-covered Cacao Nibs are beyond the beyond.

- DAGOBA ORGANIC CACAO NIBS: Fine, organic, and divine.

UNSWEETENED CHOCOLATE/BAKING CHOCOLATE

This is pure chocolate that has been processed by conching and tempering (see "Divine Process" on page 109) and is generally sold in bars and squares. On average, it contains 45 percent cocoa solids and 55 percent cocoa butter.

BITTERSWEET CHOCOLATE/SEMISWEET CHOCOLATE

Bittersweet chocolate is also called semisweet chocolate and contains at least 35 percent chocolate liquor and up to 50 percent cocoa butter, sugar, and lecithin. It is typically sold in bars, and the sweetness varies with different makers.

DARK CHOCOLATE

Standards set by European manufacturers state that dark chocolate must contain a minimum of 35 percent chocolate liquor. In the United States, it must contain a minimum of 15 percent. Sugar and lecithin content vary with different brands, as does the complexity of flavor, aroma, and texture.

- DOLFIN: Any of their dark chocolates are about as good as it gets, especially Noir 70% de Cacao à la Nougatine (with little nibs in the bar, yum!); Noir au Gingembre Frais (with ginger); and Noir aux Feuilles de Menthe (with mint leaves).

- GREEN & BLACK'S: Any of their dark chocolate bars.

- VOSGES: These bars feature exotic blends of spices. The Black Pearl is exquisite with wasabi and toasted black sesame.

Storing Chocolate

Chocolate is happiest stored in a cool, dry place between 59° to 63°F (15° to 17°C). Because it absorbs other flavors, chocolate should be wrapped or sealed tightly. Stored properly, most chocolate will last for more than a year. The darker and purer the chocolate, the longer it will keep. Poor storage can result in the surface of the chocolate blooming with a cloudy gray layer. This is actually the result of the crystals of cocoa butter melting and migrating to the surface of the chocolate. Bloom will not affect the taste much, but it can impair the smooth texture of fine chocolate.

Chocolate can be wrapped or sealed tightly and kept in the fridge during hot months or frozen for long-term storage. If you do choose cold storage, allow the chocolate to come to room temperature before eating it to let the flavors and aroma emerge.

Balancing the Earth: Composting Scraps of Gold

Kitchen scraps returned to the earth are like organic gold that enriches the soil, and healthy soil is key to strong plants and spry, blooming flowers. Fortifying the earth with compost inoculates it with organisms that balance the complex living ecosystem of soil, enabling plants to absorb nutrients and minerals and grow with vitality (much the way the beneficial microorganisms in our guts provide nutrient assimilation in our bodies).

Plants feed from more than 20 minerals found in healthy soil. Artificial and chemical fertilizers typically replace only three to six of those minerals. Artificial fertilizers are usually high in nitrogen; although it increases a plant's ability to draw up extra water from soil, nitrogen does not necessarily help uptake extra nutrients. On the other hand, composting returns *all* of the minerals a plant needs to the soil for a well-rounded feast. Returning compost to the earth supports healthy soil ecology not only by feeding itty-bitty soil-borne microorganisms, but also by providing for little critters like earthworms that naturally aerate the soil for proper plant growth.

Composting does not have to be messy or expensive and establishes the responsible and valuable cycle of feeding the earth, which feeds us. In most households, about 30 percent of the garbage is viable to compost into rich, healthy soil. Kitchen scraps, plant trimmings, grass clippings, and yard waste can be recycled into rich fertilizer for the garden, flowers, and houseplants. A 5-gallon bucket with a lid is all you need to start collecting food scraps from the kitchen to grow your own organic gold.

If composting seems like more than you want to get into, a vendor at your local farmer's market will likely be happy to be the recipient of your treasure trove of kitchen scraps. It does require a little effort to get into a cycle of collecting and depositing, but it is a noble endeavor worth pursuing.

Elements of a Healthy Compost Pile

GREEN MATTER: Green matter is nitrogen-rich material like grass clippings, weeds, vegetable and plant trimmings, and manure.

BROWN MATTER: Brown matter is found in carbon-containing material like wood chips, dried leaves, straw, and hay.

FOOD SCRAPS: Almost anything from the kitchen, including vegetable and fruit peels, cores, and tops, coffee grinds, and tea bags. Unbleached paper towels and paper napkins are even okay. Leave out any animal foods like meat, as they will likely attract unwelcome pests and rummaging neighborhood dogs.

Three Stages of Composting

INITIAL PHASE: 1 to 2 days. The temperature of "waste" rises, breaking down and decomposing easily degradable material and compounds.

THERMOPHILIC STAGE: 1 to 3 months. The tougher material, like the fibrous cellulose of organic "waste," is broken down.

CURING AND STABILIZATION PHASE: The temperature reduces and stabilizes. Decomposition slows and stabilizes. Mesophyllic and microorganisms recolonize, thrive, and stabilize.

Easy Composting in Your Yard

An empty corner of the yard is a perfect spot for a compost pile. There are also handy bins for neat and easy composting, available in garden stores and online. Some are cylindrical bins on legs that can be easily turned to churn up scraps of gold in no time.

What you need:

- 3 to 4 square feet of space
- Wire metal fence material or chicken wire to keep domesticated and feral creatures out

Coffee Grounds for Plants and Flowers!

Used coffee grounds are delicious food for certain plants and flowers. Acid-loving flowers such as azaleas, gardenias, orchids, and jasmine and plants such as holly and fern will especially thrive.

- Add 2 tablespoons to orchids and other acid-loving flowers once a month.
- Add ¼ cup around the base of small and medium acid-loving plants once a month.
- Add ½ cup around the base of larger plants once a month.
- Fertilize and watch 'em bloom!

- Green and brown matter; food scraps
- A pitchfork (or other tool for turning compost)

To begin:

- Fence in 3 to 4 square feet of space to contain the compost.
- Make a mixture of equal parts green and brown matter about 6 inches deep in the plot. This can be done in a large tub or directly on the earth. A neighborly piece of advice is to choose an inconspicuous place in the yard away from your house and your neighbor's house, so the wafting aromas will not drift and offend.
- This mixture will breed healthy microbes and generate a toasty 150° to 160°F temperature that will quickly break down all varieties of organic matter.
- Keep tossing food scraps onto the pile until they are about 6 to 9 inches deep.
- Cover the food scraps with another layer of the green and brown mixture. Continue the layering as long as you produce scraps.
- Turn the pile over every few weeks with a pitchfork to keep things going. Turning the pile once a week will speed up the process even more. Water the pile to keep it moist and damp for quicker breakdown.

Depending on conditions and how often you turn and water the compost, it will break down within 1 to 3 months, leaving you with rich, healthy fertilized soil for the garden, flowers, and houseplants.

Composting Indoors

Composting indoors in apartments or during cold months can be clean, simple, and rewarding. Use a 5-gallon bucket with a sealing lid to keep the situation tidy and odor-free.

Pureeing food scraps to a pulp in a food processor, Vita-Mix, or blender will expedite easy breakdown. Mix ground food scraps with some green and brown matter in a 5-gallon bucket. A florist or nursery is a good place to get a bag of plant trimmings to help the compost break down. Be sure to get organic trimmings because some flowers from florists are heavily sprayed with chemicals. Add a scoop of soil to provide healthy microbes and bacteria. Mix in food scraps daily, keeping the compost mixture moist but not soggy. In a matter of weeks, the compost will begin to eat itself and shrink into rich, earthy fertilizer. Your houseplants will thank you.

Fire: Balanced Methods of Cooking

Fire is the most transformative of the elements. It is not surprising, then, that the catalytic properties of heat and fire in cooking dramatically affect food's nutrient content, texture, color, and flavor. Good cooking can tenderize texture, brighten color, and marry flavors, as well as aid digestion, increase absorption, and please the senses. Too much heat, however, can spoil the aesthetics and erode the nutrients in a dish. Moist heat and dry heat have different effects, which can be tailored to suit the food and dish. Bringing out the best attributes of food with the right cooking techniques opens a playground of variables for fantastic creations in the kitchen. As always, bringing balance to the plate is the ideal. Most vegetables are happiest when:

- Cooked for the shortest amount of time
- Cooked in the least amount of liquid
- Served as soon as they are done

Granted, there are always exceptions, so let the food speak for itself.

Nutrient Content

Heat has an irrevocable effect on the valuable nutrients and delicate enzymes in food. While cooking with heat can make certain foods, like beans, easier to digest by softening tough fibers and subsequently making more nutrients available, on average, raw vegetables are the best bet for good health. Neither water-soluble vitamins nor enzymes can stand up to heat. The challenge is to prepare food that is enjoyable to eat and easy to digest without destroying the good stuff in the process. Take a piece of broccoli, for example. Raw broccoli has more nutrients than cooked broccoli. However, the tough fiber in raw broccoli can cause uncomfortable bloating or gas for the unfortunate many. No fun. However, lightly steaming broccoli, just until it turns bright green, softens that rough fiber and makes it easier to digest without destroying its nutrients. Moreover, a double-blind study shows that most people prefer cooked broccoli over raw. Kidding. But it does seem to be the last contender on the crudités plate.

Texture

Cooking can soften tough fibers; however, overcooking can completely destroy the fibers and reduce their appealing bulk. Think of that bright green, perfectly steamed broccoli versus the same broccoli overcooked into a pile of mush. Finding balance of form, function, and fiber is the key.

Steamed and blanched vegetables are at their best when cooked *al dente,* tender but still crisp. Firm vegetables like winter squash, beets, and sweet potatoes, which have a bit more starch and sweetness, usually benefit from texture a few degrees softer than al dente. And without exception, the melting fibers from the slow, low heat used to properly caramelize onions yield a savory tenderness to indulge gastronomical dreams.

Color

Apt cooking enhances the natural color of vegetables. The deep green of leafy vegetables, branched florets of broccoli, elegant spears of asparagus, and tender haricots verts springs to brightness when lightly steamed or blanched. Even the warm orange of carrots comes brightly alive. The trick is not overdoing it. Less is more. To retain the bright color of properly cooked veggies, remove them just before they are ready, as they will continue to cook slightly when they're away from the heat source. Shocking veggies under cold running water or giving them a plunge in ice water is another way to capture the perfect color.

Taste

Cooking alters the taste of food, melding and marrying flavors, drawing forward attributes of some tastes and muting the presumption of others. Part of this is due to the chemical change heat inspires. For instance, using a slow, low heat to roast tomatoes or caramelize onions brings out the natural sugars to blossom on the palate. Dry-roasting cumin

seed to enhance its dynamic flavor or infusing the sweet pungency of bay leaf in soup are delicious examples of the beneficial seduction of fire. Of course, certain foods are at their best without the help of fire, such as tender fresh herbs like basil and cilantro. But, following the theme, balance is the enchanted epitome. Pairing sweet fresh cilantro with lightly dry-roasted coriander, the seeds of the same plant, can bring out the best qualities of both in the right dish. There is alchemical magic in this, with a universe of possibilities.

Moist Heat

Moist heat produces tender, flavorful foods by pampering them with steam or in a bath of hot water. Sounds like a nice kitchen spa treatment for your veggies. Proper cooking with moist heat lends delicacy; overcooking can leech flavor and nutrients into the water. Including the vegetable cooking liquid in a sauce, stock, or soup will allow you to make the most of flavor and recapture some of the nutrients lost in liquid, even for aptly cooked veggies.

Steaming

Steaming brings out a warm, moist quality of vegetables that contributes more warmth to the body than vegetables in their raw state. Steam, circulating around lovely vegetables suspended over boiling water, offers a nice, moist environment that helps foods retain most of their natural flavors and juices. Lightly steaming vegetables preserves the most nutrients of any cooking technique (emphasis on *lightly*). If you want to get fancy about it, adding stock, wine, or herbs to the liquid will infuse a light and lovely flavor. (P.S. Don't use the '61 Rothschild, but you probably knew that.)

There are a few pieces of equipment that can be used for steaming.

- A steaming pot looks like a saucepan with holes in the bottom for steam to rise through. It sits comfortably on top of a saucepan that water is boiled in and is fitted with a lid to trap the steam.
- Metal steaming baskets are my favorite. They fit inside a variety of sizes of saucepans as the edges of the basket fold together or open up to fit the pan. Handy. They can also be easily stored inside a pan in the cabinet to reduce clutter.
- Bamboo steaming baskets are another option. Round and made from bamboo, they have a loose weave like a basket on the bottom to allow steam to pass through and reach the veggies. One or more is stacked over a saucepan of boiling water and covered with a tightly woven lid. Very zen looking. I like the idea of using bamboo, but the fiber seems to absorb some of the moisture and heat, inhibiting the efficacy of the steam, and over time they get a little funky.
- Prepared vegetables can also be steamed

in the oven by placing them in a preheated casserole dish and pouring a small amount of hot water over them. Cover, to hold the steam, and place in the oven on medium heat (350°F). This is a nice method to nourish the body with warmth, especially in the colder seasons—not to mention warm the kitchen! Serve in the casserole dish. No mess, no fuss.

Blanching

Blanching is a very hot, quick bath to tenderize the fiber, bring out the flavor, and brighten the color of vegetables. It brings a warm, moist element to raw vegetables and preserves their natural flavors and crisp texture.

Large leafy greens like collard greens can be blanched and then used to make great wraps and rolls (page 237). Asparagus is another great contender, as steaming long stalks can be awkward without breaking them. Edamame (whole soybeans in their pods) can be blanched to warm and freshen just before serving.

To blanch, fill a pan with enough water to cover the vegetables completely. Once the water boils, gently toss in the veggies and wait 30 seconds to 5 minutes (depending on the veggie and cut). Watch lovingly. Generally, I do not cover the pot so I can see what is going on, but covering will contain the heat and shorten the cooking time.

The trick to blanching is to not overcook. Drain or remove the veggies a split second before they are done, as they will continue to cook a bit from their own heat. Shocking blanched vegetables in cold running water or plunging them in ice water will arrest the cooking and halt the texture at its peak. *Perfetto*.

Water Sautéing or "Pan Steaming"

Vegetables can be sautéed in water instead of oil for lighter results. Water sautéing is a combination of steaming and blanching with fast action. Some call it pan steaming, as the results are just like steaming, but done directly in the pan. It is great for serving *à la minute*, for naturally tender or thin specimens, or for veggies cut into small, uniform pieces. It brings a warm, watery element to vegetables and requires a shorter cooking time than steaming.

To water sauté, place a small amount of water in a skillet over medium-high heat and bring to a scald, just below boiling. Add seasonings like garlic, onion, herbs, or citrus zest if desired to infuse a gentle flavor.

Moist Heat Cooking Tips

- Use filtered water to steam for pure water vapor.
- Make sure the water level is not so high as to touch the veggies while steaming them (the water will thieve the nutrients and flavor). One inch of water is plenty to generate a good steam.
- Bring the water to a rolling boil before adding the veggies to the steaming basket or pan.
- The smaller a vegetable is cut, the more quickly it cooks.
- Different vegetables take different amounts of time to cook. For the best results, steam vegetables individually, rather than mixing them together.
- Small veggies, like baby squashes, baby carrots, and small potatoes can be steamed whole for an attractive whole foods presentation.
- It is better to steam two batches for larger servings, rather than trying to steam a smothered pile of veggies, as they will not steam evenly.
- Don't overdo it! Al dente, crisp veggies are the best. Overcooked veggies lose their flavor, texture, and precious nutrients.
- The cooking water contains valuable vitamins, minerals, and nutrients. Use it for soup, stock, or sauces. Or put it in a watering can to feed the plants.

> The kitchen is the great laboratory of the
> household, and much of the "weal and woe" as far
> as regards bodily health depends on the nature of
> the preparations concocted within its walls.

—ISABELLA BEETON (1836–1865)

Add prepared veggies, reduce the heat, and simmer until bright-colored and just on the verge of tender. Covering the pan will contain the heat and trap the steam for even faster action. A cover prevents a good view of what is going on, though, so be mindful and attentive. Remove the veggies from the heat a split second before they're done, as they will continue to cook a bit from their own heat.

Water-Oil Sautéing

Water-oil sautéing uses a combination of water with a little oil for flavorful results without overheating the oil. It is a hybrid approach bringing moist warmth to the body, especially in cold weather.

To prepare foods in this fashion, cover the bottom of a skillet with water. Heat to a simmer. Add a little oil, then seasonings. Follow with vegetables and sauté as usual, being careful not to overheat the oil.

Simmering and Boiling

Simmering and boiling vegetables is a method I use mostly for soups, when the precious nutrients that leak into the cooking liquid can be preserved. Boiling vegetables sounds criminal to me and reminds me of the overcooked vegetables I dutifully ate as a youth in the middle school cafeteria. But eat them I did, and they hardly required chewing, which was convenient. In fact, I believe that mushy green beans may be just the dish the plastic "spork" was invented for.

Potatoes are about the only vegetable I boil—for mashed potatoes (page 276), which are down-home good in any season.

Nishime: Long Japanese Water-Sauté

Nishime is a Japanese technique of sautéing vegetables in water with seasonings like salt, shoyu (soy sauce), or tamari; it is valued for its ability to fortify and strengthen the body. The difference from a more traditional water-sauté is that the veggies should not be disturbed while they are cooking, giving them a soothing quality, tender texture, and mildly sweet taste. See Nishime Carrot and Lotus Root on page 261 for a lovely expression of this technique.

With nishime, a heavy pot should be used

with a lid that fits nicely. Traditionally, a 6-inch strip of kombu seaweed is used to fortify and gently flavor the veggies. The kombu is cut into 1-inch squares and placed in the bottom of the pot with about a half-inch of water. Vegetables are cut to the desired size and placed on top. A bit of sea salt, shoyu, or tamari is added for seasoning. The pot is covered and put over high heat until steam is generated, then the heat is lowered to simmer for 15 to 20 minutes. After that time, a little more shoyu or tamari is added and a touch more water if all of it has evaporated. The pot is then shaken, covered, and cooked over low heat for another 2 to 5 minutes. Finally, the pot is removed from the heat and uncovered; the veggies are left to stand for a few minutes to evaporate and absorb any remaining water.

Almost any vegetable can be cooked this way, and though this technique is simple and mild, its results are very delicious and fortifying.

Dry Heat

Dry fire methods do not use liquid to cook and thus seal the outside of the food, lock-

Tips for Baking

- Vegetables are best baked whole or cut in large pieces so they do not dry out.
- If you do cut the veggies, do so uniformly so they cook evenly.
- Leave the skins on to prevent them from drying out or getting scorched.
- Thick-skinned vegetables are best suited for baking, like potatoes, winter squashes, and eggplant, because they stay nice and moist inside. Their skins should be pierced a few times with a fork before baking so heat can escape.
- Winter squashes can be cut in half and placed facedown in a casserole dish to bake. Adding a little water to the dish will help keep them moist.
- Try rubbing a little salt and pepper or crushed garlic on the surface of vegetables destined for baking to infuse a gentle flavor.
- Generally, vegetables are done when they are easily pierced with a fork.
- Use glass dishes or stainless steel baking sheets. Avoid aluminum or coated dishes, pans, and sheets.
- Serve baked dishes as soon as possible (within 20 to 30 minutes) to avoid excessive evaporation and dried-out veggies.

Tips for Roasting

- Vegetables may be roasted whole or cut into pieces.
- When cutting vegetables, be sure they are uniform for even cooking.
- Covering the pan for the first half of cooking can speed up the process, though it is not appropriate for all dishes as some vegetables, such as potatoes and onions, will sweat and become soft and unsavory.
- Baste or stir occasionally for even cooking and distribution of flavor.
- Cranking up the heat of the oven for the last 10 minutes can lend a nice, crisp outside, but it is not appropriate for all dishes.
- Allow roasted foods to rest for 15 minutes before serving so that the flavor can settle and the juices can redistribute evenly in the food.
- Deglaze the pan after taking the veggies out by adding a splash of water or stock to the pan and stirring to loosen the flavorful drippings. Use them in a sauce.

ing in moisture and flavor. Oil and seasonings may be used, which is done to impart flavor, not act as a cooking medium. The end result is a highly flavored, sometimes crusty or crispy exterior and a moist, succulent interior.

Baking

Baking brings out the natural sweetness of foods and reduces their moisture. Similar to roasting, baking surrounds the food with hot, dry air, but uses no oil, seasonings, or sauces. In vegetables, the moisture carries the heat from the exterior to the interior. The result is a nice, highly flavored exterior and a tender, moist interior. The absence of water makes baking more warming for the body than cooking methods that include water, which is especially nourishing in cold seasons.

Roasting

Roasting is also done in the oven, uncovered. Roasted veggies are seasoned and usually include a bit of oil, which imparts and carries flavor and seasoning, but does not act as a cooking medium. Roasting cooks food by surrounding it with hot air and, because it includes some oil, yields the most warming nourishment for the body of any cooking method.

Sautéing

Sautéing is accomplished on the stovetop in a skillet. Generally a little oil is used to seal in the natural flavors and juices of food, though water, stock, or wine may also be used. Cooking over heat with a little oil brings drier warmth to the body than "moist" methods. Though oil is technically liquid, it acts differently than liquids like water, stock, or wine. I consider it a "dry" method because it seals the outside of the food to lock in flavor, whereas "moist" methods keep vegetables tender outside.

Sautéing is a treat for me and draws out the flavor of certain foods like onions and mushrooms. Yum! I refrain from cooking with oil too often because oil has a delicate nature and is so much more nutritious fresh, unrefined, and uncooked in its place at the table.

Dry Roasting

Dry roasting is a performance staged on the stovetop over low heat. It is generally reserved for seeds and whole spices. Whole spices (like cumin, caraway, mustard seeds, coriander, and even black pepper) will release their fragrance when lightly roasted in a dry pan over low heat. Seeds like sesame seeds and pumpkin seeds open their delicate flavors and lend drying warmth to the body. Roasted sesame seeds and sea salt are ground in a classic combination for the staple macro-

Tips for Sautéing

- Cut veggies uniformly for even cooking.
- Add different vegetables according to the time they need to cook if using more than one ingredient.
- For best results, let the pan warm up before adding the oil.
- Use high-quality olive oil, unrefined sesame oil, or cold-pressed coconut butter or oil, and never let it get so hot that it smokes.
- Garlic is a delicious, popular seasoning to sauté with, though it tends to burn at too high a heat—adding a little wine or stock will reduce this tendency.
- Stir regularly and don't overcook the goods! Everything tastes better when cooked with care.
- Add salt near the end or after cooking so it does not interfere with the process.

Tips for Dry Roasting

- Use a heavy pan over low heat.
- Stir regularly with a wooden spoon or paddle for even results.
- Seeds should not pop when roasting, or the heat is too high.
- Try adding a little seasoning, like umeboshi plum vinegar or shoyu (soy sauce), to pumpkin seeds at the last minute to infuse them with dynamic flavor. See the Umeboshi Pumpkin Seeds recipe on page 291.

biotic condiment called gomasio (see the recipe on page 280). On the other hand, using the oven to toast nuts is the best kind of heat to bring out their maximum flavor and crunch.

Low-Temperature Heating

Dehydrating and Low-Temperature Baking

Dehydrating and low-temperature baking are done at temperatures below 120°F to preserve valuable heat-sensitive nutrients and minerals as well as delicious flavors. Although these techniques take much longer than traditional baking, the upside is that they do not require constant and immediate attention. The temperature can be set low enough and contained in a unit so that it can be safely left unattended.

I have been using an Excalibur dehydrator for more than a decade, and I highly recommend one (see the Resource Guide on page 378). There are 4-, 5-, and 9-tray models, all of which have a temperature gauge and fan to circulate the air evenly.

Dehydrating and low-temperature baking can be done in an oven set at the lowest temperature, though even the lowest temperature in most ovens is about 200°F, which exceeds the safe zone for sensitive nutrients and enzymes to survive. Some gas ovens have a pilot light, which will keep the oven warm enough to dehydrate without turning the oven on. The best are convection ovens; Jenn-Air and KitchenAid sell models that can be set low enough to dehydrate in. Fancy!

Double Boiling

Traditionally, double boilers are used for their gentle regulation of heat, which is good for delicacies like melted chocolate or to keep sauces and soups warm without applying direct heat and to prevent burning and overcooking. Double boiling is also a great way to preserve heat-sensitive nutrients and enzymes and bring gentle, moist warmth to food and the body. Double boiling warms up raw and living foods, such as a lovely raw soup (see the soup recipes beginning on page 176), without technically cooking them. The temperate heat of double boiling can also help kick-start and speed up dishes that require marinating for a long time.

A double boiler consists of two saucepans, or a pot and a heat-tolerant bowl, that fit together. The bottom pan is filled with water that is heated to a simmer or boil, and the rising steam warms the pan that nests on top. It is likely that you have pots and pans that can be rigged up for this action without going out to purchase anything special. I often use a stainless steel bowl, which will conduct the heat, over a regular old saucepan.

A Note about Heat Sources

The source of heat for cooking is the protagonist in the ongoing culinary saga. Both gas and electric burners and ovens have their advantages and disadvantages. It is just to say that most chefs prefer gas burners by a long shot, as the temperature is easier to control. As for ovens, the jury is out.

Stovetop Heat Sources

Every stove and oven has variations, so it is a good idea to get friendly with your own equipment. The marks for settings like "low" and "medium" are not absolute on stovetops. In the recipes in this book, these marks work as guidelines, but use your own judgment to gauge the process, and remember that the pan used also plays a major role in how well and evenly the heat is conducted and distributed.

Oven Heat Sources

All ovens have some degree of variation. Electric ovens will vary no more than 15°F before the thermostat triggers an automatic correction. Gas ovens vary a bit more, sometimes more than 20°F before correcting themselves. Convection ovens (gas or electric) are the most even of all and are equipped with a fan that continuously circulates hot air. Either way, it is helpful to familiarize yourself with the idiosyncrasies of your own kitchen pals. An oven thermometer, available for purchase at almost any kitchen supply store, can tell you how well the oven is calibrated by showing you the actual temperature inside the oven versus what the setting reads. Studying a sheet of browned cookies or breadcrumbs is also a good way to reveal your oven's individual hot spots.

Air: Wholesome Balance for Health and Happiness

Fresh air is indubitably one of the most essential elements of life, health, and, if you ask me, happiness. There is nothing like a pure deep drink of fresh air to smooth down the feathers and lift up the spirit. As warm-blooded creatures, we can go some time without food and water, but we'll last less than 5 minutes without air. The air we breathe as we live, sleep, and work is subtle, silent nourishment, and full of more than our lungs' desire. Air is an element we cannot live without.

Air pollution is forlorn reality. Smog alerts and car emissions are part of the price paid in the industrialized world. But what about indoor air? The Environmental Protection Agency (EPA) currently ranks indoor air pollution as one of the top five threats to health. There are a few primary sources of poor indoor air quality:

- Hermetically sealed buildings and houses with poor ventilation, often constructed in a sincere effort to maximize energy efficiency following the oil embargo and energy crunch of the 1970s.

Coping with Airplane Air: The Traveler's Companion Face Spray

Airplanes have drier air than the driest desert on earth. A clever ploy to combat these dried-out conditions is carrying a simple face spray to spritz your pretty puss with as often as you remember. There are some great products on the market, but I just make my own by mixing distilled water and a few drops of pure essential oils, like calendula, rose, or chamomile, in a small spray bottle that I can use again and again. Of course, water alone may be used for a simple, fragrance-free misty hydration. Sometimes I add a wee bit of vegetable glycerin, which actually pulls moisture from the air, for your skin. I use only a little drizzle (too much feels sticky), which is excellent for skin that errs on the dry side, though not always great for oilier skin. If you do make your own, be sure to use pure essential oils that agree with your skin type, and use only a few drops, as essential oils are potent and the skin of your face is delicate. If you opt to purchase prefab face spray, be sure it does not have chemicals or preservatives or other sneaky ingredients like perfume. Almost every time, my seatmate will ask what I am up to and want some too.

- Emissions from modern synthetic materials in our homes and offices and the glues and resins that hold them together, including a growing number of electronic devices that comfort, entertain, and make our lives possible.
- Humans are part of the pollution: We emit substances from natural processes, like carbon dioxide from breathing (and another 150 volatile substances, according to Russian and American space scientists).

What We Are Breathing

Ever wonder about that distinctive smell of a new car or a freshly painted room? What about the whiff of a document fresh off the press from the computer printer?

Albeit for different reasons, NASA wondered the same thing, too, and has subsequently conducted the most extensive tests on air quality to date. In the late 1970s, NASA was smitten with the hope of manning space stations. With the primary task of creating a sustainable ecosystem to treat and recycle air and wastewater for long trips away from home in confined spaces, NASA pulled back the invisible curtain to look into something that all humans must have: clean air.

They went about testing closed spaces and sealed rooms, which had all of the things one would need to survive in space. What they found was hundreds of volatile chemicals in everyday indoor air, which compete with oxygen in a fight for space.

The chemicals detected in these trials are the same compounds emitted from the creature comforts and high-tech gadgets of our homes, schools, and offices, such as formaldehyde, benzene, and a bevy of noxious and carcinogenic compounds that no one wants to breathe.

After intense stretches of sophisticated research and untold funding, the ironic conclusion emerged that the technology required to advance futuristic space stations was a simple return to the earth: plants.

Superhero Houseplants

The atmosphere of our homes, offices, and schools is host to a long list of chemical compounds, produced from upholstery, carpet, cleaning products, plastic bags, ceiling tiles, printers, copy machines, and the glue and resins that hold everything together, to name just a few culprits. The results are commonly called indoor air pollution, and we innocently breathe this stuff for hours and hours, day in and out. Indoor air pollution is so often overlooked as a villain of aggravated allergies and chronic health problems. But have no fear, plants are here!

Plants are agreeable companions, softening the geometry of a room and bringing organic life to the dull spaces of our offices, foyers, and corners of our homes. But beyond their aesthetic appeal, they are doing more than they appear. Houseplants are unsung superheroes. Though these docile pretties appear calm, unwitting, and rather helpless save for our occasional watering, fettering, and cooing, they are in constant action as nature's cleaning machines:

- Producing fresh air and oxygen
- Reducing carbon dioxide in air
- Reducing and removing chemical vapors emitted from synthetic materials, like formaldehyde, benzene, and ammonia
- Offering healthy, microbe-free humidity to dry indoor air
- Reducing airborne bacteria, mold spores, and mildew
- Fostering a calm, peaceful environment, with measurable benefits including reduced stress,[66, 67] more productivity in the workplace,[68, 69] and quicker recovery time for hospital patients.[70]

Plants Create Their Own Mini-Ecosystems

From ancient old-growth trees to a simple potted houseplant (most of which originated underneath the canopy of dense forests), all plants create a little ecosystem around them. Coupled with oxygen and water vapor, plants produce a complex cloud of helpful substances around their leaves and roots to provide for their protection and well-being.

To our naked eye, houseplants seem static and unmotivated. (I have heard the occasional insult comparing reduced human intelligence to that of a houseplant, but at times, I think the offense is to the plant.) In reality, plants are brilliant, complex organisms that improve the very essence of our lives and give a gift that keeps giving: fresh air.

Plants Grow Fresh Air

One of the most beneficial natural by-products of a plant's personal ecosystem is oxygen! When humans breathe, we consume precious oxygen and exhale noxious fumes like carbon dioxide. Plants, on the other hand, are very clever. They use our carbon dioxide waste and turn it back into oxygen. Through photosynthesis, plants use sunlight to split water (H_2O) into hydrogen (H) and

Healing Plants for Speedy Recovery

More and more hospitals in Japan are planting "ecology gardens." Recent studies reveal that plants not only clean and improve air quality, but also have beneficial psychological effects on humans, significantly improving a patient's recovery time. Plants are medicine, in more ways than one.

oxygen (O). They use that hydrogen with the carbon dioxide emissions in the air to form sugars (which they eat), and in turn release oxygen. Brilliant.

Nature's Air Purification: Transpiration

Plants clean and humidify the air through *transpiration:* consuming air-polluting substances and moving it to their roots, and moving water up from their roots to their leaves and releasing it in the air. They literally absorb chemical vapors from the synthetic materials found in virtually every home, office, and school. As they skillfully produce fresh air, they simultaneously regulate a lovely balance of ambient humidity. Forty to 60 percent humidity is a healthy ideal. Most indoor air is much drier than that, especially when centrally heated or air-conditioned. Parched air is harsh on vulnerable mucous membranes in the nose and throat and leads to a higher susceptibility to germs, bacteria, and sickness, as well as skin problems and other chronic health conditions.

Plants offer healthy humidity. Critics might say that plants can cause too much humidity (think of a dank, moist greenhouse) and cause mold and mildew, but studies prove the exact opposite is true. Even with elevated levels of humidity, rooms with plants have

Airborne Battle: Formaldehyde and Benzene

Modern living inoculates the air with chemical vapors from the many synthetic materials inhabiting our homes, schools, and offices. Formaldehyde is a toxic chemical that the EPA states has "the greatest human exposure in the United States"; it is the most common toxin in indoor air. Formaldehyde is in everything: insulation, plywood, particleboard, decorative panels, grocery bags, waxed paper, facial tissue, paper towels, cleaning products, floor covering, carpet backing, adhesive binders, glue, and resins.

Benzene, a component of petroleum, is runner-up to formaldehyde as the most toxic air contaminant at home. Benzene is commonly found in gasoline, ink, oil, paint, plastic, rubber, detergents, and dyes.

So what is the best way to remove formaldehyde and benzene from your home and office? Plants. Plants actually remove these harmful chemicals, and many more, while producing oxygen and maintaining a healthy humidity. Studies show that ferns are the most effective for removing formaldehyde and benzene, followed by chrysanthemums, but palms, ivy, lilies, tulips, philodendrons, and spider plants will all do the trick.

Those who contemplate the beauty of the earth find reserves of strength that will endure as long as life lasts. There is something infinitely healing in the repeated refrains of nature—the assurance that dawn comes after the night and spring after winter.

—RACHEL CARSON

much lower levels of mold spores and mildew than rooms without.

Along with water, plants release natural compounds, like *phytochemicals,* which are healthfully effective for controlling airborne microbes and mold spores surrounding them.

Research shows that plant-filled rooms contain 50 to 60 percent fewer airborne mold spores and bacteria than rooms without plants.[71] And they do all of this without a neocortex or thumbs. Wow.

How Many, How Much

How many plants does it take to clean a room? It depends a bit on the conditions, but this is a helpful start.

Per 100 Square Feet:
- 2 or more medium to large plants, or
- 3 or 4 small to medium plants

Rooms with a lot of upholstery or wall-to-wall carpeting, offices with copiers or printers, or any room that is subject to chemical cleaners will benefit from more greenery. Beyond cleaning and humidifying the air, the organic aesthetic of flora offers a placid ease. Every room has a different fit. To a reasonable degree, the more, the merrier. And as long as everybody gets watered, we can all breathe deeply.

The charts on the following pages will help you choose the right houseplants for your home and provide handy guidelines for plant love and care. Each plant characteristic is rated on a scale from 1 to 10, with a higher number equaling a greater performance level.

A g a v e s   *Agavaceae family*

TYPES	CHARACTER
CORN PLANT *Dracaena fragrans* APPEARANCE: Solid woody stem; shiny rosettes, similar to leaves of corn, some with yellow stripe in the center.	Removal of Chemicals: 8 Easy to Grow: 7 Resistance to Insects: 8 Transpiration: 7
DRACAENA *Dracaena deremensis* APPEARANCE: Rosette of dark-green leaves from a thick, segmented stem; Compacta variety 1–3 ft; Janet Craig up to 10 feet.	Removal of Chemicals: 8 Easy to Grow: 9 Resistance to Insects: 8 Transpiration: 7
DRAGON TREE *Dracaena marginata* APPEARANCE: Smooth gray, erect stalk; narrow, glossy, dark-green, 2-foot-long leaves with red edges.	Removal of Chemicals: 6 Easy to Grow: 7 Resistance to Insects: 8 Transpiration: 7
SNAKE PLANT *Sansevieria trifasciata* APPEARANCE: Stiff, spearlike leaves that stand erect and rigid; 2–4 feet high, 2 inches wide; tiger stripes of green, trimmed in yellow.	Removal of Chemicals: 3 Easy to Grow: 10 Resistance to Insects: 10 Transpiration: 2

LOVE AND CARE

LIGHT: Semi-shade (can tolerate bright light or dim light as well).

HAPPY TEMPERATURE: 60°–75°F (16°–24°C); can tolerate as low as 50°F (10°C) for short periods of time.

WATERING: Do not let dry out. Likes to be moist, but not soggy; water less often in winter. Loves to be misted or wiped with a damp cloth.

FEEDING: Liquid fertilizer every few weeks during growth period in spring and summer; do not feed in winter.

PEST PROBLEMS: Few to none; spider mites and aphids in dry, centrally heated air.

Ferns *Polypodiaceae family*

TYPES	CHARACTER
BOSTON FERN *Nephrolepis exaltata* APPEARANCE: Classic fern leaves; stiff fronds that arch out, naturally droop with age; happiest in a basket or on a pedestal.	Removal of Chemicals: 9 Easy to Grow: 5 Resistance to Insects: 9 Transpiration: 9
KIMBERLY QUEEN FERN *Nephrolepis obliterata* APPEARANCE: Classic fern leaf (similar to Boston fern, but less temperamental); graceful, drooping fronds.	Removal of Chemicals: 9 Easy to Grow: 4 Resistance to Insects: 8 Transpiration: 9

LOVE AND CARE

LIGHT: Partial sun/semi-shade.

HAPPY TEMPERATURE: Day: 65°–75°F (18°–24°C); night: 50°–65°F (10°–18°C).

WATERING: Do not let dry out; likes to be moist with frequent watering, but not soggy. Likes room-temperature water (rainwater is its favorite); loves to be misted.

FEEDING: Feed once a month during spring through fall and sparingly in winter.

PEST PROBLEMS: Few to none.

Figs *Moracae family*

TYPES	CHARACTER
RUBBER PLANT *Ficus robusta* APPEARANCE: Large, oval, thick, dark-green, leathery leaves. Can reach up to 8 feet in height.	Removal of Chemicals: 9 (one of the best) Easy to Grow: 9 Resistance to Insects: 8 Transpiration: 7
WEEPING FIG *Ficus benjamina* APPEARANCE: Dark-green leaves, graceful drooping branches. Bush, tree, and braided-trunk varieties are widely available.	Removal of Chemicals: 8 Easy to Grow: 6 Resistance to Insects: 6 Transpiration: 6

Figs—Continued

FICUS ALII *Ficus macleilandii "Alii"* APPEARANCE: Similar to weeping fig (but less finicky and more perky); slender, dark-green leaves; bush, tree, and braided-trunk varieties.	Removal of Chemicals: 7 Easy to Grow: 7 Resistance to Insects: 9 Transpiration: 8

LOVE AND CARE

LIGHT: Full sun/partial sun.

HAPPY TEMPERATURE: Day: 60°–80°F (16°–27°C); night: 55°–68°F (13°–20°F).

WATERING: Allow to dry between watering, then water thoroughly.

FEEDING: Feed every few weeks from midsummer to fall only.

PEST PROBLEMS: Few to none; scale insects and spider mites in too dry an environment, common with centrally heated air; too much water causes root rot.

Flowering Houseplants *Full sun/partial sun*

TYPES	CHARACTER
BEGONIA *Begonia semperflorens* APPEARANCE: Waxy, rounded, dark-green leaves; fleshy, almost succulent stems. Healthy plants bloom all year; flowers like a loose rose with fewer petals; colors range from pink, red, and orange, to yellow, white, and a combination of any of these.	Removal of Chemicals: 4 Easy to Grow: 8 Resistance to Insects: 9 Transpiration: 7
GERBERA DAISY *Gerbera jamesonii* APPEARANCE: Dark-green leathery leaves; blooms in summer; large, handsome red or orange daisy flowers on sturdy stalks.	Removal of Chemicals: 9 Easy to Grow: 4 Resistance to Insects: 8 Transpiration: 8
MUMS *Chrysanthemum moriflorum* APPEARANCE: Dark oak-leaf foliage; colorful flowers, like large daisies, in just about every color of the rainbow. Annual varieties bloom only once for 6 to 8 weeks in autumn; perennial varieties bloom every year for 6 to 8 weeks in autumn.	Removal of Chemicals: 9 Easy to Grow: 4 Resistance to Insects: 8 Transpiration: 8

Flowering Houseplants—Continued

LOVE AND CARE

LIGHT: Full sun/partial sun.

HAPPY TEMPERATURE: Day: 60°–75°F (16°–24°C); Night: 45°–50°F (7°–10°C).

WATERING: Likes to be slightly damp with regular watering.

FEEDING: Feed every few weeks in spring and summer with fertilizer for flowering plants; generally let rest in the fall to bloom again.

PEST PROBLEMS: Few to no insect problems; root rot from overwatering; occasional spider mites and aphids in too dry an environment.

Flowering Houseplants *Partial sun/semi-shade*

TYPES	CHARACTER
PEACE LILY *Spathiphyllum* APPEARANCE: Stiff stalks, dark-green broad foliage; reliably blooms indoors.	Removal of Chemicals: 8 Easy to Grow: 8 Resistance to Insects: 7 Transpiration: 8
ORCHIDS *Dendrobium species* APPEARANCE: Beautiful, zen appearance; broad, waxy, deep green leaves. Flowers vary dramatically.	Removal of Chemicals: 6–7 Easy to Grow: 4 Resistance to Insects: 6–7 Transpiration: 3–5
POINSETTIA *Euphorbia pulcherrima* APPEARANCE: Brilliant red flowers (actually its leaves); think Christmas; green foliage year-round.	Removal of Chemicals: 3 Easy to Grow: 6 Resistance to Insects: 7 Transpiration: 5

LOVE AND CARE

LIGHT: Partial sun/semi-shade.

HAPPY TEMPERATURE: Day: 60°–75°F (16°–24°C); night: 55°–68°F (13°–20°C).

WATERING: Like to be evenly moist; some like a soak and dry cycle; all like mist a lot.

FEEDING: Every few weeks during growth from spring to fall; sparingly or not at all during winter.

PEST PROBLEMS: Few to none; if air is too dry they are vulnerable to scale insects and spider mites.

Tropical Plants *Araceae family*

TYPES	CHARACTER
DUMBCANE *Dieffenbachia maculata, 'Exotica Compacta'* APPEARANCE: Wide, long, lance-shaped leaves, variegated with cream splotches (which will fade without sufficient light). Called dumbcane because chewing any part of the plant will numb the mouth, due to the calcium oxalate in its sap. This sap is also toxic, so keep dumbcane out of the reach of children and pets.	Removal of Chemicals: 2 Easy to Grow: 9 Resistance to Insects: 10 Transpiration: 2
GOLDEN POTHOS *Epipremnum aureum* APPEARANCE: Large, heart-shaped leaves like philodendron; dark green, sometimes with some yellow. Grows like a vine; good in hanging baskets and can be trained to climb or cascade.	Removal of Chemicals: 9 Easy to Grow: 10 Resistance to Insects: 8 Transpiration: 7
PHILODENDRON *Red Emerald (P. erubescens)* *Lacy Tree (P. selloum)* *Heart-Leaf (P. scandens oxycardium)* *Elephant Ear or Spade Leaf (P. domesticum, P. tuxla)* APPEARANCE: Grows like a vine; leaves ample and dark green; narrow, rounded, heart-shaped, or like oak leaves depending on variety; loves water-absorbent poles to climb on (made from wire and sphagnum moss).	Removal of Chemicals: 6 Easy to Grow: 9 Resistance to Insects: 8 Transpiration: 5

LOVE AND CARE

LIGHT: Partial sun/semi-shade; except aloe, which likes full sun/partial sun.

HAPPY TEMPERATURE: 60°–80°F (16°–27°C), not below 50°F (10°C).

WATERING: Likes to be moist but not soggy (except aloe, which likes to be watered only moderately); water less in winter. Likes to be misted often (will reduce likelihood of insects); wipe leaves occasionally with a damp cloth.

FEEDING: Once every month or two in spring and summer; do not feed in fall and winter.

PEST PROBLEMS: Few to none; occasional scale insects, mealybugs, and aphids in too dry an environment. Root rot from cold, wet soil.

Palms *Arecaceae family*

TYPES	CHARACTER
ARECA PALM *Chrysalidocarpus lutescens* APPEARANCE: Also called yellow butterfly palm; stalky, canelike clusters of feathery green fronds. Up to 6 feet tall.	Removal of Chemicals: 8 Easy to Grow: 8 Resistance to Insects: 8 Transpiration: 10! (1 quart of water every 24 hours)
LADY PALM *Rhapis excelsa* APPEARANCE: Large palm with fans, 6–12 inches wide with a hand of shiny leaves. Hairy main trunk, thin arching stems.	Removal of Chemicals: 7 Easy to Grow: 9 Resistance to Insects: 10 Transpiration: 8
BAMBOO PALM *Chamaedorea seifrizii* APPEARANCE: Looks like bamboo, with clusters of slender, small canelike stalks like graceful fans. Grows up to 6 feet tall.	Removal of Chemicals: 9 Easy to Grow: 8 Resistance to Insects: 8 Transpiration: 9
PARLOR PALM *Chamaedorea elegans* APPEARANCE: Small, stiff trunk, 8-inch light green fronds. Average height 3 feet, can grow up to 6 feet tall.	Removal of Chemicals: 4 Easy to Grow: 8 Resistance to Insects: 8 Transpiration: 7

LOVE AND CARE

LIGHT: Partial sun.

HAPPY TEMPERATURE: 60°–75°F (16°–24°C); not below 50°F (10°C).

WATERING: Like to be watered regularly to keep moist, but not soggy; like to be misted to keep fresh.

FEEDING: Fertilize monthly, but not in winter.

PEST PROBLEMS: Relatively pest-free; spider mites and brown-tips in too dry an environment; too much water causes root rot.

Vines and Ivy

TYPES	CHARACTER
ARROWHEAD VINE (Also Called Butterfly Plant) *Syngonium podophyllum* APPEARANCE: Similar to philodendron, but with green-white or silver-white variegated leaves; young leaves are shaped like arrows.	Removal of Chemicals: 4 Easy to Grow: 9 Resistance to Insects: 8 Transpiration: 7
ENGLISH IVY *Hedera helix* APPEARANCE: Classic ivy leaves, with 3 to 5 lobes per leaf; climbing vine, grows aerial roots which will attach to just about anything.	Removal of Chemicals: 9 Easy to Grow: 8 Resistance to Insects: 8 Transpiration: 7
OAK LEAF IVY *Cissus rhombifolia* APPEARANCE: Vining plant, grows rapidly; more compact than other ivy; deeply lobed leaves that look like oak leaves (dark green with a slightly reddish tint).	Removal of Chemicals: 4 Easy to Grow: 7 Resistance to Insects: 7 Transpiration: 9

LOVE AND CARE

LIGHT: Partial sun/semi-shade.

HAPPY TEMPERATURE: 60°–75°F (16°–24°C); do not allow below 55°F (13°C).

WATERING: Water thoroughly and allow to dry slightly between waterings; water less in fall and winter. Likes to be misted, especially when the air is dry in winter.

FEEDING: Feed every few weeks from spring to fall with a complete fertilizer; do not feed in winter.

PEST PROBLEMS: Few to none; aphids and spider mites if environment is too dry.

Water: Pure, Clean Balance

Water is arguably the most important and precious element of life. Both our bodies and our planet are made up of about 70 percent water, and both intimately depend on it for health and harmony. Water gives life to everything that grows.

Good ol' H_2O is the "universal solvent" and the predominant transport for delivery of nutrients and minerals in the body. Water is part of every metabolic process in the body, from digestion and absorption to circulation and regeneration. In addition, water is essential for flushing cellular waste and a major element for elimination and excretion. Without adequate amounts of water, our own metabolic waste will poison our bodies. So drink deeply!

We absolutely must stay hydrated and restore water that is continuously lost through sweat and elimination. The quality of water we use to replenish our bodies greatly determines how well our bodies function and are replenished. Pure, clean water is the spring of life for a pure, clean body.

Facts about Water, the Human Body, and Our Planet

- As infants, our bodies are about 80 percent water. As adults, we are about 70 percent water. Part of the aging process is a slow dehydration. Staying juicy and hydrated means staying young.
- Pure water is 7.0 pH—perfectly neutral and just right, neither acid nor alkaline.
- Water dissolves more substances than any other fluid. It carries minerals and nutrients, chemicals and toxins into the body, within the body, and out of the body.
- Eight cups of pure water every day is the ideal goal. It is nature's beautifying tonic.
- Fresh juicy foods, like raw fruits and vegetables, are a great source of organic water to keep the body hydrated.
- We can survive almost a month without food, but less than a week without water.
- By the time you actually feel thirsty, you have lost about 1 percent of the total water in your body, which is pretty extreme.
- Caffeine is a mild diuretic, which prevents water from traveling to where it needs to be in the body. So if you enjoy tea or coffee, up the ante on your water intake.
- Seventy to 75 percent of the earth's surface is covered with water. Only 1 percent of all the water on the planet is accessible fresh water. The other 99 percent is either seawater or frozen in glaciers and icebergs.

- There is more freshwater underground than on the earth's surface.
- The amount of water on the planet does not change. There are roughly 326 million cubic miles of water that circulate around the planet in one form or another. Disturbingly, more and more of it is contaminated and polluted every day.
- On average, every American uses 160 gallons of freshwater every day.
- The United States uses 80 percent of the nation's water for irrigating industrial agriculture and cooling thermonuclear power plants, both of which are leading causes of water pollution.
- Half of all US public water violates one or more pollutant limits.
- Lead in drinking water contributes to 480,000 cases of learning disabilities in children, according to the EPA.[72]
- On average, most American tap water contains more chlorine than recommended to disinfect a swimming pool.

The Truth about Fluoride

Most of us have been raised to believe that fluoride in the water is a good thing for pearly white teeth and strong bones. However, fluoride is actually a lethal poison—and it's been added to most public water supplies since 1961.

The chemical used to fluoridate water is an industrial waste product of the phosphate fertilizer industry and is contaminated with a number of toxins, including arsenic. It is also a notoriously toxic compound commonly used in rat poison and insecticide. What's more, fluoride was a key chemical in atomic bomb production.

Proponents of fluoridating water will argue that it is good for teeth and bones, especially for children, but there is no scientific evidence to prove this claim. Studies do show that sodium fluoride and fluorosilicic acid contribute to osteoporosis, Down's syndrome, and cancer and are known to yellow, pit, and mottle teeth.

The governmental body delegated to mon-

Pesticides and Water Pollution

More than 800 million pounds of pesticides and more than 54 million tons of chemical fertilizer are used annually on American farmland, much of which filters into our freshwater supplies. Tragically, 120,000 miles of rivers in America are now polluted by the commercial agricultural industry.

In summary, we hold that fluoridation is an unreasonable risk. That is, the toxicity of fluoride is so great and the purported benefits associated with it are so small—if there are any at all—that requiring every man, woman, and child in America to ingest it borders on criminal behavior on the part of governments.

—DR. J. WILLIAM HIRZY, SENIOR VICE PRESIDENT, HEADQUARTERS UNION, UNITED STATES ENVIRONMENTAL PROTECTION AGENCY, MARCH 26, 2001

itor substances in our food and water supply, called the Delaney Congressional Investigation Committee, stated, "Fluoridation is mass medication without parallel in human history."

Two-thirds of public water in the United States is fluoridated. In contrast, 98 percent of Europe has banned fluoridating water. Whether or not the jury is out on fluoride, the best bet is to filter it out until the evidence is in.

There's Something in the Water

According to the EPA, there are 2,100 known contaminants and toxic chemicals in American drinking water, several of which are known poisons and carcinogens.[73] Synthetic compounds, pharmaceutical drugs, and radioactive substances currently found in many public water supplies pose major problems, but are generally ignored as health or safety concerns by public agencies and officials. Though most public water is disinfected from bacteria and viruses, it is done with the use of chlorine and additives, which have their own set of risks. The following is a general classification of contaminants commonly found in drinking water.

Microbes and Pathogens

- Bacteria that cause giardiasis, dysentery, and cholera
- Viruses
- Cysts of parasites like *Cryptosporidium* produced from human and animal waste

Inorganic Compounds

- Heavy metals like lead, mercury, cadmium, and cyanide from pipes and industrial processes
- Poisons like arsenic and asbestos from industrial manufacture
- Nitrates and nitrites from fertilizer industrial agriculture

Safe Water Is Your Right

The "Right to Know Amendment" was passed into federal law on October 1, 1999, and it requires all water utilities to provide each and every customer with a detailed report of what is in their water. When you receive it, it will likely read that the contaminants present "do not necessarily pose a health risk." However, a National Cancer Institute report to the Surgeon General counters that, "No level of chemical carcinogens should be considered toxicologically insignificant to humans." For more information, call the EPA Safe Drinking Water Hotline at 800-426-4791.

Synthetic Compounds

- PCBs, dioxins (from bleach), pesticides, trihalomethanes (from a reaction of chlorine and other compounds)
- Other chemicals like MTBE, a gasoline additive, now widely showing up in our water supply

Radioactive Substances

- Radon, radium, and other radioactive material

Water Additives

- Chlorine, fluoride, and others

Pharmaceutical Drugs

- These are passed into our water through urine, and they circulate freely now that so much of the population takes pharmaceutical drugs.

If these contaminants sound a bit scary, they are. The good news is that it is easy to filter out these nasties. The simple effort of filtering water at home is deeply worth every drop.

Water Filters

There is a wide range of water filters available for the home. Before purchasing, make sure you consider the efficacy versus the cost. A solidly performing filter should remove bacteria as well as additives like chlorine and fluoride and compounds and chemicals like pesticides and herbicides. The better models will also remove heavy metals and nitrates. A good system will cost anywhere from $50 to $500. Most filters will last 9 to 12 months before needing new cartridges or service.

Carbon Filtration

How it works: Carbon filtration uses pulverized carbon that is pressed into a block to form a porous maze that captures and removes impurities and contaminants from the water as it passes through. Carbon filters remove only basic impurities. Therefore, in areas where water is heavily contaminated, carbon filters are best used in combination with another filter.

What is filtered out: Reduces chlorine, organic chemicals, pesticides, herbicides, bacteria, and microbes. Carbon filters reduce, but do not necessarily remove, heavy metals, nitrates, some bacteria, and cysts.

How long it lasts: Filters need to be replaced every few months.

Installation and cost: Easy to install. Reasonably priced.

- Faucet model: $25 to $50
- Under-the-counter model: $100 and up

Charcoal Filtration

How it works: Charcoal filters use charcoal derived from coconut husk as a medium to absorb impurities and contaminants as the water passes through. Activated charcoal filters are the best, as the charcoal has been treated with oxygen to open up millions of tiny pores to make it more effective at absorbing impurities. Charcoal filters are good rudimentary filters best used in combination with another filter for thorough purification.

What is filtered out: Removes most dangerous contaminants, bacteria and microbes like *Giardia*, and cysts like *Cryptosporidium*.

How long it lasts: Filters need to be replaced every few months.

Installation and cost: Very easy to install under the sink or on the counter; reasonably priced ($40 to $100).

Distillation

How it works: Water is raised to its boiling point and condensed, leaving all contaminants behind, including sediments, toxic metals, nitrates, and microbes.

What is filtered out: Everything. However, the water tastes very flat.

How long it lasts: Many years, depending on the manufacturer.

Installation and Cost: Countertop distillers cost $200 to $1,200, depending on size, and require no installation per se as they are self-contained units. They require a lot of energy, so electrical cost should be considered.

Ultraviolet Light Treatment

How it works: Ultraviolet (UV) light is used to disinfect water and kill bacteria. UV is usually used in combination with other filters, as it disinfects water but does not remove contaminants.

What is filtered out: Bacteria.

How long it lasts: UV treatment systems last for years but require regular maintenance and cleaning.

Installation and cost: Reasonably easy to install, but should be professionally maintained, which can be expensive.

Reverse Osmosis

How it works: Pressurized water is forced through the superfine pores of a membrane that measures ten-millionths of an inch (itty-bitty!). Reverse osmosis (RO) not only filters the impurities but also actually rejects contaminants and repels them from the surface of the filter membrane. Water is then sent to a holding tank to be used. RO is very effective and one of the best systems available. I have one in my home and highly recommend it.

What is filtered out: All bacteria, microorganisms, heavy metals, radium, radon, and uranium. Even single molecules of organic compounds are removed with RO.

How long it lasts: An RO system and holding tank will last more than a dozen years. Membranes must be changed every few months for best results.

Installation and cost: Must be professionally installed and serviced.

- Counter model: $150 to $250
- Under-the-sink model: $500 to $1,500

Shower Filters for Bathing Beauties

A warm shower opens the pores of your skin beautifully, which aids circulation, but open pores make permeable skin more vulnerable to chlorine and additives in the water. So it's a good idea to install a water filter in your shower and protect your precious hide.

What a shower filter will do for you:

- *Reduce and remove chlorine and other chemicals.* More chlorine is absorbed into the body through the skin than through drinking water. Chlorine is more stable as a gas and is, therefore, released into the air when sprayed from a showerhead. Spraying chlorinated water produces chloroform (a deadly poison), which is not good to inhale, even in small amounts. Breast cancer studies show that women with breast cancer have an average of 50 to 60 percent more chlorine in their breast tissue than women without breast cancer.
- *Keep your skin and hair soft and supple.* Chlorine has a harsh, drying effect on the skin and hair and is a common cause of skin irritation and rashes.
- *Improve the air quality of the whole house* by reducing and removing chemical vapors from spraying water.

Danger: Bleach! Alternative: Oxygen!

Bleach is praised for its ability to make whites whiter and for its miraculous disinfectant powers. It is less known as a toxic culprit that produces dangerous fumes and poisonous dioxins that literally never degrade. The toxins in bleach are directly linked to the growing rates of cancer, birth defects, and environmental poisoning. Safe, ecofriendly alternatives like "oxygen" bleaches are just as effective and available in your local natural food store.

Green Cleaning

Every home should be safe—an inviolable nest that is a cloister from the outside world and free from the harm of chemicals and toxins. But under the average kitchen sink lurk chemical invaders cloaked in a promise to protect. Although they may indeed sanitize and deodorize, commercial cleaning agents are also laden with toxic poisons and chemicals poised to rain on your wholesome parade.

Green Cleaners: Thinking Beyond the Drain

Commercial soaps and cleaners are produced from harmful chemical compounds and petroleum products, which put our personal and planetary health in danger. The primary ingredients of commercial soaps and cleaners are oil-derived phosphates that do not break down and end up in our freshwater supplies and oceans forever. Not only are petroleum products a nonrenewable resource fueling the world's heated political duels, they are also toxic to produce and reluctant to go away.

Chemical soap, detergent, and cleaning agents not only wreck the environment but also irritate skin and instigate allergic reactions. Beyond topical affliction, chemical compounds in standard cleaning agents contribute to much deeper health concerns. One of the growing number of examples clearly linked to extensive research is the direct impact of "estrogen-like" chemicals found in petroleum-based commercial soap and chemical cleaners on reproductive and endocrine damage and disease, including breast and prostate cancer, birth defects, infertility, and reproductive problems. Yikes!

Each of us can make a personal and global difference by choosing "green" soaps and cleaners. Green cleaners are earth-friendly, plant-based, fully biodegradable, and gentle to human skin and senses. They are made from effective, nontoxic materials that begin to break down into harmless carbon and water long before recirculating back into the freshwater system of our rivers, lakes, streams, and aquifers. It is a big, beautiful world to keep clean, beginning with the kitchen sink. Thinking beyond the drain and cleaning with ecofriendly agents will sustain a spanking clean household as well as a sound future for our planet. Our great-grandkids would thank us.

The Basic Six of Green Cleaning

My home is my sanctuary, and I freely admit to having a bit of a hygiene fetish. I like it clean, and I don't care for chemicals. Fortunately, there are plenty of nontoxic solutions for even the cruddiest cleaning and unkempt quarters.

Natural Soap: It almost sounds too simple to be true, but good ol' soap is one of the oldest and most effective cleaning agents there is. Soap is a surfactant (derived from "surface active agent") that removes dirt and stains and cuts grease. According to my daddio (who is a king of cleaning), soap makes water wetter. Loosely put, soap causes the molecules of water to get closer together by lowering the surface tension of the water, causing the water to become thinner to be able to get under dirt and grime and wash it away.

Soap is made from an oil base of natural materials, though many commercial brands now contain petroleum oil as well as chemicals and perfume. Until about 60 years ago, all soap was nontoxic and mostly coconut-based. During World War II, coconut importing came to a grinding halt, and a snappy team of American chemists invented a bevy of modern chemical detergents for every household in America to replace the tried-and-true scrub-a-dub of natural soaps. These chemical super-detergents have not left our homes since, and they are directly contributing to the deterioration of freshwater supplies, wildlife, marine life, and increasing chemical exposure in the safety of our own homes. Boo-hiss. None of the modern additives actually improves the plain power of natural soap to tackle all kinds of dirt, dishes, surfaces, and so forth.

Biodegradable Detergent: Like soap, detergent is a surfactant that removes stains and cuts grease. Detergent has a different composition than soap and reacts less to the minerals naturally found in water, especially hard water. Washing clothing with soap can leave a residue, but detergents will wash away. Likewise, detergents are used in automatic dishwashers to reduce residue buildup and render sparkling clean dishes and glasses.

Detergent is made from phosphates, which are organic and synthetic materials, and may also contain abrasives for scouring action, oxidants to bleach, and enzymes to digest dirt or soften fabrics. Although detergents act as a powerful cleaning agent at home,

Castile Soap

Castile soap is a mild soap that was originally made from olive oil, though today it's made from any vegetable oil. Although castile soap seems thin and watery, it is powerfully potent and a little goes a long way. Castile soap is especially good for cutting grease and oil and cleaning surfaces.

they can cause a host of problems in the environment if they are not biodegradable. One big problem with nonbiodegradable detergent is that plants love the phosphates in them and they grow out of control (though please don't go about watering the houseplants with detergent!). On the surface this sounds pretty good, but phosphates in fresh-water sources and the ocean cause serious algae blooms, which snuff out natural species and severely mess up the balance of the ecosystem.

Given the ongoing action of detergents after they go down the drain, it is only responsible to use biodegradable detergents for a clean future.

2. BAKING SODA AND WASHING SODA

Baking soda and washing soda are two tried-and-true, old-school mineral cleaners that still work as well as when Grandma used them.

BAKING SODA, OR SODIUM BICARBONATE, is slightly alkaline with a pH of 8.1. It is a mild abrasive, with soft crystal molecules that dissolve easily in water so it won't scratch surfaces. Baking soda is the best scrub for cleaning cutting boards and tile in the kitchen as well as the tub and shower. It also brilliantly absorbs and neutralizes odors. I keep an opened box of it in my fridge to absorb roaming smells.

WASHING SODA, OR SODIUM CARBONATE, is a little more hard-core. It is extremely caustic with a pH of 11, which falls just shy of being labeled with a toxic warning, but it gives off no fumes. This means that you should wear gloves when using it. It is the best green cleaner for heavy-duty scouring and removing serious stains. It should not be used on fiberglass or marble, as it will scratch. Washing soda makes easy work out of tough jobs like cleaning greasy ovens and oil spills in the garage, and removing wax and waxy substances like lipstick. It is too powerful to use on waxed floors, however, unless you plan to strip them.

3. VINEGAR

Vinegar is a classic cleaning agent used through the ages to remove grime, clean stains, and neutralize odors. Distilled white wine vinegar is the safest bet to clean without the risk of staining. Vinegar should be diluted with water in a 1:1 ratio for most jobs. Mixing it in a spray bottle is convenient for easy use. The strong smell of vinegar dissipates quickly, leaving a crisp, sanitary wake.

4. CITRUS-BASED CONCENTRATED CLEANER

Concentrated citrus-based cleaners are highly effective for all-purpose cleaning. The active ingredient is a natural solvent made from citrus peels, and these cleaners contain minerals and plant-based ingredients that are completely biodegradable.

The cleaner brilliantly removes stubborn stickers off of glass jars. Just a few drops of the concentrate can be diluted with water in a spray bottle to clean glass, surfaces, no-wax floors, carpets, and upholstery. The concentrate will even remove ink, blood, and chewing gum. It is also available for sale in a diluted form, but why not save a buck and add water at home?

Ecofriendly brands: Citrisolve, 7th Generation, and Earth Friendly.

5. OXYGEN BLEACH AND HYDROGEN PEROXIDE

Natural oxygen bleach and hydrogen peroxide are great alternatives to chemical bleach. *Sodium percarbonate,* made from hydrogen peroxide, is what makes oxygen bleaches work. They are nontoxic and effective for whitening and brightening clothes. Oxygen bleach is color-friendly, but test your clothes on a hidden seam first to make sure there is no adverse reaction.

Hydrogen peroxide is a natural disinfectant commonly used to clean cuts. It literally eats dirt. It fizzes little white bubbles where there is grime that show it is working. It is brilliant for combating mold and mildew and will really brighten white clothing (see "Natural Laundry Solutions" on page 151 for some great formulas). Hydrogen peroxide is also great for cleaning narrow-necked bottles, especially water dispensers, and very effective for scrubbing porous materials such as cutting boards, wooden utensils, and wooden salad servers.

6. ANTISEPTIC ESSENTIAL OILS

Antiseptic essential oils kill bacteria and mold. A few drops added to liquid cleaning agents will help eradicate the dankest funk. Tea tree oil is the most effective with antibacterial, antiseptic, and antifungal properties. It does have a strong smell, which will dissipate within a day or so. Essential oils of lemon, lemongrass, cinnamon, oregano, eucalyptus, and thyme are also very effective and smell fantastic.

Recipes for Green Cleaning

Cleaning from scratch is easier than cooking from scratch. A few basic ingredients will tackle any cleaning task in the house, and all of the ingredients are cheap, easy to find, and naturally effective.

Mold Buster

Four basic ingredients will eliminate mold and mildew from even the dankest corners: tea tree oil, grapefruit seed extract, hydrogen peroxide, and distilled white vinegar. Spray this army of green cleaners on problem areas. There's no need to rinse.

2   teaspoons tea tree oil

½   cup hydrogen peroxide or distilled white vinegar

2   cups water

25   drops grapefruit seed extract (optional, for full-strength problems)

In a clean spray bottle, mix together the tea tree oil, hydrogen peroxide or vinegar, water, and grapefruit seed extract (if desired) and shake to blend. Spray on mildew-stricken and moldy areas. Do not rinse. The tea tree oil has a strong smell, which will dissipate within a day or two.

NOTE: Hydrogen peroxide loses its potency when exposed to oxygen, so make sure the top of the bottle is screwed on tightly. Distilled white vinegar can be used instead of hydrogen peroxide with an indefinite shelf life. For a fragrance-free formula, eliminate the tea tree oil and increase the amount of grapefruit seed extract to 40 drops.

Fresh Disinfectant Deodorizer

This is a great disinfectant to spray in bathrooms for a fresh, clean smell. Essential oils of lavender and peppermint are antiseptic and antibacterial for squeaky-clean surfaces and sweet-smelling air.

½ teaspoon essential oil of lavender

½ teaspoon essential oil of peppermint

2 cups water

In a clean spray bottle, mix together the lavender essential oil, peppermint essential oil, and water and shake to blend. Spray on surfaces such as the toilet bowl, vanity, and sink after cleaning. No need to wipe off. Be careful not to get the mist in your eyes because the essential oils are very strong.

Clean Sponges and Scrubbies

Sponges are a breeding ground for funk, mold, and bacteria. Yuck. I consider it a minor investment to break out a new dish sponge regularly and recycle the old ones.

- Use different-colored sponges for an easy system to get the longest and most hygienic life out of a sponge: one for dishes, one for counters and surfaces, one under the sink for floor mishaps.
- Rotate the sponges every 2 weeks. The dish sponge becomes the counter-surface sponge. In turn, the counter-surface sponge is demoted to the floor sponge.
- Sponges with a scrubby side are more versatile and seem to last longer.
- Rinse out the sponge when finished using it and give it a good squeeze to dry. Sponges that are left wet will get funky more quickly.
- A designated scrubber for vegetables will keep grunge and soap away from lovely veggies and fruit. A natural-bristle scrub brush is best.

All-Purpose Glass Cleaner

This all-purpose glass cleaner is as good as anything in the store. Try adding a few drops of the essential oils of your choice for a fresh smell. Use newspaper to clean and dry glass and windows as it leaves no trace of lint.

¼   **cup distilled white vinegar**

½   **teaspoon castile soap or liquid detergent**

2   **cups water**

6   **drops essential oil, such as peppermint, lavender, lemon, or lemongrass (optional)**

In a spray bottle, mix the vinegar, soap or detergent, water, and essential oil (if desired), and shake to blend. Spray on glass and wipe dry with newspaper or a squeegee.

Natural Laundry Solutions

Lemon-Fresh Whites!

Lemon juice lightly bleaches clothing and works best when the clothes are hung on the line to dry in the sun. Add ½ cup of strained lemon juice to the rinse cycle of a medium load of laundry.

Oxygenated Whites!

Hydrogen peroxide acts as a natural bleaching agent and disinfectant for laundry. A basic bottle of hydrogen peroxide is a 3 percent solution and is usually on a shelf near the adhesive bandages. Add ½ cup of hydrogen peroxide to the rinse cycle of a medium load of laundry.

    Note: Do not use on dark laundry as it will bleach away color.

10 Green Cleaning Solutions

PRODUCT	RISKS	HEALTHY SOLUTION
AEROSOL CANS	PROPELLANTS LIKE ISOBUTANE AND PROPANE ARE TOXIC TO THE BRAIN, HEART, AND CENTRAL NERVOUS SYSTEM.	DO NOT USE. USE A PUMP SPRAY, NONAEROSOL SPRAY, LIQUID, OR ROLL-ON, OR APPLY BY HAND.
SURFACE CLEANERS	AMMONIA AND CHLORINE ARE FOUND IN MANY ALL-PURPOSE CLEANERS. AMMONIA IRRITATES LUNGS. CHLORINE FORMS CANCER-CAUSING COMPOUNDS WHEN RELEASED INTO THE ENVIRONMENT. MIXED TOGETHER, THEY FORM A DEADLY CHLORA-MINE GAS.	USE NATURAL SURFACE CLEANERS OR VINEGAR. FOR SCOURING, USE BAKING SODA OR SALT AND WATER.
FURNITURE/ FLOOR POLISH	MOST WOOD POLISH CONTAINS PHENOL, WHICH CAUSES CANCER. RESIDUAL VAPORS STICK AROUND FOR A LONG TIME. PHENOL DAMAGES THE LIVER AND KIDNEYS AND IS ASSOCIATED WITH HEADACHES, DEPRES-SION, AND WEAKNESS.	DUST WITH A DAMP CLOTH. USE MINERAL OR VEGETABLE OIL AND VITAMIN E AS AN ALTERNATIVE.
GLASS CLEANERS	MOST ARE POISONOUS. MOST CONTAIN AMMONIA, WHICH IS DANGEROUS TO INHALE. LUNG AND EYE IRRITANT.	USE A NONTOXIC VERSION. OR TRY DILUTED APPLE CIDER VINEGAR IN A SPRAY BOTTLE.
DISINFECTANTS	DAMAGE THE BRAIN. CAN CAUSE NAUSEA, DIZZINESS, CHEST PAIN, SKIN PROBLEMS, AND CANCER.	AIR AND LIGHT ARE THE BEST DISINFEC-TANTS. OR TRY A MIXTURE OF BORAX AND HOT WATER.
METAL POLISH	BURNS THE EYES AND SKIN. FUMES FROM PHOSPHORIC AND SULFURIC ACIDS ARE DANGEROUS TO BREATHE.	**SILVER:** USE BAKING SODA + SALT + WATER. **BRASS:** USE SALT + FLOUR + VINEGAR. **COPPER:** USE LEMON JUICE + SALT. **CHROME:** USE RUBBING ALCOHOL. **ALUMINUM:** USE LEMON.
MOTHBALLS	TOXIC TO THE BRAIN, LIVER, AND BLOOD. KNOWN TO ACCUMULATE IN THE BODY.	USE CEDAR BLOCKS AND CHIPS. BAGS OF LAVENDER, CLOVES, ROSEMARY, AND DRIED LEMON PEELS ARE NATURAL ALTERNATIVES.
DRAIN CLEANER	HARSH INGREDIENTS CAN BURN TISSUE AND EYES, CAUSING PERMANENT DAMAGE. ESPECIALLY DANGEROUS FOR CHILDREN. FLAMMABLE AND CAN EXPLODE.	USE DRAIN BASKETS FOR PREVENTION. USE A METAL DRAIN SNAKE. OR TRY 1 CUP OF BAKING SODA FOLLOWED BY ½ CUP OF VINEGAR. LET SIT FOR 15 MINUTES AND FLUSH WITH HOT WATER.
OVEN CLEANER	MOST PRODUCTS CONTAIN LYE AND HYDROCHLORIC AND SULFURIC ACID, WHICH CAN BURN TISSUE AND CAUSE PERMANENT DAMAGE. HARMFUL TO THE EYES AND LUNGS.	USE A SELF-CLEANING OVEN. OR USE A PASTE OF BAKING SODA AND HOT WATER WITH STEEL WOOL.
AIR FRESHENER	DAMAGES THE LIVER, KIDNEYS, AND BRAIN. CAUSES CANCER. BUILDS UP IN THE BODY.	PLANTS ARE THE BEST AIR FRESHENER. TRY USING FRESH FLOWERS OR POTPOURRI.

PART TWO

Recipes for the Balanced Plate

Happy and successful cooking doesn't rely only on know-how; it comes from the heart, makes great demands on the palate, and needs enthusiasm and a deep love of food to bring it to life.

—GEORGES BLANC, *MA CUISINE DES SAISONS*

My passion for food is innate and eternal. Although I am not a conventionally trained chef, I have dined and worked alongside some of the greats, and I humbly acknowledge their influence on my own alternative approach to the culinary arts and integrative nutrition—my life's pursuit. I have been working with food professionally for more than a decade and independently studying and teaching nutrition over the same course of time, and still I feel that no matter the lengths of my stroke, I am just on the edge of a deep ocean.

I compare my relationship with food to one of my greatest joys: living on Maui. It is like standing in the place where so many have stood before, none of it new, yet always open to endless possibility. I moved to Maui more than 10 years ago, in a leap of faith, hopeful to find work as a chef. What I found was so different from what I imagined, having never been here before. And what I continue to find is so far beyond my wildest dreams. Previous to moving here, I had a finite concept of island life. I figured that after some spell of time, I would have explored every beach, eaten every fruit, hiked every trail, walked in every circle. Yet what continues to unfold is in inverse proportion. What I realize is that even if I did not globe-trot as much as I do—if I spent the rest of my days exploring just this one island surrounded by 3,000 miles of blue Pacific waters, where time has stood still in certain places and the veils are thin—it would only be a taste. Island life, like the preparation and enjoyment of good food, unfolds into quiet nooks and crannies, where secrets and great discoveries are born.

I will ask your forgiveness in advance. I offer many variations, substitutions, and options in the recipe pages that follow. My hope is not to foster confusion, but to free up choices for what works for you. The treasure is that each of us is different; the seasons change; sometimes the avocados just aren't ripe enough, and creativity comes into play. I invite you to use these recipes verbatim or as inspiration. Above all else, trust your senses and instincts, work with what you have, and embrace the unexpected. Remember: Fruits and vegetables are like snowflakes, no specimen alike.

These recipes have grown from my heart, from a deep passion for food, and with sincere respect for culinary tradition, nutrition, and healing systems. I triumphantly believe that healthy food and delicious food are not mutually exclusive. True health, in the holistic sense, is contingent on thorough enjoyment, and that real joy brings real health. I believe that nutritious food can be truly delicious, and great food can be made healthy. That is the essence of the balanced plate.

May the spine of this book soften with a lifetime of use and the pages become stained with the paw prints of love and engagement. As the Dalai Lama said, "Approach love and cooking with reckless abandon."

How to Use These Recipes

The purpose of this key is to help you develop a deeper connection to your food and allow you to experiment with the different whole foods dietary systems outlined in Chapter 2. Remember that balance is not an absolute science. What may work for me may not work for you and vice versa. I encourage you to use these recipe classifications as a guide to discovering which whole foods ingredients and techniques suit you. Build a purely macrobiotic menu or mix it up! Try eating all raw for a few of the dog days of summer, or prepare at least one raw recipe at each meal. Rather than following a strict regimen, follow your senses for a great adventure en route to good health and good food.

 Macrobiotic: Gently balanced seasoning and preparation in accord with the traditional macrobiotic system (see page 29)

 Raw-friendly: Containing fresh, living ingredients, prepared at room temperature or low temperature, or variations in the procedure for low-temperature preparation (see page 36)

 A-Vata: Balancing for Ayurvedic vata types (see page 40)

 A-Pitta: Balancing for Ayurvedic pitta types (see page 40)

 A-Kapha: Balancing for Ayurvedic kapha types (see page 40)

 Integrated: These recipes draw from the best of all worlds using traditional techniques with clean, whole foods ingredients.

 Gluten-sensitive: These recipes include grains or flour, but are gluten free or can be made using low-gluten options for those with sensitivities.

 Low-glycemic: These recipes feature slower-burning carbohydrates and are less likely to cause a spike in blood-sugar levels.

CHAPTER 4

Drink Deeply

Tell me what you eat, and I shall tell you what you are.

—JEAN-ANTHELME BRILLAT-SAVARIN

Lemon Cucumber Spa Hydrator

Fresh lemon juice and cucumber blend into pure hydration for beautiful cells and skin. Lemon is juicy with electrolytes to rehydrate the body, especially after a good workout. Just a pinch of sea salt lifts the flavor and actually allows your cells to drink deeply.

YIELDS: 4 SERVINGS (A BIT MORE THAN A QUART)

2 **medium cucumbers, peeled and roughly chopped (about 4 cups)**

1 **lemon, peeled and seeded**

1–2 **tablespoons agave nectar**

¼ **teaspoon sea salt**

3 **cups filtered water**

Blend the cucumbers, lemon, agave, salt, and water at high speed until smooth.

Pour through a fine strainer or sieve.

Serve chilled.

NUTRITION AT A GLANCE

Per serving: 20 calories, 0 g total fat, 0 g saturated fat, 1 g protein, 4 g carbohydrates, 1 g dietary fiber, 150 mg sodium

---

Agave!

Agave is the sticky-sweet juice naturally extracted from the agave cactus. Grown for thousands of years in Mexico, agave yields a sap like a thin honey and is the source for distilling tequila. Agave is sweeter than sugar but is a low-glycemic food, meaning it is metabolized slowly and doesn't jack blood sugar levels around as much as other simple sugars. It dissolves easily in water, making it a fine choice for even the frostiest of beverages. It's widely available in natural food stores and online.

- Sometimes called agave "nectar" or agave "syrup." Same stuff.
- Lighter-colored agave has a more neutral sweetness; darker agave tastes more of minerals.
- Can be substituted 1:1 for honey and maple syrup.
- If using to bake, reduce the oven heat by 25°F.
- For diabetics: 1 teaspoon agave = a free food; 2 teaspoons = ½ carbohydrate exchange

Raspberry Lavender Lemonade

The delicate aroma of lavender flowers blossoms in the arms of this bright raspberry lemonade. Dried lavender flowers are often sold in the dried herb section of natural food stores or for the bath. Be sure to look for organic lavender. This makes a fantastic raspberry lemonade on its own, even without the lavender. Thawed organic frozen raspberries may be used in lieu of fresh raspberries if they're not available.

YIELDS: 4 SERVINGS (A BIT MORE THAN A QUART)

2	**tablespoons dried lavender flowers**
2	**cups boiled filtered water**
2–3	**tablespoons maple syrup**
2–3	**tablespoons agave nectar or raw honey**
½	**teaspoon nonalcoholic vanilla extract**
1	**pint raspberries (2 cups)**
2	**cups filtered water**
¾	**cup fresh lemon juice**
	Pinch of sea salt
	Sprigs of fresh mint for garnish

Steep the lavender flowers in the hot water for 3 to 5 minutes. Do not steep longer or it will turn bitter. Strain.

Mix in the maple syrup, agave or honey, and vanilla. Set in the freezer to chill for 15 minutes or in the fridge for 20 minutes, or until cool to the touch.

Meanwhile, in a blender, blend the raspberries, filtered water, lemon juice, and salt until smooth.

Pour through a fine mesh strainer or sieve. Press down on the pulp with the back of a large spoon to extract as much liquid as possible.

Mix the cooled, sweetened tea and the raspberry-lemon mixture together. Add a bit more maple syrup or agave or honey if desired.

Serve in tall glasses or wine glasses over ice with sprigs of fresh mint.

NUTRITION AT A GLANCE
Per serving: 70 calories, 0 g total fat, 0 g saturated fat, 1 g protein, 19 g carbohydrates, 4 g dietary fiber, 45 mg sodium

Green Lemon Ginger Beauty Tonic

At first sight, this juice is shockingly green, but it has a very mild taste. Both cleansing and fortifying, this tonic flushes and hydrates the system for beautiful hair and glowing skin.

YIELDS: 4 SERVINGS (ABOUT A QUART)

1	head romaine lettuce
1	cucumber
2	organic green apples
6	ribs celery
½	bunch parsley
1	lemon
1"	fresh ginger

Separate the romaine and cut the stem into pieces that will fit through a juicer. Cut the cucumber into quarters lengthwise. Cut the apples into sections that will fit through the juicer.

Juice the romaine, cucumber, apples, celery, parsley, lemon, and ginger in a vegetable juicer, alternating for easy processing.

Drink as fresh as possible.

NUTRITION AT A GLANCE
Per serving: 70 calories, 0 g total fat, 0 g saturated fat, 3 g protein, 18 g carbohydrates, 5 g dietary fiber, 80 mg sodium

Pure Pomegranate Antioxidant Punch

Pomegranates are a champion source of antioxidants, sweeping the body of free radicals from pollution and metabolic waste to keep cells and skin young and beautiful.

YIELDS: 2 SERVINGS (ABOUT 3 CUPS)

3	pomegranates, quartered
¼	cup apple juice, apple cider, or filtered water

Separate the pomegrante seeds from the skin and pith.

Place the seeds in a blender with the apple juice, cider, or water. Blend until smooth.

Pour through a mesh strainer or sieve and press with the back of a large spoon to extract as much juice as possible. Serve chilled.

NUTRITION AT A GLANCE
Per serving: 170 calories, 0.5 g total fat, 0 g saturated fat, 2 g protein, 43 g carbohydrates, 1 g dietary fiber, 10 mg sodium

Honey Ginger Ale

This homemade ginger ale has the clean, clear kick of fresh ginger, which is so good for digestion and circulation. Adjust to taste: I am an avid fan of strong ginger and mild sweetness, but for kids I usually mellow out the ginger and amp up the sweet.

YIELDS: 4 SERVINGS (A BIT MORE THAN A QUART)

4–8 tablespoons ginger juice (see "Ginger Juice," below)

¼ cup lemon juice, fresh is best

4–6 tablespoons raw honey

2–4 tablespoons agave nectar

Pinch of sea salt

1 liter sparkling water, chilled

Mix together the ginger juice, lemon juice, honey, agave, and salt.

Pour ¼ cup or more in each glass and add the sparkling water. Serve with ice.

NUTRITION AT A GLANCE
Per serving: 70 calories, 0 g total fat, 0 g saturated fat, 0 g protein, 19 g carbohydrates, 0 g dietary fiber, 40 mg sodium

---

Ginger Juice

For a small amount of ginger juice, I recommend finely grating fresh gingerroot and squeezing out the juice. One inch of fresh ginger will yield about 1 tablespoon of juice. Younger ginger has more tender fiber and more juice.

Scrub or peel the ginger (the edge of a spoon works brilliantly). Grate the ginger very finely. A microplane grater works wonders. Place in a cheesecloth and squeeze firmly to extract as much juice as possible.

Larger amounts of ginger juice can be extracted in a blender using a little water, then straining and squeezing the juice out—though the ginger juice will be slightly diluted. For ¼ cup ginger juice, chop ⅓ cup peeled ginger (about 6 inches). Place in a blender with 2 to 3 tablespoons of filtered water. Blend in pulses at first to get it going, then at high speed until it's as smooth as possible. Line a strainer with cheesecloth and pour the blended ginger through. Gather the edges of the cheesecloth together and squeeze firmly to extract as much juice as possible. Store leftovers in a tightly sealed jar in the fridge for up to a week. Shake well before using.

Stone Julius Smoothies and Popsicles

This smoothie conjures up nostalgic childhood memories of Creamsicles on a hot summer afternoon. The lecithin and flax oil are optional, but they add a dose of healthy oils for beautiful cells and skin. For a lighter smoothie, blend the nuts and orange juice and strain to remove the pulp, then add in the rest of the ingredients. Blend as a decadent creamy smoothie, or pour into popsicle containers for the kids. I prefer frozen peaches, though frozen bananas are usually a hit with the little 'uns.

YIELDS: 4 SERVINGS (ABOUT A QUART) OR 10–12 POPSICLES

½ cup raw macadamia nuts or raw cashews, soaked 1 hour in filtered water and drained

2½ cups fresh orange juice

2 oranges, peel and pith removed

1 teaspoon orange zest (be sure the oranges are organic!)

2 tablespoons agave nectar (optional)

1–2 teaspoons nonalcoholic vanilla extract

1 tablespoon lecithin granules (optional)

2 teaspoons flax oil (optional)

Pinch of sea salt

2½ cups ice or frozen peaches, skin removed

In a blender, combine the nuts and orange juice and blend until smooth.

Cut the oranges into quarters and remove any seeds as they are very bitter and will impose on the flavor. Add the oranges to the blender along with the orange zest, agave (if desired), vanilla, lecithin granules (if desired), flax oil (if desired), and salt. Blend until very smooth.

Add the ice or frozen peaches and blend again until thick and smooth.

Serve immediately or stash in the freezer.

NUTRITION AT A GLANCE
Per serving (based on 4 servings): 220 calories, 13 g total fat, 2 g saturated fat, 3 g protein, 27 g carbohydrates, 3 g dietary fiber, 40 mg sodium

Each popsicle (based on 10 popsicles): 90 calories, 5 g total fat, 1 g saturated fat, 1 g protein, 11 g carbohydrates, 1 g dietary fiber, 15 mg sodium

Virgin Bell Mary

The Virgin Bell is the benevolent cousin of a Bloody Mary. Add a pinch of cayenne if you like a kick. Perfect for Sunday brunch, straight or spiked!

YIELDS: 4 SERVINGS (ABOUT A QUART)

4   cups red bell peppers, stems, seeds, and veins removed (2–3 peppers)

1   cucumber, quartered

6   ribs celery

4–6   sprigs cilantro

4–6   sprigs parsley

1   clove garlic

1"   fresh ginger

Pinch of cayenne pepper

Pinch of sea salt

Freshly ground black pepper

4   ounces vodka (optional)

4   ribs celery (optional, for garnish)

Juice the bell peppers, cucumber, celery, cilantro, parsley, garlic, and ginger in a juicer.

Stir in the cayenne, salt, and pepper to taste.

Serve immediately, or add 1 ounce of good-quality vodka (Grey Goose, Belvedere, or Kettle One are excellent choices) to each serving to de-virginize. Serve with a tender rib of celery.

NUTRITION AT A GLANCE
Per serving: 70 calories, 0 g total fat, 0 g saturated fat, 3 g protein, 16 g carbohydrates, 5 g dietary fiber, 115 mg sodium

Smooth Bell Gazpacho Soup

The Virgin Bell Mary makes a succulent base for a smooth soup.

YIELDS: 2 SERVINGS

2 cups seeded, diced tomato

1 avocado, peeled and pitted

1 tablespoon olive oil

1 teaspoon agave nectar

Blend until smooth and season with sea salt and freshly ground black pepper.

NUTRITION AT A GLANCE
Per serving: 190 calories, 3 g total fat, 0 g saturated fat, 1 g protein, 8 g carbohydrates, 9 g dietary fiber, 125 mg sodium

Bancha Blood Sugar Balancer

This is a classic macrobiotic tonic used to stabilize blood sugar from too many sweets. It is very helpful to balance over-acidic conditions and aid digestion and is prized for purifying and balancing the blood. Umeboshi plum vinegar is prized for its balancing properties and shoyu for stimulating natural digestion. Drink one cup in the morning or after eating too much sugar to relieve imbalance.

Bancha tea is a green tea, widely available in natural grocery stores.

YIELDS: 2 SERVINGS

2   **cups filtered water**

1   **bancha tea bag**

2   **teaspoons shoyu (soy sauce)**

1   **teaspoon umeboshi plum vinegar**

Bring the water to a boil and turn off the heat. Cool for a moment and pour over the tea bag. Steep for 5 minutes. Squeeze out the tea bag. Add the shoyu and vinegar. Stir and drink hot.

NUTRITION AT A GLANCE
Per serving: 5 calories, 0 g total fat, 0 g saturated fat, 0 g protein, 0 g carbohydrates, 0 g dietary fiber, 790 mg sodium

Green Tea Chai Frappé

Chai is a delicious blend of spices traditionally served sweet and creamy with black tea. Using fresh, whole spices launches the flavor into a divine stratosphere. Though green tea does have some caffeine, it is an excellent source of antioxidants and naturally occurring fluoride. Fresh almonds make a positively delicious milk. For a quick fix if soaked almonds are not on hand, just use raw almond butter and blend. Blend with ice to make a frozen frappé (you may need to add a touch more sweetness as the ice will dilute the flavor), or warm gently on a cool fall day.

YIELDS: 4 SERVINGS (ABOUT A QUART)

2   green tea bags

2   cups boiled filtered water

1   cup raw almonds, soaked 8 hours in filtered water, drained, and rinsed, or 4 tablespoons raw almond butter

2   cups filtered water

1–1½   tablespoons chopped ginger

1–2   cinnamon sticks (each 3"), broken, or 2 teaspoons ground cinnamon

¼   whole nutmeg, roughly cut, or ½ teaspoon ground nutmeg

2   whole cloves or ⅛ teaspoon ground cloves

2–3   tablespoons maple syrup

2–3   tablespoons agave nectar or raw honey

Pinch of sea salt and a bit of freshly ground black pepper

Steep the tea bags in the hot water for 3 to 5 minutes. Remove the tea bags and squeeze them out to extract as much liquid as possible. Cool the tea in the fridge or freezer unless you intend to serve it warm.

In a blender, add the cooled tea, almonds or almond butter, filtered water, ginger, cinnamon, nutmeg, cloves, maple syrup, agave or honey, and salt and pepper and blend until supersmooth. Start with less sweetener and add more as you please.

Pour through a strainer or sieve. Press on the pulp with the back of a large spoon to extract as much liquid as possible.

Return the liquid to the blender and blend with ice for a frosty frappé, or warm over low heat to soothe the spirit.

NUTRITION AT A GLANCE
Per serving: 130 calories, 9 g total fat, 1 g saturated fat, 2 g protein, 11 g carbohydrates, 0 g dietary fiber, 110 mg sodium

Milk Chocolate Milk

This smooth-as-silk milk made from creamy nuts and laden with pure cocoa powder is both decadent and a great source of energy—truly delectable warmed up on a cold winter day, or blended with ice for a cool frozen treat. Almonds are naturally a little sweet, creamy, and full of heart-healthy oils and protein. Raw cashews yield an even more rich, creamy, and decadent milk. More water may be added for a lighter milk. A touch of balsamic vinegar and shoyu (soy sauce) may seem unusual, but they lend a depth of flavor and an exceptional je ne sais quoi. For kids, I recommend leaving them out.

YIELDS: 4 SERVINGS (ABOUT A QUART)

1½ cups raw almonds, soaked 8 hours in filtered water, drained, and rinsed, or 2 cups raw cashews, soaked 2–4 hours, drained, and rinsed

4 cups filtered water

4–6 tablespoons organic cocoa powder (Green and Black is choice)

2–4 tablespoons maple syrup

2–4 tablespoons agave nectar

1 teaspoon shoyu (soy sauce) or nama shoyu (unpasteurized soy sauce) (optional)

½ teaspoon balsamic vinegar (optional)

½ teaspoon nonalcoholic vanilla extract (optional)

Place the nuts in a blender with the filtered water. Blend at high speed until smooth.

Pour through a mesh strainer lined with cheesecloth. Squeeze out as much liquid as possible. Set the pulp aside. The pulp can be used to make a second batch using half the amount of all of the other ingredients or used to make flour (see "Almond Flour" on page 167).

Rinse out the blender and return the nut milk to it. Add the cocoa powder, maple syrup, agave, shoyu (if desired), vinegar (if desired), and vanilla (if desired). Blend until smooth. Add more cocoa for a rich, darker chocolate and more maple syrup or agave for a sweeter taste.

NUTRITION AT A GLANCE
Per serving: 100 calories, 4 g total fat, 0.5 g saturated fat, 2 g protein, 19 g carbohydrates, 3 g dietary fiber, 160 mg sodium

Pure Almond Milk

Almond milk is smooth as cream. A great source of calcium, heart-healthy fats, and easily digestible protein, this milk is a fresh alternative to soy milk, rice milk, or cow's milk and perfect as the base for a smoothie, with cereal, and of course, with cookies! You can substitute other nuts for the almonds, such as cashews, or even hulled hemp seeds. The leftover pulp can be recycled for a second batch, or dried and ground into flour for cookies and cakes (see "Almond Flour," opposite page).

YIELDS: 4 SERVINGS (1 QUART)

1¼ cups raw almonds, soaked 8 hours in filtered water, drained, and rinsed

4 cups filtered water

Pinch of sea salt

2 tablespoons maple syrup (optional)

2 tablespoons agave nectar (optional)

Pinch of freshly ground cinnamon (optional)

½ teaspoon nonalcoholic vanilla extract (optional)

Place the almonds in a blender with the filtered water and salt. Blend at high speed until smooth.

Pour through a mesh strainer lined with cheesecloth. Squeeze out as much liquid as possible. Set the pulp aside. The pulp can be used to make a second batch using half the amount of all of the other ingredients or used to make almond flour (see "Almond Flour").

Drink as is, or rinse out the blender and return the nut milk to it. Add the maple syrup and/or agave, and the cinnamon and/or vanilla and blend again until mixed.

Store in a tightly sealed jar in the fridge for 2 to 3 days.

NUTRITION AT A GLANCE
Per serving: 60 calories, 3 g total fat, 0 g saturated fat, 1 g protein, 8 g carbohydrates, 1 g dietary fiber, 190 mg sodium

Almond Flour

The pulp left over from straining nut milk can be dried until crumbly and used as flour for cookies, pie crusts, and other sweets.

Spread the nut meal thinly on a dehydrator tray and dehydrate at 112°F until completely dry (12 to 20 hours or as needed). Or spread on a cookie sheet and place in the oven, set at the lowest temperature, for 3 to 4 hours, or until it is dry enough to crumble when pinched. If your oven has a pilot light, it may be warm enough to use without turning the oven on. Let cool completely. As is, it is a coarse flour and may be ground into a fine meal in a food processor. Store in a tightly sealed jar, container, or bag in the fridge for up to 2 weeks or tightly sealed in a double bag in the freezer for up to 2 months.

Daikon Dissolver

This formula is very helpful to dissolve fat and mucus in the body. Daikon is a generous variety of radish with firm, white flesh and a characteristically spicy flavor. It's prized for its cleansing and stimulating properties. Small, red-skinned radishes may be used, though daikon is the best for this tonic. Carrot may be added for a gentle, natural sweetness.

YIELDS: 2 SERVINGS

2   cups finely grated daikon

½   cup finely grated carrot

2   cups filtered water

2   teaspoons umeboshi plum vinegar

½   teaspoon shoyu (soy sauce)

1   nori sheet, torn into pieces (optional)

Place the daikon and carrot in a saucepan with the water and bring to a gentle boil.

Reduce the heat and simmer for 2 to 3 minutes.

Add the vinegar, shoyu, and nori (if desired). Simmer for 30 seconds and remove from the heat.

Strain (or leave pulpy) and drink hot.

NUTRITION AT A GLANCE
Per serving: 50 calories, 0 g total fat, 0 g saturated fat, 2 g protein, 13 g carbohydrates, 4 g dietary fiber, 85 mg sodium

Molokai Chai

I always say that I leave a piece of my heart on Molokai, a sleepy island of old Hawaii, where a beautiful friend and advanced yogi, Karen Noble, taught me to make chai from whole spices. Whole spices are the key. This brew is far better than anything available in a store. I add fresh vanilla bean or extract; star anise, which has a lovely licorice flavor; and black peppercorns for a spicy kick. I often make a generous batch of the spice concentrate, which stores well in the refrigerator for more than a week.

YIELDS: 4 SERVINGS (ABOUT A QUART)

2   cups Chai Spice Concentrate

2   tea bags (green, white, or black tea)

2   tablespoons maple syrup, honey, or agave, or to taste

2   cups unsweetened Pure Almond Milk (page 166) or soymilk

In a saucepan, bring the chai spice concentrate to a boil and turn off the heat. Steep the tea bags in the concentrate for 3 to 5 minutes. Remove the tea bags and squeeze out any liquid into the tea. Stir in the maple syrup, honey, or agave to taste. Add the almond milk or soymilk. Warm over medium-low heat until piping hot.

CHAI SPICE CONCENTRATE

YIELDS: 1 QUART

4–5   cinnamon sticks (each 3"), broken

1   vanilla bean, split in half, or 2–3 teaspoons pure vanilla extract

1   whole nutmeg, coarsely chopped

6–8   whole cardamom pods (1 teaspoon whole seeds may be used)

3   whole star anise, roughly broken

2–4   tablespoons finely shredded ginger

3   black peppercorns, bruised

3   whole cloves

    Pinch of sea salt

6   cups filtered water

Place the cinnamon, vanilla bean or extract, nutmeg, cardamom, star anise, ginger, peppercorns, cloves, salt, and water in a stockpot and bring to a boil.

Reduce heat to low and simmer for 25 to 30 minutes. Strain through a fine strainer or sieve. If there is a lot of sediment, try straining through a strainer or sieve lined with cheesecloth. The brew may be simmered longer to reduce volume and concentrate the flavor.

NOTE: *The spices may be used again for a second batch, reducing the water by half.*

NUTRITION AT A GLANCE
Per serving (1 cup): 60 calories, 1.5 g total fat, 0 g saturated fat, 1 g protein, 11 g carbohydrates, 0 g dietary fiber, 100 mg sodium

Flu-Buster Tonic

This homemade version of expensive tincture formulas sold in natural food stores has quite a kick! It stimulates circulation and really stands up to an assault on the immune system.

YIELDS: 8 SERVINGS

½   cup apple cider vinegar

1–2   cloves garlic (optional)

¼   cup finely shredded ginger

2   teaspoons wasabi powder, or to taste

1   teaspoon cayenne pepper, or to taste

2–4   tablespoons raw honey

In a blender, combine the vinegar, garlic (if desired), and ginger and blend until smooth. Pour through a fine strainer and press with the back of a spoon to extract as much juice as possible. Discard pulp.

Whisk in the wasabi, cayenne, and honey. Store in a glass jar in the refrigerator.

Serve 2 tablespoons at a time on an empty stomach. Add to 1 cup hot water for a warming tonic.

NUTRITION AT A GLANCE
Per serving: 25 calories, 0 g total fat, 0 g saturated fat, 0 g protein, 7 g carbohydrates, 0 g dietary fiber, 5 mg sodium

Ginger Ume Kudzu

This tonic soothes stomach and digestive disorders. Kudzu, an Asian root vegetable that is ground and dried into a white powder, is used as a thickening agent and energy source.

YIELDS: 2 CUPS

2   heaping teaspoons kudzu

2   cups filtered water, divided

1   tablespoon umeboshi plum vinegar

1   teaspoon umeboshi plum paste (optional)

1–2   teaspoons shoyu (soy sauce)

1–2   teaspoons finely shredded ginger

In a saucepan, dissolve the kudzu in ¼ cup water.

Add the remaining water and bring to a boil over medium heat, whisking constantly to avoid clumping, until the mixture is clear.

Reduce the heat to as low as possible and stir in the vinegar, plum paste, shoyu, and ginger. Gently simmer for 2 minutes. Drink hot.

NUTRITION AT A GLANCE
Per serving: 15 calories, 0 g total fat, 0 g saturated fat, 0 g protein, 3 g carbohydrates, 0 g dietary fiber, 1,710 mg sodium

Pomegranate Ginger Saketini

This beautiful, scarlet cocktail is abundant in antioxidants from the fresh pomegranate juice. It's perfect in the autumn, when pomegranates are at their peak. Just a touch of ginger is gorgeous, but too much will pierce the other flavors too strongly. A touch of maple syrup is lovely, especially if the pomegranate is tart.

YIELDS: 2 SERVINGS (A BIT MORE THAN A PINT)

1   **pomegranate**

1   **teaspoon finely chopped ginger**

1–2 **teaspoons maple syrup (optional)**

1   **cup sake, chilled**

      Thin slices of pear

Cut the pomegranate into quarters. Separate the seeds from the skin and pith. Place the seeds in a blender or food processor with the ginger and maple syrup (if desired). Blend until fairly smooth. It may be necessary to add a bit of sake to help get it going.

Pour through a strainer or sieve to separate the juice from the pulp. Press the pulp with the back of a large spoon to extract as much juice as possible. The strainer or sieve may be lined with cheesecloth, which can be used to squeeze the pulp to extract as much juice as possible.

Mix the pomegranate-ginger juice with the sake and serve with a thin slice of pear.

NUTRITION AT A GLANCE
Per serving: 240 calories, 0 g total fat, 0 g saturated fat, 1 g protein, 27 g carbohydrates, 0 g dietary fiber, 15 mg sodium

Old-World Sangria

My friend Lavinia inspired this recipe, which has been in her family for a few generations. We would make it in late summer and early fall when the days are still hot and the fruit in the orchard is ripe. I recommend an average merlot or cabernet as the complexity of a big wine will get lost in the fruit, plus it is served chilled, which will snuff out the subtleties. Make this sangria at least an hour ahead so the flavors have time to meld.

YIELDS: 4 SERVINGS (A BIT MORE THAN A QUART)

1   bottle red wine, a fruity Merlot or Cabernet works well

1   sweet apple, cored and cut into ½" cubes

1   firm pear, Anjou or Bosc are nice, cored and cut into ½" cubes

12   grapes, halved

2–4   plums, pits removed, cut into ½" cubes

2–4   tablespoons agave nectar, maple syrup, or a mixture of both (optional)

1   orange, cut into ⅛" slices, seeds removed

In a large glass pitcher, mix together the wine, apple, pear, grapes, plums, agave and/or maple syrup (if desired), and orange.

Allow to chill in the fridge for at least an hour before serving, though it's best left overnight.

Serve over ice in a red wine goblet.

NUTRITION AT A GLANCE
Per serving (without fruit): 210 calories, 0 g total fat, 0 g saturated fat, 0 g protein, 6 g carbohydrates, 0 g dietary fiber, 10 mg sodium

Summer Sangria Blanco

*This white wine sangria is reminiscent of a zurra from the south of Spain.
I recommend a dry white wine such as chardonnay or sauvignon blanc. Peaches,
nectarines, and apricots are my favorite, but by all means, use any ripe, seasonal
fruit that strikes your festive fancy.*

YIELDS: 4 SERVINGS (A BIT MORE THAN A QUART)

1	bottle dry white wine, like chardonnay or sauvignon blanc
1–2	peaches, pits removed, cut into ¼" pieces
1–2	nectarines, pits removed, cut into ¼" pieces
2–4	apricots, pits removed, cut into ¼" pieces
12	green grapes, quartered
1	lemon, cut into ⅛" slices, seeds removed
2–4	tablespoons agave nectar (optional)

In a large glass pitcher, mix together the wine, peaches, nectarines, apricots, grapes, lemon, and agave (if desired).

Allow to chill in the fridge for at least an hour before serving, though it's happiest when left overnight.

Serve over ice in wine goblets.

NUTRITION AT A GLANCE

Per serving (without fruit): 200 calories, 0 g total fat, 0 g saturated fat, 0 g protein, 5 g carbohydrates,
0 g dietary fiber, 10 mg sodium

If fruit is consumed: 250 calories, 0 g total fat, 0 g saturated fat, 1 g protein, 16 g carbohydrates,
1 g dietary fiber, 0 mg sodium

Fresh Lime and Sake Margarita

There are many tales of just how the margarita was invented, but my favorite is that it was made for silver-screen beauty Rita Hayworth, whose full name was Margarita. A classic margarita is made with tequila, Triple Sec, and lime juice with a salted rim. I concoct it with fresh orange and lime juice, and sake, with the occasional splash of tequila. I wax and wane in favor of salting the rim of the glass. It is delicious, but it makes me thirsty, and I've been known to suck it down a little too fast from time to time.

YIELDS: 2 SERVINGS (ABOUT A PINT)

Medium-ground sea salt (optional for salted rim)

Lime wedges (optional for salted rim)

Ice

½ cup freshly squeezed orange juice

¼ cup freshly squeezed lime juice

1–2 tablespoons agave nectar (optional)

1 cup sake, chilled

1 ounce tequila, like Silver Patrón

If you prefer a salted rim: Place enough salt on a small plate to coat the rim of a tumbler glass. Use a wedge of lime to moisten the rim of the tumbler and press the rim into the salt. Repeat with the second glass.

Fill each tumbler with ice.

In a large pitcher, stir together the orange and lime juices, agave (if desired), sake, and tequila (if desired). Distribute evenly between the glasses and serve immediately.

NUTRITION AT A GLANCE
Per serving: 190 calories, 0 g total fat, 0 g saturated fat, 1 g protein, 15 g carbohydrates, 0 g dietary fiber, 0 mg sodium

---

Salt is born of the purest of parents:
the sun and the sea.

PYTHAGORAS (580 BC–500 BC)

Silver Mint Mojito

This is a new twist on a classic cocktail choosing sake and tequila over rum because they burn more cleanly with less hangover. Using sake solo makes it milder, but for extra-festive occasions, I add tequila, which is made from the same cactus as agave and is actually a stimulant where all other alcohol is a depressant. Silver Patrón is my choice because it is smooth with a refreshing kick of fruit and in moderation burns cleanly in the body.

YIELDS: 2 SERVINGS (ABOUT 1½ PINTS)

1½   cups fresh mint leaves, washed

1¼   cups freshly squeezed lime juice

6   tablespoons agave nectar, or to taste

1¼   cups sake, chilled

2   ounces Silver Patrón tequila (optional)

Ice

8   ounces sparkling water

Divide the mint, lime juice, and agave evenly between 2 glasses. Mash with a wooden pestle, muddler, or spoon. Divide the sake, tequila (if desired), ice, and sparkling water between the 2 glasses. Serve immediately.

NUTRITION AT A GLANCE
Per serving (1½ cups): 290 calories, 0 g total fat, 0 g saturated fat, 1 g protein, 36 g carbohydrates, 0 g dietary fiber, 10 mg sodium

---

Velvet Nutmeg Nog

Traditional eggnog is laden with heavy cream and eggs, and enough cholesterol to kill a moose. This creamy, sweet nog delivers all of the festive holiday cheer without clogging your precious arteries. Fresh nutmeg and vanilla intoxicate the senses. Traditional eggnog is spiked with rum, but sake is my passion and is less likely to cause a foggy morning-after. By all means, this recipe is decadent and delicious even as a virgin. Add the coconut butter for a silkier drink, or skip it for a lower-fat version.

YIELDS: 4 SERVINGS (1 QUART)

1   cup raw cashews, soaked 2 hours in filtered water, drained, and rinsed

3   cups filtered water

1   tablespoon Omega Nutrition coconut butter (optional)

3–4   tablespoons maple syrup

2–4   tablespoons agave nectar

1   teaspoon freshly ground nutmeg

2   teaspoons nonalcoholic vanilla extract

Pinch of sea salt

1–2   cups sake

2–4   ounces rum (optional)

Place the cashews, water, coconut butter (if desired), maple syrup, agave, nutmeg, vanilla, and salt in a blender. Blend at high speed until smooth. Pour through a strainer or sieve and press with the back of a large spoon to extract as much liquid as possible. If the strainer is not fine enough to separate the pulp, you may want to line it with cheesecloth, which can be used to squeeze the pulp to extract as much liquid as possible.

Pour into a pitcher and add the sake and the rum, if desired.

Cheers!

NUTRITION AT A GLANCE
Per serving: 140 calories, 4 g total fat, 0.5 g saturated fat, 2 g protein, 10 g carbohydrates, 0 g dietary fiber, 45 mg sodium

CHAPTER 5

Soups for All Seasons

Soup is to the meal, what the hostesses' smile of welcome is to the party. A prelude to the goodness to come.

—LOUIS P. DE GOUY

Stocks

Soup is a staple in my kitchen. I keep homemade stock in the fridge or the freezer at all times. It's a flavorful, fortified foundation for so many recipes, including quick soups that taste like you worked through the night. These stocks can be easily modified using what you have on hand to create the flavor you want. Light-colored vegetables will create a pale stock with a subtler flavor. Vegetables can be roasted first for a darker, richer stock. You can even caramelize vegetables for stock with a deep amber color. The possibilities are endless, and the bounty of each season brings new delights for nourishment and pleasure.

Kombu Dashi

Kombu dashi is a delicate, clear Japanese soup stock. It is used in many traditional dishes and is a fortified base for miso soup. Kombu is a type of kelp, rich in minerals with a deep, gentle flavor. You can store the stock in a sealed jar in the fridge for up to 4 days.

YIELDS: 4 SERVINGS

1   6" strip kombu seaweed

4   cups filtered water

5   dried shiitake mushrooms

In a stockpot, soak the kombu in the water for 2 hours. Heat to a gentle boil. Add the dried mushrooms. Turn off the heat, cover, and let stand for 20 minutes. Strain or remove the kombu and mushrooms with a slotted spoon. Discard the kombu. The mushrooms can be sliced and used in the soup or reserved for another dish.

NUTRITION AT A GLANCE
Per serving: 15 calories, 0 g total fat, 0 g saturated fat, 0 g protein, 4 g carbohydrates, 0 g dietary fiber, 15 mg sodium

Light Vegetable Stock

This clear, pure stock is a lovely base for any vegetable soup, especially matched with seasonal spring and summer ingredients. As with all of my stocks, this should be made without salt, to keep the flavors unadulterated as they concentrate.

YIELDS: 12 SERVINGS (1 GALLON)

1 bunch celery, washed and coarsely chopped, including base

3 large yellow onions, papery skin removed, coarsely chopped

2 leeks, split lengthwise, washed, and coarsely chopped, including greens

1 bulb garlic, unpeeled, cloves separated and cut in half

4 carrots, tops cut off, scrubbed and coarsely chopped

4–6 new potatoes, fingerling potatoes, or Jerusalem artichokes, scrubbed and coarsely chopped

1 bunch flat-leaf parsley, including stems

1 fennel bulb, feathery leaves removed, coarsely chopped (optional)

2 bay leaves

Place all of the ingredients in a large stockpot (or two) and add enough filtered water to cover by 2", leaving a few inches at the top of the pot so the stock doesn't boil over.

Bring to a boil. Reduce the heat and simmer for at least 1 hour (the longer you simmer, the more concentrated the flavor).

Cool and strain the stock through a sieve or strainer. Press with the back of a spoon to extract as much liquid as possible.

Once the stock has cooled completely, store in sealed glass jars in the refrigerator for 3 to 4 days, or in sealed containers or freezer bags in the freezer for 6 to 8 weeks.

NUTRITION AT A GLANCE
Per serving: 15 calories, 0 g total fat, 0 g saturated fat, 0 g protein, 4 g carbohydrates, 0 g dietary fiber, 20 mg sodium

Hearty Vegetable Stock

Thanks to an abundance of fall and winter root vegetables, this stock has a beautiful deep color and a complex flavor.

YIELDS: 12 SERVINGS (1 GALLON)

2	red onions, papery skin removed, coarsely chopped
1	yellow onion, papery skin removed, coarsely chopped
6–8	shallots, papery skin removed, coarsely chopped
1	bunch celery, washed and coarsely chopped, including base
1	bulb garlic, unpeeled, cloves separated and cut in half
4	carrots, tops discarded, scrubbed and coarsely chopped
2	parsnips, tops discarded, scrubbed and coarsely chopped
2	turnips, tops discarded, scrubbed and coarsely chopped
1	pound mushrooms, coarsely chopped
4–6	sun-dried tomatoes (optional)
1	bunch flat-leaf parsley, including stems
4	bay leaves
2	stems fresh thyme
2	teaspoons whole black peppercorns

Place all of the ingredients in a large stockpot (or two) and add enough filtered water to cover by 2", leaving a few inches at the top of the pot so the stock doesn't boil over.

Bring to a boil. Reduce the heat and simmer for at least 1 hour (the longer you simmer, the more concentrated the flavor).

Cool and strain the stock through a sieve or strainer. Press with the back of a spoon to extract as much liquid as possible.

Once the stock has cooled completely, store in sealed glass jars in the refrigerator for 3 to 4 days, or in sealed containers or freezer bags in the freezer for 6 to 8 weeks.

NUTRITION AT A GLANCE
Per serving: 20 calories, 0 g total fat, 0 g saturated fat, 1 g protein, 4 g carbohydrates, 1 g dietary fiber, 30 mg sodium

Roasted Vegetable Stock

YIELDS: 12 SERVINGS (1 GALLON)

1   red onion, papery skin removed, cut into 8 wedges

2   yellow onions, papery skin removed, cut into 8 wedges

6–8   shallots, papery skin removed, or 1 leek, trimmed and cut into 1" pieces

1   bunch celery, washed and coarsely chopped, including base

1   bulb garlic, papery skin removed and pointed top cut off

4   carrots, scrubbed, trimmed, and cut into 1" pieces

2   potatoes, scrubbed and cut into 8 wedges

2   turnips, scrubbed, trimmed, and cut into 8 wedges

1   celery root, scrubbed, trimmed, and cut into 8 wedges (optional)

1   pound mushrooms

¼   cup extra-virgin olive oil

1   bunch flat-leaf parsley, including stems

2   bay leaves

2   teaspoons whole black peppercorns (optional)

NOTE: *The veggies can be roasted (or technically baked) without oil, though the oil seals in the flavor, moisture, and the nutrients.*

Preheat the oven to 375°F.

Toss the red onion, yellow onions, shallots or leek, celery, garlic, carrots, potatoes, turnips, celery root, and mushrooms with the olive oil. This may be done in one or two batches in a large bowl, or in a large stockpot, which will be used to cook the stock in after roasting (to save washing extra dishes!).

Arrange the vegetables in a single layer in one or two roasting pans or on baking sheets. If you overcrowd the pans, the vegetables will steam instead of roasting and caramelizing.

Bake for 20 to 25 minutes, or until tender, golden, and fragrant.

Place the roasted veggies in a large stockpot (or two) with the parsley, bay leaves, and peppercorns, if desired, and add enough filtered water to cover by 2", leaving a few inches at the top of the pot so the stock doesn't boil over.

Bring to a boil. Reduce the heat and simmer for at least 1 hour (the longer you simmer, the more concentrated the flavor).

Cool and strain the stock through a sieve or strainer. Press with the back of a spoon to extract as much liquid as possible.

Once the stock has cooled completely, store in sealed glass jars in the refrigerator for 3 to 4 days, or in sealed containers or freezer bags in the freezer for 6 to 8 weeks.

NUTRITION AT A GLANCE
Per serving: 50 calories, 2.5 g total fat, 0 g saturated fat, 1 g protein, 7 g carbohydrates, 1 g dietary fiber, 35 mg sodium

Onion Stock

This stock captures the pure, sweet essence of onions and fills the kitchen with a comforting aroma. Different onions will yield different flavors: My favorite is a mixture that includes sweet onions. The onions may be roasted first for a sweeter, richer stock.

YIELDS: 8 SERVINGS (2 QUARTS)

8–10   **onions (red, yellow, white, sweet, or a mixture), peeled and cut into ½" wedges**

Olive oil (if desired)

If you wish to roast the onions first:

Preheat the oven to 350°F. Toss the wedges with just enough olive oil to lightly coat. Arrange the onions in a single layer in one or two roasting pans or on baking sheets. Bake for 20 to 25 minutes, or until tender.

Place the prepared onions in a large stockpot, and add enough filtered water to cover by 2", leaving a few inches at the top of the pot so the stock doesn't boil over.

Bring to a boil. Reduce the heat and simmer for at least 1 hour (the longer you simmer, the more concentrated the flavor).

Cool and strain the stock through a sieve or strainer. Press with the back of a spoon to extract as much liquid as possible.

Once the stock has cooled completely, store in sealed glass jars in the refrigerator for 3 to 4 days, or in sealed containers or freezer bags in the freezer for 6 to 8 weeks.

NUTRITION AT A GLANCE
Per serving: 50 calories, 3.5 g total fat, 0 g saturated fat, 0 g protein, 5 g carbohydrates, 0 g dietary fiber, 0 mg sodium

Mushroom Stock

A rich mushroom stock can be used as a substitute in many soups that traditionally call for beef stock. Any and all mushrooms may be used. I find the addition of dried mushrooms (especially porcini mushrooms) cedes a savory complexity. The mushrooms may be roasted for 20 to 30 minutes at 350°F before adding them to the stockpot to enrich the flavor.

YIELDS: 6 SERVINGS (1½ TO 2 QUARTS)

4   **pounds fresh mushrooms, including stems**

1   **cup dried mushrooms**

Place the mushrooms in a stockpot and add enough filtered water to cover by 2", leaving a few inches at the top of the pot so the stock doesn't boil over.

Bring to a boil. Reduce the heat and simmer for at least 1 hour (the longer you simmer, the more concentrated the flavor).

Cool and strain the stock through a sieve or strainer. Press with the back of a spoon to extract as much liquid as possible.

Once the stock has cooled completely, store in sealed glass jars in the refrigerator for 3 to 4 days, or in sealed containers or freezer bags in the freezer for 6 to 8 weeks.

NUTRITION AT A GLANCE
Per serving: 40 calories, 0 g total fat, 0 g saturated fat, 4 g protein, 6 g carbohydrates, 2 g dietary fiber, 40 mg sodium

---

Both day and night everything we encounter is our life.
Because of that, we put our life
into everything we encounter.
Our life and what we are encountering become one.

—UCHIYAMA ROSHI

Miso Soup for All Seasons

Miso broth is liquid nourishment. Simple and satisfying. Any of the many varieties of miso may be used. Darker-colored miso has a deeper and stronger flavor (a fine fall and winter choice); lighter-colored miso is more gentle and sweet (superb for spring and summer). I love to mix and match to meet my mood. Using vegetable, mushroom, or kombu dashi stock instead of water fortifies a simple miso soup with flavor and nutrients. Serving it with pickles and a small bowl of whole grain fits the order for a macrobiotic breakfast or power snack.

YIELDS: 4 SERVINGS

4   cups filtered water

¼   pound soft tofu, cut into ½" cubes (optional)

2   teaspoons dried wakame seaweed (optional)

4   tablespoons red or yellow miso

2   green onions, cleaned and sliced finely to the top

Place the water in a medium stockpot and bring to a boil. Reduce the heat to medium. Add the tofu and wakame, if desired, and simmer for 2 to 3 minutes, uncovered.

Pour ¼ cup of the hot water into a small bowl. Add the miso and stir to dissolve, preferably with a wooden spoon.

Return the miso mixture to the stockpot and add the green onions. Reduce the heat to low and allow to simmer for 1 more minute. Adjust to taste with a touch more miso or a bit more water, as desired.

Serve immediately.

NUTRITION AT A GLANCE
Per serving: 30 calories, 1 g total fat, 0 g saturated fat, 2 g protein, 4 g carbohydrates, 0 g dietary fiber, 750 mg sodium

Spring and Summer Miso Soup

YIELDS: 4 SERVINGS

4   cups filtered water, **Light Vegetable Stock (page 178),** or **Kombu Dashi (page 177)**

4   **radishes (ideally with tops), roots trimmed and thinly sliced, greens trimmed and chopped**

3   **shiitake mushrooms, stems removed and sliced (optional)**

½   **cup snap peas or tender green beans, sliced on an angle, or ½ cup shelled green peas (choose what looks best in the market)**

4   **tablespoons sweet white miso or garbanzo bean miso**

2   **green onions, cleaned and sliced finely to the top**

1   **teaspoon lemon juice**

Finely chopped parsley, cilantro, or mixture of both, as desired for garnish

Pour the water or stock into a medium stockpot and bring to a boil. Reduce heat to medium-low. Add the radish roots, mushrooms (if desired), and green beans (if using), and simmer for 5 minutes, uncovered.

Add the radish greens and snap peas or shelled peas (if using) and allow to simmer for 2 to 3 minutes, or until tender.

Pour ¼ cup of the broth into a small bowl. Add the miso and stir to dissolve, preferably with a wooden spoon.

Return the miso mixture to the stockpot and add the green onions. Reduce heat to low and allow to simmer for 1 more minute. Adjust to taste with a touch more miso or a bit more water, as desired.

Stir in the lemon juice and serve immediately garnished with parsley and/or cilantro.

NUTRITION AT A GLANCE
Per serving: 45 calories, 1 g total fat, 0 g saturated fat, 4 g protein, 9 g carbohydrates, 4 g dietary fiber, 550 mg sodium

Autumn and Winter Miso Soup

YIELDS: 4 SERVINGS

4   cups filtered water, Hearty Vegetable Stock (page 179), or Kombu Dashi (page 177)

1   turnip or parsnip, scrubbed, trimmed, and cut into ¼" pieces

1   carrot, scrubbed, trimmed, and sliced into thin rounds

1   cup finely sliced leek

¼   pound soft tofu, cut into ½" pieces (optional)

2   tablespoons dried wakame seaweed (optional)

4   tablespoons red rice or barley miso

2   green onions

Finely chopped parsley for garnish, as desired

Drizzle of sesame oil and umeboshi plum vinegar for garnish, as desired

Pour the water or stock into a medium stockpot and bring to a boil. Reduce heat to medium. Add the turnip or parsnip and simmer for 5 minutes. Reduce heat to medium-low. Add the carrot and leek and simmer for 3 to 5 minutes. Add the tofu and wakame, if desired, and simmer another 2 to 3 minutes.

Pour ¼ cup of the broth into a small bowl. Add the miso and stir to dissolve, preferably with a wooden spoon.

Return the miso mixture to the stockpot and add the green onions. Reduce heat to low and allow to simmer for 1 more minute. Adjust to taste with a touch more miso or a bit more water, as desired.

Serve immediately garnished with chopped parsley and a drizzle of sesame oil and umeboshi plum vinegar, as desired.

NUTRITION AT A GLANCE
Per serving: 60 calories, 1 g total fat, 0 g saturated fat, 3 g protein, 10 g carbohydrates, 2 g dietary fiber, 780 mg sodium

Spring and Summer House Soup

This smooth soup is a blank canvas for the bounty of spring and summer. It's also an easy weeknight dish, as the veggies are simply cut, simmered, and blended. The Jerusalem artichoke, also known as a sunchoke after its family ties to the sunflower, is a great low-starch root vegetable that blends smooth as cream.

YIELDS: 6 SERVINGS

1	onion, roughly chopped (a sweet onion like Vidalia or Walla Walla is best)
2	carrots, roughly chopped
2	ribs celery, roughly chopped
2	cups roughly chopped Jerusalem artichokes (fingerling or new potatoes may be used instead)
1	medium zucchini, roughly chopped
4	cups Light Vegetable Stock (page 178), or as needed (see note)
1	leek, roughly chopped to the top
2–3	tomatoes, quartered
3–6	tablespoons olive oil
	Coarse sea salt
1½–2	cups basil leaves; reserve a pinch for garnish
1–1½	cups parsley leaves; reserve a pinch for garnish
½	cup cilantro leaves (optional)
1	tablespoon fresh thyme (optional)
	Freshly ground black pepper

In a large stockpot, place the onion, carrots, celery, Jerusalem artichokes or potatoes, and zucchini. Cover with stock by 1". Bring to a boil. Reduce heat and simmer for 10 to 12 minutes. Add the leek and tomatoes and simmer another 8 to 10 minutes, or until the Jerusalem artichokes or potatoes are soft enough to mash with the back of a fork and the leek is soft. Be careful not to overcook or you'll sacrifice the bright flavors.

Using an emersion blender (a handheld wand blender), blend the soup until smooth. Add the olive oil, salt, basil, parsley, and cilantro and thyme (if desired). Adjust to taste.

Or, allow the soup to cool a bit and blend in batches in a blender or food processor until smooth, adding the olive oil, salt, and herbs to taste.

Season with freshly ground black pepper and garnish with chopped fresh herbs.

NOTE: *In a pinch, organic, prepared vegetable broth may be used, or filtered water and natural bouillon cubes.*

NUTRITION AT A GLANCE
Per serving: 170 calories, 8 g total fat, 1 g saturated fat, 4 g protein, 24 g carbohydrates, 5 g dietary fiber, 450 mg sodium

Autumn and Winter House Soup

This soup will warm the body and soul with round, full flavor in the colder seasons.
Easy substitutions can be made depending on what is available in the market. It is
quick to make any day of the week, and leftovers are perfect for lunch.

YIELDS: 6 SERVINGS

1   large yellow onion, diced

1   red onion, diced

4–6   shallots, peeled and chopped

3   cloves garlic, minced

2   carrots, scrubbed or peeled and roughly chopped

2   parsnips or 2 to 3 turnips, scrubbed or peeled and roughly chopped

2   ribs celery, roughly chopped

1   medium sweet potato or yam, peeled and roughly chopped, or ½ winter squash (red kuri, kabocha, or butternut), peeled and seeded

4"   sprig rosemary

2   teaspoons fresh thyme or 1 teaspoon dried

½   teaspoon ground chipotle pepper (optional)

4   cups Hearty Vegetable Stock (page 179), or as needed (see note)

4–6   tablespoons olive oil

1–1½   cups parsley leaves

2–3   tablespoons chopped fresh oregano

Sea salt

Freshly ground black pepper

In a medium-large stockpot, place the yellow and red onions; shallots; garlic; carrots; parsnips or turnips; celery; sweet potato, yam, or squash; rosemary; thyme; and chipotle (if desired). Cover with stock by 1". Bring to a boil. Reduce heat and simmer for about 15 minutes, or until the vegetables are soft enough to easily pierce with a fork.

Using an emersion blender (a handheld wand blender), blend the soup until smooth. Add the olive oil, parsley, oregano, and salt and pepper. Adjust to taste.

Or, allow the soup to cool a bit and blend in batches in a blender or food processor until smooth, adding the olive oil, herbs, and salt and pepper to taste.

NOTE: *In a pinch, organic, prepared vegetable broth may be used, or filtered water and natural bouillon cubes.*

NUTRITION AT A GLANCE
Per serving: 200 calories, 9 g total fat, 1.5 g saturated fat, 2 g protein, 27 g carbohydrates, 5 g dietary fiber, 270 mg sodium

Andalusian Gazpacho with Avocado Sorbet

There are many interpretations of gazpacho, all raw-food friendly by nature. This version is inspired by the Andalusia region of southern Spain, the home of gazpacho. The chipotle pepper lends a smoky sweet light heat that I just love, though I leave it out for friends who can't tolerate spicy foods. The avocado sorbet is absolutely divine. I eat a little bowl of the sorbet by itself when no one is looking.

YIELDS: 6 SERVINGS

GAZPACHO

1	pound tomatoes (about 4)
1	large red bell pepper
3	green onions, trimmed and cleaned
2	small cloves garlic
1	medium sweet onion
10	basil leaves
2–2½	tablespoons chopped fresh oregano or 1 tablespoon dried
2	tablespoons chopped cilantro leaves
1	teaspoon fresh thyme or ½ teaspoon dried
2–4	tablespoons extra-virgin olive oil
2	tablespoons lemon juice
1	teaspoon organic sugar or maple syrup (optional if tomatoes are really sweet)

1	teaspoon aged balsamic vinegar, or ½ teaspoon balsamic vinegar + ½ teaspoon maple syrup
1	teaspoon apple cider vinegar
¼	teaspoon prepared mustard (optional)
¼	teaspoon whole coriander seeds or ground coriander
¼	teaspoon ground chipotle pepper (optional)
¼	teaspoon salt
¼	teaspoon freshly ground black pepper
1	tablespoon chopped basil (for garnish)
1	teaspoon chopped cilantro (for garnish)

AVOCADO SORBET

2	cups cilantro leaves
½	cup chopped green onions (3–4)
¼	cup lime juice
1	teaspoon lime zest (go organic!)
1	small clove garlic
3	tablespoons olive oil

2	cups cubed avocado (about 2)
1	teaspoon shoyu (soy sauce)
1	teaspoon umeboshi plum vinegar
1	teaspoon whole cumin seeds, or ⅓ teaspoon ground cumin seed
½	teaspoon sea salt
¼	teaspoon freshly ground black pepper

TO MAKE THE GAZPACHO:

Cut the tomatoes in half. Use clean fingers to scoop out the stem and seeds. Finely dice two halves and reserve. Chop the remaining tomatoes roughly and place in a blender (preferably a high-speed model like the Vita-Mix) or a food processor.

Cut the bell pepper in half. Remove the stem, seeds, and veins. Finely dice half of the pepper and reserve. Chop the rest roughly and place in the blender or processor with the tomato.

Chop one green onion finely and reserve. Chop the others roughly and add with the garlic to the blender or processor.

Cut off the ends of the onion and peel the skin. Mince one-quarter of the onion and reserve. Roughly chop the rest and add to the blender or processor.

Add the basil, oregano, cilantro, thyme, olive oil, lemon juice, sugar or maple syrup, aged balsamic (or balsamic + maple syrup), apple cider vinegar, and mustard (if desired) to the blender.

Toast the coriander seeds in a skillet over low heat for a few minutes until fragrant. Crush in a mortar and pestle or spice grinder. Add to the blender or processor. Or, if using ground corian-der, add it directly to the blender or processor. Add the chipotle pepper, salt, and black pepper and blend until silky smooth.

Place in a large serving bowl and fold in the reserved diced tomatoes, bell peppers, green onion, and sweet onion. Add 1 tablespoon of chopped basil and 1 teaspoon of chopped cilantro. Chill for 15 minutes to 2 hours before serving. This soup can be made a day ahead and will keep for 3 to 4 days.

TO MAKE THE SORBET:

Place the cilantro in a food processor and chop finely. Add the green onions, lime juice, lime zest, garlic, olive oil, avocado, shoyu, and vinegar. Blend until smooth.

Toast the whole cumin seeds in a heavy skillet over low heat for a few minutes, or until fragrant. Crush in a mortar and pestle or spice grinder. Add to the processor. Or, add the ground cumin seed directly to the processor. Season with salt and pepper and blend until ultra-smooth.

Freeze in an ice cream machine according to the manufacturer's directions.

Serve a small scoop over the gazpacho and store any leftovers in the freezer.

NUTRITION AT A GLANCE
Per serving: 230 calories, 20 g total fat, 3 g saturated fat, 3 g protein, 14 g carbohydrates, 5 g dietary fiber, 520 mg sodium

Spring Cucumber Watercress Soup

*Fresh cucumber rounded out with creamy pine nuts and peppered with watercress
is a great, light course for a seasonal spring menu. A touch of ginger and white miso
lends lovely layers of subtle taste. English cucumbers are a longer variety with
thin skin and little to no seeds. Peel and remove the seeds of common cucumbers
to yield a fine, smooth texture.*

YIELDS: 6 SERVINGS

½   **cup pine nuts**

1   **cup filtered water, plus additional if needed**

2–4   **tablespoons olive oil**

2   **tablespoons lemon juice**

2   **teaspoons agave nectar**

2   **teaspoons white miso**

2   **teaspoons finely grated ginger**

½   **clove garlic**

4   **cups chopped English cucumbers (common cucumbers may be used)**

  Sea salt

1   **bunch watercress, cleaned and roughly chopped**

¾   **cup chopped mint leaves**

½   **cup chopped parsley leaves**

2   **green onions, cleaned and chopped**

  Freshly ground black pepper, for garnish

In a blender, blend the pine nuts, water, olive oil, lemon juice, agave nectar, miso, ginger, and garlic until very smooth.

Add the cucumbers to the blender and blend until smooth, adding additional water as necessary to achieve the desired thickness. Season to taste with salt.

Add the watercress, mint, parsley, and green onions and blend in pulses until well mixed, but pieces of herbs are still visible.

Serve chilled, garnished with freshly ground black pepper.

NUTRITION AT A GLANCE
Per serving: 140 calories, 12 g total fat, 1 g saturated fat, 3 g protein, 5 g carbohydrates, 2 g dietary fiber, 160 mg sodium

Tuscan Pomodoro Soup

*The quintessence of the Italian countryside is enveloped in this chunky tomato soup.
Caramelized onions draw out the natural sweetness of the tomatoes, and ample fresh
basil is a must. Traditionally, the soup is served with stale bread to soak up the flavor
and add body, though it is divine without the bread for a lighter course. This soup
keeps well and is almost better the second day.*

YIELDS: 8 SERVINGS

2½ cups chopped yellow onions

½ cup olive oil, divided

2 teaspoons balsamic vinegar

2 teaspoons maple syrup or organic
sugar

2–4 cloves garlic, slivered

4 pounds ripe tomatoes, chopped with
their juices, or canned organic whole
or diced tomatoes

2 cups vegetable stock, packaged broth,
or filtered water, plus additional if
needed

Sea salt

Freshly ground black pepper

½ loaf stale or lightly toasted bread

2–3 cups fresh basil leaves

In a medium-large stockpot, heat the onions and
¼ cup of the olive oil over medium heat, stirring
occasionally, for 15 minutes, or until the onions
are very soft, translucent, and caramelized.

Add the vinegar, maple syrup or sugar, and
garlic and continue to cook and stir for 2 to 3
minutes.

Add the tomatoes with juices. Stir together
and allow to simmer for 30 minutes, stirring
occasionally to concentrate the tomatoes.

Add the vegetable broth or water and bring to
a simmer again. Season to taste with salt and
pepper.

Remove the crust of the bread if it is too thick
and tough. Tear into pieces and fold into the
soup. Allow to stand until the bread absorbs the
liquid. Add more vegetable broth or water if the
soup becomes too thick.

Tear the basil leaves and stir into the soup with
the remaining ¼ cup of olive oil. Allow to cool to
serving temperature, which will let the bread
absorb the flavors of the basil and olive oil.

If desired, drizzle each serving with additional
olive oil, a pinch of sea salt, and freshly ground
black pepper.

NUTRITION AT A GLANCE
Per serving: 240 calories, 15 g total fat, 2.5 g saturated fat, 4 g protein, 26 g carbohydrates, 4 g dietary fiber,
240 mg sodium

Dubarry Crème Chowder

Traditional Dubarry is a cauliflower soup said to be named after Comtesse du Barry,
mistress of Louis XV. I always love a little scandal with my chowder, creamed with
almonds and pine nuts in this case. Excellent chilled or warmed.

YIELDS: 6 SERVINGS

5 cups filtered water

1 handful tender haricots verts (about ¼ pound), trimmed, or green beans, halved

2 ears fresh corn

1 medium head cauliflower, florets separated

1 sweet onion, coarsely chopped

2 cloves garlic, halved

3" stalk rosemary

1 bay leaf

½ fresh vanilla bean or ¼ teaspoon vanilla extract

1 cup raw almonds, soaked for 8 hours in filtered water, drained, and rinsed

½ cup pine nuts

2 tablespoons olive oil

2 tablespoons Omega Nutrition coconut butter, or additional olive oil

Sea salt

2 tomatoes, seeded and chopped

1 cup frozen edamame, thawed (whole soybeans out of the shell)

Freshly ground black pepper

In a medium-large stockpot, bring the filtered water to a boil.

Plunge the haricots verts in the boiling water for 30 seconds to 1 minute, or just until tender and bright green. Strain and immediately run them under very cold water. Set aside.

Shuck the corn. Drop in the boiling water for 2 to 3 minutes and pull out with tongs. Set aside to cool.

Reduce the heat to medium and place the cauliflower, onion, garlic, rosemary, bay leaf, and vanilla in the stockpot and bring to a gentle simmer for 10 minutes, or until the cauliflower is tender and easily pierced with a fork. Remove from the heat. Allow to cool for a few minutes.

Place a strainer in a large glass measuring cup or bowl. Pour 3 cups of the cooking water through the strainer.

Remove the bay leaf and rosemary. Split the vanilla bean in half and scrape out the seeds with a spoon. Return the seeds of the vanilla to the vegetables. Set aside.

Place the drained almonds and the pine nuts in a blender and add the reserved cooking water, olive oil, coconut butter or additional olive oil, and a pinch of salt. Blend at high speed until smooth. Pour through a fine strainer or sieve (or colander lined with cheesecloth) and press with the back of a spoon to extract as much liquid as possible. Add the nut milk to the vegetables.

Using an emersion blender (a handheld wand

blender), blend the vegetables and nut milk until smooth. They may also be blended in batches in a food processor or blender.

Return the chowder to the stockpot and place over medium-low heat. Add the haricots verts, corn, tomatoes, and edamame and gently warm. Season to taste with salt and freshly ground black pepper.

NUTRITION AT A GLANCE
Per serving: 400 calories, 32 g total fat, 3 g saturated fat, 14 g protein, 22 g carbohydrates, 7 g dietary fiber, 45 mg sodium

---

Summer Squash and Truffle Bisque

This smooth summer soup is made from a few simple ingredients and infused with the indulgence of truffle oil. Add pine nuts for a more full-bodied soup.

YIELDS: 6 SERVINGS

6 cups sliced summer squash, such as zucchini, pattypan, or crookneck

2 cloves garlic

4–5 cups Mushroom Stock (page 182), Light Vegetable Stock (page 178), packaged broth, or filtered water, as needed

¼ cup pine nuts (optional)

2 tablespoons truffle oil

2–4 tablespoons olive oil (use less if adding pine nuts, and more if not)

1½–2 cups chopped parsley leaves

½ cup chopped green onions

½ cup chopped fresh chives (additional green onions may be used instead)

Sea salt

Freshly ground black pepper, for garnish

In a medium stockpot, place the squash and garlic. Add the stock or filtered water just to cover. Bring to a gentle boil. Reduce the heat and simmer for 5 to 10 minutes, or until the squash is soft enough to easily pierce with a fork.

Use an emersion blender (a handheld wand blender) to blend the soup until smooth. If desired, add the pine nuts while blending for a more full-bodied soup. Add the truffle oil, olive oil, parsley, green onions, chives, and salt and blend until well mixed, but with flecks of parsley still visible. Adjust seasoning to taste.

Or, allow the soup to cool a bit and blend in batches in a blender or food processor until smooth, adding the pine nuts, if desired. Add the truffle oil, olive oil, parsley, green onions, chives, and salt to taste.

Garnish with chives and pepper.

NUTRITION AT A GLANCE
Per serving: 160 calories, 14 g total fat, 2 g saturated fat, 2 g protein, 7 g carbohydrates, 2 g dietary fiber, 300 mg sodium

---

Roasted Corn and Tomato Soup

This soup tastes like summer, with corn so sweet from roasting, it's like candy. Making a corn stock with the cobs, rather than a complex vegetable broth, is preferable as the flavor is clean and true.

YIELDS: 8 SERVINGS

6   ears fresh corn cobs, cut in half and kernels separated from cobs

3   tablespoons grapeseed oil or mild-tasting olive oil

    Sea salt

2   large sweet onions or yellow onions, chopped (about 5 cups)

10   cups filtered water

6   tablespoons olive oil

4   cups finely chopped tomatoes

1   tablespoon arrowroot

    Freshly ground black pepper

    Fresh oregano, chopped, for garnish

Preheat the oven to 400°F.

Place the corn kernels in a baking dish and drizzle with 1 tablespoon grapeseed oil and a pinch of salt, mixing to lightly coat. Place the cobs on a baking sheet, drizzle with 1 tablespoon grapeseed oil, and rub to lightly coat. Place both in the oven and roast for 10 minutes.

Meanwhile, toss 1 cup of onion with the remaining grapeseed oil.

After the corn has roasted, sprinkle the cup of onion over the cobs and return to the oven for 7 to 10 more minutes (about 20 minutes total). Remove the cobs from the oven, leaving the kernels in for another 8 to 15 minutes (for a total of 25 to 35 minutes), or until fragrant, soft, and caramelized. Stir the corn once or twice during cooking for even roasting, then remove from the oven and set aside.

While the kernels finish roasting, place the cobs and onions in a stockpot and cover with water. Cover and bring to a boil. Reduce heat

and uncover to simmer for 45 minutes to 1 hour. The liquid will reduce by half.

As the stock simmers, warm 3 tablespoons of the olive oil in a large saucepan over medium heat. Add the remaining onions. Cook until soft and translucent, 5 to 10 minutes. Add the corn kernels and cook for 5 to 10 minutes, stirring occasionally.

Add the tomatoes to the onions and cook, stirring occasionally, for 15 to 20 minutes, or until the tomatoes are concentrated. Ladle in a spoonful of corn stock if more liquid is needed.

Remove the cobs from the stock with tongs and discard. Pour the hot stock into the tomato-corn mixture and cook, stirring occasionally, for 10 minutes or so.

Sprinkle in the arrowroot (make sure it does not have any lumps), and stir vigorously. Cook another 5 minutes, stirring occasionally, while the soup thickens.

Add the remaining 3 tablespoons of olive oil.

Use an emersion blender (a handheld wand blender) to blend the soup until it's partially smooth (it should still have quite a bit of texture with whole or partial corn kernels visible). Or, pour half of the soup into a blender or food processor and blend until fairly smooth and return to pot. Season to taste with sea salt and pepper. Serve warm, garnished with oregano.

Mushroom Barley Soup

I dedicate this soup to my husband. He loves it so much that I wish I was soup when he is eating it. Rich with niacin to protect and build a healthy heart, barley is well known to lower cholesterol. Barley is rich in complex carbohydrates for long-term fuel and has plenty of fiber for a healthy digestive system. It is also one of the best sources of selenium, a valuable trace mineral vital to our thyroid, immune system, and antioxidant defense systems. The barley does not absolutely have to be soaked overnight, but I recommend it because it cuts the cooking time in half.

YIELDS: 6 SERVINGS

1½ cups pearled barley, soaked in 4 cups filtered water overnight, drained, and rinsed

1 yellow onion, chopped

3 ribs celery, cut into ½" pieces

2 carrots, scrubbed or peeled, sliced in half lengthwise and cut into ½" pieces

3 cups sliced cremini mushrooms

4 cups Light Vegetable Stock (page 178), Hearty Vegetable Stock (page 179), or Mushroom Stock (page 182, see note)

2 cups filtered water

Sea salt

In a medium-large stockpot, place the drained barley, onion, celery, carrots, and mushrooms. Add the stock and 2 cups of filtered water.

Bring to a boil. Reduce the heat and simmer for 45 to 50 minutes, or until the barley is completely cooked and thickened. Season to taste with sea salt. Add more water or stock if the soup is too thick for your liking.

NOTE: *In a pinch, organic, prepared vegetable broth may be used, or filtered water and natural bouillon cubes.*

Baby Lima Bean and Chard Soup

Here's a nourishing, hearty soup with tender baby lima beans and vitamin-packed chard that's reminiscent of a rustic Italian ribollita soup. Soaking the beans for 4 to 6 hours reduces the cooking time significantly. In a real pinch, canned beans may be used.

YIELDS: 8 SERVINGS

1 cup dried baby lima beans, soaked, drained, and rinsed (see "Soaking Beans," opposite page)

3 cups filtered water

4" strip kombu seaweed (optional to tenderize beans)

2 cloves garlic, halved

3 cups vegetable stock, packaged broth, or filtered water

4 tablespoons olive oil + additional for garnish

2 medium red onions, peeled and chopped

4 ribs celery, chopped

2 carrots, scrubbed or peeled, halved and chopped

3 cups parsley leaves, chopped

4 Roma tomatoes or 2 tomatoes, chopped with their juices

2–3 teaspoons fresh thyme

2 bay leaves

1 bunch Swiss chard, stems removed and leaves coarsely chopped

Sea salt

Freshly ground black pepper

In a medium stockpot, cover the beans with 3 cups of filtered water and bring to a boil. Reduce the heat and simmer for 10 minutes. Drain.

Return the beans to the pot with the kombu and garlic and cover with the vegetable stock, broth, or filtered water by 2". Bring to a boil. Reduce the heat and simmer, covered, until the beans are tender, 40 to 75 minutes. (If the beans were soaked first, they will require less time to cook.) Skim off any foam that arises while cooking.

Heat the olive oil in a large saucepan and add the onions, celery, carrots, and 2 cups of the parsley. Sauté for 20 minutes, until the flavors meld. Add the tomatoes, thyme, and bay leaves and cook over a gentle heat for 15 minutes. Add the Swiss chard and half of the cooked beans with enough of their cooking liquid to cover. Simmer for 20 minutes.

In a food processor, puree the remaining beans and cooking liquid until smooth. Mix into the soup. Season to taste with salt and pepper. Add additional vegetable stock or filtered water if the soup is too thick.

Fold in the remaining parsley and a bit more olive oil, if desired, just before serving.

NUTRITION AT A GLANCE
Per serving: 190 calories, 7 g total fat, 1 g saturated fat, 7 g protein, 26 g carbohydrates, 8 g dietary fiber, 250 mg sodium

Soaking Beans

Soaking dried beans shortens cooking time and improves digestibility. Soaking also softens the skins of beans and breaks down *phytic acid,* which liberates nutrients and minerals to be more available. Gas-causing enzymes and *trisaccharides* (complex sugars) are also released in the soaking water, making the beans easier to digest.

SOAKING TIPS

- Use 3 cups of filtered water for every cup of beans. Drain and rinse the beans before cooking.
- Generally, all beans can be soaked overnight, or minimally: Small beans should be soaked at least 4 hours; large beans should be soaked at least 6 hours.
- Quick soaking: Bring water and beans to a boil for 1 minute. Remove from heat and let stand 1 hour. Drain and rinse. Proceed with cooking as directed.
- Lentils, mung beans, and split peas do not need to be soaked to improve their digestibility.

You don't have to cook fancy
or complicated masterpieces—
just good food from
fresh ingredients.

—JULIA CHILD

Golden Squash Bowl with Pestou Blanc

This velvet soup is gently seasoned to perfection and can be made in no time. Butternut squash is gorgeously loaded with the antioxidant vitamins A and C and chock-full of potassium, manganese, folate, and B vitamins, including B_1, B_3, B_5, and B_6! A dollop of smooth white pestou cream is just the right adornment.

YIELDS: 6 SERVINGS

GOLDEN SQUASH BOWL

¼   **cup pine nuts**

    Sea salt

1   **tablespoon whole coriander seeds**

1   **teaspoon freshly ground black pepper + additional for garnish**

1   **medium butternut squash, peeled, seeded, and cut into 1" cubes**

2–4   **cloves garlic, chopped**

1   **medium leek (white part only), split lengthwise, cleaned, and chopped**

2   **bay leaves**

4"   **sprig rosemary**

3–4   **cups filtered water, Light Vegetable Stock (page 178), Hearty Vegetable Stock (page 179), or packaged broth**

2   **tablespoons white miso**

2   **tablespoons olive oil**

2   **tablespoons truffle oil (optional for sensuous flavor, or use additional olive oil)**

1   **tablespoon maple syrup**

1   **teaspoon balsamic vinegar**

PESTOU BLANC

½   **cup pine nuts**

1   **small clove garlic**

¼   **cup filtered water (add a touch more as necessary)**

2   **tablespoons olive oil**

    Pinch of sea salt

In a dry skillet on medium-low heat, toast the pine nuts, a pinch of salt, the coriander seeds, and 1 teaspoon of black pepper until fragrant (2 to 4 minutes). Use a wooden spoon to stir for even toasting. Be careful not to brown the pine nuts too much. Set aside.

In a stockpot, place the squash, garlic, leek, bay leaves, and rosemary. Add enough water or stock to just cover the ingredients and a pinch of salt. The amount of liquid will depend on the size of the squash. The less water added, the thicker the soup. For a thinner soup, add more water or stock at the end.

Place the stockpot over medium-high heat and

bring to a gentle boil, then reduce the heat and simmer until the squash is easily pierced with a fork, 15 to 20 minutes.

Meanwhile, prepare the Pestou Blanc: In a food processor or blender, combine the pine nuts, garlic, water, olive oil, and salt. Process or blend until smooth. Add a touch more water only if necessary to blend the pestou to a smooth consistency. Set aside.

When the squash is tender, remove the bay leaves and rosemary.

In a food processor or blender, blend the squash in batches until smooth, adding the toasted pine nut–spice mixture, miso, olive oil, truffle oil (if desired), maple syrup, and vinegar. Season to taste with salt as desired. Return to the stockpot and place over low heat to keep warm.

Serve warm with a spoonful of Pestou Blanc and freshly ground black pepper to taste.

NUTRITION AT A GLANCE
Per serving: 340 calories, 25 g total fat, 2.5 g saturated fat, 5 g protein, 28 g carbohydrates, 5 g dietary fiber, 260 mg sodium

PINE NUTS

Pine nuts are a scrumptious delicacy harvested from the cones of certain pine trees. With 31 percent protein, pine nuts are the highest source of protein of all nuts. The type of healthy fat found in pine nuts is very satisfying and satiates the appetite, so a little goes a long way. These little guys are also a great source of iron, magnesium, and thiamin (B_1), which is a coenzyme that helps metabolize carbohydrates.

I love pine nuts for their delicate, smooth flavor and texture, which finds a suitable home in so many recipes. Lily-white in color, they blend into a beautiful cream that offers a healthy alternative to dairy creams, which are laden with saturated fat. Cheers to a healthy heart, supple skin, and fantastic flavor!

1 teaspoon pine nuts

Calories: 20

Protein: 0.86 gram

Carbohydrate: 0.5 gram

Total Fat: 1.8 grams

Fiber: 0.16 gram

Savory French Onion Soup
with Pine Nut Medallion Crusts

Savory marinated onions bathe in a buttery broth with a bloom of flavor. Onions are a valuable source of phytonutrients, flavonoids, and heart-healthy saponins. Though this is a "raw" soup, it is delicious when warmed. The pine nut crusts lend a great texture, though the soup is fantastic on its own.

YIELDS: 4 SERVINGS

SAVORY ONIONS

1   tablespoon nama shoyu (unpasteurized soy sauce)

2   tablespoons olive oil

2   teaspoons maple syrup

2   teaspoons fresh thyme or 1 teaspoon dried

2   sweet onions, such as Vidalia, sliced

1   red onion, sliced

1   yellow onion, sliced

Pinch of Celtic sea salt

BUTTERY BOUILLON BROTH

¼   cup whole raw cashews, soaked 1 hour in filtered water, drained, and rinsed

1   bay leaf, soaked in ¼ cup warm water for 1 hour

¼   cup pine nuts

1   clove garlic

1½   cups chopped carrot

1   rib celery, chopped

1   cup parsley leaves

¼   cup cilantro leaves

2   teaspoons rosemary

1   teaspoon thyme

½   teaspoon ground chipotle pepper

2½–3   cups filtered water

1½   tablespoons olive oil

1   tablespoon Omega Nutrition coconut butter, or additional olive oil

1   tablespoon apple cider vinegar

2   teaspoons nama shoyu (unpasteurized soy sauce)

1   teaspoon red miso

1½   teaspoons maple syrup

Pinch of Celtic salt

Freshly cracked black pepper

PINE NUT MEDALLION CRUSTS

¼ cup whole raw cashews, soaked 1 hour and drained

¼ cup pine nuts

¼ cup lemon juice

1 teaspoon nutritional yeast

¼ cup filtered water

Pinch of Celtic sea salt

TO MAKE THE ONIONS:

In a large bowl, mix the shoyu, olive oil, maple syrup, and thyme. Fold in the Vidalia, red, and yellow onions and salt.

Allow to marinate for 1 to 2 hours (ideally in a dehydrator set at 108°F). If not using a dehydrator, allow to soften and warm in a double boiler for 30 minutes (see page 125 for double boiler methods).

TO MAKE THE BROTH:

In a blender, place the soaked and drained cashews, soaked bay leaf and water, pine nuts, garlic, carrot, celery, parsley, cilantro, rosemary, thyme, chipotle, water, olive oil, coconut butter or additional olive oil, vinegar, shoyu, miso, and maple syrup. Blend at high speed until smooth. Pour through a strainer or sieve. Season to taste with salt and pepper.

The broth may be warmed gently in a dehydrator or double boiler, or over low heat.

TO MAKE THE MEDALLION CRUSTS:

In a blender or food processor, combine the cashews, pine nuts, lemon juice, and nutritional yeast, adding water only as necessary to blend smooth. Season to taste with sea salt.

Spread by spoonfuls into 3½" rounds on lightly oiled parchment paper or nonstick sheets designed for a dehydrator. Dehydrate at 108°F for 4 to 8 hours, or until firm enough to transfer to the mesh sheet of the dehydrator to speed up the process. Return to the dehydrator for another hour or until crisp. This can also be done on a baking sheet in the oven set at the lowest temperature for 2 hours or until crisp.

TO SERVE:

Divide the Savory Onions among 4 serving bowls. Pour the Buttery Bouillon Broth over the onions and top with a Pine Nut Medallion Crust.

NUTRITION AT A GLANCE
Per serving: 440 calories, 35 g total fat, 4.5 g saturated fat, 9 g protein, 31 g carbohydrates, 5 g dietary fiber, 600 mg sodium

CHAPTER 6

New and Classic Salads

To make a good salad is to be a brilliant diplomatist—the problem is entirely the same in both cases. To know how much oil one must mix with one's vinegar.

—OSCAR WILDE

Three Quick Vinaigrettes

Vinaigrette is a classic dressing with scores of variations. It's brilliant on any fresh greens for a fabulous, no-fuss salad. High-quality oil is essential, and a sense of adventure is recommended. Store leftovers in a tightly sealed jar in the fridge for up to a week.

Balsamic Vinaigrette

YIELDS: 8 SERVINGS (2 TABLESPOONS PER SERVING)

3   tablespoons balsamic vinegar

2   tablespoons aged balsamic vinegar, or 1 tablespoon balsamic + 1 tablespoon maple syrup

2   cloves garlic, pressed

1½ tablespoons chopped fresh thyme or 2 teaspoons dried

2   teaspoons chopped fresh oregano or 1 teaspoon dried

½   cup extra-virgin olive oil

¼   teaspoon sea salt, or to taste

    Freshly ground black pepper

Whisk together the balsamic, aged balsamic (or balsamic + maple syrup), garlic, thyme, oregano, and olive oil or shake vigorously in a jar. Season to taste with salt and pepper.

NUTRITION AT A GLANCE
Per serving: 140 calories, 14 g total fat, 2 g saturated fat, 0 g protein, 4 g carbohydrates, 0 g dietary fiber, 75 mg sodium

French Vinaigrette à Mr. Verge

YIELDS: 8 SERVINGS (2 TABLESPOONS PER SERVING)

2   tablespoons + 1 teaspoon red wine vinegar

1½   teaspoons Dijon mustard

½   teaspoon honey or agave nectar

2   tablespoons minced shallot

1   tablespoon chopped fresh thyme

½   cup extra-virgin olive oil

¼   teaspoon sea salt, or to taste

Freshly ground black pepper

Whisk together the vinegar, mustard, honey or agave, shallot, thyme, and olive oil, or shake vigorously in a jar. Season to taste with salt and pepper.

Try adding 1 tablespoon chopped tarragon leaves for a variation.

NUTRITION AT A GLANCE
Per serving: 120 calories, 14 g total fat, 2 g saturated fat, 0 g protein, 1 g carbohydrates, 0 g dietary fiber, 95 mg sodium

Ginger Vinaigrette

YIELDS: 8 SERVINGS (2 TABLESPOONS PER SERVING)

1   tablespoon grated peeled ginger

3   tablespoons shoyu (soy sauce) or tamari

2   tablespoons umeboshi plum vinegar

2   tablespoons rice vinegar

2   teaspoons lemon juice

2   tablespoons chopped cilantro

½   cup sesame oil (not toasted)

Sea salt

Freshly ground black pepper

Whisk together the ginger, shoyu or tamari, umeboshi plum vinegar, rice vinegar, lemon juice, cilantro, and sesame oil, or shake vigorously in a jar. Season to taste with salt and pepper.

Try adding 1 teaspoon of toasted sesame oil for a toasty, rich flavor.

NUTRITION AT A GLANCE
Per serving: 130 calories, 14 g total fat, 2 g saturated fat, 0 g protein, 1 g carbohydrates, 0 g dietary fiber, 1,080 mg sodium

Wild Rice Salad with Cranberries and Hazelnuts

The long, dark, slender grains of wild rice are unusual for a grain, which is not surprising considering it is actually the seed of an aquatic grass of the Great Lakes. Power-packed with protein, B vitamins, and minerals like calcium and magnesium, wild rice is a wonderfully rich source of folate. Like a true rice, it contains no gluten and has an exquisite, nutty flavor and delicate texture. In this recipe, it is matched with cranberries, prized for their potent antioxidant properties, and hazelnuts, which add a crunchy complement and are full of heart-healthy oils, vitamin E, and plant sterols, which are believed to play a role in cancer prevention.

YIELDS: 6 SERVINGS

1	**cup hazelnuts**
1	**cup dried cranberries**
½	**cup orange juice**
	Sea salt
1–2	**shallots, finely chopped (about 2 tablespoons)**
1	**clove garlic, pressed**
1	**tablespoon balsamic vinegar**
1	**tablespoon umeboshi plum vinegar**
1	**teaspoon maple syrup**
¼	**cup walnut oil or extra-virgin olive oil**
	Freshly ground black pepper
4	**cups cooked or sprouted and blanched wild rice**
1½	**cups chopped flat-leaf parsley**

Preheat the oven to 350°F. Spread the hazelnuts in a baking pan. Bake for 12 to 15 minutes, stirring a few times for even toasting. Immediately pour the toasted nuts onto one-half of a cloth kitchen towel on a work surface. Fold the other half over the nuts and rub vigorously to remove as much of the skins as possible. Chop roughly and set aside.

Toss the cranberries with the orange juice and a pinch of salt. Let stand, stirring occasionally, for 15 minutes to soften.

Whisk together the shallots, garlic, balsamic and umeboshi plum vinegars, and maple syrup. Drizzle in the oil a little at a time while whisking until it emulsifies. Add a pinch of salt and pepper.

Toss the dressing with the wild rice, parsley, hazelnuts, and cranberries (including the extra orange juice). Season with salt and pepper.

NUTRITION AT A GLANCE
Per serving: 400 calories, 22 g total fat, 2 g saturated fat, 8 g protein, 48 g carbohydrates, 6 g dietary fiber, 540 mg sodium

Marinated Beets on Arugula

Beets are a nonstarchy root vegetable with loads of minerals such as iron; they are also wealthy in beta-carotene (a precursor of vitamin A), which is responsible for their gorgeous color. Boiling the beets to tenderize them takes a little time, but not too much attention, and the skin will then easily slip off. It is best to pick beets of similar size so they cook in accord. Oh so good on a bed of baby arugula, which packs a peppery punch, or watercress when in season.

YIELDS: 6 SERVINGS

4	medium beets, halved (about 4 cups)
8	cups filtered water
1¼	cups finely chopped green onions (5–6)
1	cup basil chiffonade (see note)
¼	cup chopped cilantro
1–2	tablespoons chopped fresh mint (optional)
3	tablespoons olive oil
1–2	cloves garlic, pressed
1	tablespoon ginger juice (page 160)
1	tablespoon umeboshi plum vinegar
1	tablespoon aged balsamic vinegar, or 2 teaspoons balsamic + 1 teaspoon maple syrup
1	tablespoon balsamic vinegar
1½	teaspoons maple syrup
2	teaspoons shoyu (soy sauce)
	Sea salt
	Freshly ground black pepper
4	cups baby arugula
1	cup pine nuts (lightly toasted) or Pine Nut Crumble (see opposite page), optional

Place beets in a medium to large saucepan and fill with filtered water. The beets should be well submerged as some of the water will cook off, but leave some room at the top of the pan, so it does not boil over.

Bring to a rolling boil and reduce heat to a gentle boil. Cook until the beets are tender enough to easily pierce with a fork and the skins will easily slip off, 8 to 10 minutes.

Drain the water. It may be saved for drinking, to color a lemonade pink, or to water plants, since it is rich in minerals. (See the note on page 220.)

Allow the beets to cool enough to comfortably handle. The beets can be cooked up to a day ahead of time.

Cut the tops from the beets and slip off the skin. Use a paring knife to help remove any stubborn spots.

Cut each beet half in half from top to bottom. Slice across into ¼" pieces. Place in a bowl. Add the green onions, basil, cilantro, and mint (if desired).

In a separate bowl, whisk together the olive oil, garlic, ginger juice, umeboshi plum vinegar, aged balsamic (or balsamic + maple syrup), balsamic vinegar, maple syrup, and shoyu. Pour over beets and toss well. Season to taste with salt and freshly ground black pepper. Let stand at least 10 minutes to develop flavor. Will keep fresh in a sealed container in the fridge for at least 2 days.

Serve on a bed of arugula and top with toasted pine nuts or Pine Nut Crumble, if desired.

NOTE: *To chiffonade basil, stack the leaves, roll up like a cigar, and slice thinly to yield beautiful ribbons.*

NUTRITION AT A GLANCE
Per serving: 100 calories, 7 g total fat, 1 g saturated fat, 2 g protein, 9 g carbohydrates, 2 g dietary fiber, 680 mg sodium

PINE NUT CRUMBLE

Use a sprinkle of this condiment as you would Parmesan or feta cheese in a more traditional salad. When ground, it adds a flavorful, moist texture to crumble on a salad—similar to feta cheese. Another step is to dehydrate or bake it at a low temperature, to preserve the delicate oils and flavor, until dry and crumbly—which results in a texture more like Parmesan cheese. When dried, it can be stored in a sealed container in the fridge for up to 2 weeks. Nutritional yeast is loaded with protein and B-complex vitamins, and it's a great option to lend a subtly deep flavor, reminiscent of some cheeses. Try using smoked sea salt for a light touch of deep hickory smoke.

YIELDS: 12 SERVINGS (1½ CUPS)

1½ cups pine nuts

2 tablespoons lemon juice

1 tablespoon olive oil

1 teaspoon nutritional yeast (optional)

Pinch of sea salt or smoked sea salt

Place the pine nuts in a food processor and grind into a fine meal.

Add the lemon juice, olive oil, nutritional yeast (if desired), and a pinch of salt. Chop in pulses just until mixed.

Use as is for a moist crumble, or spread thinly on dehydrator trays and dry at 112°F for 12 hours until completely dry for a more crumbly texture and concentrated flavor. The mixture may also be spread on a baking sheet and dried in the oven set at the lowest temperature for 1 hour or more as needed.

NUTRITION AT A GLANCE
Per serving: 120 calories, 13 g total fat, 1 g saturated fat, 2 g protein, 2 g carbohydrates, 0 g dietary fiber, 10 mg sodium

Lady Spring Salad
with Wasabi Mayonnaise

The beautiful texture of fresh spring vegetables comes alive with the quiet, fiery kick of a creamy wasabi mayonnaise, the cool of mint, and warm cilantro. Pine nuts and pure olive oil blend to a silky cream, though without eggs, it does not emulsify quite the same as traditional mayonnaise. In this recipe it works perfectly, and I usually add extra wasabi when left to my own devices. This recipe yields extra mayonnaise—keep it sealed in the fridge for up to 4 days.

YIELDS: 4 SERVINGS

WASABI MAYONNAISE

2–3	tablespoons wasabi powder	2	teaspoons yuzu or additional lemon juice
4	tablespoons filtered water	2	teaspoons mirin or brown rice vinegar
½	cup pine nuts	2	teaspoons agave nectar
½	clove garlic		Pinch of sea salt
2	teaspoons lemon juice	4	tablespoons olive oil

LADY SPRING SALAD

	Pinch of sea salt	2	tablespoons finely chopped cilantro
12	stalks asparagus, trimmed	2	tablespoons finely chopped mint (optional)
8	baby carrots, thinly sliced	2	teaspoons finely chopped tarragon (optional)
6	radishes, thinly sliced		
1½	cups fresh peas, blanched (thawed frozen peas may be used)	1	head butter leaf lettuce or small head romaine lettuce, washed, dried, and torn
3–4	green onions, cleaned and thinly sliced		Radish sprouts for garnish (optional)
2	tablespoons finely chopped parsley		

TO MAKE THE MAYONNAISE:

In a small bowl, mix the wasabi powder and filtered water into a paste and allow to stand for 5 minutes to thicken and develop flavor.

In a Vita-Mix or blender, blend the wasabi paste, pine nuts, garlic, lemon juice, yuzu, mirin or brown rice vinegar, agave, a pinch of salt, and 1 tablespoon of olive oil at high speed until as smooth as possible. While still blending, slowly drizzle in the remaining 3 tablespoons of olive oil to emulsify and thicken. Set in the fridge to chill and thicken.

TO MAKE THE SALAD:

Fill a large skillet with 1" of water and a pinch of salt. Bring to a boil. Blanch the asparagus for 2 to 3 minutes, just until bright green and tender. Remove with tongs. Immediately run the asparagus under cold water or plunge in ice water to arrest the cooking and set the color. When cool, drain and set aside.

Next, blanch the carrots and radishes for 1 to 2 minutes, just until tender. This can be done using the same water, though I recommend transferring it to a medium saucepan because the vegetables will be easier to remove from the water. Remove with a slotted spoon into a colander or strainer and immediately run under cold water. Drain and set aside.

Now, blanch the peas for 2 to 3 minutes, just until bright green and tender. Remove with a slotted spoon into a colander or strainer and immediately run under cold water. Drain and set aside. If using frozen peas, blanch just for a minute to thaw.

Toss the asparagus, carrots, radishes, peas, green onions, parsley, cilantro, mint (if desired), and tarragon (if desired) together. Spoon 3 to 4 tablespoons of Wasabi Mayonnaise on the veggies and toss gently to coat well.

Place on a bed of torn lettuce and toss gently, just to let some of the dressing make its way to the bed of lettuce. This can be done on individual plates, or on a large serving plate.

Garnish with radish sprouts, if desired.

NUTRITION AT A GLANCE
Per serving: 320 calories, 26 g total fat, 3 g saturated fat, 8 g protein, 18 g carbohydrates, 6 g dietary fiber, 140 mg sodium

Chopped Summer Farm Salad

Here is a classic chopped salad seasoned with summer flavors and offering a great variety of texture. Try it with browned tempeh for a protein-packed plate (see note). It can be made a day ahead of time to allow the flavors to marry, though wait to add the avocado until just before serving. Savory Balsamic Onion Rings bring this one over the top.

YIELDS: 6 SERVINGS

1 cup loosely packed parsley leaves	3 tablespoons extra-virgin olive oil
1 cup loosely packed basil leaves	2 tablespoons lemon juice
1 tablespoon chopped oregano	1 tablespoon umeboshi plum vinegar
1 red bell pepper	2 teaspoons balsamic vinegar
4 green onions, chopped	2 teaspoons aged balsamic vinegar, or 1 teaspoon balsamic + 1 teaspoon maple syrup
3 Roma tomatoes, chopped	
2 ribs celery, chopped	2 teaspoons agave nectar
2 medium carrots, chopped	Sea salt
1 medium red onion, chopped	Freshly ground black pepper
1 teaspoon fresh thyme or ½ teaspoon dried	1–2 firmly ripe avocados, peeled and cubed

BROWNED TEMPEH

2 tablespoons extra-virgin olive oil	1 teaspoon aged balsamic vinegar, or ½ teaspoon balsamic + ½ teaspoon maple syrup
1 medium sweet onion	
1 package (8 ounces) tempeh	Sea salt
1 teaspoon shoyu (soy sauce)	4 cups washed and chopped romaine lettuce

Chop the parsley, basil, and oregano finely.

Cut the red bell pepper in half and remove the stem, seeds, and veins. Roast if desired over a flame or under the broiler until the skin is blistered and blackened. Cool by running under cold water and peel the skin away. Dice into ⅛" pieces.

Toss all of the vegetables and the thyme in a bowl and coat evenly with the olive oil, lemon juice, umeboshi plum vinegar, balsamic, aged balsamic (or balsamic + maple syrup), agave, a generous pinch or two of sea salt, and freshly ground black pepper.

Let stand for 10 to 20 minutes to develop flavor.

Meanwhile, prepare the Browned Tempeh. Warm the olive oil in a medium skillet over medium heat. Add the onion and sauté for 2 minutes, just until turning translucent. Cut the tempeh into ⅛" slices and across into ¼" pieces. Add to the onion and cook, stirring regularly, for 3 minutes. Add the shoyu and aged balsamic (or balsamic + maple syrup) and cook, stirring regularly, for another 5 to 7 minutes, or until nicely browned. Add a pinch of sea salt, remove from the heat, and let cool 5 minutes before serving.

TO ASSEMBLE THE SALAD:

Fold the avocado into the salad with the Browned Tempeh. Season to taste with sea salt and freshly ground black pepper, as desired.

Toss with the romaine lettuce just before serving.

NOTE: *Tempeh is made from soybeans or grains and is a great source of protein. One 8-ounce package has more than 40 grams of protein! It has a mild, nutty flavor and a porous texture that absorbs marinades well, and it browns up nicely.*

NUTRITION AT A GLANCE
Per serving: 280 calories, 21 g total fat, 3 g saturated fat, 10 g protein, 19 g carbohydrates, 6 g dietary fiber, 620 mg sodium

Savory Balsamic Onion Rings

These savory onions are to live for! Touching on four corners of flavor, all of the good stuff is preserved using low temperatures to dry. I typically double the recipe as they store well and are fantastic on practically any soup or salad.

YIELDS: 4 SERVINGS (ABOUT 2 CUPS)

2 tablespoons balsamic vinegar

2 tablespoons shoyu (soy sauce)

1 tablespoon maple syrup

4 cups sliced sweet onions, ¼" thick

Mix together the vinegar, shoyu, and maple syrup.

Toss with the sliced onions. Let stand 15 minutes to 1 hour to marinate.

Spread out on dehydrator trays and dehydrate at 112°F for 12 hours or until dry.

Alternatively, spread on a baking sheet and dry in the oven set at the lowest temperature for 4 to 6 hours, or until dry. The onions take some time to prepare, but they're tantalizingly delicious! Store in a tightly sealed container or bag in a cool, dry place.

NUTRITION AT A GLANCE
Per serving: 80 calories, 0 g total fat, 0 g saturated fat, 2 g protein, 18 g carbohydrates, 2 g dietary fiber, 400 mg sodium

Salade Tapenade

This salad sweeps me away to fond memories of living on the Riviera, where tapenade is as much a kitchen staple as ketchup is in America. Tapenade is a classic condiment for the balanced plate, rich with health-giving flavor. Olives, the primary ingredient in tapenade, are easy to digest and full of heart-healthy oils and the mighty antioxidant power of vitamin E, which grows and protects beautiful skin and cells. Olives also boast beneficial polyphenols and flavonoids, which have anti-inflammatory properties and are believed to ward off cancer. Yet another benefit is that this tapenade will keep fresh for up to a week when stored tightly covered in the fridge.

YIELDS: 4 SERVINGS

TAPENADE

1 cup kalamata or niçoise olives, rinsed and pitted

½ cup extra-virgin olive oil

1 cup loosely packed basil leaves

½ clove garlic

2 tablespoons pine nuts

1 teaspoon red wine vinegar

Sea salt

Freshly ground black pepper

SALAD

2 heads endive or 1 head heart of romaine

4 cups loosely packed arugula, washed

1 medium cucumber, peeled, seeded, and cut into chunks

1 bulb fennel, trimmed, quartered, and thinly sliced

4 radishes, trimmed and thinly sliced

2 green onions, trimmed and thinly sliced

1 rib celery, trimmed and thinly sliced

2 cups cherry tomatoes, halved

1 red bell pepper, roasted and cut into thin strips (organic jarred peppers are a real time-saver)

¼ cup loosely packed torn basil leaves

1 teaspoon finely grated lemon zest

¼ cup lemon juice

2 tablespoons extra-virgin olive oil

Coarse sea salt

Freshly ground black pepper

TO MAKE THE TAPENADE:

Place the olives, olive oil, basil, garlic, pine nuts, and vinegar in a food processor and blend until smooth. It may be necessary to scrape the walls of the food processor with a rubber spatula and continue to blend until you have a smooth puree. Taste, then season with salt and pepper. The olives may provide enough salt, but a few twists of ground pepper bump up the flavor beautifully. Set aside.

TO ASSEMBLE THE SALAD:

Cut the bottom off of the endive or heart of romaine. Cut into ½" pieces across the head.

Remove any tough stems from the arugula.

In a large bowl, gently toss together the endive or romaine, arugula, cucumber, fennel, radishes, green onions, celery, cherry tomatoes, bell pepper, and basil. Toss with the lemon zest, lemon juice, olive oil, and a pinch of salt and pepper to coat.

Gently fold into half of the tapenade. Taste and add more to your liking. Dot the plates with tapenade and serve the rest in a small bowl.

NUTRITION AT A GLANCE
Per serving: 450 calories, 43 g total fat, 6 g saturated fat, 5 g protein, 19 g carbohydrates, 6 g dietary fiber, 310 mg sodium

---

Cooking is an art and patience a virtue. . . . Careful shopping, fresh ingredients, and an unhurried approach are nearly all you need. There is one more thing—love. Love for food and love for those you invite to your table.

—KEITH FLOYD

Soba Noodle Salad

Buckwheat soba noodles make this dish a gluten-free, nutrient-enriched delight. Arame seaweed is a champion source of precious minerals, trace elements, and protein, though the salad fares well without it if you have trouble finding it at the market.

YIELDS: 4 SERVINGS

¼   **cup tamari or shoyu (soy sauce)**

¼   **cup lemon juice**

2   **tablespoons unrefined sesame oil**

2   **teaspoons toasted sesame oil**

1   **tablespoon maple syrup**

2   **tablespoons mirin, sake, or brown rice vinegar**

2   **tablespoons umeboshi plum vinegar**

3   **tablespoons finely shredded ginger**

2   **teaspoons white miso**

1   **teaspoon yuzu (optional)**

1   **teaspoon wasabi powder (optional)**

6   **ounces buckwheat soba noodles**

¼   **cup dried arame seaweed**

¼   **cup prepared Gomasio (page 280)**

12   **snow peas, julienned**

3–4   **green onions, trimmed and cleaned, sliced thinly on an angle**

2   **shiso leaves, julienned**

½   **cup prepared smoked tofu, cubed (optional)**

4   **cups salad greens (optional)**

¼   **cup Ume Pumpkin Seeds (optional, page 291)**

In a bowl or pitcher, whisk together the tamari; lemon juice; sesame oils; maple syrup; mirin, sake, or brown rice vinegar; umeboshi plum vinegar; ginger; miso; and yuzu and wasabi, if desired. This dressing can be stored in a tightly sealed jar or container in the fridge for at least a week.

Cook the soba noodles according to the package directions. Drain and rinse.

Toss the noodles with the dressing while still warm. Place in the fridge to begin chilling.

Cover the dried arame with filtered water and soak until soft (5 to 10 minutes). Drain off the water and reserve to water plants. Rinse the arame and drain.

Fold the Gomasio into the noodles along with the drained arame, snow peas, green onion, shiso leaves, and smoked tofu, if desired. Chill.

Serve chilled over a bed of baby greens, topped with Ume Pumpkin Seeds as you wish.

NUTRITION AT A GLANCE
Per serving: 340 calories, 14 g total fat, 2 g saturated fat, 11 g protein, 46 g carbohydrates, 3 g dietary fiber, 3,130 mg sodium

Soba Noodle Soup

Leftover Soba Noodle Salad is transformed into a quick, nourishing soup for a comforting pick-me-up in the cooler months.

YIELDS: 1 SERVING

1½ cups filtered water

2 teaspoons white miso

1 cup Soba Noodle Salad

Bring the water to a boil in a small saucepan. Remove from heat. Pour ¼ cup into a small bowl or pitcher and stir in the miso until dissolved. Return to the saucepan and add the Soba Noodle Salad. Warm over low heat as necessary to warm up the soba noodles. Serve or stash in a thermos for lunch to go.

NUTRITION AT A GLANCE

Per serving: 370 calories, 14 g total fat, 2 g saturated fat, 12 g protein, 51 g carbohydrates, 3 g dietary fiber, 3,390 mg sodium

Nothing will benefit human health and increase chances for survival of life on Earth as much as the evolution to a vegetarian diet.

——ALBERT EINSTEIN

Endive, Fennel, and Blood Oranges with Seasoned Walnuts

I have a thing for this salad. It embodies a great posse of texture and flavor and looks just gorgeous on a simple plate. Of course, I would munch a big ol' bowl of it with some great black olives on the side as a light meal and be pleased as punch. Oranges or tangerines may be used when blood oranges are out of season, and can be colored with a little beet juice for colorful pizzazz. The walnuts can be done at a low temperature in the dehydrator to preserve all of the precious oils and nutrients, or toasted in the oven for quicker preparation.

YIELDS: 4 SERVINGS

¼   cup olive oil

1½ tablespoons aged balsamic vinegar, or 2 teaspoons balsamic + 2 teaspoons maple syrup

1   tablespoon red wine vinegar

1   tablespoon finely chopped shallot

2   teaspoons fresh thyme or 1 teaspoon dried

    Sea salt

    Freshly ground black pepper

2   blood oranges, or dyed oranges (opposite page)

1   medium bulb fennel, trimmed

½   pound endive, trimmed

In a large bowl, whisk together the olive oil, aged balsamic (or balsamic + maple syrup), red wine vinegar, shallot, thyme, and a pinch of salt and pepper. Let stand for 10 minutes to develop flavor.

Cut the ends off of the oranges and cut away the rest of the peel with a paring knife to remove all of the white pith. Cut each section between the membranes to end up with nice, clean wedges. Do this over a bowl to catch the juices. Whisk any extra juice into the dressing.

Cut the fennel into quarters and slice as thinly as possible by hand or on a mandoline.

Separate the endive leaves.

Whisk the dressing and gently toss it with the orange sections, fennel, and endive leaves.

Serve on salad plates topped with seasoned walnuts. Voila!

SEASONED WALNUTS

⅔   cup walnuts

2   cups filtered water

1   teaspoon shoyu (soy sauce)

1   teaspoon umeboshi plum vinegar

1   teaspoon balsamic vinegar

1   teaspoon maple syrup

1   teaspoon fresh thyme or ½ teaspoon dried

1   tablespoon finely chopped shallot

    Freshly ground black pepper

LOW-TEMPERATURE PROCEDURE:

Soak the walnuts in 2 cups of filtered water for 4 to 6 hours. Drain and rinse. Chop roughly.

Toss the walnuts with the shoyu, umeboshi plum vinegar, balsamic, maple syrup, thyme, shallot, and a bit of pepper. Spread in a shallow dish and dehydrate at 112°F for 12 to 20 hours until dry, stirring occasionally for even coating.

TOASTING PROCEDURE:

Preheat the oven to 275°F.

Chop the walnuts roughly and toss with the shoyu, umeboshi plum vinegar, balsamic, maple syrup, thyme, shallot, and a bit of pepper. Let stand for 15 minutes, stirring occasionally to coat and allow the walnuts to absorb flavor.

Spread out in a baking dish and bake for 8 to 15 minutes, stirring after 5 minutes for even coating, until fragrant and dry.

NUTRITION AT A GLANCE
Per serving: 320 calories, 25 g total fat, 3 g saturated fat, 5 g protein, 23 g carbohydrates, 8 g dietary fiber, 390 mg sodium

---

No Blood Oranges at the Market?

If you are after the scarlet beauty of blood oranges when they are not available, orange oranges can be dyed naturally with beet juice.

To do so, cut the ends off of the oranges and cut away the rest of the peel with a paring knife to remove all of the white pith. Cut each section between the membranes to end up with nice, clean wedges. Do this over a bowl to catch the juices. A good, sharp knife will help to avoid smashing the orange to smithereens in the process.

Grate ½ cup of beet as finely as possible. A wide microplane works best. Squeeze through a double-layer section of cheesecloth to extract as much juice as possible.

Place the orange sections in a bowl and cover with the beet juice and a pinch of sea salt. Fold gently and let stand for 15 minutes to 1 hour. Though this will not dye the oranges through and through, it lends a beautiful crimson color for just the right dishes.

Wild Mushroom à la Truffle Florentine Salad

Fresh chanterelle, porcini, and morel mushrooms are the ideal for this salad, though cultivated mushrooms such as oyster mushrooms or cremini mushrooms are easier to find year-round and quite a bit less expensive. The truffle oil definitely bumps it up a notch, but a good olive oil will stand on its own. Leftover dressing should be stored in a tightly sealed container in the fridge for up to 2 weeks.

YIELDS: 4 SERVINGS

AGED BALSAMIC AND TRUFFLE DRESSING

2 tablespoons olive oil	1 teaspoon lemon juice
1 tablespoon pine nuts	1 teaspoon shoyu (soy sauce)
1 teaspoon truffle oil	1 teaspoon umeboshi plum vinegar
1 tablespoon + 1 teaspoon aged balsamic vinegar, or 2 teaspoons balsamic + 2 teaspoons maple syrup	1 medium clove garlic
	2 teaspoons fresh thyme leaves
2 teaspoons balsamic vinegar	

WILD MUSHROOMS AND WHITE WINE CARAMELIZED ONIONS

2 tablespoons extra-virgin olive oil	Sea salt
1 medium sweet onion, sliced	Freshly ground black pepper
2 cloves garlic	4 cups baby spinach
½ cup white wine, like a light chardonnay	Pinch of smoked salt or flaky sea salt
8 ounces fresh wild mushrooms, sliced	

TO MAKE THE DRESSING:

Place 2 tablespoons of the olive oil, pine nuts, truffle oil, aged balsamic (or balsamic + maple syrup), balsamic, lemon juice, shoyu, umeboshi plum vinegar, garlic, and thyme in a blender. Blend until very smooth. If the dressing seems too thick, add a touch more olive oil. Taste and adjust seasoning. Set aside.

TO MAKE THE MUSHROOMS:

Warm the olive oil in a medium skillet over medium heat. Add the onion and stir with a wooden spoon or paddle to coat. Cook, stirring occasionally, for 6 to 8 minutes, until savory and soft.

Add the garlic, stirring frequently for just about a minute until fragrant.

Add the wine and cook, stirring occasionally, for about 2 minutes.

Add the mushrooms to the pan. Sprinkle with

a pinch of salt. Stir to coat and cook, stirring gently and occasionally, until the liquid has almost completely reduced. Remove from heat. Season to taste with salt and pepper.

TO ASSEMBLE THE SALAD:

Toss the spinach with the dressing. Start with half of the dressing and add more to taste.

Place a small bed of mushrooms on a serving plate. Top with a nice mound of tossed spinach. Top generously with freshly ground black pepper and a pinch of smoked salt or flaky sea salt. Serve immediately.

> **NUTRITION AT A GLANCE**
> Per serving: 230 calories, 18 g total fat, 2.5 g saturated fat, 3 g protein, 12 g carbohydrates, 2 g dietary fiber, 410 mg sodium

Yuzu Sunumono

This side salad is an interpretation of sunumono, a traditional Japanese cucumber salad with a light vinegar dressing. I add yuzu, a dynamic Japanese citron juice with a peppery kick; tender wakame seaweed, which is loaded with calcium; ginger juice; and green onion. White shoyu keeps this simple salad a pure, clean color, though traditional shoyu (soy sauce) may be used. Lemon juice and a touch of wasabi can substitute for the yuzu in a pinch. Best served chilled.

YIELDS: 2 SERVINGS

2   **tablespoons dried wakame seaweed**

1   **cucumber, peeled, seeded, and sliced**

1   **tablespoon white shoyu or shoyu (soy sauce)**

2   **teaspoons yuzu, or 2 teaspoons lemon juice + ⅛ teaspoon wasabi powder**

1   **teaspoon ginger juice (page 160)**

1   **teaspoon agave nectar**

1   **green onion, finely chopped (optional)**

Cut the wakame into small pieces if necessary. Cover with filtered water and soak until soft (5 to 15 minutes). Drain and set aside the water for other uses or to water plants.

Cut the cucumber in half lengthwise and slice into ¼" pieces.

Mix together the shoyu, yuzu or lemon juice and wasabi powder, ginger juice, and agave. Toss with the cucumber and wakame. Allow to stand in the fridge for 20 minutes or more. Top or toss with the green onion, if desired.

> **NUTRITION AT A GLANCE**
> Per serving: 35 calories, 0 g total fat, 0 g saturated fat, 2 g protein, 7 g carbohydrates, 2 g dietary fiber, 480 mg sodium

Sea Salad

Sea veggies contain 10 to 20 times the minerals of land plants and an abundance of vitamins. Both hijiki and arame contain more than 10 times the calcium of milk and eight times the iron of beef, and they are an excellent source of iodine for healthy thyroid function, zinc, and B-complex vitamins, notably B_{12} and B_3. Seaweed is also a solid source of simple protein with a full profile of amino acids. Arame has a milder flavor than hijiki, though hijiki has almost twice as much calcium and iron. Both are available dried in natural food stores and Asian markets.

YIELDS: 4 SERVINGS

1   ounce dried hijiki (about ½ cup) or arame (about 1 cup)

3   tablespoons shoyu (soy sauce) or tamari

2   tablespoons sesame oil (not toasted)

1   teaspoon toasted sesame oil (optional)

2   tablespoons rice vinegar

1   tablespoon umeboshi plum vinegar

1   teaspoon maple syrup or agave nectar

1   teaspoon finely chopped ginger

1   clove garlic, pressed

2   green onions, trimmed and chopped to the top

2   tablespoons chopped cilantro

2   tablespoons chopped parsley

2   tablespoons sesame seeds or Gomasio (page 280)

Cover the hijiki or arame with filtered water or broth by just more than 1". Soak until soft. Arame will take 5 to 10 minutes, hijiki 10 to 15. Warm water or broth will speed up the soaking. Drain and reserve the soaking water (see note).

Whisk together the shoyu or tamari, sesame oil, toasted sesame oil (if using), rice vinegar, umeboshi plum vinegar, maple syrup or agave, ginger, and garlic. Toss together with the drained seaweed until well coated. Toss in the green onions, cilantro, and parsley. Let stand for 10 minutes before serving. Meanwhile, place the sesame seeds in a heavy skillet over low heat and cook, stirring frequently, for about 5 minutes, or until fragrant but not popping.

Top salad with the toasted sesame seeds or Gomasio. Store leftovers in a tightly sealed container in the fridge for up to 4 days.

NOTE: *The water used to soak seaweed is rich with precious minerals and trace elements too good to throw away. I consider it a liquid vitamin-mineral supplement and just knock back an ounce or two as medicine or I save it to use in a fortified soup. At the least, it can be put in the watering can and used as a fertilizing drink for houseplants. I try feeding it to my cat, but she mostly swishes her tail and canters off.*

NUTRITION AT A GLANCE
Per serving: 120 calories, 9 g total fat, 1.5 g saturated fat, 2 g protein, 7 g carbohydrates, 4 g dietary fiber, 1,440 mg sodium

Three Bean Salad

Beans are a premium source of protein for clean-burning energy. With plenty of cholesterol-lowering fiber, they are also great for your heart.

YIELDS: 6 SERVINGS

¼ cup extra-virgin olive oil

1 tablespoon lemon juice

1 tablespoon red wine vinegar

2 teaspoons Dijon mustard

1 teaspoon maple syrup

2 tablespoons minced fresh thyme or 2–3 teaspoons dried

Sea salt

Freshly ground black pepper

1½ cups cooked or sprouted and blanched garbanzo beans (page 197)

1½ cups cooked or sprouted and blanched adzuki beans (page 197)

1½ cups shelled edamame

½ red onion, finely chopped (about 1 cup)

2 shallots, finely sliced

2 green onions, finely chopped

2 ribs celery, thinly sliced

½ cup chopped parsley

¼ cup chopped cilantro (optional)

¼ pound green beans

Whisk together the olive oil, lemon juice, vinegar, mustard, maple syrup, thyme, a pinch of salt, and a few twists of pepper.

Toss together the garbanzo beans, adzuki beans, edamame, red onion, shallots, green onions, celery, parsley, and cilantro (if desired). Pour the dressing over this mixture and toss to coat.

Snap the stems off of the green beans. Cut them into 1½" pieces on an angle. Bring a saucepan of filtered water and a pinch of salt to a boil. Blanch the green beans in the boiling water for 2 to 3 minutes, or just until tender and bright green. Drain and shock by running under cold water immediately to arrest cooking and keep the color bright.

Toss the green beans in with the mixture. Season with salt and pepper to taste as desired.

Serve at room temperature or chilled on a bed of lettuce or à la carte. Store leftovers in a sealed container in the fridge. Keeps for 4 days.

NUTRITION AT A GLANCE
Per serving: 120 calories, 9 g total fat, 1.5 g saturated fat, 2 g protein, 7 g carbohydrates, 4 g dietary fiber, 1,440 mg sodium

CHAPTER 7

Wraps, Rolls, and Balanced Starts

The true cook is the perfect blend, the only blend, of artist and philosopher. He knows his worth; he holds in his palm the happiness of mankind, the welfare of generations yet unborn.

—NORMAN DOUGLAS (1868–1952)

Roasted Beet Carpaccio with Frisée

Roasting the beets whole, with the skin on, captures their juicy, sweet essence and rich minerals. Frisée is a decorative member of the chicory family with a slightly bitter nuttiness and pale green, almost wiry leaves. If you are lucky enough to find mâche in the market, it works beautifully in frisée's place, though chopped endive or field mix can substitute if neither are available.

YIELDS: 4 SERVINGS

4   **medium beets**

2   **teaspoons + 2 tablespoons extra-virgin olive oil**

½   **teaspoon truffle oil**

1   **teaspoon aged balsamic vinegar, or 2 teaspoons balsamic + 1 teaspoon maple syrup**

3   **teaspoons lemon juice**

½   **teaspoon yuzu, or ½ teaspoon lemon juice + ⅛ teaspoon wasabi powder**

½   **teaspoon smoked salt or sea salt**
    Freshly ground black pepper

4   **cups roughly chopped frisée (mâche or chopped endive may be used)**

Preheat the oven to 350°F.

Scrub the beets. Rub with 1 teaspoon olive oil and place in a baking dish. Roast beets for 25 to 35 minutes, or until tender and able to be pierced with a fork. Remove from the oven and let cool for 15 minutes. While still warm but comfortable to handle, trim the top and bottom off of each beet. Peel away the skin with your fingers if possible; use a paring knife if necessary.

Slice the peeled beets into ⅛" pieces.

Place the beets in a bowl and drizzle with 1 tablespoon of olive oil, the truffle oil, aged balsamic (or balsamic + maple syrup), 1 teaspoon of lemon juice, yuzu (or lemon juice and wasabi powder), ¼ teaspoon smoked salt or sea salt, and a few twists of pepper. Fold together gently with your fingers. Let stand 15 minutes to 1 hour to absorb and develop flavor.

A few minutes before serving, toss the frisée with the remaining olive oil, the remaining lemon juice, the remaining smoked salt or sea salt, and a few twists of pepper.

Arrange the beets on serving plates, overlapping in a 4" to 5" circle. Top with a nice little mound of tossed frisée. Season with pepper, if desired.

NUTRITION AT A GLANCE
Per serving: 130 calories, 10 g total fat, 1.5 g saturated fat, 2 g protein, 10 g carbohydrates, 4 g dietary fiber, 300 mg sodium

Pan-Seared Mushrooms in Leek Skin with Pale Pesto

This recipe first came about in the kitchen with my dearest muffin-love, Alicia. We are both mushroom lovers and big leek fans, so these morsels were an ideal combination, and they've grown quite a fan base. Leeks have a delicate fiber and make a perfect, thin skin to hold the goodies inside. Any type of mushroom can be used, but oyster and shiitake are our favorite combination. The pesto is light on the herbs to take a supportive role rather than center stage. Perfect as a taster or appetizer, especially for a dinner party or cocktail hour.

YIELDS: 8 SERVINGS (16–24 BITE-SIZE ROLLS)

1   large or 2 medium leeks, white part only

2   tablespoons + 1 teaspoon extra-virgin olive oil

Pinch of sea salt

2   cloves garlic, finely minced

4   cups sliced mushrooms (shiitake, oyster, and/or portobello)

¼   cup white wine, vegetable stock, or filtered water

1   teaspoon balsamic vinegar

1   teaspoon shoyu (soy sauce)

½   teaspoon maple syrup

½   cup Pale Pesto, or as needed (opposite page)

Trim the top and bottom of the leek and remove the outermost skin.

Cut the white part of the leek into 1½" sections (with a large leek you will get about 4 sections, a smaller leek about 3).

Slice halfway into the leek lengthwise (with the fiber).

Separate the layers to end up with 4 to 6 skins from each section (the closer to the heart of the section, the smaller the pieces).

Place the skins in a basket for steaming. Steam over rapidly boiling water until tender-crisp (2 to 3 minutes). Watch them carefully because they cook quickly and if overdone will become too soggy.

Let cool and blot with a clean, dry towel or paper towel (laying them flat on a towel and placing another towel over to press gently is a good technique). Drizzle with 1 teaspoon of olive oil and a sprinkle of salt. Fold gently to coat evenly. Set aside.

Warm the remaining 2 tablespoons of olive oil in a medium skillet. Add the garlic and sauté until soft, not brown.

Add the mushrooms, toss to coat, and cook for about 30 seconds.

Add the wine, stock, or water; balsamic, shoyu, and maple syrup. Cook, stirring occasionally, until all of the liquid has evaporated. Remove from the heat and set aside.

Lay a piece of leek skin flat on a clean work surface. Lay a few pieces of mushroom across the skin and dollop with a teaspoon of pesto.

Roll into a cylinder.

Serve at room temperature or warm in the oven at 350°F to serve.

NUTRITION AT A GLANCE
Per serving: 120 calories, 11 g total fat, 1.5 g saturated fat, 2 g protein, 4 g carbohydrates, 0 g dietary fiber, 45 mg sodium

Pale Pesto

With just a bit of basil, this pesto keeps a pale complexion and a milder taste than traditional pesto. I often double or triple the recipe to stash in the fridge as it is great on steamed veggies, cooked grains, or just about anything. It is a versatile condiment for a balanced plate and keeps for about a week. Mix a few tablespoons with 2 tablespoons each of additional olive oil and lemon juice, and season with salt for salad dressing. If you do double the recipe, try using half of it for another variation, adding parsley, mint, watercress, or additional basil.

YIELDS: 8 SERVINGS (ABOUT ½ CUP)

¼ cup pine nuts

2 tablespoons extra-virgin olive oil

2 teaspoons lemon juice

½ cup basil leaves

1 teaspoon fresh thyme or ½ teaspoon dried

Sea salt and freshly ground black pepper

Place the pine nuts, olive oil, lemon juice, basil, and thyme in a blender or small food processor. Blend until smooth. It may be necessary to aid blending by scraping the walls of the blender or food processor with a rubber spatula and continuing to blend. Season to taste with salt and pepper.

NUTRITION AT A GLANCE
Per tablespoon: 60 calories, 6 g total fat, 0.5 g saturated fat, 1 g protein, 1 g carbohydrates, 0 g dietary fiber, 0 mg sodium

Spicy Thai Lettuce Wraps

This recipe has all of the magic of Thai flavor and a tantalizing, dynamic texture.
The list of ingredients is long, but worth it. The dressing is worth making double as it
keeps well for a few days and is delectable on a crunchy salad, steamed veggies, or to
dip anything in—my favorite is celery.

YIELDS: 6 SERVINGS (ABOUT 12 ROLLS)

1–2   heads romaine lettuce

3   tablespoons umeboshi plum vinegar

3   tablespoons unrefined sesame oil

3   tablespoons raw almond butter

1   clove garlic, pressed (garlic lovers, add another clove)

2   tablespoons peeled and finely shredded ginger (add another tablespoon if you love ginger!)

⅓   cup finely chopped green onions, including the greens

1–2   kaffir lime leaves, sliced very thinly (optional)

¼   cup lime juice + 1–2 tablespoons

1½   tablespoons shoyu (soy sauce)

1   tablespoon maple syrup

1   tablespoon agave nectar

½–1   Thai chili pepper (or other small chili pepper), seeded and finely chopped (or include the seeds if you like it spicy!)

Sea salt

1   large carrot, cut into matchsticks

1   small jicama, peeled and cut into matchsticks, or 2–3 ribs celery, cut into matchsticks

2   cups napa cabbage or Chinese cabbage, sliced finely across the leaves

1   mango or papaya, peeled, seeded, and cut into ¼" strips

2   cups mung bean sprouts

½   bunch cilantro, washed

¼   cup packed mint leaves, torn if they are large

20   basil leaves, torn

Tamarind Dipping Sauce (page 228)

Separate the 12 largest lettuce leaves from the head (save the rest for a salad).

Bring a large pot of water to a simmering boil. Submerge the lettuce leaves in the water for about 10 seconds. Remove with tongs or drain immediately. Shock under cold running water or submerge in ice water to halt the cooking and preserve the bright green color at its peak. Gently squeeze and blot with a clean, dry towel. Toss gently with 1 tablespoon of umeboshi plum vinegar to coat. Set aside.

In a bowl or measuring pitcher, mix together the sesame oil, almond butter, garlic, ginger, green onions, kaffir lime (if available), lime juice, the remaining 2 tablespoons of vinegar, shoyu, maple syrup, agave, and chili pepper. Season to taste with sea salt. This can be made ahead of time and will keep for 2 days in a sealed container in the fridge. (P.S. Very delicious over crunchy chopped lettuce. Yum!)

Toss the carrot, jicama or celery, and cabbage with the dressing.

Lay one of the romaine leaves flat on a cutting board with the rib facing up. Trim away the protruding rib of the leaf with a paring knife.

Use a drinking glass, bottle of wine, or rolling pin to flatten the rib so it will be flexible enough to roll.

Make sure the stem end of the leaf is facing you. Place ¼ to ⅓ cup of dressed vegetables evenly across the bottom half (the stem end) of the leaf. Top with a few strips of mango or papaya, a small bunch of mung bean sprouts, a few sprigs of cilantro, a few mint leaves, and pieces of basil leaves. (The tendency is to overfill it, but less is actually more here.) Fold the flattened bottom of the leaf over the vegetables and tuck under. Fold the sides of the leaf in (like making a burrito) and roll into a cylinder. Set aside and carry on with the rest.

The rolls may be cut in half on a slight angle for beautiful presentation. Serve with Tamarind Dipping Sauce.

NUTRITION AT A GLANCE

Per serving (2 rolls): 200 calories, 12 g total fat, 1.5 g saturated fat, 4 g protein, 22 g carbohydrates, 5 g dietary fiber, 1,830 mg sodium

TAMARIND DIPPING SAUCE

Tamarind, also called an Indian date, tastes both sour and sweet, which makes it a very versatile flavoring. Fresh tamarind is available in Asian and East Indian markets, but you may have better luck finding it in dried blocks or as a concentrate in the ethnic food aisle of your gourmet grocer. If you use reconstituted pulp in this recipe, you will likely need to add a touch more maple syrup to balance the flavor.

YIELDS: 6 SERVINGS (ABOUT ½ PINT)

½ cup tamarind pulp (fresh or in a block), or ⅓ cup tamarind concentrate + 2 large pitted dates

3 umeboshi plums, pitted, or 1½ tablespoons umeboshi plum paste

3 tablespoons maple syrup

1 tablespoon shoyu (soy sauce)

1 tablespoon unrefined sesame oil

If using fresh tamarind, remove the skin, veins, and seeds. If using a block, break into pieces and remove any seeds. Cover with filtered water until softened, about 15 to 30 minutes. Work the tamarind with clean fingers to dissolve as much as possible. Pull out any extra pulp and squeeze out any extra liquid and discard. Drain the pulp and reserve the soaking liquid.

Place the softened tamarind, umeboshi plums or plum paste, maple syrup, shoyu, and sesame oil in a blender. Blend at high speed until smooth. Add a touch of the tamarind soaking water if necessary. This sauce should be nice and thick.

If using tamarind concentrate and dates as an alternative, pit the dates and cover in filtered water for 10 minutes or until soft. Drain off the water and reserve. Place the tamarind concentrate, softened dates, umeboshi plums or plum paste, maple syrup, shoyu, and sesame oil in a blender. Blend at high speed until smooth. Add a touch of the date soaking water if necessary.

Serve in a dipping bowl with Spicy Thai Lettuce Wraps, or store covered tightly in the refrigerator for up to a week.

NUTRITION AT A GLANCE
Per serving: 80 calories, 2.5 g total fat, 0 g saturated fat, 0 g protein, 13 g carbohydrates, 0 g dietary fiber, 390 mg sodium

Endive Cups with Pine Nut Crème Fraîche, Fresh Figs, and Olives

These little boats of endive are delicious bites of pure joy. Perfect as an appetizer, gourmet snack, or a simply divine starting course. Olives stand well on their own when fresh figs are not available. For a lighter version, try using a bit of fresh Sweet Pea Mole (page 242) with just a dollop of dairy-free Crème Fraîche topped the same. Oooh, yum!

YIELDS: 12 SERVINGS (2 DOZEN)

CRÈME FRAÎCHE

2   cups pine nuts

¼   cup lemon juice, plus more as needed

1   tablespoon Omega Nutrition coconut butter or extra-virgin olive oil

Sea salt

Filtered water

ENDIVE CUPS

3   heads endive

6   fresh figs

1   cup kalamata olives, pitted and roughly chopped

2   tablespoons torn cilantro leaves (optional)

1   tablespoon chopped tarragon leaves (optional)

Coarse sea salt

Freshly ground black pepper

TO MAKE THE CRÈME FRAÎCHE:

Place the pine nuts, lemon juice, coconut butter or olive oil, and a pinch of salt in a food processor or a high-speed blender. Blend until ultra-smooth, adding 1 or 2 tablespoons of filtered water as necessary to achieve the correct consistency. It should be very smooth, like a thick sour cream. It will thicken more when chilled. The Crème Fraîche may be stored in a tightly sealed container in the fridge for 2 days.

TO ASSEMBLE THE ENDIVE CUPS:

Separate the endive leaves.

Trim the figs and cut into thin wedges.

Spoon a dollop of Crème Fraîche onto each endive leaf and spread. Top with fig wedges and chopped olives. Sprinkle with torn cilantro and tarragon leaves if desired and a few grains of coarse sea salt and freshly ground black pepper.

Serve immediately.

NUTRITION AT A GLANCE
Per serving: 210 calories, 19 g total fat, 1.5 g saturated fat, 4 g protein, 9 g carbohydrates, 2 g dietary fiber, 125 mg sodium

Buddha Nori Maki Roll
with Jicama-Parsnip "Rice"

Nori makes a scrumptious home for this perfectly balanced bite, boasting 38 percent protein and ample amounts of vital minerals including calcium and iron. Serve this knockout roll with Wasabi and Ponzu Dipping Sauce (opposite page) and Pickled Ginger (page 232).

YIELDS: 4 ROLLS

JICAMA-PARSNIP "RICE"

2½ cups peeled and roughly chopped jicama

2 cups peeled and roughly chopped parsnips

½ cup pine nuts

1 teaspoon sea salt

3 tablespoons brown rice vinegar

1 tablespoon lemon juice

2 tablespoons agave nectar

1 tablespoon wasabi powder (optional)

NORI MAKI

4 sheets nori

8 stalks asparagus, trimmed and blanched for 1–2 minutes

1 small cucumber, peeled and seeded, cut into matchsticks

1 carrot, cut into matchsticks

1 avocado, sliced

TO MAKE THE RICE:

In a food processor, chop the jicama into rice-size fragments. Cut a 12" piece of cheesecloth. Place the chopped jicama in the center of the cloth and gather the edges to squeeze out a bit of juice. If you don't have cheesecloth handy, place the jicama between two clean dish towels or paper towels and press down to release some of the moisture. Place the jicama in a medium bowl.

Toss the parsnips into the food processor and chop into rice-size fragments. Place in the bowl with the jicama.

Grind the pine nuts into a fine meal in the food processor and fold into the jicama and parsnips. Add the sea salt, vinegar, lemon juice, and agave and mix thoroughly. Let stand at least 20 minutes to develop flavor. If you love wasabi as much as I do, mix the wasabi powder with enough filtered water to make a paste and let stand for at least 5 minutes to develop flavor. Fold into the rice (or serve on the side to spread on each roll).

TO MAKE THE ROLLS:

Lay a sheet of nori flat on a bamboo rolling mat with the shiny side down and the rough side up. Spread 1 cup of the "rice" evenly across the bottom third of the nori sheet to the edges, leaving 1" of nori exposed at the bottom. Lay 2 stalks of asparagus, a few cucumber and carrot matchsticks, and 2 slices of avocado across the middle of the rice. For a nice touch, place the asparagus with the tips and a few matchsticks extending ½" past the edge of the sheet for decorative end pieces.

Fold the bottom edge of the nori sheet up over the veggies. Gently tuck under and roll another inch by hand. Fold the bamboo mat over the roll. Hold the roll and gently tug the far end of the mat to tighten. Moisten the top edge of the nori with wet fingers and roll closed. Hold the roll in the mat for a moment to dry and seal.

With a sharp, serrated knife, cut the roll in the middle and work your way out to one side, then the other. Wipe the knife between cuts to keep it from sticking.

Serve face-up for a pretty view, and do so immediately as the nori will become soggy if it hangs around too long. If you maul it a bit, sprinkle some black and white sesame seeds over the rolls to camouflage! It gets easier with practice, and soon you will roll them in your sleep.

NUTRITION AT A GLANCE
Per serving: 300 calories, 19 g total fat, 2 g saturated fat, 6 g protein, 29 g carbohydrates, 11 g dietary fiber, 610 mg sodium

Wasabi and Ponzu Dipping Sauce

I typically double this recipe, because the kick gets me so good and leftovers keep for up to a week. Add 2 tablespoons of sesame oil for a rockin' salad dressing.

YIELDS: 4 SERVINGS (¼ CUP)

2–3 teaspoons wasabi powder

1–2 teaspoons filtered water

2 tablespoons shoyu (soy sauce)

1 tablespoon brown rice vinegar

1 tablespoon mirin, or 2 teaspoons brown rice vinegar + 1 teaspoon agave

1 teaspoon agave nectar

1 teaspoon yuzu (optional)

Mix together the wasabi powder and water to form a paste. Let stand for 5 to 10 minutes to thicken and develop flavor.

Whisk the remaining ingredients into the wasabi paste and serve in small dipping bowls. Store leftovers in a sealed jar in the fridge for up to a week.

NUTRITION AT A GLANCE
Per serving: 10 calories, 0 g total fat, 0 g saturated fat, 1 g protein, 1 g carbohydrates, 0 g dietary fiber, 390 mg sodium

Pickled Ginger

Refreshing, spicy, and cool, pickled ginger clears the palate between bites. Traditionally served as a garni with sushi, I unabashedly enjoy it with many foods. Ginger is an excellent digestive aid and promotes good circulation. Sugar is a customary ingredient, but you can replace it with agave nectar, which is a little less sweet and will only gently impose on the flavor. Younger ginger is choice as it is less fibrous than more mature roots. Keeps fresh for weeks in the fridge.

YIELDS: 24 SERVINGS (ABOUT 3 CUPS)

2 nice "hands" of fresh ginger, peeled (see note)

1 teaspoon sea salt

1 cup brown rice vinegar

6 tablespoons organic sugar or 8 tablespoons agave nectar

Cut the ginger into 1" pieces and toss with the salt. Let stand for 30 minutes in a bowl.

Mix together the vinegar and sugar or agave in a freshly cleaned glass jar. If using sugar, stir until all of the sugar crystals are dissolved.

Place the ginger in the sweet vinegar mixture. Cover and give it a good shake. Let stand 1 week. This may be done on a cool counter or in the fridge.

After that time, slice the ginger as thinly as possible across the fiber. Return to the sweet vinegar mixture. May be used at this time or can be marinated several more days. Will keep fresh for at least 2 months, covered in the fridge.

Note: Peel the ginger using the edge of a spoon! This is really the best way to get in the nooks and crannies of a gnarly root and ensure you don't cut your pretty little paws.

NUTRITION AT A GLANCE
Per tablespoon: 10 calories, 0 g total fat, 0 g saturated fat, 0 g protein, 2 g carbohydrates, 0 g dietary fiber, 50 mg sodium

Scallion-Stuffed Roasted Shiitake Mushrooms with Ume Natto Miso

Tender shiitake mushrooms are natural immune system boosters. Here, they are marinated and stuffed with scallions and natto miso, a chunky, whole-grain miso (see Resource Guide on page 378). Natto miso is worth seeking out for this recipe, although a white or yellow miso may also be used. Try to choose mushrooms of the same size so no one gets jealous!

YIELDS: 6 SERVINGS (12 STUFFED MUSHROOMS)

12 shiitake mushrooms, stems removed

3 tablespoons raw sesame oil

2 tablespoons shoyu (soy sauce)

2 teaspoons brown rice vinegar

1 teaspoon maple syrup or agave nectar

4 tablespoons white sesame seeds

1 cup cleaned and finely chopped scallions, including greens

3 tablespoons natto miso

2 umeboshi plums, torn, or 2–3 teaspoons umeboshi plum paste

1 tablespoon finely grated ginger

1–2 cloves garlic, pressed

Pinch of sea salt (optional)

Maple syrup or agave nectar (optional)

Preheat the oven to 375°F.

Toss the mushrooms with the sesame oil, shoyu, vinegar, and maple syrup or agave. Place in a glass baking dish in the oven for 10 to 12 minutes, stirring once or twice for even roasting.

Meanwhile, toast the sesame seeds in a heavy skillet over low heat, stirring constantly, until fragrant. The seeds should not pop, or the heat is too high. Grind in a suribachi (a grooved Japanese mortar and pestle), a spice grinder, or a small food processor. Mix together with the scallions, natto miso, umeboshi plums, ginger, and garlic. Season with sea salt and maple syrup or agave to taste, if desired, to bring up the flavors.

Remove the mushrooms from the oven and crank up the heat to 425°F. Drain off any extra marinade and set it aside.

Stuff each mushroom with about 2 tablespoons of scallion filling to form a small mound. Place back in the baking dish, and drizzle with any remaining marinade.

Bake for 5 to 7 minutes, or just until turning golden brown.

Serve hot.

NUTRITION AT A GLANCE
Per serving: 60 calories, 5 g total fat, 0.5 g saturated fat, 2 g protein, 2 g carbohydrates, 0 g dietary fiber, 135 mg sodium

Crisp Spring Rolls with Plum Dipping Sauce

Cabbage is a rich source of phytonutrients that protect against disease; it's braised here with carrots and sweet onion for a tender fiber, which supports a healthy heart and happy digestion. By all means, packaged veggie broth can be used. The rolls can be cut into bite-size pieces to go farther in larger circles. Best served warm and in good company.

YIELDS: 4 SERVINGS (8 ROLLS)

2 tablespoons + ¼ cup unrefined sesame oil

1 sweet onion, cut lengthwise into thin crescents (about 1½ cups)

1 tablespoon finely chopped ginger

4 cups shredded green cabbage

3 cups coarsely shredded carrot

¼ cup sake or mirin

1 tablespoon shoyu (soy sauce) or tamari

1½ cups Light Vegetable Stock (page 178) or broth

Sea salt

2 tablespoons chopped cilantro

2 tablespoons chopped mint

2 tablespoons chopped basil

2 teaspoons agave nectar

1 package (16 ounces) spelt, whole wheat, or wheat phyllo dough, thawed

2 teaspoons toasted sesame oil (optional for a toasted flavor)

1½ tablespoons sesame seeds

4 lettuce leaves (optional for garnish)

Plum Dipping Sauce (opposite page)

1–2 green onions, finely chopped (optional for garnish)

3 tablespoons Pickled Ginger, julienned (page 232, optional for garnish)

Heat 2 tablespoons of the sesame oil over medium heat. Add the onion and sauté, stirring occasionally, for about 2 minutes, until slightly softened. Add the ginger and stir, cooking another minute. Add the cabbage and carrot and cook, stirring occasionally, for 4 minutes, or until they soften. Add the sake or mirin, shoyu or tamari, and vegetable stock. Turn up the heat to medium-high and cook, stirring occasionally, until all of the liquid has cooked off, about 8 minutes. Remove from the heat, season to taste with salt only if necessary, and let cool to room temperature. Fold in the cilantro, mint, and basil.

Preheat the oven to 400°F.

Line a baking sheet with parchment paper or lightly grease with sesame oil.

Mix together the remaining ¼ cup unrefined sesame oil and the agave in a small bowl.

Lay a sheet of phyllo dough on a clean, dry work surface. Cover the remaining dough with a towel to keep it moist.

Use a pastry brush to coat the sheet lightly with the oil mixture. Lay another sheet on top and brush lightly with the oil. Repeat until there are 4 layers.

Place a 1"-wide by 1"-thick layer of the filling across the bottom of the phyllo, leaving 1" of phyllo exposed. Fold the bottom edge of the phyllo over the filling and roll into a cylinder.

Use a serrated knife to cut the roll into 4" pieces. The rolls can be cut smaller to go farther.

Place on a lined or greased baking sheet. Brush the tops of the rolls with toasted sesame oil, if desired, and sprinkle with sesame seeds.

Bake for 15 minutes, or until golden brown.

Let cool for a few minutes before serving.

Serve on lettuce leaves with Plum Dipping Sauce and garnish with green onions and Pickled Ginger, if desired.

PLUM DIPPING SAUCE

This sauce is sweetened with plums and thickened with arrowroot.
I highly recommend organic citrus, as the peel is used for zest.

YIELDS: 24 SERVINGS (ABOUT 3 CUPS)

1   tablespoon finely chopped ginger

1   clove garlic, minced

⅓   cup shoyu (soy sauce) or tamari

4   tablespoons agave nectar

¼   cup lime juice or lemon juice

1   teaspoon lime zest or lemon zest

2   tablespoons umeboshi plum vinegar

1   cup vegetable stock or broth

4–6   ripe dark-skinned plums, pitted and cubed (about 1½ cups)

1–2   teaspoons dried chili flakes (optional)

1   teaspoon arrowroot

1   tablespoon filtered water

Place the ginger, garlic, shoyu or tamari, agave, lime or lemon juice, lime or lemon zest, vinegar, stock or broth, plums, and chili flakes (if desired) in a saucepan. Bring to a boil. Reduce the heat to medium-low and simmer for 30 minutes or until the plums are completely soft.

Whisk together the arrowroot and filtered water until dissolved. Add to the pot and cook, stirring constantly, for 5 minutes, or until thickened. Let cool for a few minutes before transferring to a blender to blend until very smooth.

Let cool to room temperature before serving. Store in a tightly sealed jar or container in the fridge for up to a week.

Potato Cannelloni with Roasted Eggplant

Thin slices of potatoes embrace a succulent, tender filling as a nouveau cannelloni.

YIELDS: 4 SERVINGS (8 ROLLS)

2   extra-large Idaho potatoes, peeled

6   tablespoons extra-virgin olive oil

1   eggplant (about ¼ pound), peeled

1   large portobello mushroom

2   cloves garlic, pressed

2   tablespoons chopped thyme

Sea salt

Freshly ground black pepper

1   small sweet onion, sliced

20 cherry tomatoes, cut in half

Watercress Parsley Pesto (page 277, optional to accompany)

2   cups sautéed spinach (optional to serve over pesto)

Preheat the oven to 350°F.

Slice the potatoes thinly on a mandoline or by hand. You need at least 16 slices.

Brush each side with a total of 2 tablespoons of olive oil and lay on cookie sheets that have been oiled or lined with parchment paper. Make sure the slices are not overlapping.

Bake for 10 minutes to soften.

Remove them from the cookie sheets and let cool on a plate. It is okay to layer them.

Meanwhile, cut the eggplant into 2" batons. Remove the stem and gills of the mushroom and slice into 8 slices.

Mix together the remaining olive oil, the garlic, thyme, and a pinch of salt and pepper.

Toss the eggplant, mushroom, and onion with the olive oil mixture and fold in the tomato halves. Spread out on a cookie sheet and roast for 10 to 15 minutes, until tender.

Turn up the oven to 400°F.

Lay two slices of potato side-by-side, overlapping by ¼". Sprinkle with a pinch of salt and pepper. Lay a few pieces of eggplant, a slice of mushroom, and 5 tomato halves in the center. Fold the bottom edge of the potato over the filling and roll. Place on a cookie sheet. Repeat.

Bake for 15 minutes, or until golden brown.

Spoon Watercress Parsley Pesto, if desired, on a small serving plate and spread. If desired, place ¼ cup of sautéed spinach over the pesto. Serve the rolls on top.

NUTRITION AT A GLANCE
Per serving: 380 calories, 22 g total fat, 3 g saturated fat, 6 g protein, 44 g carbohydrates, 8 g dietary fiber, 25 mg sodium

Collard Wraps—Two Ways

I am a big fan of bite-size delights. These rolls are more like two or four bites, but fabulous just the same. They are excellent as hors d'oeuvres, or to take for lunch on the run. Blanched marinated collard greens make a beautiful thin wrapper for seasonal vegetables. Collard greens are incredibly nutritious, with ample amounts of minerals, vitamin C, and phytochemicals, which prevent cancer. They are a great source of folate—a disease-fighting B vitamin—and calcium. I offer two seasonal variations, though the possibilities are endless. Munch and be merry.

Collard Wrappers

YIELDS: 6 SERVINGS

1 **bunch collard greens (6 large leaves)**
1 **tablespoon extra-virgin olive oil**
1 **teaspoon umeboshi plum vinegar**
1 **teaspoon lemon juice**
Sea salt
Freshly ground black pepper

Bring a wide pot of filtered water to a simmering boil. Blanch the collard greens by submerging in the water for 1 or 2 minutes, just until they turn bright green and the ribs become tender. Pull out the greens with tongs or drain immediately. Shock by running under cold water or plunging in ice water to arrest the cooking process and preserve the bright green color. Drain.

Toss the greens with the olive oil, vinegar, lemon juice, a pinch of salt, and pepper. Set aside until ready to use (if it will be more than 20 minutes, store covered in the fridge).

NUTRITION AT A GLANCE
Per serving: 30 calories, 2.5 g total fat, 0 g saturated fat, 1 g protein, 2 g carbohydrates, 1 g dietary fiber, 180 mg sodium

Summer Collard Wraps

I came up with this recipe while visiting my folks in New Paltz, New York, when the farmer's market was in full bloom. My mom has a very snazzy gas stovetop that can be converted to a grill. Even without that luxury back at home, I continue to make this treat by roasting the vegetables under the broiler.

YIELDS: 6 SERVINGS (12 ROLLS)

1   large zucchini or 2 medium zucchini

1   large portobello mushroom, stem and gills removed, in ¼" slices

2–3   tablespoons extra-virgin olive oil

1   teaspoon balsamic vinegar

1   teaspoon umeboshi plum vinegar

1   teaspoon maple syrup

1–2   cloves garlic, pressed

1   tablespoon chopped fresh oregano or 1 teaspoon dried

2   teaspoons fresh thyme or 1 teaspoon dried

1   red onion, sliced

  Sea salt

  Freshly ground black pepper

  Collard Wrappers (page 237)

12   basil leaves, torn

  Porcini, Sun-Dried Tomato, and Basil Dipping Sauce (opposite page)

Preheat the broiler if it is electric.

Cut the zucchini crosswise into 2½" pieces. Stand each section on its end and slice into ⅛" wedges.

In a large bowl, mix together the olive oil (starting with 2 tablespoons), balsamic vinegar, umeboshi plum vinegar, maple syrup, garlic, oregano, and thyme. Toss with the vegetables to coat evenly, seasoning with a pinch of salt and pepper. Add a little extra olive oil as needed. Marinate for 15 minutes to 2 hours (the flavor gets better with more time).

Lay the marinated vegetables in two casserole dishes or a large roasting pan or a baking sheet with edges (so the juices don't drip).

Place on the top rack of the oven and broil for 5 to 7 minutes, until browning nicely. Flip the vegetables over with a spatula and cook for another 5 to 7 minutes, until savory and browned (ovens vary, so watch closely so it doesn't burn).

Remove and let cool until you can handle them comfortably.

Lay a prepared collard wrapper flat on a cutting board. Use a paring knife to slice close to the rib on either side to remove the rib. Each side can be cut in half across (4 pieces per leaf).

Lay a piece of collard with the short side facing you and place a piece or two of basil on top.

Lay a piece or two of zucchini, mushroom, and onion in the center of the wrapper. Fold the bottom edge over the vegetables and tuck under. Fold the sides in (like rolling a burrito), then keep rolling the package away from you until it is closed.

If any of the leaves have torn, try patching two together. Carry on until you have used up the greens or the veggies.

Cut the rolls on an angle for a beautiful presentation.

Serve at room temperature with Porcini, Sun-Dried Tomato, and Basil Dipping Sauce.

PORCINI, SUN-DRIED TOMATO, AND BASIL DIPPING SAUCE

YIELDS: 8 SERVINGS (1 PINT)

¼ cup sun-dried tomatoes (about 5–6 dry halves, not in oil)

¼ cup dried porcini mushrooms (about ¼ ounce)

1 Roma tomato, seeded and finely chopped

1 cup vegetable stock or broth

1–2 cloves garlic

2 tablespoons pine nuts

2 tablespoons extra-virgin olive oil

1–2 teaspoons umeboshi plum vinegar

1 teaspoon aged balsamic vinegar, or ½ teaspoon balsamic vinegar + ½ teaspoon maple syrup

½–1 teaspoon apple cider vinegar

½–1 teaspoon maple syrup

2 tablespoons chives or 1 small green onion, chopped

1½–2 tablespoons fresh oregano or 1 teaspoon dried

1 teaspoon fresh thyme leaves

1 cup basil leaves

Sea salt

Freshly ground black pepper

Cut the sun-dried tomatoes into pieces with kitchen scissors. Place in a small saucepan with the mushrooms, Roma tomato, stock or broth, and garlic. Bring to a simmer over medium heat. Reduce the heat to low and gently simmer for 5 to 8 minutes (until everything is soft and smells really good). Let cool a bit because you are going to blend it and do not want to be splatter-burned.

Pour into a blender and add the pine nuts, olive oil, umeboshi plum vinegar, aged balsamic (or balsamic + maple syrup), apple cider vinegar, maple syrup, chives or green onion, oregano, thyme, basil, and a pinch of salt and pepper. Blend until very smooth. Adjust seasoning to taste (the strength of sun-dried tomatoes and porcinis varies). If the sauce is too thick, add a little stock, broth, or water and a touch more olive oil.

Serve in a small dipping bowl with a spoon.

Winter Collard Wraps

The Wild Mushroom Dipping Sauce is wonderful served warm and is also fantastic to dress steamed vegetables or to serve with roasted potatoes. Dip, munch, and be merry.

YIELDS: 6 SERVINGS (12–20 ROLLS)

1	medium butternut squash
1	fennel bulb
1	large portobello mushroom, stem and gills removed
6	shallots
2–3	tablespoons extra-virgin olive oil
1	teaspoon balsamic vinegar
1	teaspoon umeboshi plum vinegar
1	teaspoon maple syrup

1–2	cloves garlic, pressed
2	tablespoons fresh thyme or 2 teaspoons dried
1	tablespoon finely chopped fresh rosemary or 2 teaspoons dried
	Sea salt
	Freshly ground black pepper
	Collard Wrappers (page 237)
	Wild Mushroom Dipping Sauce (opposite page)

Preheat the broiler if it is electric.

Peel the butternut squash. Cut in half and scoop out the seeds with a spoon. Cut across into 3 sections. Slice into ¼" wedges.

Remove the upper stem and feathery leaves of the fennel. Cut in half and cut out the stem at the bottom. Lay facedown on the cutting board and cut across into ¼" pieces.

Cut the mushroom into ¼"-thick slices.

Mix together the olive oil (starting with 2 tablespoons), balsamic vinegar, umeboshi plum vinegar, maple syrup, garlic, thyme, and rosemary. I recommend putting the squash in one bowl and the rest of the veggies in another. Distribute the marinade evenly between the bowls and toss it with the vegetables to coat evenly, seasoning with a pinch of salt and pepper. Add a little extra olive oil as needed. Marinate for 15 minutes to 2 hours (the flavor gets better with more time).

Lay the squash in one casserole dish and the rest of the veggies in another.

Place on the top rack of the oven and cook for 6 to 8 minutes, until browning nicely. The squash might take a few minutes extra to brown. Flip the vegetables over with a spatula and return to the broiler for another 5 to 7 minutes, until savory and browned (ovens vary, but this is worth watching closely so it doesn't burn).

Remove and let cool enough so that you can handle them comfortably.

Lay a prepared collard wrapper flat on a cutting board. Use a paring knife to slice close to the rib on either side to remove the rib. Each side can be cut in half across (to get 4 pieces per leaf).

Lay a piece of collard with the short side facing you (long side running away from you).

Lay a piece or two of squash, a nice pinch of fennel and shallot, and a slice or two of mushroom in the center of the wrapper. Fold the bottom edge over the vegetables and tuck under. Fold the sides in (like rolling a burrito), then keep rolling the package away from you until it is closed.

If any of the leaves have torn, try patching two together.

Carry on until you have used up the greens or the veggies.

Cut the rolls on an angle for a beautiful presentation.

Serve at room temperature with Wild Mushroom Dipping Sauce.

WILD MUSHROOM DIPPING SAUCE

YIELDS: 6 SERVINGS (1 PINT OR SO)

¼ cup dried wild mushrooms (about ¼ ounce), a mixture of porcini and morel is ideal

4 large dates, pitted and torn into pieces

1¼ cups Mushroom Stock (page 182), Hearty Vegetable Stock (page 179), or Roasted Vegetable Stock (page 180)

2 tablespoons pine nuts

3 tablespoons extra-virgin olive oil

6 shallots, thinly sliced (about 1¼ cups)

2 cloves garlic, minced

¼ cup white wine

2 teaspoons balsamic vinegar

1 teaspoon shoyu (soy sauce)

1 teaspoon maple syrup

1 tablespoon finely chopped fresh thyme or 2 teaspoons dried

1 teaspoon Dijon mustard

  Sea salt

  Freshly ground black pepper

Place the mushrooms and dates in a small saucepan with the stock. Bring to a gentle simmer over medium heat. Reduce heat to low and let simmer for 10 minutes, or until the mushrooms are completely soft.

Place the pine nuts in a medium skillet and toast over low heat, stirring regularly, for 3 to 4 minutes, until fragrant but not browned. Set aside.

In the same skillet, warm the olive oil over medium heat. Add the shallots and cook, stirring frequently, for 5 minutes, or until soft and turning translucent. Add the garlic and cook for 1 minute, until fragrant but not browned. Add the wine, balsamic, shoyu, and maple syrup. Turn the heat up to medium-high and continue to cook, stirring occasionally, for 7 to 10 minutes, or until almost all of the liquid has cooked off. Add the softened mushrooms and dates with their cooking stock. Cook, stirring occasionally, for about 10 minutes, or until about half of the liquid has reduced. Add the thyme, mustard, and a pinch of salt and pepper (be mindful not to

(continued)

oversalt if the stock has salt in it already). Stir and remove from the heat.

Let cool for a few minutes. Use an emersion blender or transfer to a blender to blend until smooth. Season with salt and pepper only if needed. Use as is, or pass through a sieve for a more delicate texture.

Serve warm or at room temperature. Store leftovers in a sealed container in the fridge for up to 3 days.

NOTE: *In a pinch, organic, prepared vegetable broth may be used, or filtered water and natural bouillon cubes.*

NUTRITION AT A GLANCE
Per serving: 130 calories, 9 g total fat, 1 g saturated fat, 3 g protein, 9 g carbohydrates, 0 g dietary fiber, 140 mg sodium

---

Sweet Pea Mole

This simple spread is brilliant on the Endive Cups with Pine Nut Crème Fraîche, Fresh Figs, and Olives (page 229), on top of a thick slice of a juicy summer tomato, or as a complement to guacamole and salsa. Of course, I am happy with just a bowlful and a spoon.

YIELDS: 6 SERVINGS (2 CUPS)

2	**cups sweet peas**
1½	**cups cilantro leaves**
2	**tablespoons lime juice**
1–2	**teaspoons lime zest**
1	**tablespoon extra-virgin olive oil**
	Sea salt
	Freshly ground black pepper

If using fresh peas, blanch in hot water for a few minutes until they turn bright green. Drain and shock under cold running water. If using frozen peas, simply thaw to room temperature.

Finely chop the cilantro in a food processor. Add the peas, lime juice, lime zest, and olive oil and chop in pulses until pummeled, but not completely smooth.

Season to taste with salt and pepper.

Serve fresh as the color will fade.

NUTRITION AT A GLANCE
Per serving: 60 calories, 2.5 g total fat, 0 g saturated fat, 3 g protein, 7 g carbohydrates, 2 g dietary fiber, 240 mg sodium

---

Edamame Hummus

Edamame are sold shelled, usually in the freezer section. Blended and seasoned with fresh herbs, green onion, and a smattering of pine nuts, these protein-rich beans are lovely, light, and easy to digest. I sincerely advise to purchase organic or GMO-free edamame (and all soy), as soybeans are a primary crop subject to genetic engineering.

YIELDS: 12 SERVINGS (ABOUT 3¼ CUPS)

3 cups organic edamame, shelled (thaw if using frozen beans)

3–4 tablespoons pine nuts, may be lightly toasted to bring up the flavor

3 green onions, trimmed, cleaned, and chopped to the top

1 small clove garlic

2–4 teaspoons peeled, finely grated ginger (to taste)

1–2 tablespoons raw sesame oil or olive oil

1 tablespoon umeboshi plum vinegar

2 teaspoons shoyu (soy sauce)

1 teaspoon brown rice vinegar or lemon juice

1 cup chopped parsley leaves

¼ cup chopped cilantro leaves (optional)

Sea salt

In a food processor or a high-speed blender (such as the Vita-Mix), combine the edamame, pine nuts, green onions, garlic, ginger, sesame or olive oil, umeboshi plum vinegar, shoyu, and brown rice vinegar or lemon juice. Blend until very smooth.

Add the parsley and cilantro (if using). The herbs may be blended in completely or blended in pulses so pieces of leaves are visible.

Season and adjust to taste, adding a bit of salt, a touch more oil, ginger, and so forth until you are pleased as punch. Serve with pita, crackers, and/or veggie crudité.

NUTRITION AT A GLANCE
Per serving: 70 calories, 5 g total fat, 1 g saturated fat, 5 g protein, 3 g carbohydrates, 0 g dietary fiber, 310 mg sodium

Smoked Pine Nut Farmer's Cheese

Seeds and nuts may be used to make a soft cheese sans dairy, but with the slightly tangy taste similar to cottage cheese. The fermenting action breaks down the protein and fats, which are teeming with healthy microorganisms for good digestion.

YIELDS: 24 SERVINGS (ABOUT 3 CUPS)

2	Lapsang Souchong tea bags	1½	tablespoons lemon juice
3	cups hot filtered water	2	tablespoons Omega Nutrition coconut butter or olive oil
3	cups pine nuts (see note)		Smoked salt or sea salt
2	teaspoons white miso		

Steep the tea bags in the hot water for 5 minutes. Allow the tea to cool slightly, but not completely. It is helpful if the tea is a bit warm to get the fermenting action going.

Place the pine nuts in a blender. Add the miso and tea. The liquid should cover the pine nuts by ½" or so. Blend until fairly smooth.

Line a colander or mesh strainer with two layers of cheesecloth, allowing 3" or more hanging over each side to cover the cheese while it is fermenting. Place the colander over a bowl to catch liquid (called *whey*) as the cheese ferments. Pour the blended mixture into the colander.

Set in a warm spot (75° to 95°F) for 8 to 10 hours, or until it begins to smell a little ripe and the cheese is firm like a thick hummus. The top may become discolored from oxygen; just scrape it off. In warm climates and seasons, an out-of-the-way place on the counter may be just right. This may also be done in a dehydrator that has a temperature setting, or in an oven with a pilot light (to keep warm), with the door slightly ajar

(to be sure it does not get too warm!).

If the cheese is still quite moist, press down on the cheesecloth to extract excess liquid (save the whey to use in dressings or to drink as a fortified probiotic).

Mix in the lemon juice and coconut butter or olive oil by hand or blend until ultra smooth in the food processor or a high-speed blender (like the Vita-Mix). Season to taste with smoked salt.

The cheese will firm up in the fridge.

Serve as a dip, on slices of ripe tomato with chopped basil, or layered with seasoned, steamed or baked sliced vegetables in a strata or lasagna. Do not heat the cheese above 120°F as the cultured microorganisms cannot survive.

NOTE: *Pine nuts are choice for this recipe, but they cost a pretty penny, so buy in bulk! Check out www.pinenut.com for wild-harvested, organic pine nuts grown in America. Or try using raw cashews in place of half of the pine nuts to conserve your purse. Cover 1½ cups raw cashews with 2 cups filtered water for 1 hour. Drain and rinse. Carry on as directed.*

NUTRITION AT A GLANCE
Per serving: 130 calories, 13 g total fat, 1 g saturated fat, 2 g protein, 2 g carbohydrates, 0 g dietary fiber, 15 mg sodium

Quick Smoked Pine Nut Spread

This version of the farmer's cheese is simpler and does not require fermenting the cheese. Though the added benefits of a flurry of enzymes, healthy bacteria, and predigested protein are curbed, it is delicious and takes a short time to prepare. I recommend Omega Nutrition's coconut butter, which does not have a strong coconut smell; otherwise, a good olive oil is perfect.

YIELDS: 24 SERVINGS (ABOUT 3 CUPS)

1 Lapsang Souchong tea bag, or any smoked tea

1 cup hot filtered water

3 cups pine nuts

2 tablespoons lemon juice

2 tablespoons Omega Nutrition coconut butter or olive oil

Smoked salt or sea salt

Steep the tea bag in the hot water for 5 minutes. Squeeze the tea bag to extract as much tea as possible. Allow the tea to cool until you can touch it comfortably.

Grind the pine nuts into a fine meal in a food processor. Add the cooled tea, lemon juice, and coconut butter or olive oil and blend until smooth. Season to taste with smoked salt or sea salt.

NUTRITION AT A GLANCE
Per serving: 120 calories, 13 g total fat, 1 g saturated fat, 2 g protein, 2 g carbohydrates, 0 g dietary fiber, 0 mg sodium

Whey Out!

Most of us consider dairy whey to be a great source of protein, and so is this whey. As an added benefit, the whey from this cheese is full of probiotics, or healthy microorganisms. These helpful bacteria encourage a vital population of healthy flora in our intestines, which are largely responsible for digesting food and nutrients small enough to be passed through our intestinal walls and used by our bodies. Refined food, alcohol, stress, and antibiotics all kill off the good guys. A healthy ecology of microbes in our guts not only improves digestion, it boosts the immune system as well. Replenishing and nourishing our friendly flora is a smart measure, especially when doing so tastes delicious!

Winter Squash Butter

*This velvety copper-colored butter is lovely to spread on any kind of bread or cracker.
For an innovative use of leftovers, add ½ cup of squash butter to 1 cup of vegetable
stock and warm for a serving of smooth soup. Winter squash provides great fuel with
easy-to-digest complex carbohydrates and gentle fiber. As you might guess from their
bright orange-yellow color, they are a prime source of vitamin A in the form of
beta-carotene, a natural antioxidant, as well as vitamin C, and they're rich in minerals
such as potassium and magnesium. This spread keeps fresh in a tightly sealed container
for up to 4 days in the fridge or for up to a month in the freezer.*

YIELDS: 4 CUPS

1   large winter squash, such as kabocha, blue hubbard, red kuri, or butternut (about 6 cups of cubes)

2   tablespoons olive oil

1   clove garlic

1   teaspoon finely grated ginger

1–2   tablespoons fresh thyme leaves

1   teaspoon fresh rosemary

    Sea salt

    Freshly ground black pepper

Scrub the squash. It is easier to peel after cooking so leave the skin on.

Cut in half and scoop out the seeds with a spoon. Cut into 1" wedges or cubes. Place in a medium-large saucepan and cover with filtered water by 2". Bring to a boil over high heat. Reduce the heat and simmer for 6 to 9 minutes, or until tender and easily pierced with a fork.

Drain (reserve the liquid for other uses such as making a vegetable stock or at least watering houseplants!) and let cool.

Cut away the skin with a paring knife. Place in a food processor with the olive oil, garlic, ginger, thyme, and rosemary. Blend until very smooth. Season to taste with sea salt and pepper.

NUTRITION AT A GLANCE
Per cup: 220 calories, 7 g total fat, 1 g saturated fat, 4 g protein, 43 g carbohydrates, 7 g dietary fiber, 15 mg sodium

Spring Carrot, Fennel, and Leek Spread

*Fennel is abundant in vitamin C and lots of disease-fighting compounds and
phytonutrients. Steam the vegetables first for a lighter spread with a clean finish,
or roast them to bring out the natural sweetness and aromatic essence.*

YIELDS: 8 SERVINGS (ABOUT 4 CUPS)

3   medium carrots, chopped

1   medium fennel bulb, cut into wedges

1   leek, white part only, chopped

2–3   tablespoons olive oil

    Sea salt

¼   cup almonds (may be soaked for
    8 hours in filtered water to improve
    digestibility; see page 251)

1   teaspoon whole coriander seeds

1   teaspoon white miso

1   tablespoon lemon juice

2   tablespoons fresh dill, or more to taste

2   tablespoons chopped cilantro, or
    more to taste

3   tablespoons finely chopped chives

TO STEAM THE VEGETABLES:

Bring 1½" of water to a rolling boil in a medium
saucepan. Steam the carrots just until tender (3
to 5 minutes). Remove and shock by running
under cold water. Set aside. Steam the fennel just
until tender (3 to 4 minutes). Remove and shock
by running under cold water. Set aside. Steam
the leek just until tender (2 to 4 minutes). Remove
and shock by running under cold water.

TO ROAST THE VEGETABLES:

Preheat the oven to 350°F.

In a bowl, toss the prepared vegetables with 1
tablespoon of olive oil and a pinch of salt. Spread in
one layer in a glass casserole dish or roasting pan.

Bake for 15 to 20 minutes, or until tender and
just able to be pierced with a fork.

TO MAKE THE SPREAD:

Place the almonds and coriander seeds in a food
processor or blender and grind into a fine meal.

Add the prepared vegetables, 2 tablespoons of
olive oil, miso, and lemon juice and blend until
very smooth. Season to taste with salt.

Add the dill, cilantro, and chives and blend in
pulses, just until mixed.

Serve at room temperature or chilled.

NUTRITION AT A GLANCE
Per serving: 80 calories, 6 g total fat, 0.5 g saturated fat, 2 g protein, 7 g carbohydrates, 2 g dietary fiber,
55 mg sodium

Roasted Garlic and Zucchini Baba Ghannouj

Baba ghannouj is a Middle Eastern spread made from roasted eggplant, typically served with or in the same manner as hummus. This baba ghannouj features sweet, creamy roasted garlic. Two bulbs may seem like a ton of garlic, but roasting mellows the flavor. Serve with Sesame Poppy Seed Pita Crisps (opposite page).

YIELDS: 10 SERVINGS (1½ PINTS)

1 **eggplant (about 1 pound)**	1 **large onion**
4 **tablespoons extra-virgin olive oil, plus a little more as needed**	¼ **cup sesame seeds**
1 **teaspoon sea salt**	2 **teaspoons whole cumin seeds**
2 **medium zucchini**	3 **tablespoons lemon juice**
2 **bulbs garlic**	1 **tablespoon chopped fresh oregano (optional for variation)**

Preheat the oven to 400°F.

Cut the eggplant in half lengthwise. Rub the face with a little olive oil and a sprinkle of salt and place facedown in an oiled glass casserole dish or roasting pan.

Cut the ends off of the zucchini and rub with a little olive oil. Add to the eggplant.

Rub the garlic bulbs to loosen and remove the papery outer skin. Cut off the pointed top of the garlic bulbs, leaving the cluster of cloves intact. Place in a separate casserole dish (big enough to accommodate the onion as well) and drizzle and rub each head with 1 teaspoon of olive oil.

Cut the ends off the onion and peel. Cut in quarters and rub with 1 teaspoon of olive oil, keeping the quarters intact. Place in the same dish with the garlic bulbs.

Place both dishes in the oven for about 45 minutes, or until everything is savory and soft through and through.

Remove from the oven and let cool for 10 minutes or until cool enough to handle.

Cut the zucchini into 1" pieces and place in a strainer over a bowl.

Use a large spoon to scoop the flesh of the eggplant out of the skin and into the same strainer. Allow the excess juices to drip for 15 to 20 minutes.

Lightly toast the sesame seeds and cumin seeds in a skillet over low heat just until fragrant. Let cool for a few minutes. Place in a food processor and grind into a fine meal.

Peel the garlic and add to the food processor with the onion, eggplant, zucchini, 3 tablespoons of olive oil, the lemon juice, 1 teaspoon of sea salt, and oregano (if desired). Blend until smooth.

NUTRITION AT A GLANCE
Per serving: 100 calories, 8 g total fat, 1 g saturated fat, 2 g protein, 7 g carbohydrates, 2 g dietary fiber, 5 mg sodium

SESAME POPPY SEED PITA CRISPS

These are deliciously yummy and perfect with dips or with Mediterranean dishes. Try replacing the sesame and poppy seeds with ground pine nuts for a variation and adding a bit of oregano or rosemary for Italian fare. If you like a little heat, try sprinkling with a bit of crushed dried chili pepper.

YIELDS: 6 SERVINGS (ABOUT 5 CUPS)

4 pitas

⅓ cup extra-virgin olive oil, or as needed

3 tablespoons sesame seeds

2 tablespoons poppy seeds

2 teaspoons dried thyme

½ teaspoon sea salt

Preheat the oven to 350°F.

Split the pitas in half along the seam to end up with flat rounds.

Place the olive oil in a little dish and use a pastry brush to lightly coat both sides of the pita rounds.

Place with the rough side up on baking sheets.

Crush the sesame seeds, poppy seeds, thyme, and salt in a mortar and pestle. This may also be done in a food processor. (If using pine nuts as a variation, grind them into a fine meal in a food processor.)

Sprinkle the mixture evenly over the pita halves.

Bake for about 10 minutes, until golden brown. Cut into triangles while still warm.

Store in an airtight container or bag in a cool, dry place (in the unlikely event of leftovers).

NUTRITION AT A GLANCE
Per serving: 180 calories, 14 g total fat, 2 g saturated fat, 2 g protein, 11 g carbohydrates, 2 g dietary fiber, 290 mg sodium

White Almond Hummus—Three Ways

Okay, this is not really hummus in the traditional sense as it does not contain beans of any sort (although you can certainly substitute chickpeas for the almonds in each recipe; see "Soaking Beans" on page 197). Almonds are rich in protein, calcium, antioxidants, and heart-healthy properties. Soaking the almonds first makes them light, alkaline, and easy to digest. Removing the skin offers a pale white smoothness. Peeling them by hand, however, takes some time. Blanching the almonds helps the skin slip off easily (check out "All about Almonds" for friendly advice).

Simple White Almond Hummus

YIELDS: ABOUT 1 PINT

2 cups almonds, soaked and peeled (see "All about Almonds" on opposite page)

¼ cup lemon juice

2–3 tablespoons extra-virgin olive oil

1 clove garlic

Sea salt

Place the almonds, lemon juice, olive oil, and garlic in a high-speed blender or food processor. Blend until silky smooth. Add a touch more oil or filtered water to aid blending if necessary. Season to taste with sea salt.

This hummus can be stored in a tightly sealed container in the fridge for 3 to 4 days.

NUTRITION AT A GLANCE
Per tablespoon: 60 calories, 5 g total fat, 0 g saturated fat, 2 g protein, 2 g carbohydrates, 0 g dietary fiber, 0 mg sodium

All about Almonds

Inside every little almond rests the potential energy of a great big almond tree. Soaking almonds wakes up that dormant energy, unleashing nutrients and enzyme activity, as well as converting the nut's nutrition into a more bioavailable form. Soaked almonds are easier to digest for a few reasons. First, they swell up with water, making them much less dense. Second, the soaking process wicks away self-protective compounds in the skin called enzyme inhibitors, like tannic acid, which slow down digestion. When you soak almonds for more than a few hours, you will see the soaking water turn an amber color, indicative of the leached enzyme inhibitors. Last but not least, soaking nuts like almonds changes the very nature of the food. Once a sleeping seed, it is now in a growing, metabolic state of changing into a plant. The life force awakens and is unleashed.

Soaking Almonds for Greater Nutrition and Easy Digestibility

- Start with raw almonds. Organic are best.
- Cover each cup of almonds with 2 cups of filtered water.
- Use good water as the almonds will soak up most of it.
- Soak for 6 to 12 hours at room temperature.
- Drain in a colander and rinse.
- Use as needed or store in a sealed jar or container in the fridge for 3 to 5 days.

Blanching Almonds for Easy Peeling

Soaked almonds can be blanched in boiling water for a minute, which loosens the skin significantly so they pop right out. With all due respect to my years of devotion to raw foods, blanching soaked nuts in boiling water offers a very quick, gentle, moist heat. I am willing to do it because it saves 15 to 20 minutes of patient peeling. I am all for meditative practices, but rarely do there seem to be enough minutes in the hours as it is.

To blanch soaked almonds: Bring a pot of water to a boil and drop in the soaked almonds. Let the water return to a boil for about a minute. Drain in a colander and allow to cool enough so that you can handle them. Squeeze the almond with your thumb and forefinger to pop it out of the skin. Get fancy and do one with each hand at once. In no time at all, you will have peeled 2 cups. Carry on!

Scallion, Ginger, Parsley, and Tarragon Hummus (Spring)

The south of France meets Asia in this tangy, creamy springtime dip.
For a unique treat, serve with Lemongrass Coconut Chips (page 256).
This recipe is also a prize using chickpeas.

YIELDS: ABOUT 1½ PINTS

1½   cups almonds, soaked and peeled (see "All about Almonds" on page 251), or chickpeas

¼   cup raw tahini or pine nuts (optional for extra-creamy texture)

1½   tablespoons finely grated ginger

1   small clove garlic

2   tablespoons umeboshi plum vinegar

2   tablespoons lemon juice

2   tablespoons extra-virgin olive oil

1   tablespoon mirin or a sweet sake or 2 teaspoons brown rice vinegar + 1 teaspoon agave

2   scallions, trimmed and cleaned, white part chopped roughly, green part chopped finely

¼   cup finely chopped chives or an additional scallion finely chopped

½   cup finely chopped parsley

1   tablespoon finely chopped tarragon (optional)

    Sea salt

    Freshly ground black pepper

Place the almonds or chickpeas, tahini or pine nuts (if desired), ginger, garlic, umeboshi plum vinegar, lemon juice, 2 tablespoons of olive oil, mirin or sake (or brown rice vinegar + agave), and the white part of the scallions in a high-powered blender or food processor. Blend until silky smooth. Add additional olive oil and/or filtered water to aid blending if necessary. It may be necessary to scrape the walls of the blender or food processor and continue to blend to achieve an even, smooth consistency. Fold in the green part of the scallions, the chives (or an additional scallion), parsley, and tarragon (if desired). Season to taste with salt and pepper.

This hummus can be stored in a tightly sealed container in the fridge for 3 to 4 days.

NUTRITION AT A GLANCE
Per tablespoon: 40 calories, 3.5 g total fat, 0 g saturated fat, 1 g protein, 1 g carbohydrates, 0 g dietary fiber, 135 mg sodium

White Almond and Artichoke Heart Hummus

I'm a big fan of artichoke hearts, so this splendiferous spread embodies my heart's and taste buds' desires. Fresh artichoke hearts are best procured when in season and can be marinated, steamed, or roasted to taste. You can use store-bought (organic) artichoke hearts to save time. Look for water-packed or oil-packed artichoke hearts over those marinated with vinegar. If you choose to buy the artichoke hearts and the only kind available involves vinegar, they can be rinsed to mellow the flavor so it doesn't overpower all else. This recipe is also great using chickpeas.

YIELDS: 1½ PINTS

1½ **cups almonds, soaked and peeled (see "All about Almonds" on page 251), or chickpeas**

2 **tablespoons raw tahini or pine nuts**

4 **artichoke hearts, divided (see "Artichoke Hearts—Three Ways" on page 254)**

Extra-virgin olive oil or filtered water

Sea salt

Place the almonds or chickpeas, tahini or pine nuts, and 3 of the prepared artichoke hearts in a high-speed blender or food processor. Blend until silky smooth. Add olive oil and/or filtered water to aid blending if necessary. It may be necessary to scrape the walls of the blender or food processor and continue to blend to achieve an even, smooth consistency. Season to taste with sea salt. Chop the remaining artichoke heart and fold into the hummus.

This hummus can be stored in a tightly sealed container in the fridge for 3 to 4 days.

NUTRITION AT A GLANCE
Per tablespoon: 35 calories, 3 g total fat, 0 g saturated fat, 1 g protein, 1 g carbohydrates, 0 g dietary fiber, 10 mg sodium

Artichoke Hearts—Three Ways

Getting to the heart of the artichoke takes a bit of doing. Cut off the top
third of the leaves using a serrated knife, which will make it easier to
saw through the tough leaves. Remove all of the leaves. Trim away any
tough pieces left on the heart. Use a spoon to scrape the furry material
from the top of the heart. I offer you three ways to prepare these prized
hearts to fit your fancy.

Marinated Artichoke Hearts

YIELDS: ABOUT 2½ CUPS

4 artichoke hearts, cleaned

3 tablespoons lemon juice

2 tablespoons extra-virgin olive oil, or
   1 tablespoon Omega Nutrition coconut
   butter + 1 tablespoon flax oil

1 teaspoon fresh thyme or ½ teaspoon
   dried

1–2 cloves garlic, pressed

1 bay leaf

Sea salt

Thinly slice the artichoke hearts.

Toss with the lemon juice, olive oil (or coconut butter + flax oil), thyme, garlic, bay
leaf, and a pinch of sea salt until well coated.

Let stand at least an hour or overnight before using. Don't forget to remove the bay
leaf!

NUTRITION AT A GLANCE
Per serving (½ cup): 60 calories, 6 g total fat, 1 g saturated fat, 1 g protein, 2 g carbohydrates,
0 g dietary fiber, 55 mg sodium

Steamed Artichoke Hearts

YIELDS: ABOUT 2½ CUPS

4 artichoke hearts, cleaned

¼ cup lemon juice

2 tablespoons extra-virgin olive oil, or
    1 tablespoon Omega Nutrition coconut
    butter + 1 tablespoon flax oil

1–2 cloves garlic, pressed

1 teaspoon fresh thyme or ½ teaspoon
    dried

Sea salt

Slice the hearts into ¼" pieces.

Steam over boiling water for 3 to 5 minutes just until tender.

Toss with the lemon juice, olive oil (or coconut butter + flax oil), garlic, thyme, and a pinch of sea salt. Let stand for 15 minutes to absorb flavor before using.

NUTRITION AT A GLANCE
Per serving (½ cup): 60 calories, 6 g total fat, 1 g saturated fat, 1 g protein, 2 g carbohydrates, 0 g dietary fiber, 55 mg sodium

Roasted Artichoke Hearts

YIELDS: ABOUT 2½ CUPS

4 artichoke hearts, cleaned

3 tablespoons lemon juice

2 tablespoons extra-virgin olive oil

1 teaspoon fresh thyme or ½ teaspoon dried

1–2 cloves garlic, pressed

1 bay leaf

Sea salt

Preheat the oven to 350°F.

Slice the artichoke hearts into ¼" pieces.

Toss with the lemon juice, olive oil, thyme, garlic, bay leaf, and a pinch of sea salt.

Spread in a casserole dish or roasting pan.

Bake for 20 to 25 minutes until golden brown. Let cool 15 minutes before using.

NUTRITION AT A GLANCE
Per serving (½ cup): 60 calories, 6 g total fat, 1 g saturated fat, 1 g protein, 2 g carbohydrates, 0 g dietary fiber, 55 mg sodium

Lemongrass Coconut Chips

Lemongrass and coconut meet in the heavenly crunch of these chips. Ground flaxseed, which is packed with protein and beautifying oils, lends a nutty snap. These chips are perfect alongside a salad, soup, or with guacamole and salsa.

YIELDS: 12 SERVINGS (6 CUPS)

4½ tablespoons dried lemongrass or 4 lemongrass tea bags

4 cups hot filtered water

2 cups ground golden flax seed (brown flax may be used, but it will make the chips darker)

3 cups dried coconut

1 cup chopped cilantro

1 cup finely chopped green onion

1½ teaspoons sea salt, or to taste

Steep 3 tablespoons of dried lemongrass or 4 tea bags in the hot water for 10 to 20 minutes. Strain. Let cool until you can use your finger to comfortably test the temperature.

Place the ground flaxseed in a bowl. Grind the coconut and remaining 1½ tablespoons of lemongrass (if using) into a powder. Add the tea and blend until smooth. Pour into the bowl with the ground flaxseed and fold together until well mixed.

Fold in the cilantro and green onion. Season to taste with salt. I prefer to keep these crackers less salty, so I sprinkle the tops with salt after spreading, when they're ready to dehydrate.

Let stand for 10 minutes to absorb liquid.

Spread the mixture ⅛" thick on dehydrator trays lined with nonstick sheets. Use clean, wet hands or a rubber spatula for easy spreading.

Sprinkle with salt if desired.

Dehydrate at 108°F for 12 to 20 hours, or until mostly dry. Peel away the nonstick sheets and cut the cracker sheets into triangles, rectangles, or squares. Return to the dehydrator without the nonstick sheets and dry for another few hours until crispy. (Climate, temperature, and humidity make the necessary time variable.)

Alternatively, the mixture may be spread on cookie sheets and dried in the oven set at the lowest temperature for 4 to 6 hours, or until completely dry.

Store in a zip-top bag in a cool, dry place. If the chips get soft and soggy from storing, freshen up by dehydrating or baking until dry again.

NUTRITION AT A GLANCE
Per serving: 240 calories, 21 g total fat, 11 g saturated fat, 5 g protein, 11 g carbohydrates, 9 g dietary fiber, 310 mg sodium

CHAPTER 8

On the Side

The qualities of an exceptional cook are akin to those of a successful tightrope walker—an abiding passion for the task, courage to go out on a limb, and an impeccable sense of balance.

—BRYAN MILLER, *NEW YORK TIMES*

Ginger-Glazed Carrots

Rarely am I shy with ginger. It is a magical rhizome (a type of root) that grows on my island home and produces beautiful, exotic flowers. Ginger is prized for stimulating and easing digestion. Essential minerals such as calcium, potassium, sodium, and phosphorus are concentrated in and just under the skin of carrots, though the skin is sometimes tough and bitter. Take a bite of the carrot raw and peel as you please. Brown rice syrup lends a nice glaze, though agave nectar or maple syrup may be used if you don't have brown rice syrup on hand. For a beautiful presentation, choose young, tender bunches of carrots with the greens still attached and simply slice them in half lengthwise. For extra crunch, serve topped with whole or chopped Teriyaki Almonds (opposite page).

YIELDS: 4 SERVINGS

1½   **tablespoons raw sesame oil or olive oil**

1½   **tablespoons ginger juice (page 160)**

1   **tablespoon peeled, finely grated ginger**

1–2   **cloves garlic, pressed or very finely minced**

2   **tablespoons shoyu (soy sauce) or tamari**

1   **tablespoon brown rice syrup, or 2 teaspoons agave nectar or maple syrup**

1   **bunch young carrots, greens removed and scrubbed or peeled, sliced in half lengthwise, or 2–4 medium carrots, scrubbed or peeled, sliced ¼" thick on an angle**

  Sea salt

Preheat the oven to 375°F.

In a bowl, mix together the oil, ginger juice, grated ginger, garlic, shoyu or tamari, and brown rice syrup (or agave or maple syrup).

Fold the carrots into the glaze marinade.

Place in a glass casserole dish, cover with a lid or foil, and bake for 12 to 15 minutes. Uncover and stir the carrots to keep them coated and bake uncovered for another 7 to 15 minutes, or until tender (it will depend a bit on how thick the carrots are). They may be baked until quite soft and easily pierced with a fork, or left al dente, as desired. Season to taste with sea salt.

NUTRITION AT A GLANCE
Per serving: 90 calories, 5 g total fat, 1 g saturated fat, 1 g protein, 11 g carbohydrates, 1 g dietary fiber, 450 mg sodium

Teriyaki Almonds

Teriyaki is a dynamic flavor where sweet, salty, and a touch of spiciness meet. Soaking the almonds wakes up their nutrition and enzymes, making them lighter and more digestible, and dehydrating at low temperatures preserves the precious good stuff. These take a bit of time, but they store well and make the ultimate snack. I usually double the recipe and stash some in the freezer. Yum!

YIELDS: 12 SERVINGS (3 CUPS)

2 cups almonds, soaked in filtered water for 8 hours and drained

2 tablespoons nama shoyu (unpasteurized soy sauce)

1 tablespoon umeboshi plum vinegar

1 tablespoon maple syrup

1 tablespoon agave nectar

2 teaspoons brown rice vinegar

½ teaspoon chili powder

Pinch of cayenne pepper

Toss the almonds with the shoyu, umeboshi plum vinegar, maple syrup, agave, brown rice vinegar, chili powder, and cayenne pepper. Allow to marinate for 1 to 3 hours.

Spread in a shallow dish and dehydrate at 112°F for 12 to 20 hours, or until completely dry. Or spread on a cookie sheet and place in the oven with only the pilot light on for 12 to 20 hours, or in the oven set at the lowest setting for 4 to 8 hours.

These will keep for at least 2 weeks in a tightly sealed container or bag in a cool, dry place or in the freezer for up to 2 months.

NUTRITION AT A GLANCE
Per serving: 150 calories, 12 g total fat, 1 g saturated fat, 5 g protein, 6 g carbohydrates, 3 g dietary fiber, 270 mg sodium

Kinpira Gobo Burdock

Kinpira Gobo is a braised burdock dish with a tender texture and balanced earthy flavor, popular in good Japanese restaurants. Burdock is a long, tapered root with rough brown skin prized for its strengthening properties and known to build and cleanse the blood. Good burdock should be firm and not flexible. Using a little toasted sesame oil deepens the flavor, which I favor in cold weather; in warm seasons, I prefer it without.

YIELDS: 8 SERVINGS (3 CUPS)

2   teaspoons unrefined sesame oil

1   teaspoon toasted sesame oil (optional)

2   cups burdock, peeled and cut into matchsticks

1   medium carrot, cut into matchsticks

2   cloves garlic

2   tablespoons peeled sliced ginger

¼   cup mirin or sake

2   tablespoons shoyu (soy sauce) or wheat-free tamari

1   tablespoon maple syrup

¼   sheet nori, cut into thin strips, for garnish (optional)

1–2   tablespoons Gomasio (page 280), for garnish (optional)

Warm the unrefined sesame oil and the toasted sesame oil (if desired) in a skillet over medium heat. Add the burdock, carrot, garlic, and ginger and sauté for about 8 minutes, or just until the garlic is beginning to brown. Remove the garlic and add the mirin or sake, shoyu or tamari, and maple syrup. Add a bit of filtered water so the burdock and carrots are partially covered with liquid but not submerged. Cook about 15 minutes, or until almost all of the liquid has evaporated and been absorbed. Remove from the heat. Let stand for 10 minutes to absorb any extra liquid and allow the flavor to settle.

This dish is traditionally served chilled or at room temperature.

Garnish with the nori or Gomasio, if desired.

Store leftovers covered in the fridge for up to a week.

NUTRITION AT A GLANCE
Per serving: 60 calories, 1 g total fat, 0 g saturated fat, 1 g protein, 11 g carbohydrates, 1 g dietary fiber, 200 mg sodium

Nishime Carrot and Lotus Root

The macrobiotic system recognizes that the way a food is cooked influences what it does for the body. Nishime cooking strengthens the body and restores vitality (see page 121 for more on Nishime methods). Lotus root is a lacy, tactile treat. If you can't find it at the market, use burdock root, turnips, daikon radish, Jerusalem artichokes, onions, or winter squash.

YIELDS: 4 SERVINGS

1	strip (5–7") kombu seaweed
2–3	carrots, scrubbed or peeled and sliced into ½" pieces
1–2	fresh lotus roots, scrubbed or peeled and sliced into ½" pieces
3	tablespoons shoyu (soy sauce)
2	tablespoons agave or maple syrup
1	tablespoon brown rice vinegar
1	tablespoon umeboshi plum vinegar

In a small bowl, cover the kombu seaweed with filtered water and soak for 30 minutes, until it is soft. Using warm water will speed up this process to about 15 minutes). When the seaweed is soft, cut into 1" pieces.

Place the softened, cut kombu and its soaking water in the bottom of a heavy pot with a lid.

Add the carrots, lotus roots, shoyu, agave or maple syrup, brown rice vinegar, and umeboshi plum vinegar. Add enough filtered water just to cover.

Cover with a lid and place over high heat for 2 to 3 minutes until a good steam is generated.

Reduce the heat to cook gently, covered, for 15 minutes, more or less. If all of the water evaporates during cooking, add a touch more.

When the vegetables are soft and lovely, add a few dashes more of shoyu and shake the pot to toss the veggies. If desired, add a dash of umeboshi plum vinegar and a drizzle of agave or maple syrup as well and toss to mix. Cover again and cook another 3 to 5 minutes.

Remove the cover and let stand a few minutes. Most or all of the water should have evaporated. If there is any liquid left over, serve with the veggies as it is delicious.

NUTRITION AT A GLANCE
Per serving: 50 calories, 0 g total fat, 0 g saturated fat, 2 g protein, 11 g carbohydrates, 3 g dietary fiber, 1,520 mg sodium

Japanese Eggplant with Sweet Miso

This is one of my favorite dishes to order in a good Japanese restaurant.
Japanese eggplants are thinner, longer, and often more tender than standard eggplants.
Of course, any eggplant will do in this recipe.

YIELDS: 4 SERVINGS

4   tablespoons raw sesame oil

2   tablespoons white miso

1   tablespoon maple syrup or agave nectar (or 1 tablespoon each)

1   teaspoon brown rice vinegar

2   cloves garlic, pressed

1   tablespoon finely shredded ginger

3   green onions, cleaned and chopped to the top

4   Japanese eggplants (about 1 pound)

Preheat the oven to 350°F.

Mix together the sesame oil, miso, maple syrup or agave, brown rice vinegar, garlic, ginger, and green onions.

Peel or cut the tops off of the eggplants. Cut in half lengthwise.

Use a paring knife to cross-hatch the flesh inside the skin, being careful not to cut into the skin.

Spoon and spread the sesame-miso mixture on each half.

Place in a baking dish, cover with a lid or foil, and bake for 20 to 25 minutes. Test with a fork for tenderness.

Raise the oven temperature to 425°F, uncover, and bake for 10 to 15 minutes, or until golden on top.

Serve hot.

NUTRITION AT A GLANCE
Per serving: 180 calories, 14 g total fat, 2 g saturated fat, 2 g protein, 15 g carbohydrates, 3 g dietary fiber, 240 mg sodium

Shaved Brussels Sprouts and Leeks

Brussels sprouts are the unsung hero of the table. I think they are a great test of character: Anyone who loves them must have good taste. My mom (a fantastic cook and my first culinary influence) makes a delicious version of this recipe adding toasted, chopped pecans. To be as great as her, spread out 1 cup of pecans on a baking sheet and toast at 350°F for 5 to 10 minutes. Chop 'em and toss in with the Brussels sprouts and leeks before serving. Yum. Thanks, Mama.

YIELDS: 6 SERVINGS

4 cups sliced Brussels sprouts

1 nice leek, sliced into ½" pieces, including the green

3–4 tablespoons olive oil

1 tablespoon umeboshi plum vinegar

2 teaspoons aged balsamic, or 1 teaspoon balsamic + 1 teaspoon maple syrup

1 teaspoon shoyu (soy sauce)

Sea salt

Steam the Brussels sprouts for about 5 minutes, or until just tender enough to pierce with a fork. Remove from the pot and shock under cold, running water just after steaming to arrest the heat to prevent overcooking.

Then steam the leek for about 4 minutes, until perky green and tender. The time will vary depending on the size of the veggies and the cut of each. Remove from the pot and shock.

Toss in a bowl with the olive oil, umeboshi plum vinegar, aged balsamic (or balsamic + maple syrup), and shoyu. Adjust to taste and season with sea salt as desired.

Excellent warm or at room temperature.

Stores well for a day or two.

NUTRITION AT A GLANCE
Per serving: 100 calories, 7 g total fat, 1 g saturated fat, 4 g protein, 8 g carbohydrates, 3 g dietary fiber, 590 mg sodium

---

Umeboshi Daikon Bowl

Daikon is a very long, large member of the radish family with firm white flesh. It is a nonstarchy root vegetable, which makes it very easy to digest. Its characteristically peppery, slightly spicy bite mellows when it is steamed. All radishes are rich in sulfur, which helps maintain beautiful skin and aids cellular repair. Daikon is also prized for its ability to dissolve mucus and fat deposits in the body. Umeboshi and ginger are both excellent digestive aids and keep the metabolism pumping; try topping with Wasabi Ginger Pumpkin Seeds (see opposite page) for an extra kick of flavor and texture. Toss any leftover daikon into tomorrow's salad.

YIELDS: 4–6 SERVINGS

1	daikon, scrubbed and trimmed, cut in half lengthwise and into ¼" pieces
6	red radishes, scrubbed and trimmed, whole or halved
1	leek, cut into ¼" pieces
1–1½	tablespoons flax oil
2–3	teaspoons raw sesame oil or olive oil
1–1½	tablespoons umeboshi plum vinegar
2	umeboshi plums, torn (optional)
2	teaspoons ginger juice (page 160)
1–2	teaspoons shoyu (soy sauce)
	Sea salt

Steam the daikon, radishes, and leek separately in a steaming basket over boiling water for 3 to 4 minutes, or until they are tender and a fork can just pierce them, but they're not too soft. Their resident heat will cook them a bit more, so it's best to remove them from the heat when they're a hair underdone.

Toss immediately with the flax oil, sesame or olive oil, umeboshi plum vinegar, umeboshi plums (if desired), ginger juice, and shoyu. Season to taste with salt only if desired.

NUTRITION AT A GLANCE
Per serving: 70 calories, 6 g total fat, 0.5 g saturated fat, 1 g protein, 5 g carbohydrates, 0 g dietary fiber, 870 mg sodium

---

Wasabi Ginger Pumpkin Seeds

Wasabi and ginger are a match made in the heaven of exciting flavors. They're married here with pumpkin seeds for a champion source of easy-to-digest protein, especially when soaked. Pumpkin seeds are also full of heart-healthy oils and have ample amounts of minerals such as iron, magnesium, manganese, phosphorus, and zinc.

YIELDS: 12 SERVINGS (ABOUT 3 CUPS)

½ teaspoon Celtic sea salt

4 cups + 3 tablespoons filtered water

2½ cups pumpkin seeds

1 tablespoon wasabi powder

2 tablespoons peeled and finely shredded ginger

2–3 teaspoons nama shoyu (unpasteurized soy sauce)

2–3 teaspoons umeboshi plum vinegar

1 teaspoon maple syrup (optional)

Dissolve the salt in the fresh water.

Soak the pumpkin seeds in the salt water for 4 to 6 hours. Drain and rinse.

Mix the wasabi powder and the filtered water in a small bowl. Allow to stand for 5 minutes to thicken and take on flavor.

Toss the pumpkin seeds with the wasabi paste, ginger, shoyu, vinegar, and maple syrup (if desired). Allow to marinate for 1 to 3 hours.

Spread on dehydrator trays and dehydrate at 112°F for 12 to 20 hours or until dry. May also be done on a cookie sheet in the oven with only the pilot light on (for 12 to 20 hours) or in an oven set at the lowest setting (for 4 to 8 hours).

Delicious on salad, soup, or as a crunchy snack.

They will keep in a tightly sealed glass jar, container, or sealable bag in a cool, dry place for at least 2 weeks or in the freezer for up to 2 months.

NUTRITION AT A GLANCE

Per serving (¼ cup): 60 calories, 2.5 g total fat, 0 g saturated fat, 3 g protein, 7 g carbohydrates, 0 g dietary fiber, 320 mg sodium

Green and Wax Beans
with Basil and Mint

Fresh green beans are a bookmark for summer. A mix of yellow wax beans and green beans is just beautiful. Basil and mint are my bosom buddies, simply seasoned in this recipe with olive oil, sea salt, and freshly ground black pepper with a touch of lemon juice and aged balsamic vinegar to work magic.

YIELDS: 2–4 SERVINGS

½ **pound green beans, stems snapped off (younger and tender are better)**

½ **pound yellow wax beans, stems snapped off (or additional green beans)**

2–3 **tablespoons olive oil**

1 **teaspoon lemon juice**

1 **teaspoon aged balsamic vinegar, or ½ teaspoon balsamic + ½ teaspoon maple syrup**

1 **cup chopped basil**

½ **cup chopped mint**

Sea salt

Freshly ground black pepper

Steam the green beans and wax beans for about 5 minutes, or just until bright and tender, but still crisp. Shock by running under cold water to arrest the cooking process.

Toss with the olive oil, lemon juice, aged balsamic (or balsamic + maple syrup), basil, and mint and season to taste with sea salt and black pepper.

NUTRITION AT A GLANCE
Per serving: 200 calories, 14 g total fat, 2 g saturated fat, 4 g protein, 18 g carbohydrates, 9 g dietary fiber, 5 mg sodium

Old-World Ratatouille

This is a slow-cooked, old-world dish that tastes even better the day after, when the flavors have had time to marry. Use leftovers to layer with phyllo dough for an amazingly delicious spanakopita or with a thin-crust pizza (see Chapter 10).

YIELDS: 8 SERVINGS

1	nice eggplant, peeled and cut into 1" cubes
1	teaspoon sea salt
8	Roma or plum tomatoes or 5 common tomatoes
2	medium zucchini
1	yellow onion, thinly sliced
1	red onion, thinly sliced
2–4	cloves garlic, minced
1	red bell pepper, chopped (optional)
1	green bell pepper, chopped (optional)
1	sprig (3") rosemary
2	bay leaves
¼	cup + 2 tablespoons olive oil
3	tablespoons spelt flour (wheat flour may be used)
	Sea salt
	Freshly ground black pepper
2	cups chopped basil
2–3	tablespoons fresh thyme

Toss the eggplant with the sea salt and place in a colander over a bowl for 1 hour to draw out the bitter juices. Rinse the eggplant and squeeze gently. This step of salting is not entirely necessary, but worth the effort. It can be done a day ahead of time if necessary (the eggplant will brown a bit from oxidation, but it will be just fine to use).

Preheat the oven to 350°F.

Chop the tomatoes roughly. This is a rustic dish and they do not have to be perfect and are almost better when irregular. Place in a large glass casserole dish.

Cut the top and bottom off the zucchini. Slice in half lengthwise and cut into ½" pieces. Add to the tomatoes.

Add the onion, garlic, and peppers (if desired) to the other ingredients.

Toss in the eggplant, rosemary, and bay leaves. Drizzle in ¼ cup of the olive oil and toss gently.

Sprinkle with flour and gently toss.

Bake for 30 minutes, or until everything is savory and soft.

Allow to cool a bit. Fold in the remaining 2 tablespoons of olive oil and season to taste with salt and pepper. Fold in the basil and thyme just before serving (and don't forget to remove the rosemary and bay leaves).

NUTRITION AT A GLANCE
Per serving: 150 calories, 11 g total fat, 1.5 g saturated fat, 3 g protein, 13 g carbohydrates, 4 g dietary fiber, 300 mg sodium

Roasting Vegetables

A vegetable's firmness, freshness, and size influence its roasting time. Also remember that ovens vary in temperature—some run hotter than others despite what the setting reads, and others have "hot spots" in certain areas. So get to know your oven! It is a good friend with a lifetime of rewarding returns.

BEETS		
BABY BEETS AND SMALL BEETS	350°	25 MINUTES
MEDIUM TO LARGE BEETS	350°	30–45 MINUTES
¼" BEET SLICES	350°	10–12 MINUTES
CARROTS		
BABY CARROTS	350°	15–20 MINUTES
MEDIUM TO LARGE CARROTS	350°	25–40 MINUTES
¼" CARROT SLICES	350°	8–12 MINUTES
CORN		
ON COB	350°	35–45 MINUTES
KERNELS	350°	20–30 MINUTES
EGGPLANT		
WHOLE: SMALL TO MEDIUM	350°	25–40 MINUTES
HALVES: SMALL TO MEDIUM	350°	20–25 MINUTES
WHOLE: MEDIUM TO LARGE	350°	50–60 MINUTES
HALVES: MEDIUM TO LARGE	350°	40–50 MINUTES
1" CUBES	350°	15–20 MINUTES
GARLIC		
WHOLE BULB	350°	45–60 MINUTES
CLOVES	350°	25–35 MINUTES
ROUGHLY SLICED	350°	10–15 MINUTES
LEEKS		
WHOLE	350°	25–35 MINUTES
HALVES	350°	20–25 MINUTES
½" SLICES	350°	15–20 MINUTES
MUSHROOMS		
PORTOBELLO (WHOLE)	350°	25–30 MINUTES
PORTOBELLO (½" SLICES)	350°	12–15 MINUTES
SHIITAKE (WHOLE)	350°	15–20 MINUTES

ONIONS		
WHOLE: MEDIUM	400°	45–60 MINUTES
HALVES: MEDIUM	375°	25–30 MINUTES
½" WEDGES	375°	15–20 MINUTES
POTATOES		
WHOLE: SMALL	400°	30–40 MINUTES
WHOLE: MEDIUM TO LARGE	400°	55–65 MINUTES
1" WEDGES	400°	30–40 MINUTES
1" CUBES	400°	30–40 MINUTES
¼" SLICES (SOFT)	375°	10–15 MINUTES
¼" SLICES (CRISPY)	425°	30–40 MINUTES
SHALLOTS		
WHOLE	350°	10–15 MINUTES
¼" SLICES	350°	5–10 MINUTES
SQUASH		
SUMMER SQUASH (WHOLE MEDIUM)	350°	25 MINUTES
SUMMER SQUASH (½" SLICES)	350°	15–20 MINUTES
WINTER SQUASH (HALVES)	375°	30–40 MINUTES
WINTER SQUASH (1" WEDGES)	375°	20–30 MINUTES
WINTER SQUASH (1" CUBES)	375°	12–20 MINUTES
SWEET POTATOES		
WHOLE	400°	50–60 MINUTES
1" WEDGES	375°	15–25 MINUTES
TURNIPS		
WHOLE: SMALL TO MEDIUM	350°	8–12 MINUTES
WHOLE: MEDIUM TO LARGE	350°	15–25 MINUTES
1" WEDGES	350°	10–15 MINUTES

Melanzana and Pomodoro—Simple or Stuffed Italian Eggplant and Tomatoes

Eggplant and tomatoes are very prolific at the height of the season, and this recipe was born from my overflowing garden. I love the uncomplicated ease of simple eggplant and tomatoes with a little garlic and olive oil, but adding a stuffing of crumbly ground pine nuts is a nice authentic Italian touch. I prefer to make my own breadcrumbs out of spelt bread (see "Homemade Breadcrumbs," opposite page). If you're using one huge eggplant and you have the time, I recommend salting the eggplant first to pull out the bitter juices. Smaller eggplants are usually less bitter and don't suffer from not being salted, and Japanese eggplants (long and thin) are rarely if ever salted.

YIELDS: 4 SERVINGS

1 nice eggplant	1–2 cloves garlic, pressed
1 teaspoon sea salt	2 nice tomatoes
2 tablespoons extra-virgin olive oil, or as needed	

STUFFING

¼ cup pine nuts	1 tablespoon extra-virgin olive oil
2 tablespoons fresh oregano leaves or 2 teaspoons dried	1–2 tablespoons chopped basil
½ cup breadcrumbs (see "Homemade Breadcrumbs," opposite page)	

Preheat the oven to 350°F.

Peel the eggplant and slice into ½" slices.

Toss the eggplant with the salt and place in a colander over a bowl for 1 hour to draw out the bitter juices. Rinse the eggplant and squeeze gently. This step of salting is not entirely necessary, but worth the effort. It can be done a day ahead of time if necessary (the eggplant will brown a bit from oxidation, but it will be just fine to use).

Mix together the olive oil, garlic, and a pinch of salt (if the eggplant was salted, no need to add salt here). Toss with the eggplant, which will soak it up quickly. Add a bit more olive oil if necessary to lightly coat evenly.

Cut the tops out of the tomatoes and slice a little less thick than the eggplant.

In a ceramic or glass casserole dish, set the eggplant slices in the semblance of their original form, like a log. Place a tomato slice between each eggplant slice. It is best to finish with egg-plant slices on the ends.

It is ready to bake at this point if you do not wish to stuff it. If that is the case, skip the next few steps and proceed with baking.

TO STUFF:

Place the pine nuts in a food processor with the oregano. Grind into a fine meal. Add the bread-crumbs to the pine nuts and oregano. Chop in pulses until mixed.

Spoon a bit of the mixture in between each slice of tomato and eggplant. If there is any left-over stuffing, sprinkle it on top.

Cover with a lid or foil. Bake for 20 to 25 minutes. Uncover and bake another 10 to 20 minutes, until savory and soft.

Let cool for 10 to 15 minutes before drizzling with olive oil and sprinkling with basil.

Leftovers are great on a salad the next day.

NUTRITION AT A GLANCE
Per serving: 220 calories, 17 g total fat, 2 g saturated fat, 5 g protein, 17 g carbohydrates, 6 g dietary fiber, 630 mg sodium

---

Homemade Breadcrumbs (Oil Free!)

Most store-bought breadcrumbs have oil in them, which is unnecessary for this recipe as the pine nuts lend just the right balance.

I choose spelt bread as it has more body and nutritive value than wheat, but practically any bread will do, even pita pockets!

Preheat the oven to 350°F.

Place 4 slices of bread directly on the racks in the oven.

Toast until completely dry (15 to 20 minutes or so).

Let cool. Break into pieces and grind into a fine meal in a food processor. Voila! Breadcrumbs. Store in a tightly sealed container or bag in the fridge for up to 2 weeks or in the freezer for up to 2 months. To freshen breadcrumbs that have been stored, spread on a cookie sheet and bake at 350°F for 3 to 4 minutes.

Lotus Root and Jerusalem Artichoke Bake

Lotus roots are unexpectedly plain from the outside. But split one open, and you'll find an exquisite interior with decorative pockets that look like rustic lace. Fresh lotus root is available in good natural markets and Asian markets. Dried lotus root, which is sometimes easier to find in the Japanese or macrobiotic section of health food stores, may also be used in this recipe. The dried root must first be soaked in warm filtered water for at least an hour to reconstitute. A Jerusalem artichoke is a non-starchy root vegetable with tons of iron that looks like a nubby potato and has a crisp texture and nutty flavor.

YIELDS: 8 SERVINGS

2　lotus roots (4" to 5" each), scrubbed or peeled and sliced ⅛" thick

6　Jerusalem artichokes, scrubbed and sliced ⅛" thick

1　leek, trimmed and sliced ¼" thick (save upper green leaves for soup)

4–5　tablespoons extra-virgin olive oil, raw sesame oil, or mixture of both

2　tablespoons shoyu (soy sauce)

1　teaspoon maple syrup (optional)

1　tablespoon finely shredded ginger

2–4　cloves garlic, pressed or minced finely (see note)

　　Sea salt

NOTE: *The amount of garlic to use depends on the size of the cloves and your love of garlic—use even more than 4 cloves if you love it! The flavor mellows with long baking.*

Preheat the oven to 375°F.

In a large bowl, toss together the lotus roots, Jerusalem artichokes, and leek.

Mix the oil, shoyu, maple syrup (if desired; it lifts the flavor nicely), ginger, garlic, and just a pinch of salt. Pour over the vegetables and toss to coat evenly.

Let stand to marinate at least 20 minutes to absorb flavor, stirring occasionally. The longer it marinates, the deeper the flavor. This may be done overnight in the refrigerator. If marinating in the fridge, let stand on the counter for 20 minutes to come to room temperature before baking.

Spread on a baking sheet or in a glass casserole dish and bake for 40 minutes to 1 hour, until golden brown. Stir the veggies with a wooden spoon for even cooking 2 to 3 times while baking.

Season with salt to taste.

This dish is best served fresh from the oven, though leftovers may be freshened by drizzling with a bit of oil and baking for 10 minutes.

NUTRITION AT A GLANCE
Per serving: 180 calories, 7 g total fat, 1 g saturated fat, 4 g protein, 27 g carbohydrates, 3 g dietary fiber, 220 mg sodium

Roasted Winter Squash and Brussels Sprouts with Shallots and Thyme

Roasted vegetables warm the body (and the kitchen!) in the wintry months. Heirloom squashes are usually the most flavorful, though any winter squash may be used, including butternut, kabocha, blue hubbard, red kuri, acorn, or delicata. Try adding some cubed beets to roast for a beautiful aesthetic variation.

YIELDS: 8 SERVINGS

1   **winter squash (about 2 pounds)**

18   **Brussels sprouts, trimmed and cut in half**

6   **shallots, peeled and cut in half**

4   **tablespoons olive oil**

2–4   **cloves garlic, pressed**

2½   **tablespoons fresh thyme or 1 tablespoon dried**

   Sea salt

   Freshly ground black pepper

Preheat the oven to 375°F.

Scrub the squash briskly. There are so many valuable minerals and nutrients in the skin that I choose to leave it on rather than peel it. However, if this is too rustic of a taste or appearance for you, feel free to peel away.

Cut the squash in half and scoop out the seeds with a spoon. Cut into wedges and then into 1" cubes. Place in a glass casserole dish with the Brussels sprouts and shallots.

Mix the olive oil, garlic, thyme, and a pinch of salt. Toss in with the prepared vegetables.

Bake for 20 to 25 minutes, or until everything is tender and the squash can be pierced with a fork.

Season to taste with sea salt and black pepper.

NUTRITION AT A GLANCE
Per serving: 120 calories, 7 g total fat, 1 g saturated fat, 3 g protein, 15 g carbohydrates, 3 g dietary fiber, 15 mg sodium

Twice-Baked Yukon Gold Potatoes with Chives

There is something kind and comforting about a baked potato. Twice baked is twice as good. It surprises some folks that potatoes are very nutritious, especially the skins. A good source of vitamin B$_6$ and minerals like potassium, manganese, and copper, potatoes boast helpful antioxidants to combat free radicals. The starchy carbohydrate of root vegetables is calming for the body, and triathletes and extreme sports enthusiasts value this type of fuel for peak performance. To me, this dish is hearty enough to be an entrée, served with a crunchy romaine salad; Spinach, Mushrooms, and Caramelized Onions (page 288); Tuscan Pomodoro Soup (page 191), or sliced tomatoes and avocado.

YIELDS: 4 LARGE SERVINGS

4 **Yukon Gold potatoes**

6 **tablespoons pine nuts, lightly toasted if you desire to bring out the flavor**

4 **tablespoons cold-pressed coconut butter, such as Omega Nutrition, or olive oil**

2 **tablespoons olive oil (or truffle oil if you are feeling decadent!)**

2 **tablespoons lemon juice**

½ **cup finely chopped chives**

½ **cup finely chopped parsley**

Sea salt

Freshly ground black pepper

Preheat the oven to 400°F.

Scrub the potatoes. Prick with a fork a half-dozen times each.

Bake for 45 to 60 minutes, or until soft. Remove from the oven and cool almost completely. Leave oven on.

Lay a potato on a cutting board and cut away the top, leaving ⅔ of the potato. Scoop the softened interior into a large bowl, leaving enough behind to give the potato structure. Repeat with the remaining potatoes.

In a blender or food processor, blend the pine nuts, coconut butter, olive oil (or truffle oil), and lemon juice until smooth. Mash into the potato pulp and add the chives and parsley. Season to taste with salt and pepper.

Stuff the mixture back into the potato skins, creating a nice little mound.

Bake until browned (10 to 15 minutes).

NUTRITION AT A GLANCE
Per serving: 380 calories, 25 g total fat, 4.5 g saturated fat, 6 g protein, 33 g carbohydrates, 3 g dietary fiber, 115 mg sodium

Twice-Baked Sweet Potato Halves with Shallots, Corn Kernels, and Savory Herbs

Sweet potatoes are a nutritious comfort food, perfect for satisfying autumn and winter cravings. Rich in vitamins A and C and manganese, sweet potatoes are valued for stabilizing the blood sugar and providing an even, long-burning fuel for the body. This dish is a notable pleaser for the holidays, with savory seasoning and the sweet crunch of corn kernels and tender shallots.

YIELDS: 4 SERVINGS

2	sweet potatoes
3–4	tablespoons olive oil
2	cloves garlic, pressed
1	tablespoon ginger juice (page 160)
3	tablespoons fresh thyme or 1½ tablespoons dried
3	tablespoons chopped fresh marjoram or 1 tablespoon dried oregano
	Sea salt
	Freshly ground pepper
4–5	shallots, finely chopped
2	ears corn, cut from the cob

Preheat the oven to 400°F.

Scrub the sweet potatoes. Prick with a fork a half-dozen times each.

Bake for 45 to 60 minutes, or until soft. Remove from the oven and cool almost completely. Leave oven on.

Cut the sweet potatoes in half, lengthwise. Scoop out the inside, leaving enough behind to maintain structure.

Using the back of a large fork, mash the scooped sweet potato with the olive oil, garlic, ginger juice, thyme, and marjoram or oregano. Season to taste with sea salt and pepper.

Mix in the shallots and corn kernels.

Stuff the mixture back into the sweet potato halves, creating a little mound.

Bake until golden brown (10 to 15 minutes).

NUTRITION AT A GLANCE
Per serving: 220 calories, 11 g total fat, 1.5 g saturated fat, 4 g protein, 27 g carbohydrates, 4 g dietary fiber, 25 mg sodium

Caramelized Onion Mashed Potatoes

Mashed potatoes are one of the ultimate comfort foods. This recipe uses an ample amount of caramelized onion in the mash, resulting in a melt-in-your-mouth texture. A touch of steamed pear sounds unusual but lends a certain je ne sais quoi, for which I must offer all due respect to Mr. Roger Verge, one of the great culinary masters of all time, who passed along this secret.

YIELDS: 6 SERVINGS

4	cups peeled potatoes, cut into 1" cubes
½	cup peeled and chopped pear (choose a nice firm pear that is not grainy)
3	tablespoons olive oil
2½	cups chopped yellow onion
1	teaspoon balsamic vinegar (aged is best)
1	teaspoon shoyu (soy sauce)
½	teaspoon agave nectar or maple syrup
2	tablespoons Omega Nutrition coconut butter or olive oil (optional)
	Sea salt
	Freshly ground black pepper
1	tablespoon fresh thyme leaves (optional)

Place the potatoes in a saucepan, cover with filtered water by 2", and add a large pinch of sea salt. Bring to a boil. Reduce the heat and simmer until the potatoes are tender enough that you can easily pierce them with a fork (12 to 15 minutes).

Drain. Save at least 2 cups of the salty boiling water to cook the pear in.

Place the pear in a saucepan with the potato cooking water and bring to a boil. Reduce the heat and simmer for 3 to 5 minutes, or until tender but not falling apart. Drain. Blend until smooth in a blender or food processor.

Warm the olive oil in a medium frying pan over medium heat.

Add the onion and cook, stirring occasionally, until it starts to become soft and translucent (5 to 8 minutes).

Add the balsamic, shoyu, and agave or maple syrup and cook, stirring occasionally, until totally soft, savory, and caramelized.

Pass the potatoes, pear, and onions through a food mill, or pureé in a food processor.

Add the coconut butter or olive oil if desired and season to taste with salt and pepper.

Mix in the thyme just before serving.

NUTRITION AT A GLANCE
Per serving: 180 calories, 7 g total fat, 1 g saturated fat, 3 g protein, 27 g carbohydrates, 3 g dietary fiber, 55 mg sodium

Wasabi Miso Mashed Sweet Potatoes

Serve these flavorful potatoes as is or with Watercress Parsley Pesto (see below).

YIELDS: 6 SERVINGS

2 sweet potatoes, peeled and cubed
   Sea salt
2–4 tablespoons wasabi powder
3–6 tablespoons filtered water
2 tablespoons ginger juice (page 160)
2 tablespoons melted coconut butter
2 tablespoons raw sesame oil or olive oil
2 tablespoons white miso

Place the sweet potatoes in a saucepan. Cover with filtered water by 2" and add a teaspoon of sea salt. Bring to a boil and cook until easily pierced with a fork (5 to 10 minutes). Drain.

Mix the wasabi powder and water to form a paste. Let stand 5 minutes. Mix with the ginger juice, coconut butter, sesame oil, and miso.

Pass the sweet potatoes through a food mill. Mix in the wasabi-miso mixture and season to taste.

NUTRITION AT A GLANCE
Per serving: 130 calories, 8 g total fat, 1.5 g saturated fat, 2 g protein, 13 g carbohydrates, 2 g dietary fiber, 230 mg sodium

WATERCRESS PARSLEY PESTO

Watercress and parsley are epic sources of vitamins A, C, and K.

YIELDS: 18 SERVINGS (ABOUT 2¼ CUPS)

1 bunch watercress, cleaned
1 cup parsley leaves
4 tablespoons raw sesame oil
¼ cup chopped green onion
2 teaspoons umeboshi plum vinegar
   Sea salt
1 cup pumpkin seeds
2 tablespoons pine nuts

Toss the watercress and parsley with the sesame oil, green onion, vinegar, and a pinch of sea salt. Let marinate for 10 minutes or more.

Toast the pumpkin seeds and pine nuts over low heat, stirring regularly with a wooden spoon, until fragrant (4 to 8 minutes).

Grind all of the ingredients in a suribachi, or puree in a food processor. Add a bit more oil if necessary and season to taste with salt.

NUTRITION AT A GLANCE
Per serving: 50 calories, 4.5 g total fat, 0.5 g saturated fat, 1 g protein, 3 g carbohydrates, 0 g dietary fiber, 120 mg sodium

CHAPTER 9

Greens, Grains, and Beans

To eat is a necessity, but to eat intelligently is an art.

—FRANCOIS DE LA ROCHEFOUCAULD

Gomaae (Japanese-Style Cold Spinach)

This is a traditional Japanese dish of cold spinach. Popeye knew spinach would give him super-strength, but he might have been surprised to learn that he was protecting himself from osteoporosis, heart disease, and cancer at the same time! Along with epic amounts of vitamin K, to mineralize and build strong bones, spinach contains lots of carotenoids, known to prevent prostate cancer. Lightly seasoned with soy and sake, this dish is wonderfully simple and refreshing. Many Japanese dishes include sugar, though I recommend maple syrup for this recipe because it is naturally less refined and rich with minerals like manganese and zinc. Adding sweetness is optional here and this dish is still delicious without it. Try it with the toasted sesame seeds of Gomasio (page 280).

YIELDS: 4 SERVINGS

1	**pound spinach, cleaned**
1	**tablespoon sake or mirin**
1–2	**teaspoons shoyu (soy sauce) or wheat-free tamari**
1	**teaspoon lemon juice**
1	**teaspoon maple syrup (optional)**
1	**tablespoon Gomasio (optional, page 280)**

Bring a pot of water to a boil. Blanch the spinach leaves by submerging them in the boiling water for 30 seconds to 1 minute. Drain and shock under cold running water or by plunging in ice water to arrest cooking and preserve the bright green color. Gently squeeze and pat dry with a clean towel.

Toss with the sake or mirin, shoyu or tamari, lemon juice, and maple syrup (if desired).

Serve in a small bowl topped with Gomasio, if desired.

NUTRITION AT A GLANCE
Per serving: 20 calories, 0 g total fat, 0 g saturated fat, 2 g protein, 3 g carbohydrates, 2 g dietary fiber, 210 mg sodium

Gomasio

Gomasio is a staple on a macrobiotic table. It is prized as a balancing condiment, with the yin of the oil in the sesame seeds and the yang of the salt bringing grounded flavor to many dishes. It lends a nutty, salty flavor and a dash of protein to simple vegetable dishes, salads, grains, and soups. Patiently using a very low heat to toast the sesame seeds is key to bringing out the best qualities. I recommend making it regularly and storing in a cool, dry place to keep the oil in the sesame seeds tasting fresh and buoyant.

YIELDS: 1½ CUPS

1½ teaspoons sea salt (see note)

1½ cups sesame seeds (white, brown, black, or a mixture)

In a heavy skillet, toast the sea salt over medium heat for about 3 minutes. Keep it moving until it becomes a little shiny and off-white. Place the toasted salt in a suribachi (a Japanese grooved mortar and pestle).

Reduce the heat to low and toast the sesame seeds, stirring regularly with a wooden paddle or wooden spoon. The seeds will swell up a bit and become fragrant. It is okay if a few of the seeds pop, but if they start popping like popcorn, it is a sign that the heat is too high. Be careful not to let them burn. Remove from the heat.

First, grind the salt into a fine powder in the suribachi. Then add the toasted sesame seeds and grind until almost all of the seeds are cracked open. This will take 5 to 10 minutes and is a great task to share, as the smell is amazing. The grinding can be done in a regular mortar and pestle or in a food processor if a suribachi is not available.

Store in a glass jar in a cool, dry place.

Note: For a sweet-and-sour variation, replace the salt with 1 tablespoon of umeboshi plum vinegar drizzled over the toasted sesame seeds. Stir until the vinegar is absorbed and the skillet is dry, then grind the seeds according to the directions.

NUTRITION AT A GLANCE
Per tablespoon: 50 calories, 4.5 g total fat, 0.5 g saturated fat, 2 g protein, 2 g carbohydrates, 1 g dietary fiber, 140 mg sodium

Live Shoyu Wasabi Gomasio

If you fancy the nose-tingling kick of wasabi, this Gomasio is for you. Soaking the sesame seeds wakes up the nutrients and enzymes, which are preserved using low temperatures to dry and set the flavors.

YIELDS: 32 SERVINGS (2 CUPS)

2 cups sesame seeds (white, black, or mixture of both)

4 cups water

1 tablespoon wasabi powder (add more if you love the kick!)

3 tablespoons filtered water (if using more wasabi, use a bit more water)

2 teaspoons nama shoyu (unpasteurized soy sauce)

1 teaspoon umeboshi plum vinegar

Pinch of sea salt

In a fine strainer, rinse the sesame seeds. Place in a bowl and cover with 4 cups of water for 8 hours. Drain and rinse in a fine strainer.

Mix the wasabi powder and filtered water in a small bowl. Let stand for 5 minutes to thicken and take on flavor. Mix in the shoyu, vinegar, and salt. Toss with the sesame seeds until evenly coated.

Spread on mesh trays and dehydrate at 112°F for 8 to 12 hours, or until dry.

Alternatively, spread on a baking sheet and dry in the oven, set at the lowest temperature, for 4 hours, or until completely dry.

Grind in a suribachi (a Japanese grooved mortar and pestle) until most of the seeds are cracked, which will take 5 to 10 minutes. The grinding can be done in a regular mortar and pestle or in a food processor if a suribachi is not available.

Store in a glass jar in a cool, dry place.

NUTRITION AT A GLANCE
Per tablespoon: 50 calories, 4.5 g total fat, 0.5 g saturated fat, 2 g protein, 2 g carbohydrates, 1 g dietary fiber, 55 mg sodium

Good Greens for the Balanced Plate

Leafy greens are champions of health and an essential part of the balanced plate. Calorie for calorie, leafy green vegetables have more nutrients than any other food. They are loaded with chlorophyll, disease-fighting phytonutrients, and just about every vitamin in the book. Greens are a mighty source of the three main antioxidants found in food that disarm free radicals from causing damage in our bodies— water-soluble vitamin C to protect the aqueous environment inside and outside of cells; fat-soluble vitamin A, in the form of beta-carotene; and vitamin E, which, in combination with vitamin A, covers all essential fat-containing molecules and structures. Green leafy guys have a precious B-complex profile, especially folate, which is vital for healthy red blood cells, a proud sponsor of strong circulation, and essential for expecting mamas! Green veggies also have a full spectrum of minerals, including iron, calcium, potassium, magnesium, manganese, and precious trace minerals, and are a good source of simple protein for clean, easy-burning energy.

Collard Greens

Collard greens are anticancer champions of the brassica family, which includes giants like kale, broccoli, and cabbage. With generous, smooth green leaves, sometimes tinged with blue, collard greens are packed with sulfur-containing phytonutrients that protect against cancer and disease. Collards are an incredible source of the three main vitamin antioxidants—A, C, and E—and have a rich mineral profile. Along with cardio-protecting B vitamins, potassium, magnesium, and a good dose of zinc for hearty immune strength, collards have an ample amount of calcium to help mineralize and strengthen bones, support nerve conduction, and maintain healthy cell membranes. Just 1 cup of cooked collard greens contains half the Recommended Dietary Allowance (RDA) of manganese, the precious antioxidant trace mineral that activates enzymes, especially the one that helps our bodies use vitamin C.

Kale

Kale is one of the mightiest members of the brassica family of cruciferous veggies, a kin to cabbage, broccoli, and bok choy. All of the siblings are rich in sulfur-containing phytonutrients, which promote health and fight diseases. Standing out as a powerful anticancer food, kale, like all cruciferous veggies, triggers our livers to produce enzymes that detoxify cancer-causing chemicals in the body. Kale is one of the best sources of the antioxidant vitamins A, C, and E, as well as the precious B-complex posse, including B_1, B_3, and B_6. Chock-full of minerals such as calcium, iron, manganese, and copper, this superstar even contains the essential fatty acid omega-3.

Spinach

Popeye was right—spinach is a pure source of energy that offers great defense! With a bevy of anticancer flavonoids and carotenoids that especially fight prostate cancer and protect the eyes, just 1 cup of cooked spinach offers more than 1000 percent of the RDA of vitamin K, more than 200 percent of the RDA of vitamin A, and an ample dose of vitamin C. These delicate greens are loaded with B-complex vitamins, especially folate and riboflavin (B_5), a prime player in metabolic activity and energy production. With a flurry of resident minerals, including tons of iron, calcium, magnesium, potassium, and copper, spinach is one of the most nutritious greens of all time.

Swiss Chard

Swiss chard is one of my all-time favorite greens, for good reason. Similar to spinach and beets botanically and in taste profile, Swiss chard grows on tall stalks in a rainbow of colors and provides generous crumpled leaves loaded with good stuff. Chard has huge amounts of vitamin K for strong, mineralized bones and a bevy of B-complex vitamins, including B_1, B_2, B_3, B_5, and B_6. One cup of cooked chard contains only 35 calories but has more than 100 percent of the RDA of vitamin A, in the form of beta-carotene; more than half the RDA of vitamin C; a good dose of vitamin E; and massive amounts of minerals! Chard is loaded with potassium and magnesium, which lower blood pressure; iron to enhance oxygen distribution, keeping the immune system strong; calcium; copper; zinc; and the trace mineral manganese, which helps us produce energy from protein and carbohydrates.

Turnip Greens

Turnip greens are an unsung hero of prime nutrition. Infused with the holy trinity of antioxidant vitamins C, E, and A—known to boost the immune system and reduce cholesterol and the risk of cancer—turnip greens are the leaves of the more popular root and far too precious to discard. Turnip greens are a keen source of B-complex goodies, including folate, which builds, supports, and protects all cells, especially those with a short life span, like those of our skin and intestines and those that line our organs and cavities, including the mouth. These babies are mineralized with calcium, potassium, magnesium, iron, copper, and phosphorus and even contain the precious essential fatty acid omega-3.

Massaged Greens

Doesn't that sound nice? I love a good rubbing with oil. So do leafy greens, along with a pinch of salt and seasoning. This opportune technique allows us to serve these fortified veggies in their raw nature, made tender and tasty with a little time and a lot of love. Adjust the seasonings to taste, depending on the green of choice and desired flavor. Fresh herbs are always fabulous. Keep it simple, or add green onion, garlic, and ginger for a tasty variation. To take it up another notch in flavor and texture, try topping or tossing with Live Shoyu Wasabi Gomasio (page 281).

YIELDS: 4 SERVINGS

6   cups finely chopped greens, such as kale, spinach, chard, or a mixture (see note)

2   tablespoons olive oil, or more

1   tablespoon flax oil (or additional olive oil)

1   tablespoon umeboshi plum vinegar and/or lemon juice

2   teaspoons shoyu (soy sauce)

1   teaspoon agave nectar or maple syrup (optional)

2   green onions, chopped

1–2   cloves garlic, pressed

2–3   teaspoons finely grated ginger (optional)

Sea salt

1½   cups or more chopped herbs, such as basil or parsley

A few pinches of fresh oregano, thyme, or marjoram (optional)

Toss the greens with the olive oil, flax oil (or additional olive oil), vinegar and/or lemon juice, shoyu, agave or maple syrup (if desired), green onions, garlic, and ginger (if desired). Taste and season with salt if desired. Use freshly cleaned paws to massage with love. Pay attention to the tougher parts. Allow to stand and marinate, rubbing now and again for an hour or two. Toss in the herbs and allow to stand for 10 minutes to absorb flavor before serving.

NOTE: *Tough stems may be included or removed as desired (they have good fiber but are not as delectable to chew). The more finely you chop the greens, the more quickly they will soften in the marinade.*

NUTRITION AT A GLANCE
Per serving: 150 calories, 11 g total fat, 1.5 g saturated fat, 4 g protein, 12 g carbohydrates, 3 g dietary fiber, 960 mg sodium

Sautéed Greens

Sautéed greens are very delicious. I am conservative about cooking with oil because heat destroys so many of its good properties. A clean oil like olive oil or sesame oil offers smooth taste. Cold-pressed coconut butter is awesome for buttery flavor and can withstand higher temperatures than any oil without being damaged. Omega Nutrition is a good choice as it does not smell like coconut. Sautéing does flavor food beautifully and is a great way to introduce leafy greens to anyone who is unaccustomed or resistant to digging into a heap of greens.

YIELDS: 4 SERVINGS

2   tablespoons extra-virgin olive oil, sesame oil, or cold-pressed coconut butter

2–3 cloves garlic, minced

6   cups chopped greens, such as kale, chard, spinach, and so forth (see note)

     Sea salt

2   teaspoons shoyu (soy sauce) (optional)

1   teaspoon umeboshi plum vinegar (optional)

1   cup chopped parsley (optional)

     A few pinches chopped fresh oregano, thyme, or marjoram (optional)

     Freshly ground black pepper

Heat the oil or coconut butter in a large skillet over medium heat.

Add the garlic and push around with a wooden spoon for a minute or so.

Before the garlic browns, add the greens and a pinch of salt and toss in the skillet with tongs, or cover with a lid and shake. Cook, turning for even action, for a few minutes. If desired, add a dash of shoyu and vinegar and continue to cook until the greens wilt and turn bright green. Remove from the heat and fold in fresh herbs if desired. Season to taste with salt and pepper.

NOTE: *Tough stems may be included or removed as desired (they have good fiber, but are not as delectable to chew). The more finely you chop the greens, the more quickly they will cook.*

NUTRITION AT A GLANCE
Per serving: 120 calories, 8 g total fat, 1 g saturated fat, 3 g protein, 11 g carbohydrates, 2 g dietary fiber, 45 mg sodium

Steamed Greens

Steaming greens is a simple staple in my kitchen. Bring the water to a rolling boil and use a properly fitted lid for the best steam. Mix and match the seasonings to fit your palate and favor. Serve plain or with White Miso and Sesame Sauce (see opposite page) and Gomasio (page 280).

YIELDS: 4 SERVINGS

6   cups chopped greens such as kale, chard, spinach, and so forth (see note)

1–2 tablespoons olive oil

1   tablespoon flax oil (or additional olive oil)

     Sea salt

2   teaspoons umeboshi plum vinegar and/or lemon juice

2   teaspoons shoyu (soy sauce)

1   teaspoon agave nectar or maple syrup (optional)

2   green onions, finely chopped (optional)

1–2 cloves garlic, pressed

2–3 teaspoons finely grated ginger (optional)

1   cup or more chopped herbs, such as basil or parsley

     A few pinches fresh oregano, thyme, or marjoram (optional)

Fill a saucepan that can be fitted with a steaming basket or a steaming pan with 2" of filtered water. Bring to a rolling boil.

Add the greens and steam, turning once or twice with tongs, until they turn bright green.

Remove from the heat and toss in a bowl with the olive oil, flax oil (or additional olive oil), salt to taste, vinegar and/or lemon juice, shoyu, agave or maple syrup (if desired), green onions (if desired), garlic, ginger (if desired), and herbs to taste.

NOTE: *Tough stems may be included or removed as desired (they have good fiber, but are not as delectable to chew). The more finely you chop the greens, the more quickly they will cook.*

NUTRITION AT A GLANCE
Per serving: 120 calories, 8 g total fat, 1 g saturated fat, 4 g protein, 11 g carbohydrates, 3 g dietary fiber, 710 mg sodium

WHITE MISO AND SESAME SAUCE

This sauce is delicious over steamed veggies and greens, or as a salad dressing.

YIELDS: 8 SERVINGS (1 CUP)

2 tablespoons unrefined sesame oil or extra-virgin olive oil

2 teaspoons flax oil or additional sesame or olive oil

1 tablespoon raw tahini

2 tablespoons lemon juice

1 teaspoon umeboshi plum vinegar

1 teaspoon shoyu (soy sauce) or tamari

2 teaspoons white miso

1 clove garlic, pressed

1–2 teaspoons peeled and finely grated ginger (optional)

½ teaspoon agave nectar or maple syrup

For variation add any or all:

2 tablespoons finely chopped chives or green onions

¼ cup chopped parsley

1 teaspoon wasabi powder

2 tablespoons toasted sesame seeds

In a bowl or blender, mix together the oils, tahini, lemon juice, vinegar, shoyu or tamari, miso, garlic, ginger (if desired), and agave or maple syrup. Add filtered water to thin to desired consistency. Season to taste as desired with the suggested ingredients.

NUTRITION AT A GLANCE
Per serving: 60 calories, 6 g total fat, 0.5 g saturated fat, 1 g protein, 2 g carbohydrates, 0 g dietary fiber, 210 mg sodium

Spinach, Mushrooms, and Caramelized Onions

Typically associated with a pungent flavor, the natural sugar in onions is seduced forward with a slow, low heat and married to the underlying sweetness found in a touch of balsamic and shoyu. Cremini mushrooms are full of B-complex vitamins and minerals like copper, potassium, phosphate, zinc, and the precious trace mineral selenium, for natural antioxidant and immune boosting benefits. Baby spinach is the most tender, though the chopped leaves of mature spinach may also be used. For the next level of flavor and texture, try serving with Almond-Breaded Onion Rings (see opposite page).

YIELDS: 4 SERVINGS

2–3 tablespoons olive oil

1 nice red onion, sliced

2–3 teaspoons balsamic vinegar

1–2 teaspoons shoyu (soy sauce)

1–2 teaspoons agave nectar or maple syrup

Sea salt

2 cups sliced cremini mushrooms

6 cups baby spinach

1 cup chopped basil leaves

½ cup chopped parsley leaves

Freshly ground black pepper

Warm 2 tablespoons of olive oil in a skillet over medium heat. Add the onion (it should not sizzle too much or the heat is too high) and cook, stirring occasionally with a wooden spoon, for 5 minutes or until beginning to soften a touch. Add 2 teaspoons of balsamic, 1 teaspoon each of the shoyu and agave or maple syrup, and a pinch of salt. Cook, stirring occasionally, for 10 to 15 minutes, or until soft and becoming translucent. Add the mushrooms and continue to cook until savory and soft, stirring occasionally. It may be necessary to add a touch more oil, balsamic, shoyu, and agave or maple as the mushrooms really soak up the juices and flavor.

Add the spinach to the pan and cover, stirring once or twice, cooking just until wilted and softened. Toss with the basil and parsley and season to taste with salt and pepper.

NUTRITION AT A GLANCE
Per serving: 110 calories, 7 g total fat, 1 g saturated fat, 3 g protein, 10 g carbohydrates, 3 g dietary fiber, 140 mg sodium

Almond-Breaded Onion Rings

These onion rings are a lighter, nutritious cousin of the deep-fried original. Exceptional as a savory topping for a crunchy salad or simple green veggies.

YIELDS: 8 SERVINGS (1 PINT)

2–3 medium onions, thinly sliced (any onion may be used, sweeter is nicer)

1 tablespoon olive oil

2 teaspoons balsamic vinegar

1 teaspoon nama shoyu or shoyu (soy sauce)

3 teaspoons agave nectar

¼ teaspoon sea salt

1 cup almonds, soaked 8 hours in filtered water and drained

¼ cup pine nuts

1½ tablespoons nama shoyu (unpasteurized soy sauce)

1 teaspoon maple syrup

¼ teaspoon cayenne pepper

Toss the onions with the olive oil, balsamic, 1 teaspoon of shoyu, 1 teaspoon of agave, and salt.

Allow to marinate at least 20 minutes to develop flavor and pull out some of the juices. Meanwhile, carry on with the recipe . . .

In a food processor, grind the almonds and pine nuts into a fine meal. Add 1½ tablespoons of nama shoyu, the remaining 2 teaspoons of agave, maple syrup, and cayenne and blend until thoroughly mixed. The mixture should be crumbly, but able to stick together a little. If it is entirely too crumbly, add in a few of the onion slices and blend again.

If there is more than ½" of marinade at the bottom of the onions, pour some off and set aside.

Scoop the almond mixture into the marinating onions and toss. Everything should start to stick together. If it is too dry, add some of the marinating juices or water.

Press and scatter on dehydrator sheets lined with nonstick sheets, waxed paper, or parchment paper.

Dehydrate at 112°F until mostly dry (12 to 24 hours).

This may also be done on baking sheets in the oven with the pilot light on (for 12 to 24 hours) or in an oven set on the lowest setting for 4 to 6 hours.

NUTRITION AT A GLANCE

Per serving: 170 calories, 14 g total fat, 1 g saturated fat, 5 g protein, 8 g carbohydrates, 2 g dietary fiber, 260 mg sodium

Garlic and Ginger Bok Choy Sauté

Choose similar-size heads of bok choy for even cooking. It is best done at a high heat,
so adding some seasoning liquid will keep the garlic from burning (important!).

YIELDS: 6 SERVINGS

2 tablespoons unrefined sesame oil

1 teaspoon toasted sesame oil

2–3 cloves garlic, minced

2–3 teaspoons peeled and finely chopped ginger

4 heads bok choy, halved

2 tablespoons shoyu (soy sauce)

2 tablespoons mirin or sake

1 teaspoon maple syrup (optional)

2–3 tablespoons filtered water

Warm the oils in a wok or skillet over medium-high heat.

Add the garlic and ginger and sauté for 30 seconds, until fragrant but not browning.

Add the bok choy and toss with tongs to coat. Cook for a minute or so and add the shoyu, mirin or sake, maple syrup (if desired), and water. Toss and turn. Cook for a few minutes, just until tender and most of the liquid has evaporated. Let stand a few minutes and serve.

NUTRITION AT A GLANCE
Per serving: 130 calories, 7 g total fat, 1 g saturated fat, 9 g protein, 14 g carbohydrates, 6 g dietary fiber, 360 mg sodium

Bok Choy with Ume Pumpkin Seeds

Bok choy has all the goodies found in many of the cabbage family siblings—lots of
folate, vitamins A and C, and nitrogen compounds—as well as tons of calcium.

YIELDS: 6 SERVINGS

4 heads bok choy

2 teaspoons flax or unrefined sesame oil

2 teaspoons umeboshi plum vinegar

2 tablespoons Ume Pumpkin Seeds (see opposite page) or Gomasio (page 280)

Steam the bok choy over boiling water for 3 to 5 minutes, or just until tender and bright green. Remove from the heat. Toss with the oil and vinegar to coat evenly.

Toss with Ume Pumpkin Seeds or Gomasio.

NUTRITION AT A GLANCE
Per serving: 100 calories, 4 g total fat, 0 g saturated fat, 9 g protein, 13 g carbohydrates, 6 g dietary fiber, 750 mg sodium

Ume Pumpkin Seeds

Crunchy, nutty pumpkin seeds are loaded with healthy oils and have ample protein. Lightly toasted to draw out flavor and seasoned with umeboshi plum vinegar, they are excellent to top salad or soup, or to munch on with sliced apple. This is one of my favorite staple snacks on the go.

YIELDS: 32 SERVINGS (2 CUPS)

2 cups raw pumpkin seeds   **2–3 teaspoons umeboshi plum vinegar**

Toast the pumpkin seeds in a heavy skillet (cast-iron is best) over low heat, stirring regularly. It is worth being patient and toasting slowly for the best flavor. After about 5 minutes, the seeds will swell and become fragrant, but they should not pop or the heat is too high.

Add the vinegar and stir constantly with a wooden paddle or spoon for about 1 minute, toasting until dry.

Allow to cool completely before storing in an airtight container or bag in a cool, dry place.

NUTRITION AT A GLANCE
Per serving (1/4 cup): 160 calories, 11 g total fat, 2 g saturated fat, 6 g protein, 7 g carbohydrates, 3 g dietary fiber, 260 mg sodium

The discovery of a new dish
does more for human happiness
than the discovery of a new star.

—ANTHELME BRILLAT-SAVARIN

Mash (Bitters Pesto)

What is mash? Mash is an affectionate name for a type of mashed dish of seasoned, bitter greens introduced to me by my dear tribe, the Medeski Martin and Wood crew and family, in Woodstock, New York. It is a strong side dish, served as a condiment like chutney or pickled ginger would be served, to complement the plate and clean the palate. Mash is incredibly nutritious and an excellent digestive aid. Mash also stimulates the liver. Compounds in mash increase the flow and secretion of liver enzymes and cause the liver to secrete bile, which helps detoxify this crucial, tireless organ so everything works better.

The basic technique for mash is to finely chop the bitter greens and marinate them in a good olive oil, a bit of lemon juice, garlic, and salt until they are soft. Then, using a suribachi (a grooved, Japanese mortar and pestle), the dish is mashed with a sprinkling of delicious fatty nuts, such as pine nuts or walnuts. Fresh herbs of choice may be added as desired. It takes a while to get a good mash going, and it's always most fun to take turns with friends in a festive setting. Thank you, MMW tribe, for all of the love, music, good wine, great food, and savory-sweet memories. You nourish me deeply.

The Simply Brilliant Suribachi

A *suribachi* is a Japanese mortar and pestle with a simple, brilliant design. The grooved bowl and wooden pestle are used to grind goodies like seeds with minimal oxidation to preserve maximum nutrients. I use a suribachi to pound pesto and mash by hand, which yields the best flavor of any technique I have found. Macrobiotics posits that the way in which food is cut and cooked affects not only the flavor but the nutrition as well. I agree there is a subtle, though noticeable, difference between grinding seeds or greens in a suribachi versus a food processor. No mechanized kitchen gadget can match the magic that happens when you mindfully prepare food by hand. Grind and give thanks!

Traditional Mash

The original recipe made by Sarah Zukowski came from her father Richard's battalion of brilliance as a gifted health practitioner. Sarah uses the Pan di Zucchero, which is a type of chicory green I independently fell in love with while living in Italy, that grows in her garden. If anyone reading this knows where to purchase Pan di Zucchero, can you overnight some to me? Or I will immediately fly to you. Fortunately, any good, bitter, leafy green will work. Endive may be used in part, but it is a bit too tender to use in full.

YIELDS: 10 SERVINGS (ABOUT 2 CUPS)

4   cups finely chopped bitter greens, such as escarole, chicory, frisée, radicchio, or the like

1   cup chopped basil leaves (optional)

4   tablespoons olive oil

      Juice of 1–2 lemons

2–3   cloves garlic, roughly chopped

½   teaspoon coarse sea salt + a pinch (a touch less if the salt is finely ground)

4   tablespoons pine nuts

Toss the greens and basil, if using, with the olive oil, lemon juice, garlic, salt, and pine nuts. Let stand to marinate, tossing occasionally, until soft (15 minutes to 1 hour).

Mash the greens in a suribachi (a grooved Japanese mortar and pestle) to a pesto texture. A smooth mortar and pestle will work but takes much more patience and time.

Serve with anything as a condiment. For bitter-lovers, it is great on steamed vegetables.

NUTRITION AT A GLANCE
Per serving: 80 calories, 8 g total fat, 1 g saturated fat, 1 g protein, 2 g carbohydrates, 0 g dietary fiber, 120 mg sodium

I feel a recipe is only a theme,
which an intelligent cook can play
each time with a variation.

—MADAME BENOIT

Radish Greens and Olive Mash

The leafy tops of radishes are some of the most nutritious greens ever (and rarely) used. This mash is not nearly as bitter as the rest. I dedicate this recipe to my friend Debi Disbro, a wonderful yoga teacher with a studio in Woodstock, New York, and a lovely spirit, who flipped out over it because she loves anything to do with olives.

YIELDS: 8 SERVINGS (ABOUT 1 CUP)

Leafy greens from one bunch of radishes (about 2 cups); turnip greens also may be used

½ **cup chopped basil**

½ **cup chopped parsley**

¼ **cup chopped cilantro**

2 **green onions, chopped**

5–6 **green olives, pitted and chopped**

2 **tablespoons olive oil**

2 **teaspoons umeboshi plum vinegar**

1 **teaspoon shoyu (soy sauce)**

Pinch of sea salt

Pinch of ground chipotle pepper

Finely chop the greens. If they are very tough, they may be steamed lightly to soften.

Toss the greens with the basil, parsley, cilantro, green onions, olives, olive oil, vinegar, shoyu, salt, and chipotle. Let stand to marinate, tossing occasionally, until soft (15 minutes to 1 hour).

Mash in a suribachi (a grooved Japanese mortar and pestle) to a pesto texture. A smooth mortar and pestle will work but takes much more patience and time.

Serve with anything as a condiment.

NUTRITION AT A GLANCE
Per serving: 80 calories, 8 g total fat, 1 g saturated fat, 1 g protein, 2 g carbohydrates, 0 g dietary fiber, 150 mg sodium

Black-Eyed Peas and Collard Greens

This recipe is a staple for the southern soul. Whenever my friend Marla Henderson, a brilliant eco-interior-designer and Georgia belle, comes to the island, I start soaking black-eyed peas, 'cause I know they're her favorite. Soaking the beans first abbreviates the cooking time and makes them more digestible. I do recommend cooking the beans in broth, which may be purchased if you don't have homemade stock.

YIELDS: 4 SERVINGS (4 CUPS)

1	cup black-eyed peas
3	cups filtered water
3–4	cups Light Vegetable Stock (page 178), Hearty Vegetable Stock (page 179), or packaged broth
4	cloves garlic, split
1	bunch collard greens
	Sea salt
2–4	tablespoons olive oil (optional)

Soak the black-eyed peas in 3 cups of filtered water for 6 hours. Drain and rinse. Pick through and discard any discolored or malformed peas. If the peas were not soaked, more stock or broth will be needed and they will require additional time to cook.

Place the peas in a large saucepan with the vegetable stock or broth and garlic. Bring to a boil, partially covered. Reduce heat to low and let settle to a simmer. Scoop off any foam that rises to the surface. Cover and cook for 45 to 55 minutes, or until tender but not falling apart. If the beans were not soaked, they will require 1 to 1½ hours to cook until tender.

During that time, wash the collard greens and remove the tough stem. Stack the leaves and roll up like a cigar. Cut into ½" bundles.

When the peas are tender, fold in the greens and add 1 teaspoon of sea salt. Simmer another 6 to 8 minutes or until the greens are tender.

Remove from heat and fold in the olive oil, if desired. Season to taste with salt.

NUTRITION AT A GLANCE
Per serving: 180 calories, 1 g total fat, 0 g saturated fat, 11 g protein, 32 g carbohydrates, 6 g dietary fiber, 280 mg sodium

Mighty Grains

Whole grains are one of the cleanest sources of fuel for long-term energy. Though grains have been marginalized in recent years as starchy carbohydrates that lead to weight gain, whole grains provide a superb portfolio of nutrients, minerals, and healthy fiber. As complex carbohydrates, whole grains provide steady fuel, stabilizing blood sugars and balancing metabolism. Coupled with vegetables and beans, whole grains are a brilliant part of a complete protein, though some, such as quinoa and amaranth, are a complete protein by themselves. The hearty fiber in grains supports healthy digestion, provides a satisfying sense of feeling full without feeling heavy, and regulates the absorption of carbohydrate sugars for stable, long-burning energy.

Amaranth

Known by Aztec royalty as a miracle grain, amaranth, like quinoa, is rich in the amino acid lysine, making it a complete protein (this amino acid is typically missing from grains). These tiny, tan grains are about the size of a poppy seed and have an earthy sweetness and no gluten. Their thick, porridgelike consistency makes them most enjoyable mixed with another grain with a similar cooking time (see "Soaking, Sprouting, and Cooking Grains" on page 302); use 25 percent amaranth with quinoa or millet for a brilliant medley. Amaranth is loaded with minerals, including iron, calcium, magnesium, potassium, and phosphate, and has tons of fiber for a healthy heart and digestion, as well as nifty compounds like phytosterols, which fight all kinds of diseases. One of my favorite tricks is to pop amaranth like a mini-popcorn to sprinkle on salad or to mix in trail mix, granola, or cereal. Heat a heavy saucepan over high heat and add 1 tablespoon amaranth. Stir with a wooden spoon for a few seconds until all the grains pop. Best eaten immediately.

Barley

Barley is one of the most ancient grains and one of the most heart-healthy foods. With a slightly nutty flavor, barley has a comforting, chewy texture that is high in dietary fiber, which feeds friendly flora in our guts and lowers cholesterol levels by inhibiting the production of cholesterol and also binding to bile acids, which digest fat and cholesterol and remove it from the body. It is also rich in niacin (B_6), which protects our tickers. It is a great source of minerals, including phosphorus, manganese, copper, and especially the precious trace mineral selenium, essential for thyroid health, immune function, and protection against cancer. All that, and it is fantastic in soup!

Millet

Millet originated in northern Africa but has been valued as a nutritious grain all over the world. Rich in heart-healthy magnesium and B vitamins, namely niacin (B_6), which is known to lower cholesterol, millet is a great source of fiber and easily digestible complex carbohydrates for long-term energy. It contains no gluten. Millet is also a fine source of phosphorus, which helps our bodies metabolize fat for energy and is an essential part of all the fatty structures in our bodies, especially cell membranes and our precious nervous systems. Health-protecting antioxidants and phytochemicals run amok in these yummy grains, including prized lignans, which have shown to be wickedly effective in preventing breast- and hormone-related cancers as well as heart disease. This tiny, pale grain yields a spectrum of textures determined by the way it is prepared. When left to cook undisturbed, the grains will fluff up like rice. When it is stirred frequently during cooking and a little additional water is added, it becomes creamy like mashed potatoes.

Quinoa

Once called the gold of the Incas, quinoa is commonly called a grain but is actually a small starchy seed from a plant that is a distant relative to spinach and chard. Quinoa is rich in protein and is a "complete" protein at that, containing all nine of the essential amino acids. It contains no gluten. Quinoa provides a good allowance of B vitamins, especially B_2, which is essential for energy production in our cells. Good stuff. It is well stocked with minerals, including iron, magnesium, phosphorus, manganese, and copper, which work together as cofactors of antioxidant action. Quinoa is also full of other antioxidants, such as lignans, which are converted into cancer-fighting compounds in our guts. High in fiber, quinoa is especially good for people with diabetes and hypoglycemic tendencies.

Wild Rice

Wild rice is not actually a grain, but the seed of an aquatic grass originally from the Great Lakes. Wild rice is incredibly fortified with minerals, like potassium, calcium, phosphorus, and zinc, and has more protein and fewer calories than any other rice. With a great profile of clean-burning complex carbohydrates, wild rice has a ton of good fiber, making it a fine source of long-term fuel, and lowering cholesterol and stabilizing blood sugar in the process. It is especially rich in vitamin B_3 (niacin), which, like fellow B vitamins, is important in energy production—converting protein, fat, and carbohydrates into useable energy—and regulating blood sugar and insulin to boot.

Quinoa Pilaf with Parsley, Scallions, and Black Sesame Gomasio

The black sesame offers a nice contrast of color, but white sesame can also be used. Gently toasting the quinoa before cooking is optional and brings out its nutty flavor and prevents the grains from becoming sticky. The kombu seaweed adds another layer of taste and valuable minerals. I include a few optional ingredients to bump up the flavor. As you wish.

YIELDS: 4 SERVINGS

1	cup quinoa
2	cups filtered water or vegetable stock
1	strip (2") kombu seaweed (optional)
¼	cup black sesame seeds
¼	teaspoon sea salt
½	cup chopped parsley
2	green onions, trimmed and finely chopped, including the greens
1	teaspoon umeboshi plum paste (optional)
1½	teaspoons unrefined sesame oil (optional)
½	teaspoon toasted sesame oil, or additional unrefined sesame oil (optional)
½	teaspoon shoyu (soy sauce) or tamari

If you want to toast the quinoa lightly to bring out its nutty flavor, toast for about 5 minutes in a skillet over low heat, stirring frequently, until slightly fragrant and popping a little bit.

Place the quinoa in a heavy saucepan and add the water or vegetable stock and the kombu. Bring to a boil, covered. Reduce the heat to low and simmer for 15 to 20 minutes, covered, or until all of the water has been absorbed and little air vents form on the surface of the grain. Let stand for 10 minutes, uncovered.

Toast the sesame seeds in a heavy skillet over low heat, pushing around regularly with a wooden paddle or wooden spoon, until fragrant and a few are popping.

Crush the toasted sesame seeds and sea salt in a suribachi (a grooved Japanese mortar and pestle) or spice mill. Do so until all of the seeds are broken, but not ground into a powder.

Fold into the quinoa along with the parsley and green onions.

If you want to bump up the flavor, mix together the umeboshi plum paste, sesame oil, and shoyu or tamari. Fold well into the pilaf.

NUTRITION AT A GLANCE
Per serving: 210 calories, 7 g total fat, 1 g saturated fat, 8 g protein, 32 g carbohydrates, 4 g dietary fiber, 200 mg sodium

Pickled Daikon Radish

Daikon is one of my favorite vegetables to pickle. A generously proportioned radish, daikon is abundant in sulfur, which grows beautiful skin. Its slightly spicy nature is warming and good for digestion. These pickles keep for quite a long time in a glass jar in the fridge and make a great side dish or condiment for grain dishes, sushi, and steamed vegetables for anyone who loves a little spicy tang.

YIELDS: 12 SERVINGS (1½ TO 2 PINTS)

1 pound daikon, scrubbed or peeled

¼ cup sea salt

½ cup rice vinegar

¼ cup brown rice vinegar

¼ cup sake or mirin

1 cup filtered water

½ cup agave nectar or ¼ cup organic sugar

¼ teaspoon turmeric powder (optional, to turn the pickles a brilliant yellow)

Cut the radish in half lengthwise and slice into ¼" pieces.

Toss with the salt and place in a colander or strainer over a bowl for 1 hour.

Rinse well to remove the salt.

Mix together the rice vinegar, brown rice vinegar, sake or mirin, water, agave or sugar, and turmeric (if desired). If you are using organic sugar, it may be necessary to warm these ingredients in a saucepan so the sugar will dissolve easily, then cool to room temperature.

Place the radish in a clean glass jar and pour the sweetened vinegar mixture over it. Cover and let stand for 4 to 8 hours on the counter before transferring to the refrigerator. Stores well for at least a month in the fridge.

NUTRITION AT A GLANCE
Per serving: 35 calories, 1.5 g total fat, 0 g saturated fat, 1 g protein, 3 g carbohydrates, 0 g dietary fiber, 50 mg sodium

Moroccan Saffron Quinoa Tabbouleh

Tabbouleh is a rustic grain dish traditionally made with cracked bulgur wheat, hailing from Middle Eastern and North African regions. The ratio of herbs to grain varies depending on the province. I gravitate toward quinoa over wheat for its easily digestible high-protein content and light, nutty flavor.

I offer two options for preparation. The first is raw-food friendly and takes the extra step to sprout the quinoa for an enzyme-enhanced nutritional boost. After sprouting, the quinoa can be lightly blanched to improve digestibility. The second method follows a traditional cooking procedure for quinoa. For deeper layers of flavor, cook the quinoa in vegetable broth or stock. Store-bought vegetable stock can be used, but choose unsalted stock and season to taste with salt afterward.

YIELDS: 6 SERVINGS

2 cups cooked or sprouted and blanched quinoa (see "Soaking, Sprouting, and Cooking Grains" on page 302)

3 tablespoons extra-virgin olive oil

1 tablespoon flax oil (optional)

3 tablespoons lemon juice

4 large dates, pitted and chopped

1–2 cloves garlic, pressed

½ cup finely chopped green onions

2 tablespoons chopped fresh chives

2 teaspoons fresh thyme or 1 teaspoon dried

1½ teaspoons saffron threads

½ teaspoon dried chipotle, ground (optional for a little heat)

1½ cups chopped parsley

1 cup chopped mint

Sea salt

1 lemon

2 cups chopped tomatoes

Toss the prepared quinoa with the olive oil, flax oil (if desired), lemon juice, dates, garlic, green onions, chives, thyme, saffron, chipotle (if desired), parsley, and mint. Season to taste with sea salt.

Cut the skin of the lemon off including the white pith. Using a serrated knife, cut between the membranes to end up with lemon wedges. Gently cut into ¼" pieces.

Gently fold the lemon pieces and tomatoes into the quinoa. It is best not to overmix and mash up the tomatoes. Let stand for 15 minutes to 1 hour to develop flavor.

Excellent to serve over chopped lettuce or as part of a platter including Roasted Garlic and Zucchini Baba Ghannouj (page 248) and any of the hummus recipes (Chapter 7).

NUTRITION AT A GLANCE
Per serving: 250 calories, 9 g total fat, 1 g saturated fat, 6 g protein, 40 g carbohydrates, 6 g dietary fiber, 50 mg sodium

Coconut Jasmine Rice with Scallions and Cilantro

Fragrant jasmine rice infused with buttery coconut milk just about melts in your mouth.
Fresh coconut milk is ideal, but difficult to come by outside the tropics and subtropics.
Frozen coconut milk or canned organic coconut milk is a good stand-in.

YIELDS: 6 SERVINGS

1½ cups jasmine rice

12 ounces coconut milk

2¼ cups vegetable broth or filtered water

2 stalks fresh lemongrass, bruised (or add 1 teaspoon lemon zest + 1 tablespoon lemon juice after rice is cooked, see note)

Sea salt

¾ cup finely chopped green onions

½ cup chopped cilantro leaves

Umeboshi plum vinegar (optional)

Rinse the rice two or three times: Place in a bowl, cover with water, and stir. Drain in a colander. Repeat once or twice more.

Place the rice, coconut milk, broth or water, and lemongrass (if using) in a medium saucepan with a pinch of salt. Bring to a boil, uncovered. Stir with a wooden spoon. Reduce heat to low and cover. Cook, undisturbed, for 20 to 30 minutes. Cooking time varies with stoves and pots. Check the rice after 20 minutes. The rice is done when the liquid has been absorbed and small air-vent holes appear on the surface of the rice. Keep covered and allow to stand for 10 minutes.

Before serving, fluff the rice with a fork and fold in the green onions and cilantro. If you did not use fresh lemongrass, fold in the lemon zest and lemon juice. Season to taste with sea salt or a dash of umeboshi plum vinegar.

NOTE: *To release the essential oils in lemongrass, bruise the stalk first by banging it with a heavy skillet or the side of a chef's knife blade.*

NUTRITION AT A GLANCE
Per serving: 190 calories, 0.5 g total fat, 0 g saturated fat, 4 g protein, 41 g carbohydrates, 0 g dietary fiber, 250 mg sodium

Soaking, Sprouting, and Cooking Grains

Soaking Grains

Soaking grains before cooking abbreviates the cooking time dramatically and improves digestibility. Some grains benefit from soaking more than others do to wick away bitter compounds and wake up dormant nutrition.

- Use 3 cups of filtered water for every cup of grain. Drain and rinse before cooking.
- Generally, any type of grain can be soaked overnight for convenience. More specifically, smaller grains (such as amaranth, millet, quinoa, and teff) should be soaked at least 2 to 6 hours. Larger grains (such as barley, oat groats, rice, wild rice, whole spelt, and whole wheat berries) should be soaked at least 6 to 8 hours.
- When cooking soaked grains, reduce liquid by ¼ cup.

Sprouting Grains

Sprouting grains begins the natural process of breaking down complex carbohydrates into a simpler form, which the body can use more easily. Some raw-food enthusiasts will say that this is the only way grains should be eaten. However, sprouted grains still have a complex matrix of nutrients and tough cellulose that may be more available and easier to digest when subsequently cooked after sprouting. Every body is different, and I personally endorse an individually tailored technique to what makes sense, feels good, and works according to the body, the season, and the grain.

Not all grains sprout equally. Some grains like quinoa and wild rice are quite delicious sprouted, and others such as rice are not great to sprout and are better cooked traditionally. See the chart below for methods and procedures to sprout and blanch grains.

GRAIN	SOAK TIME PER DAY (HOURS)	RINSES	TIME UNTIL READY (DAYS)	BLANCH TIME (MINUTES)
AMARANTH	8–12	2	1–2	2–5
OAT GROATS	12	2–4	1	4–8
QUINOA	8–12	2	1	3–5
WILD RICE	8–12	2–4	1–2	10–12

Cooking Grains

After sprouting, grains can be blanched by adding them to boiling water, reducing the heat, and simmering for the directed number of minutes to improve the flavor, texture, and digestibility. Blanch sprouted grains in enough water to cover them by at least an inch.

Most grains benefit from being washed before cooking if they are not soaked. Some grains like quinoa have a protective coating that contains compounds like saponins, which have a bitter flavor when not washed away. Other grains like rice will benefit by washing away some of the extra starch so they will fluff up nicely after being cooked. Still others are just grimy—who knows who or what was touching them between harvest and their arrival in your kitchen.

To wash grains, cover the dry grain with water in a bowl or pot. Stir and let settle for a minute or two. Pour off the water and strain the grain through an appropriately sized colander. Repeat up to three times. Proceed with soaking, sprouting, or cooking as directed.

GRAIN (1 CUP DRY)	AMOUNT WATER OR STOCK (CUPS)	DRY GRAIN COOK TIME (MINUTES)	SOAKED GRAIN COOK TIME (MINUTES)	YIELD (CUPS)
AMARANTH	2½	20–25	8–12	2½
BARLEY (PEARLED)	3	50–60	30–40	3½
MILLET	3½	20–25	8–15	3½
OAT GROATS (WHOLE)	3	30–40	10–15	3½
QUINOA	2¼	15–20	5–10	2¾
BROWN RICE:				
BASMATI	2½	35–40	20–30	3
JASMINE RICE	1½	15–20	8–12	2½
LONG GRAIN	2½	45–55	30–40	3
SHORT GRAIN	2½	45–55	30–40	3
SPELT BERRIES (WHOLE)	3½	40–50	25–30	3
TEFF	3	10–20	5–10	3½
WILD RICE	3	50–60	15–20	4
WHEAT:				
BULGUR	2	15	CAN BE SOAKED IN WARM WATER FOR 1 HOUR AND USED WITHOUT COOKING	2½
COUSCOUS	1	5	1–2	2
WHOLE WHEAT BERRIES	3	2	1½	2½

Lotus Manitok Wild Rice with Mâche

This recipe has been in my repertoire since my restaurant days and is so good I wanted to share it again with a slightly new take. Mâche (also called corn salad) is a tender green and makes a delicate, downy bed for this lovely dish. Without the avocado and tomatoes, the dressed rice will keep in the fridge for 3 to 4 days (the flavor actually gets better after a day), so if you don't think you will eat it all in one sitting, set some aside to store before folding in the avocado and tomatoes.

YIELDS: 6 SERVINGS

1 teaspoon whole brown mustard seeds or 1 teaspoon prepared mustard

2 tablespoons extra-virgin olive oil

2 teaspoons flax oil (optional)

1 clove garlic, pressed

1 tablespoon nama shoyu (unpasteurized soy sauce), soy sauce, or tamari

1 tablespoon umeboshi plum vinegar

2 teaspoons aged balsamic vinegar, or 1 teaspoon balsamic + 1 teaspoon maple syrup

1 tablespoon lemon juice

2 teaspoons agave nectar

2 teaspoons maple syrup

3 cups cooked or sprouted and blanched wild rice (see "Soaking, Sprouting, and Cooking Grains" on page 302)

¼ cup finely chopped green onions, including greens

¼ cup red onion, finely chopped

2 tablespoons chopped fresh chives, or 2 tablespoons dried chives + 1 tablespoon chopped greens of a green onion

½ cup chopped parsley

½ cup chopped cilantro

½ cup chopped basil

Sea salt

Freshly ground black pepper

2 nice tomatoes or 3 Roma tomatoes, seeded and chopped

1 firmly ripe avocado, chopped

4 cups mâche, also called corn salad (field mix or baby spinach may be used)

If using whole mustard seeds, lightly toast in a skillet over low heat until fragrant and beginning to pop. Grind just to break with a mortar and pestle or spice grinder.

Mix together the ground mustard seeds or prepared mustard, olive oil, flax oil (if desired), garlic, shoyu or tamari, umeboshi plum vinegar, aged balsamic (or balsamic + maple syrup), lemon juice, agave, and maple syrup. Pour over the wild rice and fold in the green onions, red onion, chives, parsley, cilantro, and basil. Mix to coat evenly. Let stand for 10 to 20 minutes to develop flavor and season to taste with salt and pepper if needed (everybody is a little different). Reserve some to store if you don't think you will eat it all in one sitting before folding in the tomatoes and avocado.

Cut the tops off of the tomatoes. Cut in half crosswise and scoop and press the seeds out with clean fingers. Dice and fold into the rice.

Cut the avocado in half. Chop the pit with a knife and twist to remove neatly. Slice the avocado into cubes while still in the skin. Scoop out with a spoon and fold into the rice.

Serve over a bed of mâche, field mix, or baby spinach.

NUTRITION AT A GLANCE
Per serving: 210 calories, 10 g total fat, 1.5 g saturated fat, 6 g protein, 27 g carbohydrates, 5 g dietary fiber, 670 mg sodium

---

Chew Well, Live Long, and Prosper

It sounds too simple to be true, but excellent chewing is the key to getting the most out of whole grains. The deal is that saliva is essential to digesting complex carbohydrates. We produce enzymes (*ptyalin*) in our saliva that begin to break down carbohydrates and trigger reactions that happen further along in our intestines. At first, it takes a bit of practice and mindful attention to chew each bite of food thoroughly, say 30 or 40 times, but soon you'll connect with a deep sense of calm that allows your body to fully embrace this good-for-you food.

Baked Millet Croquettes with Rustic Red Wine and Olive Tomato Sauce

*Millet is a gluten-free champion grain rich in antioxidants and known to lower choles-
terol. Baked croquettes are an excellent way to renovate leftover grains.*

YIELDS: 12 SERVINGS (12 OR MORE CROQUETTES AND 3 CUPS OF SAUCE)

RUSTIC RED WINE AND OLIVE TOMATO SAUCE

6	tablespoons extra-virgin olive oil	1	sprig (3") fresh rosemary or 1 teaspoon dried
1	medium sweet onion or red onion, chopped	½	teaspoon dried chili pepper (optional)
2–4	cloves garlic, minced	½	cup chopped kalamata olives
1	cup red wine (a hearty burgundy is good)	2	tablespoons fresh thyme or 1 tablespoon dried
1	tablespoon maple syrup	2	tablespoons chopped fresh oregano or 1 tablespoon dried
2	teaspoons balsamic vinegar		Sea salt
4	cups chopped tomatoes		Freshly ground black pepper
1	bay leaf		

MILLET CROQUETTES

½	cup millet, rinsed	1	tablespoon fresh thyme or 1 teaspoon dried
1¼	cups broth or filtered water	½	teaspoon whole coriander
¼	cup pine nuts	¼	teaspoon whole cumin seeds
¼	cup pumpkin seeds	¼	teaspoon whole caraway seeds
1	cup chopped sweet onion	2	tablespoons olive oil
1–2	cloves garlic		Sea salt
½	cup parsley leaves		Freshly ground black pepper
1	tablespoon fresh oregano or 1 teaspoon dried		

TO MAKE THE SAUCE:

Warm 4 tablespoons of the olive oil in a large skillet over medium heat. Add the onion and sauté for 3 to 4 minutes, just until it begins to soften. Add the garlic and continue to cook for another minute or so, until fragrant. Add the wine, maple syrup, and vinegar. Continue to cook for 4 to 6 minutes, stirring occasionally, until the liquid has reduced in half. Add the tomatoes, bay leaf, and rosemary. Reduce the heat to medium-low and cook for 20 minutes or so, stirring occasionally, until some of the tomato juice evaporates and the sauce thickens. Add the chili pepper (if desired for a little spicy heat) and olives and cook another 3 minutes. Add the thyme and oregano and cook for another minute or so. Season with salt and pepper to taste. Adjust taste as desired, adding a touch more maple syrup to bump up the sweetness of the tomatoes. Remove the bay leaf and rosemary sprig before serving and fold in the remaining 2 tablespoons of olive oil.

TO MAKE THE CROQUETTES:

Rinse the millet well under fresh water in a fine strainer. Rinsing washes away the bitterness in the skin.

Place the millet and broth or water in a saucepan and bring to a boil. Reduce the heat to low and simmer for 15 to 20 minutes (covered), or until all of the liquid is absorbed and vent holes appear on the surface of the cooked grain. Allow to stand for 10 minutes, covered.

Meanwhile, toast the pine nuts and pumpkin seeds in a heavy skillet over low heat, stirring regularly, until fragrant and lightly browned. The pumpkin seeds should not pop or the heat is too high.

Grind the toasted pine nuts and pumpkin seeds into a fine meal in a food processor. Set aside.

No need to wash the processor. Simply add the onion, garlic, parsley, oregano, and thyme and chop finely in pulses (this may also be done by hand). Set aside.

In the skillet you just used, lightly toast the coriander, cumin seeds, and caraway seeds over low heat until fragrant, pushing around with a wooden paddle or spoon regularly for even toasting. Crush with a mortar and pestle or in a spice mill (or coffee grinder).

Preheat the oven to 375°F.

Fold together the cooked grain (while it is still hot), ground nuts, onion-herb mixture, and ground spices. Add the olive oil and season to taste with sea salt and pepper.

Lightly oil a baking sheet.

Form the millet mixture into patties by hand (less than ¼ cup each). Place on the baking sheet and clean up the edges to make a flat circumference.

Bake for 35 to 45 minutes, until turning golden brown.

Flip over and jack up the heat to 450°F for 5 minutes or so to brown nicely.

Serve immediately with the Rustic Red Wine and Olive Tomato Sauce on the side.

NUTRITION AT A GLANCE
Per serving: 200 calories, 13 g total fat, 1.5 g saturated fat, 3 g protein, 16 g carbohydrates, 3 g dietary fiber, 170 mg sodium

Red Lentil Giardiniera with Sliced Almonds

Giardiniera (Italian for "from the garden") dishes can include just about any type of sliced vegetables. This medley includes lovely red lentils and sliced almonds for a fantastic balance of texture and flavor and well-rounded nutrition. Try adding ¼ cup cooked or sprouted and blanched quinoa (see "Soaking, Sprouting, and Cooking Grains" on page 302) for a clean-burning energy source and complete protein. Toss in ¼ cup Sweet Pickles (opposite page) for the perfect boost of flavor and texture. This dish keeps beautifully for a few days and makes a brilliant lunch to take away to the office or on a picnic, especially tossed with a green salad.

YIELDS: 4 SERVINGS (3 CUPS)

2   cups cooked or sprouted and blanched red lentils

2   green onions, trimmed and finely sliced

¼   cup thinly sliced red onion

2   ribs celery, thinly sliced

4–6 baby carrots or 1 small carrot, thinly sliced

3   tablespoons chopped flat parsley

1   tablespoon extra-virgin olive oil

1   tablespoon lemon juice

    Sea salt

    Freshly ground black pepper

½   cup sliced almonds

¼   cup mild green olives (Graber are my favorite in this recipe), pitted and chopped (optional)

¼   cup cooked or sprouted and blanched quinoa (page 302, optional)

In a bowl, toss the lentils with the green onions, red onion, celery, carrots, parsley, olive oil, and lemon juice. Season to taste with salt and pepper.

The almond slices can be used raw, but light toasting brings out their flavor and aroma. If desired, toast the almonds in a skillet over low heat, stirring regularly for even cooking, just until turning golden brown and fragrant. Be mindful as they will burn quickly if unattended.

Fold the almonds and olives (if desired) into the lentil mixture. Try adding quinoa for a variation and complete protein, though I advise adding an additional ½ teaspoon each of olive oil and lemon juice, a pinch more parsley, and salt for full flavor.

This dish is best if left to stand for an hour to develop flavor, though it can be eaten right away. Serve at room temperature or chilled. Store in a sealed container in the fridge for up to 3 days.

NUTRITION AT A GLANCE
Per serving: 230 calories, 10 g total fat, 1 g saturated fat, 12 g protein, 25 g carbohydrates, 7 g dietary fiber, 45 mg sodium

Mary Harrington's Sweet Pickles

I grew up across the street from the Harringtons on Deerhaven Drive. They had chickens that laid blue eggs, and Mrs. Harrington made the best pickles. Here is her recipe, verbatim; I just added the word "organic."

YIELDS: 24 SERVINGS (1 QUART)

1 cup organic white vinegar

2½ cups organic sugar

3 pounds cucumbers, sliced (small Kirby or pickling cucumbers are best)

3 cloves garlic

1 teaspoon celery seed

1 teaspoon whole mustard seed

In a medium saucepan, bring the vinegar and sugar to a simmer, stirring occasionally to dissolve the sugar.

Let cool. Pour over the cucumbers and add the garlic, celery seed, and mustard seed.

Refrigerate. Ready to eat in 5 days.

NUTRITION AT A GLANCE
Per serving: 90 calories, 0 g total fat, 0 g saturated fat, 0 g protein, 25 g carbohydrates, 0 g dietary fiber, 10 mg sodium

Insider Italian Lentils

Lentils are a quick-cooking bean that does not require soaking. I must fondly credit the memorable periods I lived in Italy for the old-world secrets of Italian tradition that are infused in this dish. The nutmeg and bay rendere speciale. Perfect as a side dish, on a green salad, or added to a simple vegetable soup. Divertiti!

YIELDS: 6 SERVINGS

1½	cups green or brown lentils
3	cups vegetable broth
2	bay leaves
2–4	cloves garlic, minced
4–6	sun-dried tomatoes (optional)
1	teaspoon freshly ground nutmeg
	Sea salt
	Olive oil

Place the lentils, broth, bay leaves, garlic, tomatoes (if desired), and nutmeg in a saucepan.

Bring to a boil. Reduce the heat and simmer, covered, for 30 to 35 minutes, until the liquid has been absorbed and the lentils are soft.

Season to taste with salt and olive oil. Remove the bay leaves before serving.

NUTRITION AT A GLANCE
Per serving: 130 calories, 0 g total fat, 0 g saturated fat, 9 g protein, 22 g carbohydrates, 10 g dietary fiber, 240 mg sodium

---

In cooking, as in all arts, simplicity is a sign
of perfection.

—CURNONSKY

Italiane Lentil Pâté

Use leftover lentils for a creamy pâté.

YIELDS: 12 SERVINGS (2½ CUPS)

3–5 tablespoons olive oil

1 small onion, chopped

2 teaspoons balsamic vinegar

½ teaspoon agave nectar or maple syrup

1 cup Insider Italian Lentils

¼ cup pine nuts, lightly toasted

1 cup chopped parsley

2–3 teaspoons fresh oregano or 1 teaspoon dried

2–3 teaspoons fresh thyme or 1 teaspoon dried

Sea salt

Freshly ground black pepper

Warm 1 tablespoon of the olive oil in a skillet over medium heat. Add the onion and cook, stirring occasionally, for 2 to 3 minutes. Add the vinegar and agave or maple syrup and cook, stirring occasionally, for 3 to 4 minutes, until the onion is completely soft and caramelized.

Blend the caramelized onion, Insider Italian Lentils, pine nuts, remaining 2 to 4 tablespoons of olive oil, parsley, oregano, and thyme in a food processor until completely smooth. Season to taste with sea salt and pepper.

NUTRITION AT A GLANCE
Per serving: 70 calories, 5 g total fat, 0.5 g saturated fat, 2 g protein, 4 g carbohydrates, 1 g dietary fiber, 35 mg sodium

Winter Baked Adzuki Beans with Sweet Potatoes, Leeks, and Shiitake Mushrooms

These slow-baked beans provide warm, long-burning energy for the winter season. They keep well, so leftovers make a great lunch, or a spoonful makes a hearty addition to miso soup (which is really a breakfast of champions).

YIELDS: 8 SERVINGS

1 cup adzuki beans, soaked overnight in 3 cups filtered water, drained, and rinsed

2 cups filtered water

2 cups vegetable stock

1 strip (4") kombu seaweed

2 cups sweet potatoes, peeled and chopped

2 leeks (white part only), cleaned and cut into ½" pieces

2 cups sliced shiitake mushrooms

2 ribs celery, finely chopped

1 tablespoon white or yellow miso

2 tablespoons shoyu (soy sauce)

2½ tablespoons brown rice syrup or 1 tablespoon maple syrup

1 tablespoon prepared horseradish mustard or Dijon mustard

1–2 tablespoons finely chopped fresh ginger

1–2 cloves garlic, finely minced

1 tablespoon mirin, sake, or brown rice vinegar

1 tablespoon fresh thyme or 2 teaspoons dried

½ teaspoon ground allspice

Place the beans in a large saucepan with the filtered water, stock, and kombu. Bring to a boil. Reduce the heat to medium-low and simmer for 45 to 55 minutes. The beans should be whole, but easily smashed with your fingers. Drain off the extra liquid into a bowl or pitcher and set it aside to mix the seasonings in. Discard the kombu.

Place the beans in a casserole dish (preferably with a lid).

Preheat the oven to 350°F.

Toss the sweet potatoes, leeks, mushrooms, and celery with the cooked beans.

If necessary, add enough vegetable stock to the drained cooking liquid from the beans to equal 1½ cups liquid. Mix in the miso; shoyu; brown rice syrup or maple syrup; mustard; ginger; garlic; mirin, sake, or brown rice vinegar; thyme; and allspice.

Pour the mixture over the beans. Add a bit more stock if needed to just cover the beans. Cover and bake for 60 to 90 minutes, until most of the liquid is absorbed and the remaining liquid has reduced to a syrup.

NUTRITION AT A GLANCE
Per serving: 170 calories, 0 g total fat, 0 g saturated fat, 6 g protein, 36 g carbohydrates, 5 g dietary fiber, 420 mg sodium

CHAPTER 10

Winds of the World Entrées

There is no sight on earth more appealing than the sight of a woman making dinner for someone she loves.

—THOMAS WOLFE

Beet Ravioli with Pine Nut Ricotta

Raw-food enthusiasts: The beets may be sliced raw and marinated in the dehydrator, turning occasionally for 4 to 6 hours to soften if you do not want to use a steaming heat. If you do not have a mandoline, the beets may be boiled for 10 minutes to soften enough to slice very thinly by hand with a sharp knife. Then toss with the marinade ingredients.

YIELDS: 6 SERVINGS

2–3	nice round beets, peeled and sliced very thinly on a mandoline
4	tablespoons extra-virgin olive oil, plus additional for drizzling
2	teaspoons aged balsamic vinegar, plus additional for drizzling, or 1 teaspoon balsamic + 1 teaspoon maple syrup
1	teaspoon umeboshi plum vinegar
1	teaspoon shoyu (soy sauce), plus additional for drizzling
	Sea salt
2	cups pine nuts
1–2	cloves garlic
2	teaspoons truffle oil or additional olive oil
1	teaspoon cold-pressed coconut butter or additional olive oil
3–4	tablespoons lemon juice
	Smoked salt or sea salt
1½	cups basil chiffonade (plus a little extra for garnish)
¼	cup chopped sorrel (optional)
	Freshly ground black pepper
	Fresh tarragon leaves, for garnish

Steam the beets for 3 to 5 minutes, turning for even cooking. Toss with 1 tablespoon of the olive oil, the aged balsamic, umeboshi plum vinegar, shoyu, and a pinch of sea salt. Let stand to marinate, turning occasionally, for 15 minutes to 1 hour. The beets may be prepared well ahead of time and stashed in the fridge for up to 2 days.

In a food processor or Vita-Mix, grind the pine nuts and garlic into a fine meal. Add the remaining olive oil, truffle oil, coconut butter, lemon juice (start with 3 tablespoons and add more as needed to taste), and smoked salt and sea salt to taste. Blend until very smooth. Add a touch of filtered water as necessary to achieve the desired consistency, which should resemble ricotta cheese. Season to taste with additional smoked salt and sea salt.

Fold the basil and sorrel (if desired, for a lemony lift) into the Pine Nut Ricotta.

Place single slices of marinated beet on each serving plate or a platter. Spoon 2 teaspoons or so of Pine Nut Ricotta in the center of each slice. Top with another slice of beet and gently press the edges to close. Drizzle with olive oil, aged balsamic, and shoyu, and sprinkle with sea salt, pepper, a pinch of fresh tarragon leaves, and basil chiffonade. Serve at room temperature.

NUTRITION AT A GLANCE
Per serving: 430 calories, 43 g total fat, 4 g saturated fat, 7 g protein, 11 g carbohydrates, 3 g dietary fiber, 240 mg sodium

Mushroom and Tofu Clay Pot

This dish was inspired by a meal I had at a remarkable restaurant in London called Hakkasan. Very chic, very pricey, and every bite of every dish I sampled was right on the money. It was so good, we went back the next night.

Tofu takes a great position in this dish. It is a great source of protein and takes on a good marinade well. I use medium or soft tofu, which is pressed to release extra water and practically melts in your mouth. Best cooked in a traditional clay pot with a lid, though a ceramic dish with a lid will also work.

YIELDS: 4 SERVINGS

1	block medium or soft tofu
15–20	cremini mushrooms (small, evenly sized ones are better)
4	tablespoons shoyu (soy sauce)
2	tablespoons agave nectar
1	tablespoon maple syrup
2	tablespoons sake or mirin
1½–2	tablespoons ginger juice (page 160)
2–3	cloves garlic, pressed
2	tablespoons arrowroot
3	green onions, chopped

Preheat the oven to 350°F.

Drain the water the tofu is packaged in. Place the tofu on a plate, with another plate on top of it. Put a light weight on top, such as a small bottle of water. Let stand for 10 to 15 minutes to press out excess water. This will help the tofu absorb the flavor of the marinade. Drain off the water and blot the tofu dry with a clean towel. Cut into small cubes.

Place the tofu in a clay pot with the mushrooms.

In a small bowl, combine the shoyu, agave, maple syrup, sake or mirin, ginger juice, and garlic. Stir in the arrowroot until dissolved.

Pour over the tofu and mushrooms and fold gently to coat. Fold in the green onions.

Bake, covered, for 35 to 45 minutes. Serve hot!

NUTRITION AT A GLANCE
Per serving: 140 calories, 5 g total fat, 0.5 g saturated fat, 11 g protein, 14 g carbohydrates, 2 g dietary fiber, 810 mg sodium

Salade Niçoise

Salade Niçoise typifies the cuisine of the French Riviera city of Nice. The integral ingredients of dishes "à la niçoise" include tomatoes, black olives, and garlic. Salade Niçoise contains these basic ingredients plus green beans, onions, and herbs. I use cubes of tender potatoes (or Jerusalem artichokes for less starch) where tuna and hard-cooked eggs traditionally stand. A piquant dressing adorns this medley, served on a bed of crunchy lettuce. You may not need all of the dressing. Store leftovers in a sealed glass jar in the fridge. Bon appétit!

YIELDS: 4 SERVINGS

3   cups cubed potatoes or Jerusalem artichokes

1   teaspoon sea salt

24 green beans, stems snapped off

2   tablespoons pine nuts

6   tablespoons olive oil

3   Roma tomatoes, sealed and chopped

1   clove garlic

1   tablespoon aged balsamic vinegar, or 2 teaspoons balsamic + 1 teaspoon maple syrup

1   tablespoon apple cider vinegar

1   tablespoon brown rice vinegar (or additional apple cider vinegar)

1   teaspoon umeboshi plum vinegar

1   teaspoon shoyu (soy sauce)

1–2 teaspoons prepared Dijon mustard

1   teaspoon agave nectar or maple syrup

Freshly ground black pepper

1½ cups black olives, pitted (niçoise olives or kalamata olives are good choices)

⅓   cup finely chopped chives (green onions may be used if chives are difficult to find)

⅓   cup thinly sliced red onion

2–3 tablespoons fresh thyme

2–3 tablespoons fresh tarragon leaves

4   cups washed and torn lettuce (butter lettuce or crunchy romaine lettuce is great)

½   cup chopped parsley leaves

¼   cup finely chopped green onions

Place the potatoes or artichokes and 1 teaspoon of salt in a pot, cover with filtered water, and bring to a boil. Reduce the heat and simmer until easily pierced with a fork (5 to 10 minutes for potatoes; 3 to 4 minutes for artichokes). It's best not to overcook the potatoes or they will fall apart in the salad. Drain off the water and cool while preparing the salad (this can be done up to a day ahead of time and stashed in the fridge).

If you have a steaming pot that fits, you can steam the green beans over the potatoes to save time and washing an extra pot. Otherwise, steam the green beans separately. Either way, look for the beans to turn bright green and become tender. Shock the beans by running them under cold running water to arrest the cooking.

They're best al dente and still a bit crisp rather than overcooked.

In a blender, place the pine nuts, olive oil, ⅓ cup of the tomatoes, garlic, vinegars, shoyu, Dijon mustard, and agave or maple syrup and blend until very smooth. Season to taste with salt and pepper. Add a touch more mustard if you prefer the tang.

Toss the dressing gently to coat the potatoes, green beans, olives, chives or green onions, red onion, thyme, and tarragon. Allow to stand for 10 to 20 minutes to marry flavor. Fold in the remaining tomatoes.

Serve over a bed of tossed torn lettuce with the parsley and green onions.

Garnish with ground black pepper.

NUTRITION AT A GLANCE
Per serving: 390 calories, 28 g total fat, 3.5 g saturated fat, 6 g protein, 33 g carbohydrates, 7 g dietary fiber, 750 mg sodium

---

A good cook is like a sorceress who
dispenses happiness.

—ELSA SCHIAPARELLI

Tomato and Portobello Phyllo Torte

Phyllo is paper-thin sheets of dough usually found in the freezer section of the market. Look for phyllo that does not have butter or hydrogenated oil in it.

YIELDS: 6 SERVINGS

7–8	tablespoons olive oil, plus additional for drizzling
1	large sweet onion or 2 small sweet onions, sliced ¼" thick
2	teaspoons aged balsamic vinegar, or 1½ teaspoons balsamic + ½ teaspoon maple syrup
1	teaspoon agave nectar
2–3	portobello mushrooms, stems and gills removed, sliced ¼" thick, or about 4 cups sliced cremini mushrooms

2	tablespoons shoyu (soy sauce)
2	tablespoons red wine
5–8	sheets phyllo dough, thawed
1–2	tablespoons fresh oregano, roughly chopped (optional)
2–4	tomatoes, sliced ¼" thick
	Salt
	Freshly ground black pepper
	Finely chopped basil

Warm 4 tablespoons of olive oil in a skillet over medium heat. Add the onion and stir to coat. Cook for 2 to 3 minutes, stirring occasionally, until it begins to soften. Add the aged balsamic and agave. Continue to cook for 5 to 7 minutes, or until the onion is very soft and caramelized.

Add the mushrooms, shoyu, and red wine. Cook about 5 minutes, stirring occasionally, until the mushrooms are soft and have released some of their liquid, which should be cooked off. If the mushrooms are sitting in liquid, turn up the heat to high for 30 seconds to 1 minute and cook off the liquid. Remove the pan from the heat.

Preheat the oven to 350°F.

Pour the remaining 3 to 4 tablespoons of olive oil into a small dish. Set a 9" or 10" pie plate and the phyllo dough in front of you. It is a good idea to keep the phyllo dough covered with a clean, damp towel to prevent it from drying out. This is especially important if you do not use the whole

package and want to save any leftovers to use again.

Brush the pie plate lightly with olive oil, using a pastry brush. Place a single sheet in the pie plate and brush it lightly but thoroughly with olive oil. Continue with another sheet, and so forth until there are 5 to 8 layers (depending on how crusty you want the torte and how much luck you are having with the phyllo). If the phyllo breaks at all, just piece it together and brush with oil. Trim the bits of phyllo hanging over the side of the pie plate or fold over and brush with a little extra oil.

Place the mushrooms and caramelized onions in the bottom of the phyllo shell. Sprinkle with oregano, if desired.

Arrange the tomato slices to cover neatly. Cover with another pie plate or foil and bake for 20 to 25 minutes, until the mushrooms are sweating a bit. Uncover and bake another 20 to

30 minutes, until the phyllo is golden brown. Drizzle with olive oil and sprinkle with salt, pepper, and basil. Cool 10 minutes or longer before cutting and serving.

Phyllo Dough

Phyllo dough is a tissue-thin dough typically made from wheat. It is used in layers, brushed with oil (or butter, which I do not use), and baked with various tantalizing fillings both savory and sweet.

When purchasing, look at the ingredient list to avoid unhealthy fats and preservatives. There are some excellent natural phyllo doughs on the market. The Fillo Factory (www.fillofactory.com) produces several choice products—organic wheat phyllo, organic whole wheat phyllo, and spelt phyllo (perfect for gluten-sensitive folks).

Phyllo dough is generally sold frozen and must be thawed before using. Unopened frozen phyllo can be stored in the freezer for up to a year. Unopened phyllo will keep fresh in the fridge for up to 1 month. Once opened, it should be used within 4 days. After opening, store it in the fridge, as refreezing phyllo can cause it to become brittle. Frozen phyllo can be placed in the fridge to thaw a day or two before using, or it can be thawed on the counter in 20 to 30 minutes. If thawing on the counter, take it out a bit before preparing the rest of the ingredients so it is ready when you are.

Handling Phyllo Dough

It takes a little practice to handle phyllo dough well, which is quickly and deftly, but the delicate, flaky results cannot be trumped. Here are a few tips:

- Don't let the dough dry out while you are working. Keep it covered with a clean, slightly damp dishtowel.
- Avoid using wet hands to pick up the sheets as they will stick together.
- Five to 10 sheets of phyllo, brushed with oil, yield a good layer.
- Use a 1" to 1½" pastry brush for the best results.
- If the sheets tear or break, it is fine; just piece them together the best you can, and make sure they are lightly but evenly brushed with oil.
- I recommend having a bit more olive oil in a bowl than you think you need for brushing the layers.

Beets and Asparagus Smoked Pine Nut Terrine

This dish is gorgeous to look at and even more pleasing to taste. It takes a bit of time to put together but presents a stunning plate of color and texture. The beets can be steamed or marinated as in the Beet Ravioli with Pine Nut Ricotta (page 314) for a more raw-friendly version. A terrine pan, which is long, narrow, and deep, is really helpful, but something like a loaf pan will also work.

YIELDS: 8 SERVINGS

2   large beets or 3–4 medium beets

1   tablespoon + 2 teaspoons extra-virgin olive oil

1   teaspoon aged balsamic vinegar, or ½ teaspoon balsamic + ½ teaspoon maple syrup; plus additional for drizzling

3   teaspoons lemon juice, divided

1   teaspoon umeboshi plum vinegar

½   teaspoon shoyu (soy sauce)

½   teaspoon maple syrup

¼   teaspoon sea salt, plus additional for the asparagus

Freshly ground black pepper

1   bunch asparagus (young spears are best), trimmed

1   bunch spinach, cleaned

3   cups Smoked Pine Nut Farmer's Cheese (page 244) or Quick Smoked Pine Nut Spread (page 245)

Fresh thyme leaves or basil leaves, for garnish

Preheat the oven to 350°F.

Rub the beets with a little olive oil.

Place in a casserole dish, pie plate, or roasting pan and bake for 30 minutes, until tender and able to be pierced with a fork. Let cool enough to handle comfortably.

Peel away the skin and slice thinly.

Toss gently with 1 tablespoon of olive oil, the aged balsamic (or balsamic + maple syrup), 1 teaspoon of the lemon juice, the umeboshi plum vinegar, shoyu, maple syrup, sea salt, and pepper to taste. Let stand for 15 to 30 minutes to absorb and develop flavor. A bowl or plate with a weight can be placed directly on top of the marinating beets to speed up the process and help the flavor join more thoroughly. This can be done a day ahead of time if you wish.

Blanch the asparagus in boiling water for 1 to 3 minutes, just until bright green and tender, or lightly steam for similar results. Remove and shock under cold running water or plunge in ice water.

Gently toss asparagus with 2 teaspoons of olive oil, the remaining 2 teaspoons of lemon juice, and a pinch of sea salt and pepper. Set aside until ready to use.

Blanch or steam the spinach separately and shock under cold running water or plunge in ice water. Gently squeeze and set aside.

Line a terrine mold or small loaf pan (4" to 6") with plastic wrap, with enough hanging over the edges to cover the terrine when it is finished.

Line the bottom with beet slices overlapping each other so the edges begin to come up on the sides of the pan.

Place a layer of spinach leaves over the beet slices (this will keep the color of the beets from bleeding into the white of the pine nuts).

Dollop small spoonfuls of the Smoked Pine Nut Farmer's Cheese or Quick Smoked Pine Nut Spread on the spinach-covered beet slices and spread into a thin layer with a wet spatula or moist fingers so it does not stick to you or the spatula.

Lay spears of asparagus neatly in a row over the spread (it may be necessary to trim the asparagus so it fits).

Dollop small spoonfuls of the smoked pine nut cheese or spread over the asparagus spears and spread with a wet spatula or moist fingers, pushing it into the crevices between the asparagus.

Continue until you have three layers of asparagus.

Place a layer of spinach leaves over the spread. Layer beet slices over the spinach, and then another layer of spinach over the beets.

Place some beet slices on the sidewalls of the pan and cover with spinach leaves.

Start again with another row of asparagus.

Dollop small spoonfuls of the smoked pine nut cheese or spread over the asparagus and spread, pressing it into the crevices. Continue until you have three more layers of asparagus packed with cheese/spread.

Cover with spinach leaves and with beet slices.

Use the extra plastic wrap to cover the top.

Use a weight designed for a terrine pan to weight the whole thing. If using a loaf pan, place another pan of the same dimensions on top and weight with a can of beans or a sack of baker's weights.

Chill in the fridge to set for at least an hour and as long as a day.

To serve, take the weight off and unwrap the top of the terrine.

Place a serving plate upside down on the terrine mold or loaf pan. Flip the whole thing over and remove the mold or pan. Peel away the plastic.

Use a very sharp knife and an even sawing motion to cut, so as not to mash your masterpiece. Clean the knife between cuts. Pieces should be 1" to 1½" thick. Serve flat on a plate (one or two pieces per serving).

Drizzle the plate with olive oil and a little aged balsamic or balsamic and maple syrup and sprinkle the plate with fresh thyme leaves or basil leaves, as desired.

NUTRITION AT A GLANCE
Per serving: 450 calories, 41 g total fat, 3.5 g saturated fat, 11 g protein, 17 g carbohydrates, 6 g dietary fiber, 290 mg sodium

Sweet Potato Rolls with Haricots Verts, Carrots, Caramelized Red Onion Rings, and Savory Mushrooms

This signature dish could be served as an appetizer, but it's so good you'll long for a larger portion. So serve it as an entrée over a bed of wild rice. Try the long neck of a butternut squash in place of sweet potatoes for a variation.

YIELDS: 4 SERVINGS (ABOUT 10 ROLLS)

2   sweet potatoes

2   tablespoons + 2 teaspoons olive oil

Pinch of sea salt

1½ tablespoons + 2 teaspoons shoyu (soy sauce)

2   teaspoons umeboshi plum vinegar

1–2 teaspoons agave nectar or maple syrup

1   medium carrot, cut into matchsticks

30 haricots verts or 18 green beans, cut in half and sliced lengthwise

1   medium red onion, thinly sliced

6–8 shiitake mushrooms, stems removed, cut into ½" slices, or 1 portobello mushroom, gills removed, cut in half and sliced into ¼" pieces

1–2 teaspoons aged balsamic vinegar (at least 25 years), or ½–1 teaspoon balsamic + ½–1 teaspoon maple syrup or agave nectar

12 fresh basil leaves, torn in half

Freshly ground black pepper

Preheat the oven to 350°F.

Peel the sweet potatoes and cut the ends off.

Slice thinly, lengthwise. If the potatoes are too long to comfortably or easily slice whole, cut them in half.

Lay the slices flat on a baking sheet without overlapping. Bake for 10 minutes, until soft.

Allow to cool and gently rub with 2 teaspoons of olive oil and a pinch of salt. If they need to stand for any length of time, cover them after they've cooled.

In a small saucepan, mix together 1½ tablespoons of shoyu, the umeboshi plum vinegar, and agave or maple syrup. Place the carrot and haricots verts or green beans in the pan and add just enough filtered water to cover the carrot and beans. Bring to a gentle simmer, uncovered, over medium heat. Reduce the heat to low and cook for 5 to 10 minutes, or just until tender. Do not disturb the veggies by stirring while they cook. The vegetables should still be firm. Remove from the heat and let stand for 2 to 3 minutes.

Drain off the liquid and reserve to use for the onion and mushrooms. Place the veggies in the fridge to cool.

Warm the remaining 2 tablespoons of olive oil in a pan over medium heat.

Add the onion and cook for a few minutes, stirring occasionally, until it starts to become soft and translucent.

Add the mushrooms, the remaining 2 teaspoons of shoyu, and the aged balsamic (or balsamic + maple syrup or agave). Cook for 3 to 5 minutes, stirring occasionally. Add a splash of marinade from the haricots verts and carrot during that time to keep the mushrooms from drying out. Cook until soft and almost all of the liquid has cooked off.

To assemble the rolls, lay 2 pieces of softened sweet potato slices on a cutting board (not touching, short end facing you, and the length of the sweet potato running away from you).

Put a few haricots verts or green beans, some carrot matchsticks, and a few onion and mushroom slices at the bottom of one potato slice. Top the filling with a torn piece of basil. Fold the short end of the softened potato skin over the filling and roll closed. The tendency is to put too much in at once. Less is more, as it will be easier to eat and go farther.

Roll the second sweet potato slice around the bundle and secure with a toothpick.

Follow suit until everything is used.

The rolls are great as is or may be baked at 350°F for 10 to 12 minutes to warm.

Garnish with pepper.

NUTRITION AT A GLANCE
Per serving: 190 calories, 9 g total fat, 1.5 g saturated fat, 3 g protein, 24 g carbohydrates, 4 g dietary fiber, 990 mg sodium

---

The fact is that it takes more than ingredients and technique to cook a good meal. A good cook puts something of himself into the preparation—he cooks with enjoyment, anticipation, spontaneity, and he is willing to experiment.

—PEARL BAILEY

Spanakopita for Four Seasons

Spanakopita is a layered Greek delicacy traditionally made with sautéed spinach, onions, and feta cheese surrounded by a delicate crust of phyllo dough. I choose organic whole wheat or spelt phyllo dough and offer four fantastic versions for four seasons of enjoyment.

Spinach, Herb, and Mushroom Spanakopita

YIELDS: 10 SERVINGS

2   cups tightly packed parsley leaves

2   cups tightly packed basil leaves

⅓–½   cup loosely packed oregano leaves

4   cups baby spinach leaves (see note)

⅓   cup pine nuts

⅓   cup lemon juice

1½   teaspoons sea salt

1   tablespoon truffle oil (optional for truffle lovers)

8   ounces tofu (medium is best, firm a runner-up)

2   medium red onions

3   tablespoons + ½ cup extra-virgin olive oil, or as necessary

2–4   cloves garlic, minced

4   cups sliced cremini, portobello, or button mushrooms

Sea salt

Freshly ground black pepper

1   package organic phyllo dough

Preheat the oven to 350°F.

Place the parsley, basil, and oregano in a food processor. Chop finely and set aside in a large bowl. (No need to wash the food processor yet!) The spinach can be chopped in the food processor, though I find it's better to chop it a little more roughly by hand. Do as you please and mix together with the chopped herbs.

Place the pine nuts, lemon juice, sea salt, and truffle oil (if desired) in the food processor. Blend until smooth. Cut the tofu into 8 pieces and add to the pine nut mixture. Blend until smooth. Add this mixture to the herbs and spinach and fold to mix well.

Cut the ends off the onions and peel. Cut in half along the grain and slice crosswise thinly. Warm 3 tablespoons of the olive oil in a skillet over medium heat. Add the onion and stir to coat with the oil. Sauté for 2 minutes, stirring occasionally, or until the onions start to become soft and translucent. Add the garlic and sauté for 15 to 20 seconds. Add the mushrooms and stir well to coat. Cook another 2 to 3 minutes, stirring occasionally, until soft.

Fold the mushrooms and onions into the spinach mixture. Season to taste with sea salt and pepper as desired.

Brush the bottom of a 13" × 9" glass baking dish with olive oil. Place one sheet of phyllo dough in the bottom and brush lightly with olive

oil. Place another sheet on top and brush again. Repeat until you have 10 layers.

Spread the filling evenly over the dough.

Lay another sheet of phyllo over the spinach mixture and brush with oil. Continue until you have another 10 layers.

Cover with foil and bake for 25 minutes.

Remove the foil and continue to bake for another 15 to 20 minutes, or until golden brown.

Let stand for 15 minutes before serving.

NOTE: *Baby spinach is best because the stems are tender. If using mature spinach, remove the stems first.*

NUTRITION AT A GLANCE
Per serving: 360 calories, 24 g total fat, 3.5 g saturated fat, 8 g protein, 32 g carbohydrates, 3 g dietary fiber, 590 mg sodium

Old-World Ratatouille Spanakopita

YIELDS: 12 SERVINGS

4   cups nicely packed spinach

2   cups nicely packed basil leaves

Old-World Ratatouille (page 267)

1   package organic phyllo dough

½   cup extra-virgin olive oil

Preheat the oven to 350°F.

Chop the spinach and basil roughly. Fold into the ratatouille.

Brush the bottom of a 13" × 9" glass baking dish with olive oil. Place one sheet of phyllo dough in the bottom and brush lightly with olive oil. Place another sheet on top and brush again. Repeat until you have 10 layers.

Spread the filling evenly over the dough.

Lay another sheet of phyllo over the filling and brush with oil. Continue until you have another 10 layers.

Cover tightly with foil and bake for 25 minutes.

Remove the foil and continue to bake for another 15 minutes, or until golden brown.

Let stand for 15 minutes to cool before serving.

NUTRITION AT A GLANCE
Per serving: 300 calories, 19 g total fat, 3 g saturated fat, 5 g protein, 29 g carbohydrates, 4 g dietary fiber, 410 mg sodium

Roasted Corn, Bell Pepper, Sweet Onion, Leek, and Shallot Spanakopita

YIELDS: 12 SERVINGS

6 ears fresh corn, kernels removed	Sea salt
1 medium sweet onion, chopped	Freshly ground black pepper
8 shallots, quartered	2 red bell peppers
1 medium leek, sliced	2 cups nicely packed basil leaves
2 cloves garlic, minced	2 cups nicely packed parsley leaves
1 tablespoon fresh thyme or 1½ teaspoons dried	¼ cup pine nuts
¼ cup + ½ cup extra-virgin olive oil, or as necessary	¼ cup lemon juice
	4 ounces tofu (medium is best, firm is good)
1 tablespoon balsamic vinegar	1 package organic phyllo dough

Preheat the oven to 350°F.

In a large bowl, toss the corn, onion, shallots, leek, garlic, thyme, ¼ cup of the olive oil, vinegar, and salt and pepper to taste.

Spread evenly in a roasting pan. Bake for 15 to 20 minutes, until soft.

Roast the bell peppers over a flame until the skin is blistering and blackened. Allow the peppers to cool slightly. Then peel away the charred skins and remove the seeds. This can be done ahead of time, or you can buy roasted peppers (go organic!) to save time. Slice into ¼" strips and cut in half to end up with shorter strips.

Place the basil and parsley in a food processor. Chop finely. Transfer to a large bowl.

Add the pine nuts and lemon juice to the food processor and blend until smooth. Add the tofu and blend until smooth. Fold into the herbs.

When the vegetables are done roasting, fold into the herb–pine nut mixture and add the red pepper. Season to taste with sea salt and pepper.

Brush the bottom of a 13" × 9" glass baking dish with olive oil. Place one sheet of phyllo dough in the bottom and brush lightly with olive oil. Place another sheet on top and brush again. Repeat until you have 10 layers.

Spread the filling evenly over the dough.

Lay another sheet of phyllo over the filling and brush with oil. Continue until you have another 10 layers.

Cover tightly with foil and bake at 350°F for 25 minutes.

Remove the foil and continue to bake for another 15 minutes, or until golden brown.

Let stand for 15 minutes before serving.

NUTRITION AT A GLANCE
Per serving: 350 calories, 20 g total fat, 3 g saturated fat, 7 g protein, 40 g carbohydrates, 4 g dietary fiber, 200 mg sodium

Roasted Artichoke Spanakopita

8   Roasted Artichoke Hearts (see "Artichoke Hearts Three Ways," page 254)

½   cup pine nuts

2   tablespoons lemon juice

2   tablespoons extra-virgin olive oil

    Sea salt

4   cups baby spinach, chopped

1   package organic phyllo dough

Preheat the oven to 350°F.

Place half of the artichoke hearts in a food processor with the pine nuts, lemon juice, olive oil, and a pinch of salt. Blend until smooth. Transfer to a large bowl. Fold the remaining hearts and the spinach into the pine nut mixture.

Brush the bottom of a 13" × 9" glass baking dish with olive oil. Place one sheet of phyllo dough in the bottom and brush lightly with olive oil. Place another sheet on top and brush again. Repeat until you have 10 layers.

Spread the filling evenly over the dough.

Lay another sheet of phyllo over the filling and brush with oil. Continue until you have another 10 layers.

Cover with foil and bake for 25 minutes.

Remove the foil and continue to bake for another 15 to 20 minutes, or until golden brown.

Let stand for 15 minutes to cool before serving.

NUTRITION AT A GLANCE
Per serving: 450 calories, 26 g total fat, 3.5 g saturated fat, 8 g protein, 47 g carbohydrates, 3 g dietary fiber, 480 mg sodium

Shepherd's Pie

This is a rustic, satisfying dish without fancy seasoning. If it seems like a lot of directions, don't worry—it is not tough; I am just trying to get you to use as few pans and dishes as possible, so you can enjoy eating and not worry about cleaning up.

YIELDS: 12 SERVINGS

8 cups chopped potatoes

Sea salt

3 tablespoons cold-pressed Omega Nutrition coconut butter or olive oil, plus additional for drizzling (optional)

Freshly ground black pepper

8 tablespoons olive oil

3¼ cups chopped onions

1 package tempeh, crumbled into small pieces (about 1½ cups)

2 teaspoons shoyu (soy sauce)

2 tablespoons fresh thyme or 1¼ tablespoons dried

⅓ cup filtered water

4 cups sliced button or cremini mushrooms

2 cups shelled peas (thawed frozen peas may be used)

1½ cups carrots, quartered lengthwise into ¼" pieces

Preheat the oven to 400°F.

Place the potatoes in a large saucepan or stockpot and cover with a few inches of filtered water and a pinch of salt. Bring to a boil. Reduce the heat and simmer until soft enough to mash with the back of a fork (about 20 minutes).

Drain off the hot water. Mash the potatoes through a food mill and add 3 tablespoons of coconut butter or olive oil, or blend in a food processor or stand mixer until smooth. Season to taste with salt and pepper. Set aside.

In a large skillet, warm 2 tablespoons of olive oil over medium heat. Add 1 cup of onions and stir occasionally for 3 to 4 minutes, or until the onions are softened. Add the tempeh and a pinch or two of sea salt, and cook, stirring occasionally, for 10 to 12 minutes, until browning nicely. Add the shoyu, thyme, and a pinch of black pepper and continue to stir and cook for another 2 to 3 minutes, until well browned. Remove from the heat, transfer to a glass casserole dish, and set aside.

Pour ⅓ cup of filtered water into the skillet and return to the heat to deglaze by rubbing the good stuff off of the pan and into the cooking water with a wooden spoon or wooden spatula.

Add the remaining 6 tablespoons of olive oil and the remaining 2¼ cups of onion. Cook for about 7 minutes, or until most of the liquid has evaporated and the onions are soft.

Add the mushrooms and stir, seasoning with

some salt. Cook for 8 minutes, until the mushrooms are savory and soft.

Add the mushroom mixture to the browned tempeh mixture. Add the peas and carrots and stir to thoroughly mix.

Dollop the mashed potatoes evenly over the vegetables and spread smooth to cover.

Bake for 30 to 35 minutes, or until the mashed potatoes are golden brown.

Drizzle with olive oil or cold-pressed coconut butter, if desired.

Sprinkle with sea salt and pepper.

NUTRITION AT A GLANCE
Per serving: 230 calories, 15 g total fat, 2 g saturated fat, 8 g protein, 17 g carbohydrates, 5 g dietary fiber, 85 mg sodium

Laughter is brightest where food is best.

—IRISH PROVERB

Siamese Pad Thai with Shiitake Mushrooms

Pad thai is a well-loved noodle dish with the balmy breeze of Southeast Asian infusion. I approach pad thai a bit unconventionally, including a few Japanese ingredients, which yield a well-rounded flavor. A generous handful of mung bean sprouts lends just the right authentic texture and lightens the dish perfectly. I often double the sauce for future use as it keeps well and is splendid on steamed veggies.

Using all of the ingredients I recommend yields a depth of flavor and texture, but in the spirit of simplicity, I list several of them as optional. Though seasoned fish sauce (nuoc cham) is an important ingredient in regional Siamese, Vietnamese, and Thai food, a high-quality soy sauce takes a worthy position as it is fermented (like fish sauce) and has complex flavor. I find nama shoyu to be the best for this dish because it is not pasteurized and has a deep strength, though any soy sauce will work well.

YIELDS: 8 SERVINGS

4 cups cooked noodles (see note)

1 tablespoon organic peanut butter

3 tablespoons brown rice vinegar

2–3 tablespoons nama shoyu (any high-quality soy sauce can be used)

1 tablespoon lime juice

1 tablespoon umeboshi plum vinegar

1 tablespoon agave nectar

1 tablespoon maple syrup

2 teaspoons umeboshi plum paste

1 tablespoon paprika

1 teaspoon yuzu (optional)

1½ cups Mushroom Stock (page 182), broth, or filtered water

2 tablespoons sesame oil (not toasted)

4–5 cloves garlic, finely minced

2 shallots, peeled and thinly sliced

2 green onions, chopped

1 tablespoon peeled ginger, finely minced

⅓ cup finely chopped daikon or turnip (optional)

1 cup sliced shiitake mushrooms

4 ounces tofu, cut into ½" cubes (optional)

½–1 small chili pepper, finely sliced (optional)

½ cup ground peanuts

1½ cups mung bean sprouts

3 green onions, finely chopped

¼ cup chopped cilantro (optional)

Juice of 1 lime

Sea salt

Freshly ground black pepper

2–3 tablespoons peanuts, roughly chopped (optional)

Lime wedges (optional)

Prepare the noodles. If using tofu noodles, simply drain from the water they are packed in. Shake to remove as much liquid as possible or blot dry with a clean towel and set aside. Shirataki noodles should be handled in the same manner. If using mung bean noodles, cook according to package directions, but keep them on the al dente side (usually about 3 minutes). Drain and set aside. If using rice noodles, soak in warm filtered water until al dente soft (25 to 30 minutes). Drain and set aside.

In a measuring pitcher or bowl, mix together the peanut butter, vinegar, shoyu, lime juice, umeboshi plum vinegar, agave, maple syrup, umeboshi plum paste, paprika, and yuzu. Add the stock, broth, or water and whisk together with a fork. Taste and adjust seasoning, adding a touch more shoyu if you like it on the salty side. Set aside. This sauce can be stored for up to a week, and therefore doubled if desired for a future dish.

In a wok or large skillet, heat the oil and stir-fry the garlic, shallots, chopped green onions, ginger, and daikon or turnip over high heat until fragrant. Add the mushrooms, tofu (if desired), and chili pepper (if desired for spicy heat) and cook, stirring, for about 2 minutes.

Add the pad thai sauce and noodles. Continue to cook, tossing and stirring, until almost all of the liquid has cooked off.

Stir in the ground peanuts, mung bean sprouts, finely chopped green onions, and cilantro (if desired). Cook for another 15 to 30 seconds and remove from the heat. Season with the lime juice and salt and pepper to taste.

Serve hot, sprinkled with chopped peanuts and garnished with lime wedges as you wish.

NOTE: *Medium-width rice noodles are traditional, though I love tofu noodles, which are high in protein and don't need to be cooked. They are becoming more available in the refrigerated section of natural food stores and online (www.house-foods.com). Shirataki noodles (found in Japanese markets) made from yam and konnyaku root are excellent, being very low in calories and high in fiber, though they're a little difficult to find. Mung bean noodles, which look like thin rice noodles, are a great choice to serve up easily digestible protein.*

NUTRITION AT A GLANCE
Per serving: 260 calories, 9 g total fat, 1.5 g saturated fat, 4 g protein, 40 g carbohydrates, 2 g dietary fiber, 760 mg sodium

Wild Rice Pilau with Brussels Sprouts and Leeks in Caramelized Onion Broth

I must admit that I am a huge Brussels sprouts fan. They are one of the most nutritious vegetables and have remarkable taste and texture when prepared well. This dish is deeply satisfying and hearty, without being overly heavy. The complex, naturally sweet flavor of the caramelized onions infuses the wild rice with an incredible layer of flavor that greets the Brussels sprouts and leeks in autumnal heaven. Store-bought onion broth, vegetable broth, or even bouillon cubes can be used to save the step of making your own, though I highly recommend using one with organic ingredients.

YIELDS: 4 SERVINGS

CARAMELIZED ONION BROTH

4 tablespoons extra-virgin olive oil	1 stem (3") fresh rosemary
4 large sweet or yellow onions, sliced	2 bay leaves
8 cups filtered water	6 black peppercorns
2 sprigs fresh thyme	

PILAU

1 cup wild rice	1 leek, trimmed and cleaned
Sea salt	Extra-virgin olive oil or Parsley-Thyme Oil (opposite page)
Freshly ground black pepper	
12 Brussels sprouts	

TO MAKE THE BROTH:

Warm the olive oil in a large stockpot. Add the onions and sauté to caramelize, stirring occasionally, for 25 to 30 minutes.

Add the water, thyme, rosemary, bay leaves, and peppercorns. Bring to a boil. Reduce the heat and simmer, partially covered, for 1 to 2 hours. Strain and return to the stockpot to simmer and reduce to about 4 cups, about 20 to 25 minutes.

TO MAKE THE PILAU:

Add the wild rice to the reduced broth and bring to a boil, covered. Reduce the heat to low and simmer, covered, for 30 to 40 minutes, or until the wild rice is split and tender. The rice will absorb a lot of the broth, though there should be some excess in the pot. Remove from the heat and season to taste with salt and pepper.

While the wild rice is cooking, trim the Brussels sprouts and remove one layer of outer leaves.

Cut into quarters. Steam in a basket over boiling water until tender, 4 to 6 minutes. Remove from the heat and shock by running under cold water.

Cut the leek into ½" pieces through the middle of the greens. Steam just until tender. Remove from the heat and shock by running under cold water.

Fold the Brussels sprouts and leeks into the wild rice and warm over low heat if necessary.

Serve with a ladle in a deep plate, including a bit of extra broth.

Drizzle with extra-virgin olive oil or Parsley-Thyme Oil.

NUTRITION AT A GLANCE
Per serving: 350 calories, 16 g total fat, 2 g saturated fat, 8 g protein, 48 g carbohydrates, 5 g dietary fiber, 35 mg sodium

Parsley-Thyme Oil

This is a beautiful bright green oil infused with the sweet essence of parsley and the savory depth of thyme. Blanching the parsley captures the color at its peak. This oil is best refrigerated for a day before straining, though it may be strained right off and used.

YIELDS: 12 SERVINGS

1 bunch parsley, stems removed
1¼ cups extra-virgin olive oil

1 teaspoon fresh thyme

Blanch the parsley in boiling water for 15 seconds. Strain and shock by running under cold water or plunging in ice water.

Place in a blender with the olive oil and thyme. Blend at high speed until smooth.

It may be strained and used as is, though it's better if you place it in a sealed container in the fridge overnight, then warm it to room temperature and strain.

Drizzle over Wild Rice Pilau or any soup for a delicate infusion of bright flavor.

NUTRITION AT A GLANCE
Per serving: 200 calories, 23 g total fat, 3 g saturated fat, 0 g protein, 0 g carbohydrates, 0 g dietary fiber, 0 mg sodium

Thin-Crust Pizza—Four Ways

This pizza takes an easy shortcut using prepared flatbread rather than making dough from scratch. In the kitchen of a gourmand, it could be considered cheating, but the results are crispy and delicious and ready to eat in no time (versus making pizza dough from scratch, which involves yeast and many steps of allowing the dough to rise, punching it down, rising again, rolling, and so forth).

One of my favorite flatbreads is a rectangular, paper-thin barley bread made by a company called Mountain Bread and Food (www.mountainbread.com). They also produce similar breads made from whole wheat, corn, rye, oats, and rice. Another great one is a very thin 12" flatbread made by Indian Life (www.indianlife.com), producers of fantastic naan bread as well.

Tortillas can be used in place of the flatbread, which sounds odd but is tasty beyond belief. I usually choose whole wheat over white tortillas. Sprouted tortillas even work well. My favorite wheat-free option is Rudi's Organic Bakery Spelt Tortillas, which are excellent for gluten-sensitive folks. Many roads, one idea: delicious, thin-crust, semi-homemade pizza with all of the trimmings.

Rustic Tomato Thin-Crust Pizza with Roasted Zucchini, Portobello Mushroom, and Red Onion

There are some great organic jarred tomato sauces on the market, but a homemade sauce can't be beat. I offer a Quick Rustic Tomato Sauce (page 336), which is quite simple and cooks quickly, or try the Rustic Red Wine and Olive Tomato Sauce (page 306) for a change of pace.

YIELDS: 4 SERVINGS

3 tablespoons + 2 teaspoons extra-virgin olive oil

1–2 cloves garlic, pressed

1 teaspoon balsamic vinegar

1 teaspoon shoyu (soy sauce)

½ teaspoon maple syrup

2 teaspoons fresh thyme or 1 teaspoon dried (optional)

1 large portobello mushroom, gills removed, thinly sliced

1 medium zucchini, thinly sliced

Sea salt

Freshly ground black pepper

1 round flatbread (12"), 2 tortillas (9"), or 1 square flatbread (9")

½ cup tomato sauce, purchased or homemade

⅓ cup thinly sliced red onion

6 cherry tomatoes, sliced (optional)

Preheat the broiler.

In a small bowl, mix together 1½ tablespoons of the olive oil, the garlic, balsamic, shoyu, maple syrup, and thyme (if desired). Pour over the mushroom and toss to coat evenly. Let stand for 10 minutes or more to absorb and develop flavor.

In a separate bowl, toss the zucchini with 2 teaspoons of olive oil. Sprinkle with a pinch of salt and pepper.

Place both the mushroom and zucchini on a baking sheet under the broiler until browned beautifully, 10 to 12 minutes. Set aside to cool.

COOK DA PIZZA!

Preheat the oven to 500°F.

Brush one side of the bread or tortillas with the remaining 1½ tablespoons of olive oil. Place the oiled side facedown on a baking sheet (or pizza stone). This will make it crisp nicely.

Spread the sauce evenly over the bread or tortillas, leaving just a ¼" border at the edge.

Distribute the mushroom, zucchini, red onion, and cherry tomatoes evenly.

Bake on the middle rack for 15 to 20 minutes, until the edges are golden brown.

Let cool enough to cut and serve.

NUTRITION AT A GLANCE
Per serving: 220 calories, 15 g total fat, 2 g saturated fat, 4 g protein, 18 g carbohydrates, 3 g dietary fiber, 320 mg sodium

Quick Rustic Tomato Sauce

Preparing this sauce in a skillet speeds up the cooking time, but it needs to be stirred frequently so it does not stick and burn. Bay leaf lends great flavor to this chunky, old-world sauce.

YIELDS: 6 SERVINGS

2–3 tablespoons olive oil

3 cloves garlic, thinly sliced

4–6 tomatoes, chopped

1 bay leaf

Sea salt

Freshly ground black pepper

1 teaspoon agave nectar (optional)

Handful of fresh basil leaves, torn

Generous pinch of fresh chopped oregano or medium pinch of dried

Heat 1½ tablespoons of the olive oil in a medium skillet over medium-high heat.

Add the garlic and sauté just until soft, not brown (or it will burn).

Add the tomatoes, bay leaf, and a pinch of salt and pepper and cook, stirring regularly. The juices of the tomatoes will release first and it will seem quite watery. Continue to cook and stir. If the tomatoes are not at their sweetest peak, add agave. When most of the liquid has evaporated, remove from the heat. Add the remaining ½ to 1½ tablespoons of olive oil and the basil and oregano and season to taste with salt and pepper.

NUTRITION AT A GLANCE

Per serving: 60 calories, 4.5 g total fat, 0.5 g saturated fat, 1 g protein, 4 g carbohydrates, 1 g dietary fiber, 5 mg sodium

Pine Nut Pesto Thin-Crust Pizza with Artichoke Hearts, Olives, and Plum Tomatoes

Store-bought artichoke hearts tossed with 2 teaspoons of extra-virgin olive oil, 1 clove of pressed garlic, and a pinch of sea salt can be used if you don't have time for roasting, though the roasted ones are beyond the beyond.

YIELDS: 4 SERVINGS

Pale Pesto (page 225)

3   cups basil leaves

1   round flatbread (12"), 2 tortillas (9"), or 1 square flatbread (9")

1½   tablespoons extra-virgin olive oil, for brushing

1½   cups Roasted Artichoke Hearts (page 254) or ½ cup chopped olives (Graber or kalamata are best)

2   plum tomatoes or Roma tomatoes, sliced

Blend the Pale Pesto and basil in a food processor until smooth.

COOK DA PIZZA!

Preheat the oven to 500°F.

Brush one side of the bread or tortillas with olive oil. Place the oiled side facedown on a baking sheet (or pizza stone if you have one). This will make it crisp nicely.

Spread the pesto evenly over the bread or tortillas, leaving just a ¼" border at the edge.

Distribute the sliced artichoke hearts or olives and the tomatoes evenly.

Bake on the middle rack for 15 to 20 minutes, until the edges are golden brown.

Let cool enough to cut and serve.

It is unlikely that there will be leftovers, but they are great (even cold!) the next day.

NUTRITION AT A GLANCE
Per serving: 270 calories, 22 g total fat, 2.5 g saturated fat, 4 g protein, 16 g carbohydrates, 4 g dietary fiber, 230 mg sodium

Roasted Red Pepper and Caramelized Onion Thin-Crust Pizza with Baby Spinach and Cremini Mushrooms

This one makes my toes curl with delight. Organic store-bought roasted peppers can be used to save a step. Caramelizing the onion brings out the sweetness of everything with savory full-bodied flavor. I started making this recipe as a bruschetta, which is brilliant as an appetizer (opposite page), but it found its way to an incarnation as a pizza with a following.

YIELDS: 4 SERVINGS

4½ tablespoons extra-virgin olive oil

1 large red onion, sliced

¼ cup white wine or vegetable stock

1 teaspoon balsamic vinegar

1 teaspoon shoyu (soy sauce)

½ teaspoon maple syrup

2 large roasted red bell peppers, store-bought (go organic!) or homemade

2 tablespoons pine nuts

2 cloves garlic, minced

1 cup basil leaves

2 tablespoons fresh oregano or 2–3 teaspoons dried

2 teaspoons fresh thyme or 1 teaspoon dried

1 teaspoon apple cider vinegar or lemon juice

¼ teaspoon ground chipotle pepper or dried chili pepper (optional)

Sea salt

Freshly ground black pepper

2 cups sliced cremini mushrooms

2 cups baby spinach, roughly chopped

1 round flatbread (12"), 2 tortillas (9"), or 1 square flatbread (9")

Chopped basil leaves, for garnish

Warm 2 tablespoons of the olive oil in a skillet over medium heat.

Add the onion and cook, stirring occasionally, until starting to soften (5 to 6 minutes). Add the wine (or stock), balsamic, shoyu, and maple syrup. Cook, stirring occasionally, until almost all of the liquid has evaporated (3 to 5 minutes). Remove from the heat and let cool for 10 minutes or more to let the flavors settle.

Place half of the onions in a food processor with the roasted peppers, pine nuts, half the garlic, half the basil, the oregano, thyme, apple cider vinegar or lemon juice, chipotle or chili pepper (if desired), and a pinch of salt and pepper. Blend until smooth. Season to taste with additional salt and pepper as necessary.

Warm 1 tablespoon of the olive oil in another skillet over medium heat. Add the mushrooms and a pinch of salt. Cook, stirring occasionally, until the mushrooms begin to soften (3 to 4 minutes). Add the remaining garlic and cook another minute or so, until it is fragrant, but not browned.

Add the spinach and cook another 30 seconds, just until it starts to wilt. Remove from the heat and fold in the remaining basil.

COOK DA PIZZA!

Preheat the oven to 500°F.

Brush one side of the bread or tortillas with the remaining 1½ tablespoons of olive oil. Place the oil side face-down on a baking sheet (or pizza stone). This will make it crisp nicely.

Spread the roasted pepper mixture evenly over the bread or tortillas, leaving just a ¼" border at the edge.

Distribute the reserved caramelized onions and the mushrooms and spinach evenly.

Bake on the middle rack for 15 to 20 minutes, until the edges are golden brown.

Let cool enough to cut and serve. Sprinkle with chopped basil.

It is unlikely that there will be leftovers, but they are great (cold even!) the next day.

NUTRITION AT A GLANCE
Per serving: 310 calories, 21 g total fat, 2.5 g saturated fat, 6 g protein, 26 g carbohydrates, 5 g dietary fiber, 190 mg sodium

---

Bruschetta

Bruschetta are lovely little munchies of Italian tradition, made of crisped sliced bread (of some sort) with something savory in nature on top (often involving tomatoes). Originally, bruschetta was just an innovative way to make use of stale bread (like French toast). They are great for appetizers and hors d'oeuvres. Delish!

Any of the pizza combinations can be used; the roasted red pepper pizza ingredients are a favorite choice of mine (though I usually leave out the spinach).

Preheat the oven to 375°F.

Use half a loaf of unsliced bread, like a baguette or pugliese bread, and slice it into thin pieces (¼" to ½" thick).

Brush both sides of the slices with extra-virgin olive oil and place on a baking sheet.

Spoon and spread your choice of recipes: Quick Rustic Tomato Sauce (page 336), Pine Nut Pesto (page 337), Rustic Red Wine and Olive Tomato Sauce (page 306), or Roasted Red Pepper and Caramelized Onion (opposite page).

Top with sautéed mushrooms (like the cremini mushrooms in the pizza on the opposite page), grilled portobello mushrooms (like in the Rustic Tomato pizza on page 335), Roasted Artichoke Hearts (page 254), or roasted red peppers.

Bake about 12 minutes, or until the bread is crispy and golden brown.

Cool and serve.

CHAPTER 11

Desserts

*I don't think a really good pie can be made without a dozen
or so children peeking over your shoulder as you stoop
to look in at it every little while.*

—JOHN GOULD

Flaky Pie Crust

I worked at this recipe with a lot of love to yield a dough that can be pressed right into a pie plate rather than rolled first. Both coconut butter and palm oil are semisolid at room temperature and very solid in the refrigerator, just like dairy butter, and they yield a flavorful flakiness in this crust without the cholesterol. Be sure not to overwork the dough or it will lose its flaky quality. All spelt flour can be used for gluten-sensitive folks, though it will yield a slightly denser and less flaky crust.

YIELDS: ONE 9" OR 10" PIE CRUST

1   cup unbleached whole wheat pastry flour

1   cup spelt flour or additional whole wheat pastry flour

2   tablespoons organic granulated sweetener, such as organic evaporated cane juice, organic sugar or brown sugar, Sucanat, or maple sugar

½   teaspoon baking powder

¼   teaspoon finely ground sea salt

8   tablespoons cold-pressed coconut butter, palm oil, or organic vegetable oil, such as grapeseed oil or safflower oil

1   tablespoon maple syrup

1   teaspoon apple cider vinegar

3–6   tablespoons filtered water

Preheat the oven to 350°F.

Sift the flours, granulated sweetener, baking powder, and salt into a bowl.

Mix in the coconut butter or oil, maple syrup, vinegar, and 3 tablespoons of the filtered water, first with a wooden spoon, then with your hands until dough forms. If the dough is too dry, add another tablespoon or two of water.

Press evenly into a 9" or 10" pie plate.

If you want to roll, flatten the dough into a disk on a piece of waxed paper large enough to wrap the dough in and refrigerate for at least 30 minutes. Roll the dough between two sheets of waxed paper. Transfer the rolled dough to a pie plate. Lightly flouring the surface of the dough and folding it in half makes the transfer easier. Press the dough into the corners of the pie plate or tart pan. Trim any excess dough from the rim of the plate or pan. Prebake the crust or fill and bake pie as directed in the recipes that follow.

NOTE: *The dough will keep fresh in the fridge for 2 days, or sealed in a bag or container and frozen for a month or two. If freezing, thaw in the fridge for a few hours before pressing or rolling.*

NUTRITION AT A GLANCE
Per serving: 240 calories, 15 g total fat, 1.5 g saturated fat, 3 g protein, 27 g carbohydrates, 3 g dietary fiber, 105 mg sodium

Tropical oils, like coconut butter and palm oil, were once branded with insidious, bad reputations for being high in cholesterol and saturated fat. The studies that allegedly proved these claims were carried out with highly refined oils, in extraordinary excess, on animals not accustomed to fat or oil in their natural diets. The results, therefore, were not favorable.

Coconut oil does contain some naturally saturated fat, which is why it is solid at room temperature, like butter. Saturated fats have stronger bonds between their molecules, which make them more stable at higher temperatures—a good thing! Coconut oil is a medium-chain fat, which is very easy for the body to digest, and provides a long-burning energy. The nature of this type of oil does not require the liver to emulsify the fat (that is, digest it into the smallest fraction of an oil or fat called a lipid). Coconut oil also contains a precious compound called lauric acid, also found in mother's milk, which is prized for its natural antibacterial properties and known to boost the immune system.

Coconut butter and coconut oil are relatively interchangeable terms. Look for unrefined, organic coconut butter or oil. Some have a very strong coconut smell (which may or may not please you; it's great for some recipes but imposing for others, especially pie crusts). Omega Nutrition's original coconut butter (not the virgin one) is a high-integrity product that is defragranced with a gentle process, leaving a buttery oil without the coconut smell.

Strawberry Rhubarb Pie

This is a classic recipe, especially in the late spring when rhubarb and strawberries are at their best. Choose fresh rhubarb as you would celery, looking for fresh, crisp stalks.

YIELDS: 8 SERVINGS (ONE 9" OR 10" PIE)

Flaky Pie Crust (page 341)

1 cup maple syrup

1 cup organic evaporated cane juice or organic sugar

2 teaspoons pure vanilla extract (optional)

½ cup filtered water

1 pound rhubarb, cut into 1" pieces (about 4 cups)

1½ cups sliced strawberries

¼ teaspoon sea salt

5 tablespoons kudzu or arrowroot

Crumble Topping (page 346)

Preheat the oven to 350°F.

Prepare the Flaky Pie Crust and bake until golden brown, 15 to 20 minutes.

While the crust bakes, mix together the maple syrup, cane juice or sugar, vanilla (if desired), and water in a large saucepan over high heat and bring to a boil, stirring. Reduce the heat to medium.

Add the rhubarb, strawberries, and salt and cook until the rhubarb begins to soften, stirring gently a few times, 5 to 10 minutes. Do not stir too much or the fibers of the rhubarb will break down and the pie will lose its body. Continue to cook, without stirring, just until the rhubarb is tender 5 to 10 minutes. You want nice chunks of rhubarb, not a puree.

Remove the rhubarb and strawberries with a slotted spoon and set aside.

Add the kudzu or arrowroot and whisk to dissolve. Reheat the syrup to a simmer and cook, stirring, until thickened and no longer cloudy.

Add the reserved rhubarb and strawberries and fold together gently.

Allow to cool for 5 minutes. Turn into the baked pie shell.

Top with Crumble Topping, if desired.

Chill well before serving.

NUTRITION AT A GLANCE

Per serving without topping: 450 calories, 15 g total fat, 1.5 g saturated fat, 4 g protein, 81 g carbohydrates, 5 g dietary fiber, 180 mg sodium

With crumble topping: 590 calories, 20 g fat, 6 g saturated fat, 6 g protein, 102 g carbohydrates, 8 g dietary fiber, 260 mg sodium

Rustic Blueberry Crostada

This good-looking tart is inspired by my mom's technique of rolling a pie crust flat; filling it with thickened, fresh seasonal fruit (without a pie plate); and folding the sides over to create a gorgeous, rustic elegance. I love a tangy lemon glaze to lift and flatter the mellow blueberries. Spelt is a great alternative for a wheat-sensitive sweet tooth, though it yields a slightly denser crust.

YIELDS: 8 SERVINGS

Flaky Pie Crust (page 341)

⅓ cup filtered water

¼ cup maple syrup

2 tablespoons lemon juice

1–2 teaspoons vanilla extract (optional)

Pinch of finely ground sea salt

4 tablespoons kudzu or arrowroot

4 cups blueberries (thawed frozen blueberries may be used)

2 tablespoons granulated sweetener (optional, if blueberries are not at the peak of sweetness), such as organic evaporated cane juice, maple sugar, or Sucanat

Lemon Glaze (opposite page)

Prepare the pie crust. Gather the dough into a ball and refrigerate for at least 30 minutes so it is firm enough to roll out with a rolling pin.

Preheat the oven to 350°F.

In a medium saucepan, mix together the water, maple syrup, lemon juice, vanilla (if desired), and salt. Whisk in 2 tablespoons of the kudzu or arrowroot until dissolved. Bring to a gentle simmer over medium heat, whisking frequently to prevent lumps. Reduce the heat to low, continuing to whisk constantly until the mixture begins to clear. Add the blueberries, fold together, take 3 deep breaths, add the remaining 2 tablespoons of kudzu or arrowroot, mix well, and turn off the heat. Add the granulated sweetener if desired, or if the blueberries are not at their super-sweet zenith. Remove from the heat. As it cools, the filling will thicken a bit.

On a lightly floured work surface, roll out the pie crust as thin as possible. It should be 10" to 12" in diameter, minimum. Slide the rolled dough onto a rimmed baking sheet (to catch any juices that escape when baking). Concerned about getting the dough on in one piece? Just fold the rolled dough in half before moving.

Scrape the thickened blueberry mixture into the center of the rolled dough. Fold the edges of the crust toward the center to hug the filling, leaving 4" to 6" of the blueberry filling exposed. If the crust cracks at all when folding, just pinch it together, so the juices do not escape while baking.

Bake for 30 to 40 minutes, or until the crust begins to brown and the blueberry juices start to bubble. Brush with Lemon Glaze and return to the oven for another 10 minutes, or until the crust is golden brown. If you are not using glaze, simply bake another 10 minutes or until golden brown.

Allow to cool for 30 minutes on a rack before transferring to a plate to cool completely.

NUTRITION AT A GLANCE

Per serving without glaze: 330 calories, 15 g total fat, 1.5 g saturated fat, 4 g protein, 48 g carbohydrates, 5 g dietary fiber, 125 mg sodium

Per serving with glaze: 345 calories, 15 g total fat, 1.5 g saturated fat, 4 g protein, 52 g carbohydrates, 5 g dietary fiber, 125 mg sodium

---

LEMON GLAZE

YIELDS: 8 SERVINGS (ABOUT ½ CUP)

2 tablespoons maple syrup

2 tablespoons lemon juice

2 tablespoons granulated sweetener (optional)

2 teaspoons lemon zest

½ teaspoon nonalcoholic vanilla extract (optional)

In a small saucepan, mix together the maple syrup, lemon juice, granulated sweetener (if desired), lemon zest, and vanilla (if desired). Simmer over medium-low heat for 2 to 3 minutes, stirring occasionally, until it thickens a touch.

Brush over the Rustic Blueberry Crostada after baking for 30 to 40 minutes. The lemon zest will likely sink to the bottom of the glaze. Scoop it up with a spoon and distribute it, especially over the exposed blueberries, where it can show off its color.

NUTRITION AT A GLANCE

Per serving (1 tablespoon): 15 calories, 0 g total fat, 0 g saturated fat, 0 g protein, 4 g carbohydrates, 0 g dietary fiber, 0 mg sodium

---

Crumble Topping

This crumbly brilliance is fantabulous on everything from pies to cakes, ice cream to sorbet, and applesauce to simply diced fresh fruit. I am a big fan of crumbles and happy as a clam just munching a little bowl of it with some slices of apple. I often double the recipe as it keeps well for snack attacks.

YIELDS: 8 SERVINGS (ABOUT 2 CUPS)

1½ cups pastry flour or spelt flour
    (or a mixture of both)
1 teaspoon baking powder
1 teaspoon ground cinnamon

Pinch of sea salt
3–4 tablespoons softened coconut oil or
    cold-pressed vegetable oil
3–4 tablespoons maple syrup

Preheat the oven to 350°F.

Mix together the flour, baking powder, cinnamon, and salt to break up any lumps.

Mix in the oil and maple syrup to a pebbly texture. Add a touch of filtered water if necessary to help achieve the correct texture. If it gets too moist, add a touch of flour.

If the texture becomes more sandy than pebbly, squeeze together a bit in your palm and crumble.

Spread on a baking sheet and bake for 10 minutes, or until golden brown. Push around the crumble with a wooden spoon or paddle halfway through for even baking.

Distribute over the filling while still hot, pressing it lightly with your fingers to let it get intimate with the dish to set and cool. Leftovers can be stored in a tightly sealed container or bag in the fridge for up to a week.

NUTRITION AT A GLANCE
Per serving: 140 calories, 5 g total fat, 4.5 g saturated fat, 2 g protein, 21 g carbohydrates, 3 g dietary fiber, 80 mg sodium

Peach Pie

*Peach pie is on my mind when I say someone is "sweet as pie." Fresh, ripe peaches
are sweetest in early summer, but thawed, frozen peaches may be used any time of year.
I peel, slice, and freeze peaches at the height of the season for the other reaches
of the year.*

YIELDS: 8 SERVINGS (ONE 9" OR 10" PIE)

Flaky Pie Crust (page 341; see note)

6–8   peaches, peeled, pitted, and sliced

2   tablespoons lemon juice

2   tablespoons maple syrup

½   teaspoon ground cinnamon

¼   teaspoon ground nutmeg

Pinch of sea salt

1   cup organic peach juice or filtered water

3   tablespoons kudzu or arrowroot

Preheat the oven to 375°F.

Prepare the pie crust. Prick the bottom of the crust with a fork a half-dozen times or so. Bake for 10 minutes.

Toss the peaches with the lemon juice, maple syrup, cinnamon, nutmeg, and salt.

In a medium saucepan, mix the peach juice or water and the kudzu or arrowroot until dissolved. Bring to a gentle boil, whisking or stirring constantly, until thickened and clear. Remove from the heat and fold in the peaches (get all of the delicious juices!).

Pile the peaches into the pie crust and smooth down.

Place the pie plate on a baking sheet to catch any drips. Bake at 375°F for 35 to 40 minutes, or until the juices are bubbling and the crust is golden.

Cool well before serving.

NOTE: *To make a lattice top crust, prepare an extra ½ recipe of the dough and roll out thinly between 2 pieces of waxed paper. Use a pastry wheel or sharp knife to cut ¾" strips and weave in a crisscross pattern over the peaches. Pinch the ends of the pieces to the pie crust. Bake as directed.*

NUTRITION AT A GLANCE
Per serving: 330 calories, 15 g total fat, 1.5 g saturated fat, 5 g protein, 48 g carbohydrates, 5 g dietary fiber, 125 mg sodium

Butternut Pumpkin Pie

Pumpkin is the traditional choice for this gently spiced autumn goodie, though any firm winter squash may be used, all of which are sweetest after the first frost, when the natural sugars emerge. Butternut squash is readily available in most markets throughout the year, or look for the prized kabocha (a squat Japanese pumpkin with dark green skin and dense, deep orange flesh), red kuri (a squat winter squash with red-orange skin and sweet, firm flesh), or sugar pumpkins in the late fall and early winter. I use agar-agar as a gelling agent, which is a clear seaweed sold in flakes or bars; it works wonders as a veggie alternative to animal-based gelatin. Agar is a good source of vitamins E, K, and B_6 and a great source of minerals like calcium, iron, magnesium, potassium, manganese, copper, and zinc. Wow! All that, and it makes a nice firm filling.

YIELDS: 8 SERVINGS

3   **pounds pumpkin**

1   **cup filtered water**

⅔   **cup maple syrup**

⅓   **cup liquid (nut milk, soymilk, coconut milk, or filtered water)**

4   **tablespoons agar-agar flakes**

2   **tablespoons softened coconut butter, safflower oil, or grapeseed oil**

2   **tablespoons kudzu or arrowroot**

1–2   **teaspoons vanilla extract**

¾   **teaspoon freshly ground cinnamon (add ¼ teaspoon more if it is already ground as the flavor is more mellow)**

1   **teaspoon finely grated ginger or ½ teaspoon ground ginger**

⅛   **teaspoon freshly ground nutmeg (add ⅛ teaspoon more if it is already ground as the flavor is more mellow)**

½   **teaspoon finely ground sea salt**

    Flaky Pie Crust (page 341)

Preheat the oven to 450°F.

Cut the pumpkin in half and place facedown in a baking dish. Pour 1 cup of filtered water into the dish. Bake for 45 minutes to 1 hour, or until tender and easily pierced with a fork.

Let cool enough to handle before removing the seeds (to discard or bake, see opposite page). Scoop out the flesh with a spoon. Or peel away the skin with a paring knife and cut the flesh into chunks, whichever is easiest.

Reduce the oven temperature to 425°F. On a cold day, leave the oven door open for a moment to allow hot air to escape and warm the kitchen.

In a small saucepan, bring the maple syrup and liquid of choice to a simmer. Add the agar-agar flakes and whisk regularly until completely dissolved (5 to 6 minutes).

Place the pumpkin in a food processor fitted with a metal blade. Add the dissolved agar mixture, coconut butter or oil, kudzu or arrowroot, vanilla, cinnamon, ginger, nutmeg, and salt and blend until very smooth.

Prepare the pie crust.

Pour the filling into the crust.

Bake for 15 minutes, then reduce the heat to 350°F and bake for 45 to 50 minutes, or until the filling is set and golden and the crust is golden brown.

Cool on a rack for a few hours to set completely. Best served chilled.

NUTRITION AT A GLANCE
Per serving: 380 calories, 18 g total fat, 2 g saturated fat, 5 g protein, 54 g carbohydrates, 5 g dietary fiber, 260 mg sodium

---

Don't Toss Those Seeds!

Toasted seeds from a fresh pumpkin are a great snack that brings many of us back to the brisk nostalgic days of our childhood, filled with leaf forts and blazing sugar maple trees. And they are loaded with minerals like zinc, iron, magnesium, and copper in a protein-rich crunch. Winter squash seeds work the same with a similar profile.

To toast 'em up, preheat the oven to 350°F. Clean them in a colander to remove any stringy flesh and pat dry with a clean towel. Then toss them with a little seasoning. Salt is a classic, but get brave and try adding a pinch of cayenne, or sweet and fancy with cinnamon and a little organic sugar. Spread on a baking sheet and bake for 25 to 30 minutes, stirring once or twice, until golden and crisp. Stash leftovers in a sealed jar, container, or bag in a cool, dry place.

Apple Crumble Tart

The montage of apple, crumble, and crust makes this tart both rustic and elegant. The wheat flour in the crumble and crust is easily replaced with spelt flour. Spelt is a bit denser and wheat a bit more fluffy and flaky. Either way, the old-fashioned flavor is fantastic and textured with sophisticated comfort.

YIELDS: 8 SERVINGS

½ recipe Flaky Pie Crust (page 341)

4 tablespoons maple syrup

1 tablespoon lemon juice

2 tablespoons kudzu or arrowroot

1½ pounds apples (see note), peeled, cored, and sliced

1 teaspoon lemon zest

1 teaspoon ground cinnamon

Pinch of finely ground sea salt

Crumble Topping (page 346), without the baking powder

Preheat the oven to 375°F.

Oil a 9" tart pan with a removable bottom. Press the pie crust dough evenly into the pan. Refrigerate the crust while preparing the filling and topping.

In a small bowl, mix the maple syrup and lemon juice with the kudzu or arrowroot until dissolved.

In a medium bowl, toss together the apples with the maple syrup mixture, lemon zest, cinnamon, and salt. Set aside until ready to bake.

Prepare the Crumble Topping, but do not bake it.

Retrieve the tart pan from the fridge. Fill evenly with the apple mixture. Crumble the topping evenly over the apples.

Bake for 45 to 55 minutes, or until the apples are bubbling and the crumble is golden brown.

Cool for at least 20 minutes on a rack before serving.

NOTE: *As always, choose what looks best at the market. Sweet apples such as Fuji, Gala, Braeburn, Red or Golden Delicious, or tart apples such as Pink Lady, Granny Smith, or Mutsu all work well in this tart.*

NUTRITION AT A GLANCE
Per serving: 300 calories, 11 g total fat, 3 g saturated fat, 4 g protein, 48 g carbohydrates, 6 g dietary fiber, 70 mg sodium

Shoofly Pie

Shoofly pie is an old Pennsylvania Dutch recipe I grew up with—my grandparents lived on the edge of Amish country in Bucks County, Pennsylvania. We used to fly-fish and drink traditional birch beer, and my granny always had a Shoofly Pie, carefully guarded while it cooled. The folklore goes that this sweet pie is so good that one must shoo away the flies. Of course I have tweaked it, but I still think the Amish contingency would be proud. If using coconut butter, be sure it has a very mild smell and taste; otherwise, use grapeseed oil. Thank you, Granny, for all the love and for being such a spicy broad to live up to.

YIELDS: 10 SERVINGS

Flaky Pie Crust (page 341)

1½ cups flour (spelt, wheat, or a mixture)

1 cup organic brown sugar or Sucanat

5 tablespoons mild cold-pressed Omega Nutrition coconut butter or grapeseed oil

1 tablespoon maple syrup

1 teaspoon cinnamon (freshly ground is best)

¼ teaspoon finely ground salt

1 cup molasses

½ cup hot filtered water

2 tablespoons arrowroot

2 teaspoons baking powder

1 teaspoon apple cider vinegar

Preheat the oven to 350°F.

Prepare the pie crust, press into a pie plate, prick the bottom of the crust with a fork a half-dozen times, and bake for 10 minutes.

Increase the oven temperature to 400°F.

Mix together the flour, brown sugar or Sucanat, coconut butter or grapeseed oil, maple syrup, cinnamon, and salt into a dry crumble. At first it will seem very dry, but keep mixing and it will moisten up a little. It should be on the dry side.

Set aside 1 cup of the crumble.

Mix together the molasses, hot water, and arrowroot in a medium bowl. Set aside.

Mix together the baking powder and vinegar (it will foam!) in another bowl. Mix into the molasses mixture.

Gently fold in the remaining dry crumble (minus the 1 cup reserve). Pour into the pie crust. Top evenly with the reserved crumble.

Bake for 25 minutes, then reduce the heat to 350°F and bake for 15 to 20 minutes, or until the crust is golden and the contents have bubbled and settled.

NUTRITION AT A GLANCE
Per serving: 490 calories, 19 g total fat, 2 g saturated fat, 5 g protein, 81 g carbohydrates, 4 g dietary fiber, 250 mg sodium

Nectarine Blueberry Cobbler

Cobbler is a winner every time and none too fussy to put together. Nectarines and blueberries are a colorful match, though almost any fruit can be substituted. Blueberries are rated as the highest antioxidant food of all time to neutralize free radicals; notably, they contain the phytonutrients anthocyanins, which give these scrumptious guys their blue color and manage healthy tissue growth; pterostilbene, known to fight cancer and lower cholesterol; and ellagic acid, which blocks the metabolic pathways that can lead to cancer. Thawed frozen blueberries can be used when the fresh ones are not in season. Pecans are a hero of nutrients, containing more than 19 vitamins and minerals, including vitamins A, C, B-complex, and folate and the minerals calcium, magnesium, potassium, phosphorus, and zinc. They also have a satisfying profile of heart-healthy monounsaturated oil and protein . . . and are ridiculously delicious.

YIELDS: 10 SERVINGS

COBBLER TOPPING

1 cup pecans	1 teaspoon ground cinnamon
1 cup spelt flour or unbleached white flour	¼ teaspoon finely ground sea salt
1¼ cups rolled oats	6–8 tablespoons softened coconut butter or grapeseed oil
½ cup organic brown sugar or maple sugar	

NECTARINE BLUEBERRY COMPOTE

1 pint fresh blueberries, washed	1 teaspoon lemon zest
2½ cups peeled and sliced nectarines	1 teaspoon vanilla extract
3 tablespoons maple syrup	1 tablespoon kudzu or arrowroot
2 tablespoons lemon juice	

Preheat the oven to 350°F.

In a food processor, grind ½ cup of the pecans, ½ cup of the flour, and ½ cup of the oats into a coarse meal. Add the remaining ½ cup of pecans, ½ cup of flour, ¾ cup of oats, the brown sugar or maple sugar, cinnamon, and salt and chop in a few pulses just to mix. Transfer to a bowl. Work the coconut butter or oil into the pecan-flour mixture until pebbly. Add more coconut butter, oil, or a touch of water if it's too dry. Set aside.

Place the blueberries and nectarines in a 12" × 9" baking dish.

The Deal with Dairy

By this time, y'all might register that dairy products do not even make a cameo appearance in these pages—no cream or milk, nor butter or cheese. I haven't eaten dairy, at least knowingly, in more than a dozen years for a few reasons. My first evasion of dairy as an animal product was on ethical grounds and supported by an aversion to the drugs, antibiotics, and hormones given to dairy cows. No thanks! Ethics aside, I have no burning need to plaster my arteries and clog my pores with saturated fat and cholesterol. Coupling the fact that more than half of the population of the world cannot even digest the lactose in dairy with the fact that heart disease kills more people than all other causes of death combined in America, I was never inspired to invite it into the cornucopia of ingredients I play with. There are so many other ingredients that can achieve full, delectable flavor and texture in a dish, sans cow's milk.

For anyone who really enjoys dairy products and feels they have a place on their plate, I soundly encourage choosing organic, especially if you have kids. Going organic will reduce exposure to chemicals, drugs, antibiotics, and growth hormones that are concentrated in animal products, especially the saturated fat. However, not all companies are the same. Federal standards for "organic" food are changing what we trust and know to be true and safe. Animal products are segregated from produce now and have looser standards, leaving producers more room to wiggle and abide by. I am a fan of researching companies I know I can trust and depending on their integrity—I hope you are, too.

Mix together the maple syrup, lemon juice, lemon zest, and vanilla. Add the kudzu or arrowroot and mix until dissolved. Pour over the blueberries and nectarines and stir until well mixed.

Spread the topping evenly over the fruit. Bake for 45 to 50 minutes, or until golden brown and the fruit is bubbling through.

NUTRITION AT A GLANCE
Per serving: 340 calories, 18 g total fat, 1.5 g saturated fat, 5 g protein, 43 g carbohydrates, 5 g dietary fiber, 60 mg sodium

Chocolate of the Gods Mousse with Raspberries and Mint

Imagine a world where decadent chocolate mousse has real value, grows beautiful skin and hair, and is actually good for you! Welcome to the rest of your life. This recipe has evolved with me over the years to become a signature dish. I made it in the movie Go Further *with Woody Harrelson, and the Web site for the film got more hits inquiring about the chocolate mousse made from avocado than anything else. Cheers to the adventurous spirit! Just a touch of balsamic vinegar and shoyu (soy sauce) may sound as unusual as a coupling with chocolate and avocados, but both draw out the subtle complexity of good chocolate. The coconut butter is optional, but it makes the mousse truly velvety smooth, with incredible, beautifying properties. I recommend Omega Nutrition coconut butter as it does not have a coconut aroma, which imposes on the balance of flavor.*

By the way, put this mousse in an ice cream maker and it is insane.

YIELDS: 8 SERVINGS

2 cups Hass avocados (about 2)

½ cup + 2 tablespoons maple syrup

2–4 tablespoons organic evaporated cane juice or organic sugar (optional, for the sweeter tooth)

2 tablespoons Omega Nutrition coconut butter (optional)

1–2 teaspoons nonalcoholic vanilla extract

1 teaspoon balsamic vinegar (aged balsamic is best)

½ teaspoon shoyu (soy sauce)

1 cup pure cocoa powder (Green & Black's is choice)

1 pint raspberries

Handful of fresh mint leaves, chopped

Scharffen Berger's Cacao Nibs (optional, for garnish)

In a food processor, blend the avocados, maple syrup, cane juice or organic sugar (if desired), coconut butter (if desired), vanilla, balsamic, and shoyu until smooth and creamy.

Add the cocoa powder and blend until smooth. Sifting the cocoa powder before adding it is a good idea to prevent lumps. A simple metal strainer works well.

Distribute half of the raspberries evenly among 4 to 8 wine goblets or martini glasses. Follow with a dollop of mousse, a sprinkle of mint, the remaining raspberries, and more mint. Top with cacao nibs, if desired.

Mmmmmmm! Euphoria . . . Leftover mousse can be stored in a tightly sealed container for up to a week in the fridge or frozen for up to a month.

NUTRITION AT A GLANCE
Per serving: 170 calories, 7 g total fat, 2 g saturated fat, 3 g protein, 29 g carbohydrates, 7 g dietary fiber, 25 mg sodium

Vanilla Bean Dark Chocolate Truffles

Truffles are sinfully delicious morsels of rich chocolate. These truffles are made with pure ingredients and a lot of love. Chocolate is a decadent source of antioxidants, phytonutrients, and compounds that make our brains very happy. Vanilla bean is one of the most prized and expensive spices in the world and takes an intoxicating position in this recipe. Together they are married in a base of cashew butter, which has a fairly neutral flavor, or almond butter, which lends a beautifully quiet sweet almond flavor, both of which are worth obsessing over and a great source of protein and heart-healthy oils. I recommend Omega Nutrition coconut butter as it does not have a strong coconut aroma, which will interfere with the flavor, and offers a buttery, melt-in-your-mouth texture and a satisfying, clean-burning source of energy.

YIELDS: 2 DOZEN

⅔ cup raw cashew butter or raw almond butter

1 cup maple syrup

4 tablespoons Omega Nutrition coconut butter

1 tablespoon aged balsamic vinegar (or 1½ teaspoons regular balsamic)

2 teaspoons nama shoyu (unpasteurized soy sauce)

1 teaspoon nonalcoholic vanilla extract

1 vanilla bean, split and seeds scraped out

1¼ cups cocoa powder, plus a bit more as necessary

Extra cocoa powder for dusting

In a medium bowl, using a wooden spoon, beat together the cashew or almond butter, maple syrup, coconut butter, balsamic, shoyu, and vanilla extract and seeds until very smooth.

Beat in the cocoa powder until very smooth. If there are any clumps in the cocoa powder, it is best to sift it in a sifter or through a mesh strainer. Add a bit more cocoa powder as necessary to achieve a smooth, stiff base.

If it is not stiff enough to handle (which can be the case in warm weather), refrigerate for an hour.

Roll 1½ tablespoons into balls and gently roll in a shallow bowl of cocoa powder to dust.

Store in the refrigerator in a sealable container lined with waxed paper. Allow to come to room temperature for 10 to 20 minutes before serving to allow the flavor and aroma to bloom. May be stored in the freezer for up to 2 months.

NUTRITION AT A GLANCE
Per serving: 100 calories, 6 g total fat, 1 g saturated fat, 3 g protein, 14 g carbohydrates, 2 g dietary fiber, 80 mg sodium

Dark Chocolate Hazelnut Ganache

This recipe was inspired by long, scrumptious jaunts in Europe, where chocolate and hazelnuts (filberts) court in sweet romance. Most hazelnut butter is roasted to bring out the natural sweetness and flavor of the filberts and reduce the bitterness that resides in the skin. Raw almond butter or raw cashew butter also works beautifully for raw-food enthusiasts. I recommend Green & Black's unsweetened cocoa powder, as it is organic, free-trade, and processed with care at low temperatures for exceptional flavor. Carob powder may be used in part or in full for a more moderate indulgence, though it influences the flavor distinctively. I vote for chocolate. A scoop of Macadamia Vanilla Bean Ice Cream (page 376) served in close quarters is where heaven meets earth. Any way you cut it, just a small slice of this euphoric ganache is intoxicating and wickedly delicious. Keep chilled until ready to serve.

YIELDS: 12 SERVINGS

CRUST

2 cups pecans	3 tablespoons cocoa powder
2½ tablespoons maple syrup	1 teaspoon ground cinnamon (freshly ground is best)
1 tablespoon Omega Nutrition coconut butter	¼ teaspoon sea salt

GANACHE

½ cup hazelnut butter (see note)	2 cups pure maple syrup
½ cup Omega Nutrition coconut butter	2 cups cocoa powder

The pecans may be soaked and dehydrated (page 359) for optimal nutrition and crunchy texture, or simply used as is.

Grind the pecans into a fine meal in a food processor. Add the maple syrup, coconut butter, cocoa powder, cinnamon, and salt and chop until well mixed. The texture should be crumbly, but sticky enough to hold its shape when pressed. If it is too dry, add a touch more maple syrup. If it is too moist, add a bit more cocoa powder.

Oil the bottom and sides of a 9" or 10" tart pan with a removable bottom or a springform pan (which also has a removable bottom) so the ganache does not stick when chilled and set for a free-standing delight. I usually line the bottom of the pan with parchment paper so it does not need to be oiled and is easy to slip off onto a serving plate when done. To do so, trace the bottom circle of the pan in pencil on parchment paper and cut out with scissors.

Gianduja Truffles

Gianduja is fine Swiss milk chocolate with hazelnuts. The base of the Dark Chocolate Hazelnut Ganache is perfect to make truffles in this tradition, oh-la-la! These decadent morsels of bite-size euphoria are especially good for dinner parties, or to simply stash in the fridge for ongoing indulgence.

To make: Follow the directions for the ganache using hazelnut butter, coconut butter, maple syrup, and cocoa powder. Chill in the fridge for an hour or two until firm enough to handle. Spoon out a tablespoon or so and roll into a ball with clean hands. A melon-baller works wonderfully! Gently roll in a dish of cocoa powder to dust. Store in a sealed container lined with waxed paper in the fridge for up to 2 weeks (or in the freezer for up to 2 months). Allow to come to room temperature for 10 to 15 minutes before serving to let the flavor and aroma bloom beautifully. Yields about 30 truffles.

Press the crust evenly into the bottom of the pan. A glass pie plate will also work, but the crust will need to be pressed around the sides as well for easier serving.

In a food processor, place the hazelnut butter, coconut butter (I recommend Omega Nutrition as it does not have a coconut aroma, which will interfere with the balance of flavor in this recipe), maple syrup, and cocoa powder. Blend until as smooth as velvet.

Spread evenly into the prepared crust. Bump the bottom of the pan on the counter so it sets without any air bubbles. Thoroughly chill in the fridge for at least 2 hours to firm and set before serving.

I recommend slicing the ganache into quarters before removing the outside ring of the tart pan or springform pan. Also, washing and wiping the knife between each cut helps for neat service. To do so, cut the ganache in half first, then each half in half to create 4 even quarters. Remove the outside ring. From there, each quarter can be sliced into 2 to 3 pieces, depending on the desired serving size.

Keep chilled until ready to serve. Leftovers should be covered in plastic wrap or in a sealed container in the fridge for up to a week.

NOTE: *Hazelnut butter can be found in most health food stores and specialty markets like Dean and Deluca and Citarella.*

NUTRITION AT A GLANCE
Per serving: 430 calories, 26 g total fat, 3.5 g saturated fat, 7 g protein, 53 g carbohydrates, 8 g dietary fiber, 110 mg sodium

Pear and Pecan Torte with Lemon Ginger Cream

Pears and pecans are well matched, especially in the autumn, when pears are at their sweetest. A simple cream, lifted by lemon and ginger, cushions the two for a lovely waltz of crispy and creamy. The pecans should be soaked, then dehydrated until crunchy for an enzyme-rich and crumbly crust, but in a pinch they can be used as is. A torte pan with a removable bottom yields a beautiful, free-standing torte, though a glass pie plate will work as well. Enjoy a slice with a steamy mug of Molokai Chai (page 168) for a real treat.

YIELDS: 10 SERVINGS (ONE 9" OR 10" TORTE)

TORTE CRUST

2 **cups pecans**	1 **teaspoon ground cinnamon (freshly ground is best)**
4 **cups filtered water**	¼ **teaspoon sea salt**
¼ **cup chopped dates**	
2 **tablespoons maple syrup**	

LEMON GINGER CREAM

2 **cups almonds, soaked and peeled (page 251)**	3 **tablespoons agave nectar**
2 **tablespoons lemon juice**	2–3 **teaspoons peeled and finely grated ginger**
1 **tablespoon lemon zest**	1 **tablespoon Omega Nutrition coconut butter (optional)**
3 **tablespoons maple syrup**	

PEARS

1 **tablespoon maple syrup**	4–6 **ripe pears, cores removed, peeled and sliced (about 5 cups)**
1 **tablespoon lemon juice**	
¼ **teaspoon ground cinnamon (freshly ground is best)**	

The pecans should be soaked and dehydrated (see opposite page) for optimal nutrition and crunchy texture, but can simply be used as is in a time pinch.

Grind the pecans and dates finely in a food processor. Add the maple syrup, cinnamon, and salt and grind until well mixed. The texture should be crumbly and sticky. If it is too dry to hold itself on its own, add a touch more maple syrup or a bit of filtered water.

Press into the bottom and sides of a torte pan with a removable bottom. It should be a thin crust. A glass pie plate will also work.

In a blender (preferably a high-speed blender like the Vita-Mix), place the almonds, lemon juice and zest, maple syrup, agave, ginger, and coconut butter (if desired) and blend until super-smooth. It may be necessary to add a bit of filtered water to aid blending. Do so 1 tablespoon at a time as this cream is best on the thick side. It will thicken nicely when chilled as well.

Spread the cream in the bottom of the torte crust.

In a large bowl, mix together the maple syrup, lemon juice, and cinnamon. Add the pears and fold gently to combine.

Arrange the pear slices over the cream.

Chill in the fridge for at least an hour before cutting and serving.

NUTRITION AT A GLANCE
Per serving: 430 calories, 32 g total fat, 2.5 g saturated fat, 9 g protein, 34 g carbohydrates, 8 g dietary fiber, 70 mg sodium

Soaking and Dehydrating Nuts for Enzyme-Rich Crunch!

Soaking nuts wakes up dormant nutrients and a flurry of enzyme activity for easier digestibility and maximum nutrition. Dehydrating soaked nuts at a low temperature reinvents their crunch with a lovely lightness, preserving all the heat-sensitive good stuff. This can be done with any nut or seed and takes some time, but not too much attention.

• Soak nuts in filtered water overnight (about 8 hours); use 3 cups of water for every cup of nuts.

• Drain and rinse the nuts.

• Spread the drained nuts on dehydrator trays and dehydrate at 112°F for 12 hours, or until completely dry and crisp. Or, spread the drained nuts on baking sheets and dry in the oven set at the lowest temperature for 6 hours until dry and crisp.

• Store in a tightly sealed jar, container, or bag in the fridge for up to 2 months or in the freezer for up to 4 months.

Crumbly Lemon Blueberry Cupcake Muffins

If ever there was a match for muffins, lemon and blueberry would take the cake. Not too sweet . . . just right. All spelt flour may be used, though the muffins may be a bit more dense. Perfect with a cup of Molokai Chai (page 168).

YIELDS: ABOUT 18

MUFFIN BATTER

¾ cup organic whole wheat flour

¾ cup organic spelt flour

2 teaspoons baking powder

¼ teaspoon Celtic sea salt

¼ cup + 2 tablespoons softened Omega Nutrition coconut butter or grapeseed oil

¼ cup agave nectar

¼ cup maple syrup

¼ cup apple juice, almond milk, soymilk, or filtered water

2 teaspoons lemon zest

2 tablespoons lemon juice

1 teaspoon vanilla extract

½ teaspoon apple cider vinegar

1 cup fresh blueberries, or thawed and drained organic frozen blueberries

STREUSEL TOPPING

¼ cup nuts (pecans, walnuts, or raw almonds)

¾ cup spelt flour

¼ teaspoon sea salt

¼ teaspoon ground cinnamon

2 tablespoons + 1–2 teaspoons softened coconut butter or grapeseed oil

1 tablespoon agave nectar

1 tablespoon maple syrup

½ teaspoon lemon zest (optional)

Preheat the oven to 350°F.

The batter will make about 18 muffins. If you have muffin pans to cover that many, line them with unbleached paper baking cups or brush the pans with coconut butter or grapeseed oil. Otherwise, you will need to bake a second batch.

In a mixing bowl, whisk together the flours, baking powder, and salt.

In another bowl, beat together the coconut butter or grapeseed oil, agave, maple syrup, apple

juice (or almond milk, soymilk, or filtered water), lemon zest, lemon juice, vanilla, and vinegar.

Beat the dry ingredients into the wet ingredients and mix just until nice and smooth. This can be done by hand or with a mixer, but be careful not to overmix or your muffins will be tough.

Gently fold in the blueberries.

Fill the muffin cups half full with batter.

Now make the streusel topping: In a food processor, grind the nuts into a fine meal. Add the flour, salt, and cinnamon and chop until well mixed. Add the coconut butter or oil, agave, maple syrup, and lemon zest (if desired) and chop in pulses just until mixed and crumbly. The texture should be like pebbles and sand. If it is too moist, add a bit of flour. If it is too dry, add a touch more oil.

Sprinkle the streusel topping evenly over the muffins.

Bake until golden, 20 to 25 minutes, or until a toothpick inserted in the center of a muffin comes out clean. Let cool before serving.

NUTRITION AT A GLANCE
Per serving: 150 calories, 8 g total fat, 0.5 g saturated fat, 2 g protein, 17 g carbohydrates, 2 g dietary fiber, 90 mg sodium

Frozen Chocolate Coconut Haystacks

These haystacks are quick to prepare and so delicious you'll want to double the recipe. They store well for up to a month in the freezer and are a great treat for well-behaved kids and adults.

YIELDS: 2 DOZEN

3 cups dried coconut

3 tablespoons raw almond butter or organic peanut butter (which is not raw, but delicious!)

4–6 tablespoons agave nectar

4–6 tablespoons maple syrup

2 tablespoons Omega Nutrition coconut butter

1 teaspoon nonalcoholic vanilla extract

Pinch of sea salt

1½ cups cocoa powder

¼ cup cacao nibs (optional)

In a food processor, grind 1 cup of the coconut into a powder.

Add the almond butter or peanut butter, agave, maple syrup, coconut butter, vanilla, and salt and blend until well mixed.

Fold in the remaining 2 cups of coconut, cocoa powder, and cacao nibs (if desired) by hand.

Roll 2 tablespoons of dough into a ball and flatten with the palm of your hand. Continue until you've used all of the dough.

Place in a sealable container lined with waxed paper. Place a piece of waxed paper between the layers of haystacks to keep them from sticking together. Freeze until firm (2 hours or more).

NUTRITION AT A GLANCE
Per serving: 100 calories, 9 g total fat, 6 g saturated fat, 2 g protein, 8 g carbohydrates, 3 g dietary fiber, 25 mg sodium

Almond Green Tea Cake with Ginger Glaze

Green tea is known as a delicious source of free-radical-combating antioxidants, notably polyphenols, and a champion antioxidant called EGCG (epigallocatechin-gallate), which guards against cell damage and fights cancer cells.

YIELDS: 10 SERVINGS

TOASTED ALMOND FILLING

1 cup sliced almonds

2 tablespoons agave nectar

2 tablespoons organic granulated sweetener, such as organic evaporated cane juice, maple sugar, organic sugar or brown sugar, Sucanat

2 teaspoons melted coconut butter or mild-tasting olive oil

Pinch of finely ground sea salt

6 large dates, pitted and chopped

1 cup hot green tea

LOVELY CRUMBLE

¾ cup spelt flour or whole wheat pastry flour

¼ cup brown rice flour

½ cup almonds

3 tablespoons organic granulated sweetener, such as organic evaporated cane juice, maple sugar, organic sugar or brown sugar, Sucanat

½ teaspoon baking powder

¼ teaspoon ground cinnamon

Pinch of finely ground sea salt

3 tablespoons agave nectar

3 tablespoons melted coconut butter or grapeseed oil

GREEN TEA CAKE

1 cup spelt flour or whole wheat pastry flour

½ cup brown rice flour

½ cup unbleached white flour or spelt flour

6 tablespoons organic granulated sweetener, such as organic evaporated cane juice, maple sugar, organic sugar or brown sugar, Sucanat

2 teaspoons baking powder

2 teaspoons baking soda

1 teaspoon ground cinnamon

½ teaspoon finely ground sea salt

¾ cup green tea (reserved from filling)

½ cup maple syrup

2 tablespoons agave nectar

⅓ cup melted coconut butter, mild olive oil, or grapeseed oil

1 tablespoon apple cider vinegar

2 teaspoons vanilla extract

GINGER GLAZE

1 tablespoon ginger juice (page 160)	1–2 tablespoons green tea
⅓ cup organic powdered sugar	

TO MAKE THE FILLING:

Preheat the oven to 350°F. Make sure the rack is in the center of the oven.

Toss together the almonds, agave, granulated sweetener, coconut butter or oil, and salt. Spread evenly on a baking sheet and bake for 8 to 10 minutes, stirring a few times to toast evenly and to keep from clumping. Cool completely. Keep the oven on.

Chop the sweetened almonds.

Cover the dates with the hot green tea for 5 minutes. Strain the tea and set aside for the cake.

Mix the softened date pieces with the almonds. Set aside until ready to bake.

TO MAKE THE CRUMBLE:

Place the flours, almonds, granulated sweetener of choice, baking powder, cinnamon, salt, and agave in a food processor fitted with the metal blade. Chop into a coarse meal.

Add the coconut butter or oil and pulse chop, just until mixed and pebbly. Do not overmix. The texture should be like sand and pebbles. If it is too moist, add a bit more flour. If it is too dry, add a drizzle of agave or oil. Set aside.

TO MAKE THE CAKE:

In a medium bowl, whisk together the flours, granulated sweetener of choice, baking powder, baking soda, cinnamon, and salt.

In another bowl, thoroughly whisk together the reserved green tea, maple syrup, agave, coconut butter or oil, vinegar, and vanilla.

Add the wet ingredients to the dry and whisk just until combined. Be careful not to overmix or your cake will be less spongy.

Oil a 9" springform pan. If you do not have a springform pan, a round cake pan may also be used, though the Lovely Crumble will have to be baked separately on a baking sheet for 12 to 15 minutes or until golden brown and put on the cake at the end.

Pour about half of the cake batter into the pan. Sprinkle the Toasted Almond Filling evenly over the batter. Pour the remaining batter over the filling and smooth with a rubber spatula to completely cover the filling. Sprinkle the Lovely Crumble evenly on top.

Bake for 50 to 60 minutes, or until a toothpick comes out clean from the center of the cake. Cool for 30 minutes on a rack. Remove the cake from the pan and cool completely. Top with Ginger Glaze, if desired, before serving.

TO MAKE THE GLAZE:

In a small bowl, mix together the ginger juice with the sugar and add a touch of green tea, as necessary, to make a thick, spoonable glaze.

Drizzle over the cooled cake and let set at least 15 minutes before serving.

NUTRITION AT A GLANCE
Per serving with glaze: 550 calories, 26 g total fat, 2.5 g saturated fat, 10 g protein, 75 g carbohydrates, 6 g dietary fiber, 510 mg sodium

Butternut Apple Coffee Cake

Mmmm . . . this coffee cake warms the kitchen with autumnal homemade aroma. The squash lends a beautiful golden color, and apple keeps the cake moist and sweet.

YIELDS: 10 SERVINGS

GOLDEN CAKE

1½ cups squash (butternut or delicata), cut into 1" pieces

½ apple, peeled, cored, and cut into 1" pieces

2 cups filtered water

½ cup organic vegetable shortening, softened Omega Nutrition coconut butter, or grapeseed oil

¼ cup grapeseed oil

½ cup organic sugar

½ cup organic brown sugar

¼ cup maple syrup

2 teaspoons apple cider vinegar

1 teaspoon pure vanilla extract

½ teaspoon yellow mustard powder

1 cup spelt flour

1 cup unbleached pastry flour

2 teaspoons baking soda

1 tablespoon cinnamon

¼ teaspoon salt

½ cup currants or raisins (optional)

½ cup chopped walnuts (optional)

APPLE STREUSEL

2 tablespoons Omega Nutrition coconut butter or grapeseed oil

4 cups apples, peeled, cored, and sliced thinly (3–5 apples depending on size)

1 teaspoon finely grated fresh ginger (optional, if you like a ginger zing)

Pinch of sea salt

1½ teaspoons lemon zest

Pinch of cinnamon

COFFEE CAKE CRUMBLE

½ cup spelt flour

½ cup unbleached pastry flour

½ teaspoon baking powder

½ teaspoon cinnamon

Pinch of sea salt

½ cup organic brown sugar

4 tablespoons melted Omega Nutrition coconut butter or grapeseed oil

LEMON GLAZE

1   cup organic powdered sugar

1   teaspoon nonalcoholic vanilla extract

1   teaspoon lemon zest

4   tablespoons filtered water, or as needed

TO MAKE THE CAKE:

Preheat the oven to 350°F.

Place the squash and apple in a saucepan and cover with the water. Bring to a boil. Reduce the heat and simmer for 5 minutes, or until the squash is easily pierced with a fork. Remove from the heat. Strain off the water and set it aside. Allow the squash and apple to cool a bit.

In a food processor, blend the squash and apple into a puree. Add the vegetable shortening, grapeseed oil, sugar, brown sugar, and maple syrup and blend until smooth.

Add the vinegar, vanilla, mustard, and ¾ cup of liquid from cooking the squash and blend again until smooth.

Whisk together the flours, baking soda, cinnamon, and salt. Add the flour mixture into the wet ingredients and beat until ultrasmooth. If you have a large enough food processor, this can be done in it. If not, do so in a large bowl, beating at least 108 times for good luck. Fold in the currants or raisins and the walnuts, if desired, until evenly distributed.

Oil two 9" cake pans and evenly distribute the batter between them.

Bake for 25 minutes, or until golden and the edges pull away from the pan. A toothpick inserted in the center should come out clean. Cool on a rack for 15 minutes before removing from the pan.

WHILE THE CAKE BAKES:

Warm the coconut butter or grapeseed oil for the streusel in a skillet over medium heat. Add the apples, ginger, and salt and cook, stirring occasionally, for about 5 minutes, or until soft. Remove from the heat and mix in the lemon zest and cinnamon. Set aside to cool.

To make the crumble, whisk together the flours, baking powder, cinnamon, and salt. Mix in the brown sugar.

Add the melted coconut butter or grapeseed oil and mix to the texture of pebbles and sand.

Spread evenly on a baking sheet. Bake for 15 minutes, or just until turning golden brown and fragrant. Let cool.

TO ASSEMBLE THE COFFEE CAKE:

In a small bowl, mix together the ingredients for the glaze. Add a touch more water only if necessary to make a thick, spoonable glaze.

Be sure the cakes have cooled completely.

Place one of the cake rounds on a cake platter. Distribute the Apple Streusel evenly to the edges. Place the second cake round on top.

Spread a thin layer of Lemon Glaze on the top and cover evenly with the Coffee Cake Crumble. Drizzle with additional Lemon Glaze.

Let stand for 30 minutes to an hour before serving.

NUTRITION AT A GLANCE
Per serving: 460 calories, 14 g total fat, 1.5 g saturated fat, 5 g protein, 85 g carbohydrates, 6 g dietary fiber, 360 mg sodium

Banana Walnut Muffins

Who can argue with banana muffins? Not I. Both delightful and wholesome, these muffins can be a breakfast of champions or an afternoon treat for a clean-burning, long-term pick-me-up. Just 1 banana serves up almost 500 milligrams of potassium power to maintain healthy fluid balance in the body and happy heart function, along with a good dose of vitamin B$_6$, C, and magnesium. Serve with Fresh Pear Butter or top with Cinnamon Crumble for a textural pleasure of homemade goodness. For the gluten-sensitive contingency, all spelt flour may be used, though the muffins will be a little more dense. Alternatively, all wheat flour may be used if spelt is not available.

YIELDS: ABOUT 18

¾ **cup spelt flour**

¾ **cup whole wheat pastry flour**

2 **teaspoons baking powder**

1 **teaspoon baking soda**

½ **teaspoon ground cinnamon, freshly ground is best**

½ **teaspoon sea salt**

½ **cup softened coconut butter or grapeseed oil**

½ **cup maple syrup**

¼ **cup agave nectar**

⅓ **cup apple juice, soymilk, or filtered water**

1 **teaspoon apple cider vinegar**

1½ **cups mashed ripe bananas**

½ **cup chopped walnuts, may be lightly toasted**

Preheat the oven to 350°F.

The batter will make about 18 muffins. If you have muffin pans to cover that many, line them with unbleached paper baking cups or brush the pans with coconut butter or grapeseed oil. Otherwise, you will need to bake a second batch.

In a mixing bowl, whisk together the flours, baking powder, baking soda, cinnamon, and salt.

In another bowl, whisk together the coconut butter or grapeseed oil, maple syrup, agave, apple juice (or soymilk or water), and vinegar.

Fold the dry ingredients into the wet ingredients just until mixed. Gently fold in the bananas and walnuts.

Spoon the batter to fill the lined or oiled muffin cups ⅔ full.

Top with Cinnamon Crumble, if desired, and bake for 25 to 30 minutes, until golden brown and a toothpick inserted into the middle of a muffin comes out clean.

NOTE: *To make Banana Walnut Bread, pour the prepared batter into an oiled 9" loaf pan, top with Cinnamon Crumble, and bake until golden brown and a toothpick inserted into the middle comes out clean, about 1 hour.*

CINNAMON CRUMBLE

½   cup walnuts

¼   cup spelt flour

¼   cup rolled oats

½   teaspoon cinnamon

¼   teaspoon sea salt

3   tablespoons softened coconut butter
    or grapeseed oil

3   tablespoons maple syrup

Place the walnuts, flour, oats, cinnamon, and salt in a food processor and grind into a fine meal.

Add the coconut butter or oil and the maple syrup and chop in pulses just until mixed. The texture should be like pebbles and sand. If it is too dry, add a tablespoon or 2 of filtered water. If it is too moist, add a touch of flour.

Crumble over muffin batter before baking.

NUTRITION AT A GLANCE
Per serving (1 muffin): 210 calories, 13 g total fat, 1 g saturated fat, 3 g protein, 23 g carbohydrates,
2 g dietary fiber, 220 mg sodium

FRESH PEAR BUTTER

5   ripe pears (apples also work
    wonderfully!)

1   cup filtered water

½   cup maple syrup

¼   teaspoon ground cinnamon, freshly
    ground is best

    Pinch of sea salt

Cut the pears into quarters. Cut away the cores and peel. Chop roughly.

Place the water and maple syrup in a heavy saucepan. Add the pears, cinnamon, and salt and bring to a boil, covered. Reduce the heat and let simmer for 15 to 20 minutes, uncovered, until the liquid is reduced in half. Let cool to room temperature. Pass through a food mill or blend smooth in a blender or food processor.

Return the mixture to a heavy saucepan and cook over the lowest heat for 1 to 1½ hours, stirring fairly regularly to avoid burning. This can also be done in a slow cooker for 2 hours.

Store covered in the fridge. Yum!

NUTRITION AT A GLANCE
Per serving (2 tablespoons): 45 calories, 0 g total fat, 0 g saturated fat, 0 g protein, 12 g carbohydrates,
0 g dietary fiber, 5 mg sodium

Mint Chocolate Wafers

These bring me back to my days in the Brownies. I never did graduate to full-fledged Girl Scouts, though I coveted their sashes and iron-on patches. Chocolate and mint are still brilliant together, and the combination is a nutritious hero here dehydrated or baked at low temperatures to preserve the delicate good stuff. The cookies can be frozen instead of dehydrated for a frosty treat, and regardless, I highly recommend doubling the recipe so you can stash a batch in the freezer.

YIELDS: 30

2 cups whole raw cashews

3 cups filtered water

6–8 tablespoons maple syrup

2–4 tablespoons agave nectar

2 tablespoons organic evaporated cane juice or organic sugar (optional)

1 tablespoon peppermint extract

½ teaspoon balsamic vinegar

¼ teaspoon Celtic sea salt or Himalayan salt

2–4 tablespoons water, as necessary to aid blending

1–1½ cups organic cocoa powder

¼ cup ground cacao nibs (optional)

Soak the cashews in 3 cups of filtered water for 2 hours. Drain and rinse.

In a food processor or high-powered blender, grind the drained cashews into a fine meal. Add the maple syrup, agave, cane juice or sugar, peppermint, balsamic, and salt and blend until smooth. Add a touch of water as necessary to aid in blending as smooth as possible.

Add the cocoa powder ¼ cup at a time and blend until smooth and as "dark" as desired.

Thoroughly mix in the cacao nibs, if desired, by hand.

Roll 1½ tablespoons of dough into a ball and place on a nonstick dehydrator sheet or plastic wrap. Wet the bottom of a glass and flatten into a ¼"-thick cookie. Continue until you've used all of the dough.

Place a dehydrator tray facedown on the nonstick sheet or plastic wrap and flip the whole thing over. This step will speed up the drying time by allowing the air to circulate more freely through the mesh sheets.

Dehydrate at 112°F for 12 to 24 hours, or until as dry as desired.

This may also be done on cookie sheets in the oven set at the lowest temperature for 2 to 3 hours or more, until a crust forms. Once dry, they can be stored in a sealed container or bag in the fridge for up to 2 weeks or frozen for up to 2 months.

The thin mints can also be frozen by rolling and flattening them on a cookie sheet, then placing them in the freezer until firm. Once firm, transfer to a sealable container and store in the freezer for up to 2 months.

Chocolate Candied Pecans

These sweet, heart-healthy nuggets are brilliant on ice cream, though I munch on them straight-up. They do take some time to dehydrate, so doubling the recipe makes good sense as they can be stored in the freezer for up to a month. Delish!

YIELDS: 12 SERVINGS (2 CUPS)

2   cups pecans

4   cups filtered water

3   tablespoons maple syrup

2   tablespoons maple sugar or organic evaporated cane juice

½   teaspoon umeboshi plum vinegar

½   teaspoon aged balsamic vinegar or ¼ teaspoon balsamic vinegar

5   tablespoons cocoa powder

2   tablespoons cacao nibs (optional)

Soak the pecans in 4 cups of filtered water for 4 to 6 hours. Drain and rinse. Pat dry with a clean towel.

Toss the pecans with the maple syrup, maple sugar or cane juice, umeboshi plum vinegar, and balsamic. Fold in the cocoa powder and cacao nibs (if desired).

Spread in a pie plate or casserole dish that will fit in the dehydrator and dehydrate at 112°F for a few hours, or until firm enough to hold their own. Place on the mesh trays of the dehydrator (which will speed up the drying time) and continue to dehydrate until crispy and dry.

Store in a sealed container, jar, or bag in the fridge for up to 2 weeks or in the freezer for up to a month.

Walnut Raisin Oatmeal Cookies

Oats are a fortified cereal grain for strength and energy, and they have some distinguished properties, including housing a fabulous fiber called beta-glucan, which is known to lower cholesterol and improve antioxidant action to reduce diseases of the cardiovascular system. The friendly fiber also stabilizes blood sugar, which is a good thing for anyone with hypoglycemic and diabetic tendencies. Laden with phytochemicals, this great grain is particularly rich in lignans, which are converted by the friendly flora in our guts to protect against hormone-dependent cancers, especially breast and ovarian cancer.

YIELDS: 1 DOZEN

1 **cup raisins**

1 **cup apple juice or filtered water**

2 **cups walnuts**

1¼ **cups rolled oats**

1½ **cups spelt flour, rice flour, or whole wheat flour**

2 **teaspoons baking powder**

1 **teaspoon ground cinnamon**

¼ **teaspoon finely ground sea salt**

½ **cup melted Omega Nutrition coconut butter, safflower oil, or grapeseed oil**

½ **cup maple syrup**

2 **tablespoons lemon juice**

½ **teaspoon lemon zest**

2 **tablespoons egg replacer or 2 tablespoons ground flax seed**

2 **teaspoons vanilla extract**

½ **cup granulated sweetener, Sucanat, organic brown sugar, or maple sugar**

Preheat the oven to 350°F.

Cover the raisins with the apple juice or water for 10 to 15 minutes to plump them up. When softened a bit, drain off the juice or water and set it aside to thin the batter as needed.

Spread the walnuts and oats on a baking sheet and toast in the oven for 6 to 9 minutes, stirring once or twice with a wooden spatula for even cooking. Let cool for a few minutes on a rack.

Place half of the walnuts and oats in a food processor and grind into a fine meal. Add the remaining walnuts and oats, flour, baking powder, cinnamon, and salt and chop in pulses a few times, just to mix together.

In a medium-large bowl, whisk together the coconut butter or oil, maple syrup, and lemon juice and zest. Whisk in the egg replacer or flax seed, vanilla, and sweetener of choice.

Fold the dry ingredients into the wet ingredients until well mixed. Add a splash of the raisin soaking juice or water if the dough is too dry. Fold in the raisins.

Lightly oil 2 baking sheets or line with parchment paper. Drop 1½ to 2 tablespoons of dough onto the sheets 2½" apart and press down gently with moistened fingers or the palm of your hand.

Bake for 15 to 20 minutes, until the edges are lightly browned.

Cool for 10 minutes on the baking sheets, then transfer to a rack or plate to cool completely.

Coconut Macaroons

Dehydrating preserves all of the good delicate oils in these yummy, raw-friendly treats. They can also be frozen instead of dehydrating for a chilled delight.

YIELDS: 2 DOZEN

3   cups dried coconut

2   tablespoons raw cashew or almond butter

2   tablespoons coconut butter

4   tablespoons agave nectar

2–3 tablespoons raw honey

2   tablespoons maple syrup

2   tablespoons brown rice syrup

1   teaspoon nonalcoholic vanilla extract (optional)

1   teaspoon ground cinnamon (optional)

   Pinch of Celtic sea salt or Himalayan salt

In a food processor, grind 1 cup of the coconut into a powder.

Add the cashew or almond butter, coconut butter, agave, honey, maple syrup, brown rice syrup, vanilla (if desired), cinnamon (if desired), and salt and blend until well mixed.

Fold in the remaining coconut by hand.

Roll 2 tablespoons of the dough into a ball and flatten one side with the palm of your hand. Continue until you've used all of the dough.

Dehydrate at 112°F for 12 to 24 hours, or until as dry as desired, or bake in the oven set at the lowest temperature possible for 2 hours or more, until a crust forms.

The macaroons can also be frozen by rolling and flattening them on a baking sheet, then placing them in the freezer until firm. Once firm, transfer to a sealable container and store in the freezer for up to 2 months.

Maple Almond Wafers

These cookies are soft and spiced to heavenly perfection. They do take some time to prepare but are well worth the effort. They are very kid-friendly and packed with protein and healthy oils, which are preserved by the gentle temperatures of dehydration.

YIELDS: 3 DOZEN

1½ cups raw almonds, soaked and peeled (page 251)

2 tablespoons raw almond butter

½ cup maple syrup

2 teaspoons nonalcoholic vanilla extract

1 teaspoon ground cinnamon

¼ teaspoon Celtic sea salt or Himalayan salt

4–6 tablespoons granulated sweetener, such as organic evaporated cane juice, Sucanat, or maple sugar

2 teaspoons ground cinnamon

1 teaspoon ground nutmeg

In a food processor, grind the almonds into a fine meal.

Add the almond butter, maple syrup, vanilla, cinnamon, salt, and 2 to 4 tablespoons of granulated sweetener and blend until as smooth as possible. Add filtered water, a tablespoon at a time, only as necessary to aid blending smooth and keep nice and thick.

Use a spoon to dollop 1½ to 2 tablespoons of dough onto nonstick dehydrator sheets or parchment. Continue until you've used all of the dough.

Sprinkle with cinnamon, nutmeg, and the remaining 2 tablespoons of granulated sweetener.

Dehydrate at 112°F for 12 to 20 hours, or until a crust forms.

Flip over and remove the nonstick sheet or parchment and return to the dehydrator for several hours until dried to the desired consistency.

This may also be done on baking sheets in the oven set at the lowest temperature for several hours, until a crust forms. Flip over and return to oven until a bottom crust forms.

NUTRITION AT A GLANCE
Per serving: 60 calories, 3.5 g total fat, 0 g saturated fat, 1 g protein, 6 g carbohydrates, 0 g dietary fiber, 20 mg sodium

Lemon Ginger Lace Cookies

A very well-respected chef said these cookies reminded him of a proper French patisserie. Indeed, they are wonderfully delicate, buttery, crispy, and good for you, thanks to a little cold-pressed coconut butter. The rice syrup binds the dough together perfectly, and spelt is a friendly option for gluten-sensitive folks. Chin-chin!

YIELDS: 2 DOZEN OR SO (DEPENDING ON HOW MUCH BATTER YOU EAT)

8	tablespoons softened coconut butter (Omega Nutrition is great)
½	cup brown rice syrup
5	tablespoons maple syrup
3	tablespoons granulated sweetener, such as organic evaporated cane juice, organic sugar, or maple sugar
1	organic lemon
2–3	tablespoons ginger juice (page 160)
2	teaspoons pure vanilla extract
1¼	cups spelt flour or pastry flour
1	tablespoon ground ginger
¼	teaspoon sea salt

Preheat the oven to 325°F.

In a nice-size bowl, cream together the coconut butter, rice syrup, and maple syrup. Mix in your granulated sweetener of choice.

With a microplane, grate the peel of the lemon directly into the batter. Cut the lemon in half, squeeze and strain the juice, and whisk it into the batter.

Add the ginger juice and vanilla and whisk to combine.

Sift the spelt or pastry flour, ginger, and salt and mix into the batter. If it is warm outside, the batter will be quite thin. If it is cold outside, the batter will be thicker.

Oil 2 baking sheets or line with parchment paper.

Spoon the batter onto the baking sheets by the tablespoon, at least 2 inches apart, as the cookies will spread thin during baking.

Bake for 12 to 15 minutes, until nicely golden brown. I recommend turning the baking sheet once or twice during baking for even browning. Be mindful as they burn easily because they are so thin. The cookies should be crunchy when cooled. Cool on a rack.

NUTRITION AT A GLANCE
Per serving: 100 calories, 3.5 g total fat, 0 g saturated fat, 2 g protein, 17 g carbohydrates, 0 g dietary fiber, 65 mg sodium

Lavender Black Raspberry Ice Cream

Black raspberry ice cream transports me to nostalgic childhood summer nights that seemed to last forever. The faint infusion of lavender, known to mellow the nervous system, is a fine match for the lavender color from the black raspberries, which are loaded with antioxidants, in this creamy frozen delight.

YIELDS: 6 SERVINGS (1 PINT)

4 tablespoons lavender flowers

1¼ cups hot water

1½ cups raw cashews

½ cup pine nuts

1¼ cups black raspberries

½ cup maple syrup

½ cup agave nectar

½ cup coconut butter

1 teaspoon nonalcoholic vanilla extract

1 teaspoon aged balsamic vinegar or ½ teaspoon balsamic

½ teaspoon sea salt

Steep 2 tablespoons of the lavender flowers in the hot water for 3 to 5 minutes. Drain off the tea and discard the flowers.

Place the lavender tea in a blender with ½ cup of the cashews and the pine nuts.

Blend at high speed until smooth. Pour through a fine mesh strainer or sieve to separate the liquid from the pulp. Use the back of a large spoon to press out as much liquid as possible. It may be helpful to line the strainer with cheese-cloth and use it to squeeze out as much liquid as possible.

Rinse out the blender and return the strained nut milk to the blender.

Add the remaining 1 cup of cashews, the black raspberries, maple syrup, agave, coconut butter, remaining lavender flowers, vanilla, balsamic, and salt. Blend until as smooth as silk.

Freeze in an ice cream maker according to the manufacturer's directions. Store in a tightly sealed container for up to a month, though the color will fade after about 2 weeks.

NUTRITION AT A GLANCE

Per serving: 390 calories, 26 g total fat, 3.5 g saturated fat, 8 g protein, 37 g carbohydrates, 2 g dietary fiber, 290 mg sodium

Agave Tequila Lime Ice Cream

I came up with this ice cream for my friend Tom, who loves good tequila. He's tall, dark, and handsome, though far from a health-minded guy, so I won't mention the other ingredients to him. Avocado provides just the right amount of fat for the perfect ice cream texture. The lime takes care of the color, and agave—made from the same cactus as tequila—adds sweetness. Delicioso!

YIELDS: 4 SERVINGS (ABOUT 1 PINT)

- 2 ripe Hass avocados, cubed (about 2 cups)
- ½ cup + 2 tablespoons agave nectar
- ⅓ cup lime juice
- 1 tablespoon lime zest (go organic!)
- 2–4 tablespoons tequila
- 2 tablespoons Omega Nutrition coconut butter (optional, but makes for a rich texture)
- ½ teaspoon nonalcoholic vanilla extract
  Pinch of sea salt
- 2 tablespoons organic sugar (optional, for the sweet tooth accustomed to sugar)

In a food processor or blender, place the avocados, agave, lime juice, lime zest, tequila, coconut butter (if desired), vanilla, and salt, and sugar (if desired). Blend until super smooth. Freeze in an ice cream maker according to the manufacturer's directions. If you don't have an ice cream maker, freeze in a sealable container until firm (it will be denser than when made with an ice cream maker, but still delish).

NUTRITION AT A GLANCE
Per serving: 150 calories, 12 g total fat, 2 g saturated fat, 2 g protein, 12 g carbohydrates, 4 g dietary fiber, 30 mg sodium

---

My advice to you is not to inquire why or whither, but just enjoy your ice cream while it's on your plate—that's my philosophy.

—THORNTON WILDER

Macadamia Vanilla Bean Ice Cream
with Cinnamon-Mace Caramel Sauce and
Orange Zabaglione

*I would happily eat any of these sweet treats out of a bowl on their own, but together
they are something extraordinary. Macadamia nuts and fresh vanilla bean is a match
made in subtropical heaven. I developed this recipe in Hawaii, where young coconuts
are easy to get for their water and meat, though young Thai coconuts are available
elsewhere in Asian markets and often in Whole Foods Markets. Mature coconuts
(hard, brown, with fibrous fur) just don't work well, so I offer substitutes. The
caramel sauce is wonderful warmed over low heat. Make extra for apple dipping!*

YIELDS: 8 SERVINGS

MACADAMIA VANILLA BEAN ICE CREAM

1½ cups raw macadamia nuts, soaked 2–4 hours in filtered water and drained

3 cups fresh coconut water (see note)

1½ cups young coconut meat (see note)

⅓ cup raw macadamia nuts

3 tablespoons coconut butter (Omega Nutrition is choice)

4 tablespoons maple syrup

4 tablespoons agave nectar

2 tablespoons raw honey

1 vanilla bean, split and seeds scraped out

1 teaspoon nonalcoholic vanilla extract

CINNAMON-MACE CARAMEL SAUCE

2 tablespoons raw almond butter

3 tablespoons maple syrup

2 tablespoons agave nectar

1 tablespoon brown rice syrup

1 tablespoon coconut butter

1 teaspoon freshly ground cinnamon

½ teaspoon mace or ¼ teaspoon nutmeg

Pinch of sea salt

Splash of coconut water or filtered water, as necessary

ORANGE ZABAGLIONE

¼ cup raw cashews, soaked 2 hours in filtered water and drained

½ cup young coconut meat (see note)

1 tablespoon Omega Nutrition coconut butter

1 tablespoon maple syrup

1–2 tablespoons agave nectar

1–2 tablespoons raw honey

½ cup orange segments

1 teaspoon orange zest

2 teaspoons nonalcoholic vanilla extract

¼ teaspoon turmeric powder (optional, for color)

TO MAKE THE ICE CREAM:

Place the drained macadamia nuts in a blender (preferably a high-speed blender like the Vita-Mix) with the coconut water. Blend until smooth. Pour through a strainer or sieve lined with cheesecloth. Squeeze out as much liquid as possible. Save the pulp to use again for milk or cookies.

Return the milk to the blender. Add the coconut meat, raw macadamia nuts, coconut butter, maple syrup, agave, honey, and vanilla bean and extract. Blend until completely smooth. Taste and sweeten more as desired. Remember that when frozen, the sweetness will be more muted, so when not frozen, it should taste very sweet.

Freeze in an ice cream maker according to the manufacturer's directions. It's usually best if left to firm in the freezer for an hour or two after freezing in the machine.

TO MAKE THE SAUCE:

Blend the almond butter, maple syrup, agave, brown rice syrup, coconut butter, cinnamon, mace or nutmeg, and salt until very smooth, adding a touch of coconut water or filtered water as necessary to achieve the desired thickness. The sauce should be quite thick, but able to be poured. I often double the recipe as it can be stored in a tightly sealed jar or container in the fridge for at least a week.

TO MAKE THE ZABAGLIONE:

In a high-speed blender, blend the cashews, coconut meat, coconut butter, maple syrup, agave, honey, orange segments and zest, vanilla, and turmeric (if desired) until silky smooth. Stash in the fridge until ready to use.

TO ASSEMBLE THE DESSERT:

Spoon the Orange Zabaglione into the bottoms of small bowls. Serve a scoop of the ice cream over it and generously drizzle with Cinnamon-Mace Caramel Sauce.

NOTE: *If fresh coconuts are not available, use 2⅔ cups filtered water + ⅓ cup agave nectar + ¼ teaspoon sea salt in place of the 3 cups of coconut water. Use ¾ cup + 1 tablespoon cashews soaked for 2 hours in filtered water + ⅓ cup macadamia nuts + ¼ cup + 2 tablespoons filtered water + 3 tablespoons maple syrup + 2 teaspoons coconut butter in place of the 2 cups of meat you need for the ice cream and zabaglione.*

NUTRITION AT A GLANCE

Per serving: 420 calories, 30 g total fat, 12 g saturated fat, 6 g protein, 40 g carbohydrates, 6 g dietary fiber, 320 mg sodium

Resource Guide

Natural Foods

EDEN FOODS
701 Tecumesh Road
Clinton, MI 49236
888-441-3336
Organic bulk foods, seaweed, vinegars, oil,
condiments

GOLD MINE NATURAL FOODS
1947 30th Street
San Diego, CA 92120
619-234-9711
800-475-FOOD
Organic, macrobiotic, and natural foods

GREAT EASTERN SUN
92 McIntosh Road
Asheville, NC 28806
800-334-5809
customersvc@great-eastern-sun.com
www.great-eastern-sun.com
Organic, natural, and macrobiotic foods and
related products

JAFFE BROTHERS
28560 Lilac Road
Valley Center, CA 92082
760-749-1133
www.organicfruitsandnuts.com
Natural and organic nuts and seeds, grains, beans,
dried fruit

MOUNTAIN ARK TRADING COMPANY
PO Box 3170
Fayetteville, AR 72702
800-643-8909
Organic foods and kitchen tools

NATURAL IMPORT COMPANY
9 Reed Street
Biltmore Village, NC 28803
800-324-1878
828-277-8870
www.naturalimport@aol.com
Organic, macrobiotic, natural foods, and related
products

SMOKEY MOUNTAIN NATURAL FOODS
15 Aspen Court
Asheville, NC 28806
800-926-0974
Organic, natural, and macrobiotic foods and
related products

WALNUT ACRES NATURAL FOODS
Penns Creek, PA
800-717-0610
Organic grains, beans, flours, dried fruit, nuts,
seeds, animal products

Chocolate

DOLFIN
Country: Belgium
Tel: +32 2 366 24 24
Fax: +32 2 366 22 42
Web: www.dolfin.be
E-mail: dolfin@link.be

GREEN & BLACK'S
Country: United Kingdom
Tel: +44 (0) 20 7633 590
Web: www.greenandblacks.com
E-mail: enquiries@greenandblacks

SCHARFFEN BERGER
Country: USA
510-981-4050
www.scharfenberger.com
pr1@scharffenberger.com

VALRHONA
Country: France
Tel: +33 (0)4 75 07 90 90
Fax: +33 (04 75 07 10 49
Web: www.valrhona.com
E-mail: info@valrhona.fr

VOSGES
Country: USA
888-301-9866
www.vosgeschocolate.com

American Organic Miso Manufacturers

AMERICAN MISO COMPANY
4225 Maple Creek Road
Rutherfordton, NC 28139
828-287-2940

MIYAKO ORIENTAL FOODS
4287 Puente
Baldwin Park, CA 91706
626-926-9633
www.coldmountainmiso.com

SOUTH RIVER MISO COMPANY
South River Farm
Conway, MA 01341
413-369-4057
Three-year barley, black soybeans, adzuki,
dandelion-leek, golden millet, chickpeas
1, 4, 9, 18, and 45# containers

YAMAZAKI MISO
4192 County Road South
Orlando, CA 95963
530-865-5979

Oil

OMEGA NUTRITION
6515 Aldrich Road
Bellingham, WA 98226
800-661-3529
www.omeganutrition.com
Organic, cold-pressed oils

Salt

CELTIC SEA SALT
www.celticseasalt.com

GRAIN AND SALT SOCIETY
PO Drawer S-DD
Magalia, CA 95954
916-873-0294
800-TOP-SALT
Hawaiian salt

SOUL OF THE SEA
www.soulofthesea.net

MALDON SALT COMPANY
www.maldonsalt.co.uk
Flake salt and smoked salt

MANY GREAT SALTS
www.saltworks.com
www.sunsalt.com
www.salttraders.com

Sea Vegetables

MAINE SEAWEED COMPANY
PO Box 57
Steuben, ME 04680
707-546-2875
Kelp, alaria, dulse, digitata kelp, and wild nori

Mendocino Sea Vegetable Company
255 Welding Street
PO Box 372
Navarro, Ca 95463
707-895-3741

Ocean Harvest Sea Vegetables
PO Box 1719
Mendocino, CA 95460
707-936-1923
Wild nori, sea lettuce, wakame, sea whip, fucus
tip, ocean ribbons, sea palm fronds, grapestone

Rising Tide Sea Vegetables
PO Box 1914
Mendocino, CA 95460
707-964-5663

Seeds

Seeds of Change
PO Box 15700
Santa Fe, NM 87506
888-726-7333
Heirloom and organic gardening seeds;
non-GMO

Spices

Frontier Cooperative
3021 78th Avenue
PO Box 299
Norway, IA 52318
800-669-3257
Bulk herb and spices, vanilla extracts, organic
coffee and teas

Eco Products for Home and Garden

Abundant Earth
888-51-EARTH
www.abundantearth.com

Lifekind Organic Mattresses
800-284-4983
www.lifekind.com

Green Cleaning Products*

Bi-O-Clean
800-477-0188
www.bi-o-clean.com
All-purpose natural and biodegradable cleaning
supplies

Citrisolve
65 Valley Street
PO Box 14258
East Providence, RI 02914
401-434-3300
800-556-6785
www.citrisolve.com
oroco@organicdye.com
All-purpose citrus-based biodegradable and heavy-
duty cleaning products

Earthfriendly Products
44 Green Bay Road
Winnetka, IL 60093
847-446-4441
www.ecos.com
All-purpose natural and biodegradable cleaning
products, Oxo Brite (color-safe oxygen bleach),
and stain-removal products

www.ecomall.com
Directory for natural products

Ecover
Ecover Belgium NV
Industrieweg 3
2390 Malle
Belgium
info@ecover.com
www.ecover.com
All-purpose natural and biodegradable cleaning
supplies

HARMONY (GAIAM)
360 Interlocken Boulevard
Suite 300
Broomfield, CO 80021
800-869-3446
www.gaiam.com

OXI-CLEAN
Box 3998
Littleton, CO 80161
www.oxiclean.com
Color-safe, readily degradable oxygen bleach and
stain-removal products and all-purpose cleaning
supplies

PLANET INC.
800-858-8449
www.planetinc.com
All-purpose natural and biodegradable cleaning
supplies

REAL GOODS
966 Mazzoni Street
Ukiah, CA 95482
800-762-7325
Books on gardening, world's most efficient
refrigerators and freezers, nontoxic cleaning
products, cloth produce storage bags

SEVENTH GENERATION
12 Battery Street, Suite A
Burlington, VT 05401-5281
802-658-3773
800-456-1191
www.seventhgeneration.com
All-purpose natural and biodegradable cleaning
supplies, recycled tissue and paper products

Organic Cotton and Clothing

ECO PLANET
Headquarters:
Box 27740
Las Vegas, NV 89126
Order Processing:
Box 1491
Glendora, CA 91740
service@ecochoices.com
www.ecoplanet.com
www.ecobedroom.com

GAIAM
www.gaiam.com

OF THE EARTH
877-HEMP-OTE
www.oftheearth.com
Hemp clothing, outdoor clothing and gear

PATAGONIA
800-638-6464
www.patagonia.com

RAWGANIQUE
Way 9000, Rayelyn Lane
Denman Island, BC V0R 1T0
Canada
877-RAW-HEMP
250-335-0050
www.rawganique.com

Healing, Education, and Rejuvenation Centers

ANN WIGMORE NATURAL HEALTH INSTITUTE
PO Box 429
Rincón, PR 00677
787-868-6307

PO Box 399
San Fidel, NM 87049
505-552-0595

HIPPOCRATES HEALTH CENTER
1443 Palmdale Court
West Palm Beach, FL 33411
800-842-2125

OPTIMUM HEALTH INSTITUTE
6970 Central Avenue
Lemon Grove, CA 91945
619-464-3346
or
Route 1 Box 339-J Cedar Road
Cedar Creek, TX 78612
512-303-4817

TREE OF LIFE REJUVENATION CENTER
PO Box 778
Patagonia, AZ 85624
520-394-2520
www.treeofliferejuvenation.com

Education and Information

Information about hazardous agricultural
chemicals:

CENTER FOR SCIENCE IN THE PUBLIC INTEREST
1501 16th Street NW
Washington, DC 20036

NATIONAL COALITION AGAINST THE MISUSE OF
PESTICIDES
530 7th Street SE
Washington, DC 20003

PESTICIDE ACTION NETWORK NEWSLETTER
965 Mission Street #541
San Francisco, CA 94103

UNITED STATES GENERAL ACCOUNTING OFFICE
Washington, DC 20548

Make your views known! Write your
congressmen and senators!

YOUR CONGRESSIONAL REPRESENTATIVE
US House of Representatives
Washington, DC 20515

YOUR SENATOR
US Senate
Washington, DC 20510

*If there are products and companies you think I should know about to spread the word,
please contact me: greencleaning@euphoricorganics.com

Notes

1. DevCan: Probability of Developing or Dying of Cancer, Statistical Research and Applications Branch, NCI 2004, http://srab.cancer.gov/devcan.

2. American Cancer Society, Cancer Statistics Presentation, 2006, www.cancer.org/docroot/STT/stt_0.asp.

3. USDA Economic Research Service, "Understanding Rural America," www.ers.usda.gov/publications/aib710/aib710g.htm.

4. Federal Reserve Board, "Rural Economic Issues," remarks by Chairman Alan Greenspan, Warrenton, Virginia, March 2004, www.federalreserve.gov/boarddocs/speeches/2004/20040325/default.htm.

5. Organic Trade Association, definition passed by National Organic Standards Board at its 1995 meeting in Orlando, Florida, www.ota.com/organic/definition.html.

6. Plunkett Research, "Food Industry Overview," February 2006, www.plunkettresearch.com/Industries/FoodBeverageTobacco/FoodBeverageTobaccoStatistics/tabid/248/Default.aspx.

7. USDA Economic Research Service, Organic Farming and Marketing, www.ers.usda.gov/Briefing/Organic.

8. Environmental Working Group, "What Government Tests Tell Us About...Pesticides in Apples," 2006, *Food News*, www.foodnews.org/highpest.php?prod=PFR20N01&.

9. National Center for Food and Agricultural Policy, Library of Pesticide Use http://CIPM.NCSU.edu.

10. EPA, "Pesticides & Food Security," April 2004, www.epa.gov/pesticides/factsheets/secrty.htm.

11. Environmental Working Group, "FDA Monitoring & Enforcing," 2006, www.ewg.org/reports/fruit/chapter1.html.

12. Dr. Virginia Worthington, "Nutritional Quality of Organic Versus Conventional Fruits, Vegetables, and Grains," *Journal of Alternative and Complimentary Medicine* 7 (2001).

13. Global Resource Action Center for the Environment, Sustainable Table Consumer Campaign, www.sustainabletable.org/issue/pesticides/.

14. Ricki Lewis, "The Rise of Antibiotic-Resistant Infection," FDA, September 1995, www.fda.gov/FDAC/features/795_antibio.html.

15. Organic Consumers Association, "Massive Use of Antibiotics in Animal Feed Threatens Public Health," January 2001, www.organicconsumers.org/toxic/massiveantibiotics.cfm.

16. Caa Peterson, Laurie E. Drinkwater, Peggy Wagoner, "The First 15 Years," The Rodale Institute Farming Systems Trial™. The Rodale Institute, 1999.

17. A. M. Andersson and N.E. Skakkebfk, "Exposure to Exogenous Estrogens in Food: Possible Impact on Human Development and Health," *European Journal of Endocrinology* 140 (1999): 477–485.

18. Cancer Prevention Coalition, "Milk: America's Health Problem," 2003, www.preventcancer.com/consumers/general/milk.htm.

19. Food Safety Network, "Safety of Hormone-Treated Beef Questioned," *CP*, July 30, 1999, www.foodsafetynetwork.ca.

20. Patti Goldman, "World Trade Organization Dispute Settlement Proceeding European Communities: Measures Concerning Meat and Meat Products (Hormones)," www.citizen.org/pctrade/gattwto/beef.html.

21. Amanda Barrett, "Added Hormones in Meat and Dairy: Do They Affect Health and If So, How?" Swedish Medical Center, 2005, www.swedish.org/111038.cfm.

22. Union of Concerned Scientists, "Hogging It!: Estimates of Antimicrobial Abuse in Livestock," January 2001, www.ucsusa.org/food_and_environment/antibiotics_and_food/hogging-it-estimates-of-antimicrobial-abuse-in-livestock.html.

23. Walter J. Crinnon, "Pesticides: Biologically Persistent Ubiquitous Toxins," Environmental Medicine series, Part 4, *Alternative Medicine Review* 5 (October 2002): 432–447.

24. American Horticultural Society, *The American Gardener*, March/April 2002, www.ahs.org/publications/the_american_gardener/0203.

25. National Resource Defense Council, "Trouble on the Farm: Growing Up with Pesticides in Agricultural Communities," cited in "Environmental and Economic Costs of Pesticide Use," *BioScience* 42 (1998): 750–59.

26. Jacques Diouf, director general of Food and Agricultural Organization of the United Nations, "Speech at Howard University of Law," October 19, 2004.

27. Craig Benjamin, "The Machu Picchu Model: Climate Change and Agricultural Diversity," Climate Ark, Fall 1999, www.climateark.org/articles/1999/makupiku.htm.

28. Californians for Pesticide Reform, "Pesticides and Human Health," www.pesticidereform.org/article.php?list=type&type=38.

29. Cancer Prevention Coalition, "Home and Garden Pesticides: Q&A," 2003, www.preventcancer.com/consumers/household/pesticides_home.htm.

30. BBC News, "Pesticides 'Can Cause Brain Damage,'" September 8, 2000, http://news.bbc.co.uk/1/hi/health/914556.stm.

31. National Institute of Environmental Health Sciences, "Environmental Contaminants and Their Relation to Learning, Behavioral and Developmental Disorders," April 2003, www.niehs.nih.gov/oc/factsheets/ceh/contamin.htm.

32. Food and Agriculture Organization of the United Nations, "Cleaning Up the Pesticides Nobody Wants, May 24,1999, www.fao.org/News/1999/990504-e.htm.

33. Global Pesticides Release Database, August 21, 2001, www.msc-smc.ec.gc.ca/data/gloperd/basic_knowledge_e.cfm.

34. Natural Resources Defense Council, "Chemicals: DDT," May 2001, www.nrdc.org/breastmilk/chem2.asp.

35. Cornell University, "Pesticides and Breast Cancer Risk: An Evaluation of DDT and DDE," fact sheet #2, April 2001, http://envirocancer.cornell.edu/FactSheet/Pesticide/fs2.ddt.cfm.

36. Association of Public Health Laboratories, "Measuring Chemicals in People," May 2004, www.aphl.org/docs/Biomonitoring.pdf.

37. Sue Blodgett and Ruth O'Neill, "Evaluating Reduced Risk Pesticides for Enhanced Biological Activity," EPA, May 2006, www.epa.gov/oppbppd1/PESP/regional_grants/2003/r8-2003.htm.

38. Rachel Carson, *Silent Spring* (Boston: Mariner Books/Houghton Mifflin Company, 2002), 62.

39. EPA, "Pesticides: Organophosphates," May 1999, www.epa.gov/pesticides/op/primer.htm.

40. Mount Sinai School of Medicine, testimony by Dr. Philip J. Landrigan to the Committee on Environment and Public Works, United States Senate, Washington, D.C., October 1, 2002, http://epw.senate.gov/107th/Landrigan_100102.htm.

41. Natural Resources Defense Council, "Putting Children First," executive summary of NRDC's April 1998 report, www.nrdc.org/health/kids/rpcfsum.asp.

42. Will Allen, "Cotton Subsidies and Cotton Problems," Organic Consumers Association, February 2004, www.organicconsumers.org/clothes/224subsidies.cfm.

43. EcoChoices, "Conventional Cotton Statistics," 2006, www.ecochoices.com/1/cotton_statistics.html.

44. CBS News, "Protect Your Kids Against Pesticides," August 12, 2000, www.cbsnews.com/stories/2000/08/10/earlyshow/saturday/main223684.shtml.

45. EPA, "Pesticides and Food: Why Children May Be Especially Sensitive to Pesticides," updated February 23, 2005, www.epa.gov/pesticides/food/pest.htm.

46. EPA, "Protecting Children from Pesticides," January 2002, www.epa.gov/pesticides/factsheets/kidpesticide.htm.

47. *Washington Times*, "Organic Diet Keeps Kids Pesticide Free," February 22, 2003, http://washtimes.com/upi/20060222-044543-1356r.htm.

48. Cornell Cooperative Extension, "Public Issues Education Project: Am I Eating GE Tomatoes?" 2003, www.geo-pie.cornell.edu/crops/tomato.html.

49. European Food Safety Authority, "EFSA Provides Scientific Advice on the Use of Antibiotic Resistance Marker Genes in Genetically Modified Plants," April 20, 2004, www.efsa.eu.int/press_room/press_release/386_en.html.

50. Alexander Haslberger, "GMO Contamination of Seeds," Institute of Microbiology and Genetics University of Vienna, *Nature Biotechnology* 19 (July 2001): 613; www.biotech-info.net/GMO_contamination2.html.

51. British Crop Protection Council, *Human Exposure to Pesticide Residues, Natural Toxins and GMOs: Real and Perceived Risk*, British Crop Protection Council Publications, 2000.

52. BBC News, Food Under the Microscope, "Genetically-Modified Q & A" April 1999, http://news.bbc.co.uk/2/hi/special_report/1999/02/99/food_under_the_microscope/280868.stm#TOP.

53. Executive Summary from the Genetically Modified Organism Exploratory Committee, Macalester College, www.macalester.edu/~montgomery/GMOs2.htm.

54. R. Meilan, C. Ma, S. Cheng, J. A. Eaton, L. K. Miller, R. P. Crockett, S. P. DiFazio, and S. H. Strauss, 2000. "High Levels of Roundup and Leaf-Beetle Resistance in Genetically Engineered Hybrid Cottonwoods," in *Hybrid Poplars in the Pacific Northwest: Culture, Commerce and Capability* (Washington State University Cooperative Extension Bulletin MISC0272, Pullman, Washington), 29–38.

55. European Food Safety Authority, www.efsa.eu.int/press_room/press_release/386_en.html.

56. BBC News, Food Under the Microscope, "GM Food: Head to Head," May 18, 1999, http://news.bbc.co.uk/1/hi/special_report/1999/02/99/food_under_the_microscope/280396.stm.

57. PBS, "Science and Health: Seeds of Conflict," October 2002, www.pbs.org/now/science/genelaws.html.

58. *Washington Post*, "How to Avoid Eating Genetically Engineered Foods: Comments by Dr. Mercola," January 12, 2006, www.organicconsumers.org/ge/avoid060202.cfm.

59. GMO Free Hawaii, "What Impact Will Genetic Engineering Have on Hawaii's Farmers?" updated 2003, www.higean.org/what-impact.htm.

60. Julie Grass, "Virus-Spliced GE Papayas Contaminating Organic Crops in Hawaii," Organic Consumers Association, October 12, 2004, www.organicconsumers.org/ge/papaya101804.cfm.

61. Michael F. Jacobson, Executive Director, Center for Science in the Public Interest, "Statement to the FDA" at a meeting on the Safety and Labeling of Genetically Modified Organisms, Chicago, November 18, 1999, www.cspinet.org/new/genetics_fda.html.

62. Neil D. Hamilton, "Legal Issues Shaping Society's Acceptance of Biotechnology and Genetically Modified Organisms," *Drake Journal of Agricultural Law* 6, no. 1 (Spring 2001).

63. Margaret Mellon, Union of Concerned Scientists, "Pharmacrop Policy: The Precautionary Principle in Action," Vienna, Austria, April 18, 2006.

64. John Hendrickson, "Energy Use in the U.S. Food System: A Summary of Existing Research and Analysis," report published by the Center for Integrated Agricultural Systems at the University of Wisconsin-Madison, www.cias.wisc.edu/pdf/energyuse2.pdf.

65. Rich Pirog and Andrew Benjamin, Iowa State University, Leopold Center for Sustainable Agriculture, "Checking the Food Odometer," paper, July 2003.

66. V. Lohr, C. Pearson-Mims, and G. Goodwin, "Interior Plants May Improve Worker Production and Reduce Stress in a Windowless Environment." Journal of Environmental Horticulture 14 (2): 97–100.

67. M. Zuckeman, "Development of Situation-specific Trait-state Test for Prediction and Measurement of Affective Responses," *Journal of Clinical Psychology* 45, no. 4 (1977): 513–23.

68. Tove Fjeld and Charite Bonnevie, "Effects of Plants and Artificial Day-Light on the Well-Being and Health of Office Workers, School Children and Health Care Personnel," presented at the Plants for People "Reducing Health Complaints at Work" symposium, June 14, 2002.

69. Joseph Mercola with Rachael Droege, "Plants Are Good for Your Health: Four Ways to Use Them to Your Advantage, May 2004, www.mercola.com.

70. B. C. Wolverton and John D. Wolverton, "Interior Plants: Their Influence on Airborne Microbes inside Energy Efficient Buildings," *Journal of Mississippi Academy of Science* 4, no. 2 (April 1996).

71. Linda Symonds, "Forty Million Americans Drinking Lead Contaminated Water," Disabled World, May 2006, www.disabled-world.com/artman/publish/water-lead.shtml.

72. Center for Study of Responsive Law, "Troubled Water on Tap," *East West*, July 1989.

Bibliography

Altman, Nathaniel. *Sacred Trees*. San Francisco: Sierra Club Books, 1994.

Anderson, William. *Green Man: The Archetype of Our Oneness with the Earth*. London: Harper Collins, 1990.

Bailey, Liberty Hyde. *Hortus Third: A Concise Dictionary of Plants Cultivated in the United States and Canada*. New York: Macmillan, 1976. Revised and expanded by the staff of the Liberty Hyde Bailey Hortorium.

Bailey, Liberty Hyde. *The Standard Cyclopedia of Horticulture*. 3 vols. New York: Macmillan, 1941. First published in 1900.

Baker, Herbert B. *Plants and Civilization*. 3rd ed. Belmont, CA: Wadsworth Publishing, 1978.

Berley, Peter, with Melissa Clark. *The Modern Vegetarian Kitchen*. New York: Regan Books, HarperCollins, 2000.

Boulud, Daniel. *Café Boulud Cookbook*. New York: Scribner, 1999.

Claiborne, Craig. *The New York Times Cookbook*. New York: Harper and Row, 1961.

Coady, Chantal. *Chocolate: The Food of the Gods*. London: Pavilion Books, 1993.

Coe, Sophie D., and Michael D. Coe. *The True History of Chocolate*. London: Thames and Hudson, 1986.

Culinary Institute of America. *The New Professional Chef*. New York: Van Nostrand Reinhold, 1991.

Haleil, Brian. *Home Grown: The Case for Local Food in a Global Market*. World Watch Paper 163, State of the World Library, 2002.

Herbst, Sharon Tyler. *Food Lover's Companion*. New York: Barrons, 2001.

Janakananda Saraswati, Swami. *Yoga, Tantra, and Meditation in Daily Life*. York Beach, ME: Samuel Weiser, 1992.

Kilham, Chris. *The Whole Foods Bible*. Vermont: Healing Arts Press, 1997.

Kimbrell, Andrew. *Fatal Harvest*. Washington, D.C.: Foundation for Deep Ecology and Island Press, 2002.

Kornfeld, Myra, and George Minot. *The Voluptuous Vegan*. New York: Clarkson Potter, 2000.

Kushi, Michio. *Macrobiotic Home Remedies*. Tokyo: Japan Publications, 1993.

Lad, Vasant. *Ayurveda: The Science of Self-Healing*. Santa Fe, NM: Lotus Press, 1984.

Lad, Vasant. *Textbook of Ayurveda: Fundamental Principles*. Albuquerque, NM: The Ayurvedic Press, 2002.

Morningstar, Amadea, and Urmila Desai. *Ayurvedic Cookbook*. Twin Lakes, WI: Lotus Press, 1990.

Nestle, Marion. *Food Politics: How the Food Industry Influences Nutrition and Health*. Berkeley, CA: University of California Press, 2002.

Newman, Nell. *The Newman's Own Organics Guide to a Good Life*. New York: Villard, 2003.

"Need an Air Freshener? Try Plants," *New York Times*, February 13, 1994.

"Plants May Play Bigger Role in Cleaning Air," *New York Times*, August 27, 1995.

Nischan, Michel. *Taste, Pure and Simple*. San Francisco: Chronicle Books, 2003.

Pitchford, Paul. *Healing with Whole Foods*. Berkeley, CA: North Atlantic Books, 1993.

Porter, Jessica. *The Hip Chick's Guide to Macrobiotics*. New York: Avery, 2004.

Rogers, Marilyn. *All about Houseplants*. San Francisco: Ortho Books, 1982.

Rogers, Ruth, and Rose Gray. *Rogers Gray Italian Country Cookbook*. New York: Random House, 1995.

Rosso, Julee, and Sheila Lukins. *The New Basics Cookbook*. New York: Workman, 1989.

Trotter, Charlie. *Charlie Trotter's Vegetables*. Berkeley, CA: Ten Speed Press, 1996.

Trotter, Charlie, and Roxanne Klein. *Raw*. Berkeley, CA: Ten Speed Press, 2003.

Tucker, Eric, and John Westerdahl. *The Millennium Cookbook*. Berkeley, CA: Ten Speed Press, 1998.

Vergé, Roger. *Cuisine of the Sun*. London: Macmillan, 1978.

Vergé, Roger. *Roger Vergé's Vegetables in the French Style*. New York: Artisan, 1992.

Wargo, John P. *Our Children's Toxic Legacy: How Science and Law Fail to Protect Us from Pesticides*. New Haven, CT: Yale University Press, 1996.

Wolverton, B.C. *How to Grow Fresh Air*. New York: Penguin Books, 1996.

General Index

Underscored page references indicate sidebars and tables.

A

Agave family plants, 132
Agni, in Ayurveda, 41, 43–44
Agriculture
industrial, 3–5, 8–9
pesticide use in (*see* Pesticides)
organic (*see also* Organic foods)
advantages of, 4
definition of, 4
productivity of, 7
Air, as essential element, 57, 127
Airplane travel, face spray for, 127
Air pollution
houseplants reducing, 128–31, 132–38
sources of, 127–28
Allergies, from GMOs, 17
All-Purpose Glass Cleaner, 151
Amaranth, 296
Anandamide, in chocolate, 111
Animal products, toxins in, 6–8, 10
Antibiotics
in animal products, 7, 8, 10
in GMO foods, 15, 16
resistance to, 16
Antioxidants, in chocolate, 110
Antiseptic essential oils, as cleaning agent, 148
Apple cider vinegar, 102
Apples, pesticides used on, 5, 11
Araceae family plants, 136
Asian fusion ingredients, 105–8
Astringent taste, in Ayurveda, 35, 47
Ayurveda, 24–25, 40–41
agni in, 41, 43–44
five elements in, 41
tridosha system in, 41–43
foods for balancing, 50–56

B

Baking, 122, 123
low-temperature, 125
Baking soda, as cleaning agent, 147

Balsamic vinegar, 103
Barley, 296
Basil, 60–61
Bay leaf, 61–62
Beans, organic canned, 27
Beauty recipes
Coconut Butter Hair Treatment, 97
Vanilla Salt Glow Scrub, 93
Bell peppers, pesticides used on, 14
Benzene, 130
Bittersweet chocolate/semisweet chocolate, 113
Bitter taste
in Ayurveda, 46–47
in macrobiotics, 35, 35
Blanching, for cooking vegetables, 119–20
Bleach
oxygen, 145, 148
toxins in, 145
Boiling
double, 125–26
of vegetables, 121
Breads, 27
Brown rice vinegar, 104

C

Cacao beans and cacao nibs, 112–13
Caffeine, in chocolate, 110
Canola oil, genetically modified, 18
Caraway, 72
Carbon water filters, 142–43
Cardamom, 85–86
Castile soap, 146
Celery, pesticides used on, 14
Celtic sea salt, 92
Charcoal water filters, 143
Cherries, pesticides used on, 11
Chewing, of whole grains, 305
Children
organic farming protecting, 9
pesticide exposure in, 13
Chili peppers, 73–74, 73

Recipe Index